Rocky Mountain Alpines

Rocky Mountain columbine, *Aquilegia saximontana*,
rare endemic of the Front Range of the
Rocky Mountains in Colorado.
Drawing by Margaret Alice Smith

Rocky Mountain Alpines

*Choice rock garden plants
of the Rocky Mountains
in the wild and in the garden*

American Rock Garden Society
and its Rocky Mountain Chapter

Denver Botanic Gardens

Publications Committee

Jean Williams, Editor

Ray Radebaugh, Chairman
Deane Hall, Picture Editor
Gwen Kelaidis, Botanical Editor
Panayoti Kelaidis, Horticultural Editor
Patricia A. Pachuta, Technical Editor

prepared for
Alpines '86
Second Interim International Rock Garden Plant Conference
June 28 to July 2, 1986; Boulder, Colorado

TIMBER PRESS
Portland, Oregon

The material for this book was prepared by

Denver Botanic Gardens

American Rock Garden Society

Rocky Mountain Chapter, ARGS

Second Interim International Rock Garden Plant Conference 1986
The Rockies—Backbone of a Continent

Sponsors:

American Rock Garden Society   Denver Botanic Gardens   Rocky Mountain Chapter, ARGS
Kenneth J. Love, President   Merle M. Moore, Executive Director   Stanley E. Metsker, President

Conference Steering Committee:
Andrew Pierce, Chairman
Sallie Allen, Panayoti Kelaidis, Kathie Lippitt, Mary Maslin, Robert Means, Maxine Metsker, Evelyn Murrow,
Patricia Pachuta, Ray Radebaugh, Lee Raden, Joan Schwarz, Sandra Snyder, Allan Taylor, Pat Thorn, Jean Williams

First Published 1986
American Rock Garden Society and Denver Botanic Gardens
909 York Street
Denver, Colorado 80206

ISBN 0-88192-058-4

Printed in Hong Kong
Book design: Sandra Mattielli

TIMBER PRESS
9999 SW Wilshire
Portland, Oregon 97225

Preface

I am honored to write on behalf of the Committees for Alpines '86 and their sponsoring organizations—The American Rock Garden Society (ARGS), the Rocky Mountain Chapter of ARGS and Denver Botanic Gardens (DBG)—and to join in welcoming rock gardeners from all over the world to the Second Interim International Rock Garden Plant Conference in Denver, Colorado, June 28–July 3, 1986. It is a pleasure to share in this rich horticultural-botanical tradition at a time and place of such intense activity.

Rock gardeners are delightful people: their spirit of camaraderie, appreciation of the natural world, devotion to botanical detail, their joy in the musical sounds of botanical Latin—their determination never to use "shrubby cinquefoil" when *Potentilla fruticosa* or *Pentaphylloides floribunda* will do—these were the first indications I had stumbled onto a vigorous subculture!

Because the Conference emphasizes visits to view our local alpines—in the mountains, at Denver Botanic Gardens and in local private gardens and nurseries—and because the Rocky Mountain region is relatively little described in rock gardening literature, the Committee decided that a preconference book highlighting Rocky Mountain alpines would be more useful than the traditional record of proceedings produced *ex post facto.* This book is the result: it was produced by a large number of dedicated people.

The first vote of thanks goes to the hard-working writer-gardeners whose work you will be pleased to find here in this volume, many of whom you will meet at the Alpines '86 Conference. Because of publishing time pressures their work had to be done on very short notice a whole year in advance: in late spring and early summer—the busiest of times for these rock gardeners, plant explorers, field botanists and alpinists of all varieties. They deserve our full appreciation for they have produced a treasure of information about Rocky Mountain alpines, along with some fascinating personal experiences.

Special recognition is also due those who are clearly indispensable to the Conference as a whole: Andrew Pierce, assistant director of DBG who serves as chairman of the committee for the Second Interim; Stan Metsker, current chairman of the Rocky Mountain ARGS Chapter; Merle Moore, executive director of DBG; and Ken Love, national ARGS chairman.

Also clearly indispensable, especially to *Rocky Mountain Alpines,* are members of the Conference Publications Subcommittee. Chairman Ray Radebaugh helped us define the scope of the Rocky Mountains and organize the layout of the book. He developed all the maps and drew many of the illustrations which introduce each chapter. He set a schedule to meet deadlines and guided the committee in working together.

Without Panayoti Kelaidis—whose encyclopedic knowledge of the world of alpine horticulture and horticulturists was indispensable, whose optimism and unflagging enthusiasm inspired us all, and who indeed conceived the book in the first place—there would quite simply have been no book at all.

Art and graphics editor Deane Hall performed a miracle of organization, correlated available photographic material with the needs of forty chapters and provided vital technical information and artistic guidance.

Patricia A. Pachuta provided expert technical editing, copyediting and proofreading, and in addition, supplied organizational skills including the essential sense of timing for the committee.

Botanical editor Gwen Kelaidis led us through a botanical wilderness of no small proportions, checking matters of style and spelling, and providing missing taxonomic information. She spent innumerable hours on a myriad of other details in the final stages of the manuscript.

Stan Metsker used his extensive knowledge of computers to compile the index for the entire manuscript.

Solange Gignac, librarian of DBG's Helen Fowler Library, was an invaluable resource, and she contributed our general bibliography. Fran Regner, of the DBG development office, provided essential liaison among those working on "the book."

My husband Peter Williams and our son Stuart also provided essential technical assistance.

A word of thanks is due also to the photographers who so kindly submitted their work for consideration, particularly those who devoted so much time ferreting out materials to fill specific photographic gaps as our deadline approached. Without the efforts of these talented volunteers, the book would have been far less interesting and complete.

Karen Ingersoll of Emery DataGraphic worked closely with the publication subcommittee to provide the maps used here. Margaret A. Smith and Mickaela Earle are acknowledged for their superb drawings used in various parts of the book.

Without long hours of work from each of these people, this book would be in far more primitive form, and indeed might not have appeared in this decade! For their professionalism and willingness to rally at deadline time to get the job done, I am grateful indeed.

Measurements are given in either the metric or the English system,   and readers may refer to the chart to make conversions.

Most authors provided a list of references following their chapters. Those books that were cited repeatedly were included in the overall bibliography only, and are indicated by an asterisk.

One detail remains: This is a book about plants. We have used their Latin names in most cases, since many do not have common names and Latin remains the international standard for nomenclature. Unfortunately, even the scientific community cannot always agree on just one name for each species, so we have given both names where two are in use. No judgment has been made as to which synonym is correct, since this frequently involves a taxonomic judgment we were unprepared to make. In other cases, the older name is simply better known to gardeners.

October 29, 1985

Jean Taylor Williams
Denver, Colorado

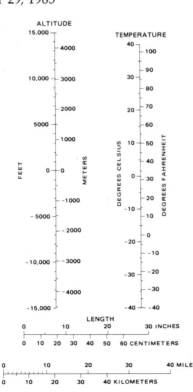

CONVERSION SCALES FOR ENGLISH-METRIC UNITS   Comparative English and metric scales for temperature and distance. Temperatures are easily converted from degrees Fahrenheit (F) to degrees Celsius (C) and back by the following formulas: $F = 9/5C + 32$ and $C = 5/9(F - 32)$. Measurements of distance are easily converted from one system to the other as follows: to convert inches to centimeters, multiply inches by 2.54; centimeters to inches, multiply centimeters by 0.394; feet to meters, multiply feet by 0.305; and miles to kilometers, multiply miles by 1.61.

Contents

H. Lincoln and Laura Louise Foster at "Millstream." Photo by Don Heiny

Foreword

by H. Lincoln Foster

It was back in 1971, at the Fourth International Rock Garden Plant Conference in Harrogate, England, that some of us, basking in the delights of a conference with rock gardening friends from around the world, agreed that a ten-year interval was much too long. We wanted to get together more frequently to share the old and the new in worldwide rock gardening. Why not an Interim Conference at the five-year mark?

The Scots and the English liked the idea of a more frequent schedule, but intimated they would welcome an interim meeting in another part of the world. In response, there was correspondence from America to other centers of rock gardening enthusiasm: Czechoslovakia, New Zealand, France, the East and West Germanys. We in America were eager for an interim conference. Others were enthusiastic also, but not quite confident about handling the details.

When at last it was decided that the American Rock Garden Society was, indeed, willing to arrange an Interim Conference, there was for a while a bit of regional rivalry for the honor of hosting the affair.

It all worked out amicably. The Northwest Chapter, based in Seattle, in combination with the Alpine Garden Club of British Columbia, prepared a program of real distinction around the theme "Alpines of the Americas." In July of 1976 a series of lectures interspersed with visits to the mountains and to local rock gardens was held at the University of Washington in Seattle. From Seattle the group moved north to Vancouver, British Columbia, for a few days at the University of Vancouver and another series of lectures and visits to outstanding gardens. There were also preconference tours into the mountains of the Northwest.

It was a memorable occasion, not only for the wonderful people in Seattle and Vancouver who rustled up the whole program, but also for the many visitors from across America and from abroad.

Now we are on the doorstep of the Second Interim International Rock Garden Plant Conference. Much has transpired between the two gatherings. The American Rock Garden Society has increased its membership, both in raw numbers, and more importantly, in distribution across this broad, complex continent. Furthermore, in my opinion, there has been a perceptible growth in rock gardening sophistication in this country. Our members are reaching out for new challenges, new plants to grow.

Together with his wife, Laura Louise Foster, **H. Lincoln Foster,** or "Linc" as he is affectionately known in rock gardening circles, has created Millstream, an idyllic and idealized natural garden encompassing a precipitous mountain in Connecticut, complete with a namesake brook. Millstream contains a wealth of alpines and woodlanders grown in a picture book setting which attracts countless visitors and was the inspiration for his book *Rock Gardening* that has already served as a "bible" for two generations of American rock gardeners.

Thanks to the active leadership of Denver Botanic Gardens and its enthusiastic staff, aided and abetted by members of the Rocky Mountain Chapter of the American Rock Garden Society, the worldwide rock gardening community is finally being educated to the rich wealth of American alpines to be found in the Rocky Mountain flora.

Along that vast spine of the American continent there is a stunning and varied array of alpines. Many of them, to be sure, are adapted to rather special habitats, and many of us elsewhere find them difficult in cultivation. I am reassured, however, by the history of introductions from other special environments. By persistent effort, especially by the use of seed, plus careful selection, many reluctant genera and species have eventually been refined to clones more adaptable to garden culture.

In a few years we may look forward to enjoying in our rock gardens such Rocky Mountain treasures as *Ranunculus adoneus, Primula angustifolia, Eritrichium aretioides,* and *Mertensia alpina,* among other wonders of the high Rockies. This conference will help to prepare us all for that happy eventuality.

May 1985

H. Lincoln Foster
Millstream
Falls Village, Connecticut

Introduction

by Panayoti Kelaidis

There is something wild, rugged, even mysterious about the Rocky Mountains. There are no grizzly bears in the European Alps, and few regions on earth possess such diversity of climates and plant communities as this long chain of mountains. The Rockies begin near the Arctic Circle, in a land of peat bogs and glaciers, and they end near the Mexican border where palm trees, agaves and a wealth of exotic arboreal cacti dominate the scene. The very diversity of the Rocky Mountains is one obstacle to growing plants from the region: you obtain seed of some interesting penstemon, for instance. Does it come from the summit of a 14,000 ft. mountain or from the alkaline desert of Utah? Fortunately, plants are sufficiently adaptable that with patience and a little luck, one can introduce plants from both extremes into far different climates.

Nevertheless, for a visitor the Rockies represent the ultimate in contrasts and contradictions. For two centuries these mountains have been a source of wonder to the European mind. Tourists come here to explore, fish, hunt and honeymoon. Over half of the land in many states here is publicly owned: this region contains the lion's share of American national parks, monuments, forests and Bureau of Land Management holdings. Indeed, the first national park ever to be so designated in the world was Yellowstone.

From the beginning of exploration here, this area has also been important for resource development and exploitation: vast mines are found throughout the West that have provided the raw materials to build our modern technological society. Coal is strip mined in huge quantities from Canada to Mexico to fuel power plants in other parts of the country. Petroleum is produced in ever larger quantities. Obviously, great care must be taken to balance the industrialization of the West with preservation of wilderness and natural areas here.

Despite tremendous development in recent decades, much of the Rocky Mountain region is probably quite similar to what it was in presettlement times. The mountains are so rugged, so valuable for watershed and tourism, that only a small percentage of forests here has ever been logged. The alpine growing season is so short that much of the tundra here simply doesn't have time to be overgrazed. Of course, the greatest number of interesting endemics occur at lower elevations. It is precisely here, in the Great Plains and the Great Basin where most of the urban development, farming, mining and overgrazing is taking place. It is a challenge for those of us who live here to learn about the natural landscape we are so quickly replacing. Since this landscape is so rich, so varied, so intricate, the task is difficult and exhilarating.

The Rockies are diverse, yet they have many unifying elements. Unlike the mountains best

Panayoti Kelaidis, curator of Denver Botanic Gardens Rock Alpine Garden, is a founding member of the Rocky Mountain Chapter of ARGS, a group he served as president for two years. His forthcoming book will be published by Timber Press, Portland, Oregon.

known to rock gardeners, the Rockies are separated from oceans and seas by huge expanses of plains, deserts and other mountain ranges. There are moist places in the Rockies: at higher elevations, perhaps, or along the widely separated river drainages. Drought can occur almost anywhere in the region at almost any time of the year.

Another feature that strikes many visitors is the dearth of trees and tree species. Whole mountain ranges in the Intermountain Region are devoid of trees, and much of the West consists of broad desert floors, sagebrush flats and endless plains. Where trees do occur, there are rarely more than a few species present: whole counties at middle elevations consist solely of lodgepole pine. Subalpine forest is invariably the twinning of Englemann spruce (*Picea englemannii*) and subalpine fir (*Abies lasiocarpa*). Nevertheless, the Rocky Mountain region is exceedingly rich in plant species.

Ten to twelve thousand species of plants occur in the region treated by this book, and practically all are dwarf woody shrubs and herbaceous plants. At the present time it would be foolish to speculate on how many of these might be amenable to or worthy of cultivation. There is no question, however, that much that grows here is attractive in bloom, form and habit.

From time to time, ranchers and city folk throughout the area have dug up plants in the wild and brought them into their gardens. This was a relatively harmless pastime when the plants they collected still outnumbered the people who collected them. The real task of studying, collecting and taming the flowers of the Rocky Mountain region has usually been done by people living elsewhere. In the field of rock gardening, the name of Carlton Worth stands pre-eminent, for no one collected a greater variety of seeds for more years throughout the Rockies than this indefatigable Professor of Mathematics from Ithaca, New York. The seed exchanges of specialist societies in Britain as well as the United States were enriched by his collections for almost three decades.

Today, the premier growers of Rocky Mountain plants can be found throughout the Pacific Northwest, the Midwest and the northeastern United States. It's possible to find superbly grown specimens of Western plants in the Pocono's, in Maryland, everywhere rock gardeners make their studies, perform mysterious rites and work their magic.

Although most of the regions in which rock gardening has traditionally been practiced are maritime in climate, it has proved possible to grow Rocky Mountain plants, provided that some care is taken in their culture. The horticultural section of this book provides a rich source of information on innovative techniques developed to grow these plants elsewhere: sand beds in central Pennsylvania, crevice gardening in Czechoslovakia and the dramatic and highly imaginative hummocks near Philadelphia which resemble whole mountains scaled down to a home landscape size.

These experiments in other regions should inspire those of us living near the Rockies to look more closely at our native flora. Natural rock gardens occur at all elevations throughout this region from the breaks throughout the Great Plains and Great Basin to the alpine tundra. This is a region where herbaceous plants not only occur in great variety, but actually constitute what ecologists call the climax, or final, undisturbed state, of the natural landscape. It is only right that we explore means to bring these plants—which are usually more heat and drought tolerant than exotics—back into the home landscape.

Rock gardening in the Rockies is sure to be different: with models like the great National Parks and Monuments nearby, rocks are sure to figure differently than they do in gentler terrains. But how appropriate it is to bring something of the majesty and beauty of the Rockies into our daily lives.

PART ONE
The Roots of the Rockies

Photo by Deane Hall

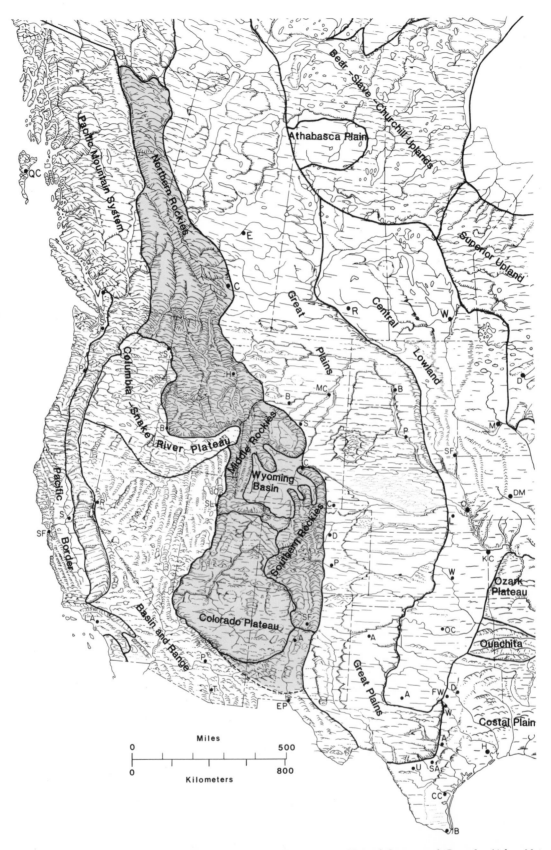

Fig. 1.1   Landforms and physiographic provinces of the western United States and Canada. (After *Natural Regions of the United States and Canada* by Charles B. Hunt, W. H. Freeman and Co., 1974.) The Rocky Mountains are defined here as the area shown in red.

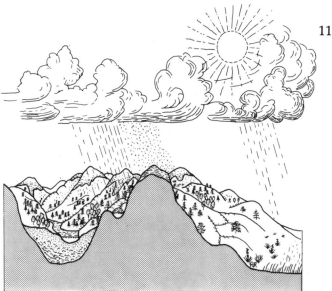

1

Geography and Climate of the Rocky Mountains

by Ray Radebaugh

Rocky slopes and rugged snow-capped peaks that rise high above vast basins, lakes and alpine meadows give the Rocky Mountains a well-deserved reputation for having some of the most magnificent mountain scenery in the world. After appreciating these classic panoramas, many discerning eyes begin to focus on the beauty of conformation and arrangement of the rocks nearby, delighting in the abundance and variety of the exquisite alpine wildflowers growing among them. To some the Rockies serve as wild rock garden models, and their superb natural beauty, ever an elusive quality in man-made gardens, inspires and challenges gardeners of all persuasions.

One of the largest mountain chains in the world, the Rockies stretch to a length of some 2,100 miles through western Canada and the United States, with a width that varies from about 75 to 400 miles. The great north-south distance contributes to a wide range of climates; consequently, a great wealth of plant species grows there. Most of the highest peaks in the United States and Canada are part of the Rocky Mountain system, and since the Continental Divide, which separates east and west drainage, lies within this great cordilleran chain, it is often called the backbone of North America. The Blackfoot Indians were less modest; they called their part of the Rockies, near Glacier National Park in Montana, the "backbone of the world."

Boundaries

The northern limits of the Rockies have never been well-defined; they vary according to the authority consulted. Some sources even label the Mackenzie Mountains of the Yukon and Northwest Territories and the Brooks Range of northern Alaska as "the Arctic Rockies." However, the northern boundary is more usually considered to lie just south of the Yukon-British Columbia border, somewhere between the 59th and 60th parallel, and these boundaries have been adopted in this study of Rocky Mountain alpines. The Liard River, which makes its southernmost bend about 30

Ray Radebaugh is a National Bureau of Standards physicist researching the production of extremely low temperatures (cryogenics); he publishes regularly in his professional field. A rock gardener for about 15 years, he was a founding member of the Rocky Mountain chapter of the American Rock Garden Society and served as president of the chapter in 1983–84. He has recently constructed a large rock garden at his home in Louisville, Colorado. The garden contains 30 tons of lichen-covered rock, and makes use of water in the form of moraines, bogs, streams, waterfalls, ponds, and mist.

miles below the Yukon border, forms a valley here that makes a natural dividing line between the Rockies to the south and the Mackenzie Mountains to the north. The Alaska Highway also runs through a part of this valley. The Kechika River joins the Liard River from the south and forms the western boundary of the Rockies in this region. From here the Rockies march south with minimal interruption through Canada and the United States into New Mexico and Arizona, down to within about 25 miles of the U.S.-Mexican border.

In accordance with the U.S. Geological Survey and most geographic references, the Rocky Mountains as they are referred to in this study are divided into the northern, middle, southern, and Colorado Plateau regions. We have also considered the Great Basin region of western Utah and Nevada and included a discussion of that area in the section on the middle Rockies. Also, some of the Basin Province of New Mexico along the Rio Grande River is considered part of the Colorado Plateau here. Figure 1.1 shows the landforms and boundaries of the Rocky Mountains and its various regions as they are discussed here. Figure 1.2 together with Table 1.1 show the location of most of the mountain ranges and other important features. Much of the land in the Rocky Mountain region is public: national forests, national parks, or national monuments.

Table 1.1. Major Mountain Ranges and Landforms within the Rocky Mountains. Numbers and letters in parentheses represent locations in Figure 1.2.

Northern Rockies
- Muskwa Range
- Hart Range
- Continental Range
- Rocky Mountain Trench
- Cariboo Mountains
- Purcell Mountains
- Selkirk Mountains
- Monashi Mountains
- (1) Kettle River Range
- (2) Pend Oreille Mountains
- Cabinet Mountains
- Salish Mountains
- (3) Whitefish Range
- Lewis Range
- (4) Mission Range
- (5) Swan Range
- Clearwater Mountains
- Bitterroot Mountains
- (6) Sapphire Mountains
- Garnet Range
- (7) Big Belt Mountains
- (8) Little Belt Mountains
- (9) Deer Lodge Mountains
- (10) Anaconda Range
- (11) Beaverhead Range
- (12) Pioneer Mountains
- (13) Tobacco Root Mountains
- (14) Madison Range
- (15) Gallatin Range
- (16) Crazy Mountains
- (17) Ruby Range
- Salmon River Mountains
- Sawtooth Mountains
- Pioneer Mountains
- (18) Lost River Range
- (19) Lemhi Range
- (20) Centennial Range

Middle Rockies
- Absaroka Range
- (21) Beartooth Range
- Bighorn Mountains
- (22) Teton Range
- (23) Owl Creek Mountains
- (25) Wyoming Range
- Wasatch Mountains
- Uinta Mountains
- Uinta Basin

Southern Rockies
- Laramie Range
- (26) Medicine Bow Mountains
- Park Range
- (NP) North Park
- Front Range
- (27) White River Plateau (Flattops)
- (28) Gore Range (Park Range)
- (MP) Middle Park
- Elk Mountains
- Sawatch Range
- (29) Mosquito Range (Park Range)
- (SP) South Park
- (GP) Gunnison Park
- San Juan Mountains
- San Luis Valley
- Sangre de Cristo Range
- (30) Wet Mountains
- (31) Jemez Mountains

Colorado Plateau
- (32) Wasatch Plateau
- Roan Plateau
- (33) Grand Mesa
- (34) Sevier Plateau
- (SRD) San Rafael Desert
- (35) La Sal Mountains
- (36) Uncompaghre Plateau
- (37) Markagunt Plateau
- (38) Paunsagunt Plateau
- (39) Aquarius Plateau
- (40) Henry Mountains
- Canyonlands
- (41) Abajo Mountains
- (42) Kaiparowits Plateau
- (43) Cedar Mesa
- (44) Kaibab Plateau
- (45) Navaho Mountains
- (46) Mesa Verde
- Grand Canyon
- (47) San Francisco Mountains
- (PD) Painted Desert
- (48) Black Mesa
- (49) Chuska Mountains
- (50) Zuni Mountains (Mt. Taylor)
- (51) Sandia Mountains
- (52) Manzano Mountains
- (53) White Mountains
- (54) Magdalena Mountains
- (55) Mogollon Mountains
- (56) Black Range
- (57) San Mateo Mountains
- (58) San Andres Mountains
- (59) Capitan Mountains
- (60) Sacramento Mountains
- (61) Organ Mountains

Fig. 1.2 Mountain ranges within the Rocky Mountains. Map by Ray Radebaugh

Fig. 1.3   View facing north along the Rocky Mountain Trench with the Rocky Mountains on the right. Drawing by Margaret Alice Smith

Fig. 1.4   A lake contained by a terminal moraine at the mouth of a glaciated canyon at the eastern foot of the Teton Range. (After *Natural Regions of the United States and Canada* by Charles B. Hunt, W. H. Freeman and Co., 1974.)

Physical Features

Because the Rocky Mountains are a relatively young mountain system, they have steep, jagged cliffs and great differences in elevation between valleys and peaks when compared to the gentler, more rounded shapes of the older Appalachian Mountains in the eastern United States. The most striking feature of the northern Rocky Mountains is the Rocky Mountain Trench (see Fig. 1.3), which is a remarkably straight valley on the west side of the mountains extending from the Liard River southward into Montana where it branches into three valleys. The Rocky Mountain Trench lies at the head of the Liard, Peace, Fraser, Columbia and Kootenai rivers. Most of the Canadian Rockies are only 75 miles wide, and drop abruptly to the Trench on the west at 2,500 ft. and nearly as abruptly to the Great Plains on the east at 3,300 ft. The highest mountain in the northern Rockies is Mount Robson, elevation 12,972 ft., which lies west of Jasper National Park in Mount Robson Provincial Park. The northern Rockies spread out considerably when they reach Idaho and Montana and form many mountain ranges of diverse shape and character and considerably lower elevations. Many glaciers and ice fields, some as long as 20 miles, fill valleys in the northern Rockies and serve as reminders that about 20,000 years ago in the Pleistocene period, the continental ice sheet and alpine glaciers covered this area, southward to about the Canada-Montana border. As a result, nearly all plant life in the Rockies north of the border is of rather recent origin.

The middle Rocky Mountains contain some of the most impressive peaks—for example, the Teton Range of northwest Wyoming. They also contain some of the lesser mountains, as well as everything in between. Diversity of form, structure, and geology is the hallmark of the region, which lies mostly in Wyoming and Utah. Few peaks in the area exceed 11,000 ft. Gannet Peak in the Wind River Range of Wyoming is the highest mountain at 13,804 ft. The Bighorn and Beartooth Mountains are impressive, rising abruptly from sagebrush-covered basins that nearly surround them. Precipitation in this region is less than that of either the northern or southern Rockies, which accounts for the abundance of sagebrush, *Artemisia,* at lower elevations, and the distinctive plants of the alpine screes, which survive on only about 30 in. of moisture per year, at higher elevations. Alpine glaciers from the Pleistocene period extended to the foot of most of the mountain ranges in the middle Rockies, and the terminal moraines deposited across the mouths of canyons now contain many lakes (see Fig. 1.4), such as Jackson Lake below the Tetons at 6,700 ft. Only the Uinta Mountains and the southern Rockies do not have lakes at the mountain bases since glaciers in these ranges did not extend to lower elevations. In those mountains the terminal moraines are located well up the canyons from the base of the mountains. The Uinta Mountains near Salt Lake City are also the only major east-west mountain chain in the Western Hemisphere, which means a different environment for plant evolution has existed there.

The southern Rocky Mountains contain most of the highest peaks in the United States and Canada, although the mountain base is also higher than in the middle and northern Rockies. Mount

Elbert in the Sawatch Range of Colorado is the highest peak in the Rockies with an elevation of 14,433 ft. The Rocky Mountains exceed the 14,000 ft. elevation only in Colorado, where there are over 50 such peaks. The southern Rocky Mountains, which lie mostly in Colorado, consist of several north-south ranges that are quite close together except at North Park, Middle Park, South Park, and the San Luis Valley. These broad, flat park areas occur at elevations of 9,000 to 10,000 ft. and are surrounded by mountains on nearly all sides. The broad San Luis Valley is drained by the Rio Grande River to the south. Extensive glaciation carved many U-shaped valleys between mountain ridges that were never covered with ice. Those high, ice-free areas, often above tree line, contain an abundance of alpine plant species that have evolved from times long before the Ice Age.

The Colorado River Plateau, or Colorado Plateau, contains high table lands with many deep, very colorful canyons. Most of the mountain peaks of the Plateau are situated around the border of the region. The presence of more national parks and monuments in this region than anywhere else in the U.S. testifies to its exceptional beauty. The arid climate has led to the evolution of drought-tolerant plants such as cacti and succulents. Elevations vary greatly. Consider, for example: the bottom of the Grand Canyon at 2,500 ft.; the surrounding plateau at 7,000 ft.; and Humphreys Peak at 12,633 ft. in the San Francisco Mountains only 60 miles to the south.

Elevations of the Rocky Mountains are displayed in the topographic map in Fig. 1.5. The north-south and west-east lines in Fig. 1.5 show the location of elevation profiles in Fig. 1.6. Also shown in the figure are tree line, the various vegetation zones, and precipitation. The elevation of tree line increases gradually from about 4,000 ft. at the northern tip of the Rockies to about 12,000 ft. at the Colorado-New Mexico border.

Vegetation Zones

North America can be divided into seven climatic zones, each with its own characteristic flora and fauna. In the West these vegetation or life zones are: the lower Sonoran zone in Mexico and the extreme southern U.S.; the upper Sonoran zone in the southern U.S.; the transition zone in the central to northern U.S.; the Canadian zone in the northern U.S. and southern Canada; the Hudsonian zone in north-central Canada; and the arctic zone in northern Canada. These vegetation zones are defined by latitude, and correspond to mountain zones defined by altitude. In general, an increase of 1,000 ft. in elevation is approximately the same as moving north by 280 miles since both are marked by a temperature reduction of about 3°F. A one-day hike into the mountains presents as much variety in vegetation as a one-year hike from Arizona to the Yukon territory. The vegetation zones in mountain areas are summarized in Table 1.2; Colorado elevations are used. Elevations for these zones in other areas are shown in Figure 1.6.

Table 1.2. Characteristics of Mountain Vegetation Zones (Elevations given are for Colorado)

Zone	Elevation	Characteristic Vegetation
Plains (east)	below 5,500 ft.	grasslands
Upper Sonoran (west)	below 6,500 ft.	sagebrush, *Artemisia*
Foothills	5,500–8,000 ft.	juniper, *Juniperus*; pinyon pine, *Pinus edulis*; sagebrush, *Artemisia*
Montane	8,000–9,500 ft.	ponderosa pine, *Pinus ponderosa*; Douglas fir, *Pseudotsuga menziesii*; aspen, *Populus tremuloides*
Subalpine	9,500–11,500 ft.	Engelmann spruce, *Picea engelmannii*; limber pine, *Pinus flexilis*; subalpine fir, *Abies lasiocarpa*
Alpine	above 11,500 ft.	tundra

Fig. 1.5   Topography of the United States and Canada. (After *Natural Regions of the United States and Canada* by Charles B. Hunt, W. H. Freeman and Co., 1974.) Red lines indicate location of cross sections shown in Fig. 1.6.

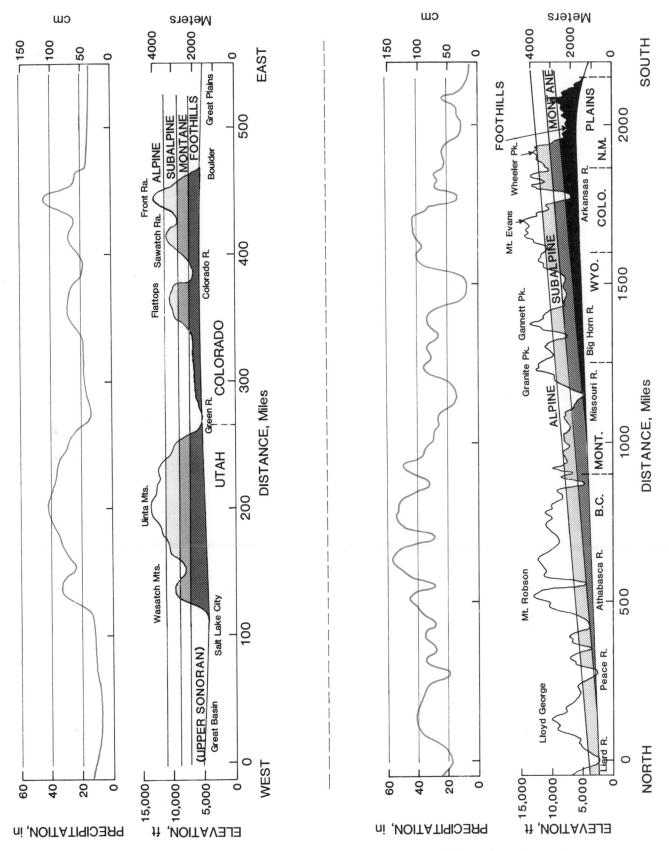

Fig. 1.6   Cross sections through the Rocky Mountains in the west-east and the north-south directions along with precipitation profiles at the cross-sections. Drawing by Ray Radebaugh

Fig. 1.7   Alpine tundra locations and limit of main ice sheet from Pleistocene glaciation.
Map by Ray Radebaugh

Of course, some intrusion of plants between zones always occurs. Often, the first sign of the next higher zone is found on north-facing slopes where there is more moisture and temperatures are lower. Since rock alpine gardeners are especially interested in plants above tree line, Figure 1.7 is included to show the extent of alpine tundra in the United States and Canada. The southern limit of the Pleistocene glaciation is also indicated in the figure. Most tundra areas north of this limit were covered with ice, whereas most of those below the line were above the alpine glaciers that filled mountain valleys. The alpine glaciers of today are remnants of that ice age of 20,000 years ago as well as from the little ice age of 1,300 years ago.

Climate

Mountain climates are harsh, with many extremes and an abundance of microclimates. There is great diversity along the 2,100 mile length of the Rocky Mountains. Because the Rockies are a considerable distance inland, they are blocked from the warm, moist air coming off the Pacific Ocean by the Coast Range, the Cascade Range, and the Sierra Nevada Range; they have a rather dry, continental climate with extreme variations in temperature over short time periods. At high elevations day and night temperatures can vary as much as 30°F. The east slopes are exposed to cold, arctic air masses which often flow down from Canada in the winter, engulfing the Rockies in subzero temperatures only a few hours after warm chinook winds blow-dry the region to temperatures as high as 65°F.

The low-temperature limit for various regions throughout the United States and southern Canada is depicted in the hardiness zone map of Figure 1.8. Such a map can give only general information for various regions, since local microclimates vary widely in the mountain areas. As an aid to the cultivation of Rocky Mountain plants abroad, we note that all regions of western Europe are zone 5 and above except for northern areas of Sweden and Finland. Japanese climates are zone 6 or

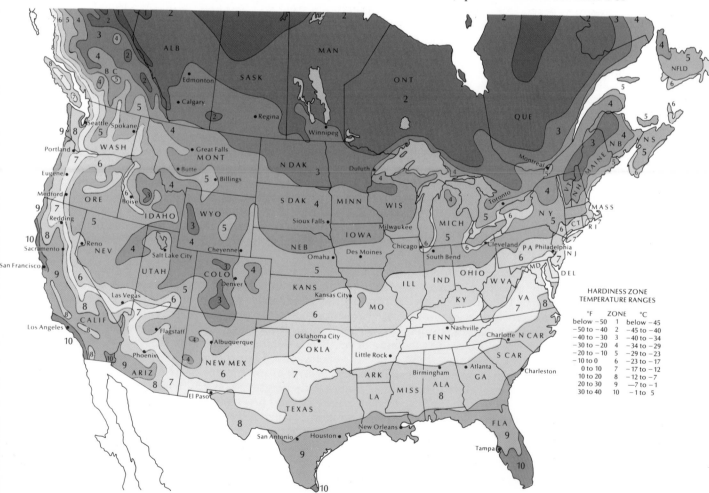

Fig. 1.8 Hardiness zones and low temperature ranges.

above. The only Rocky Mountain plants that may be too tender for some European regions are those from zones 6 and 7 in the Colorado River areas of northwest Arizona, zone 6 in southern New Mexico, and possibly the zone 6 areas of western Idaho. More often it is the need for low humidity, low moisture, high solar radiation, and sometimes for low summer temperatures, that makes some Rocky Mountain plants difficult to grow elsewhere. In most cases the mountain areas experience lower temperatures than do plains areas just to the east. However, Figure 1.8 shows that the Northern Rockies of Montana, Idaho, and southern Canada actually have a milder winter than the plains and much of the middle and southern Rockies. This phenomenon occurs because that area comes to within 300 miles of the warm Pacific Ocean.

Precipitation in the Rocky Mountains is shown in Figure 1.9. Higher precipitation rates occur at higher elevations, as shown in the profiles of Figure 1.6. These figures show that the amount of moisture available to plants of the middle and southern Rockies, and especially to those of the Colorado Plateau, is quite low. Even the high-elevation precipitation rates in the Rockies are lower than the 40–48 in. average rainfall received on the two coasts. In addition, precipitation at lower elevations often occurs in cloudbursts during which most of the water is runoff, and is not available to plants. Much of the precipitation at high elevations is in the form of snow, which often blows off exposed tundra areas. Only the northern Rockies have fairly high precipitation rates, although still less than that of the Coast Range. Having lived for many years in the semiarid southern Rockies, I was quite surprised to find ferns as tall as I while hiking near the Selway River in the Clearwater Mountains of Central Idaho. That area is a good example of a microclimate; only a few miles away the vegetation is not nearly so lush. Figure 1.9 shows a precipitation rate in excess of 48 in. there. Plants from the northern Rockies, therefore, usually require more moisture than those from other parts of the Rockies where adaptations to low moisture are commonplace.

Another aspect of the continental climate is the low humidity in most of the Rocky Mountain region. As a result, moisture that does not immediately soak into the ground evaporates quickly. The annual pan evaporation rate (the rate water evaporates from an open pan set on the ground) is influenced by temperature, humidity, sunshine, and wind. It ranges from about 40 in. per year in the northern Rockies to as high as 96 in. per year on parts of the Colorado Plateau. These evaporation rates are higher than the precipitation rate in most of the Rocky Mountain region and as much as 10 times higher in the southwestern areas of the Colorado Plateau. What these statistics mean is that moisture available to plants in this region must exist deep underground or be stored within the plant, since any water near the surface quickly disappears. The rapid evaporation prevents soluble salts from being leached out of the soil, resulting in alkaline soils.

One of the reasons for such a high evaporation rate is the bright sunshine in the region. Figure 1.10, which shows the energy density of solar radiation in the U.S., indicates that one of the unique features of the middle and southern Rockies is the intense solar radiation at high elevations where thin air and low humidity allow the sunshine to pass through the atmosphere easily. Total solar radiation increases by about 30 percent when going from sea level to 10,000 ft., while ultraviolet radiation increases by about 90 percent over the same elevation gain. An important distinction to be made here is that, in contrast to the energy of solar radiation, the actual number of hours of sunshine in the high areas of the Rocky Mountains is the same or lower than in much of the remainder of the United States because of afternoon storms that occur almost daily in the high mountains during the summer.

The final factor contributing to a harsh mountain climate and rapid evaporation is the high wind, especially in winter. Studies of wind speeds near the Alpine Visitors Center in Rocky Mountain National Park have recorded winter gusts up to 173 miles per hour and summer gusts up to 88 mph. Average wind speeds are much lower with a summer average ranging from 13 to 34 mph. Similar high winds are found a few miles farther south atop Niwot Ridge west of Boulder at 12,300 ft. where the University of Colorado's Institute of Arctic and Alpine Research (INSTAAR) has been studying the tundra climate since 1952. A typical year has only 45 frost-free days. Wet, wind-swept sites are underlain with permafrost. Precipitation can be over 40 in. annually, and for about 20 days a year, the humidity drops below 10 percent. Average summer highs are only 50°F with an extreme of 65°F. Typical Rocky Mountain tundra climate is marked by: (a) low temperatures, both winter and summer, (b) little moisture, (c) a high rate of evaporation, (d) intense sunshine, and (e) strong winds. The principal difference at lower elevations is higher temperature both summer and winter. Plants of the Rocky Mountain region have evolved to survive in such an environment. Some of the more common methods used by plants to adapt to the rigorous climate in the Rocky Mountains are: (a) dwarf, ground-hugging growth (as in moss campion, *Silene acaulis*) to escape the high winds, (b) fine hairs, (as in the alpine forget-me-not, *Eritrichium aretioides*, *E. nanum*) to reduce evaporation and trap heat as with a miniature fur coat, (c) light foliage color, (as in sagebrush, *Artemisia* spp.) to reflect the

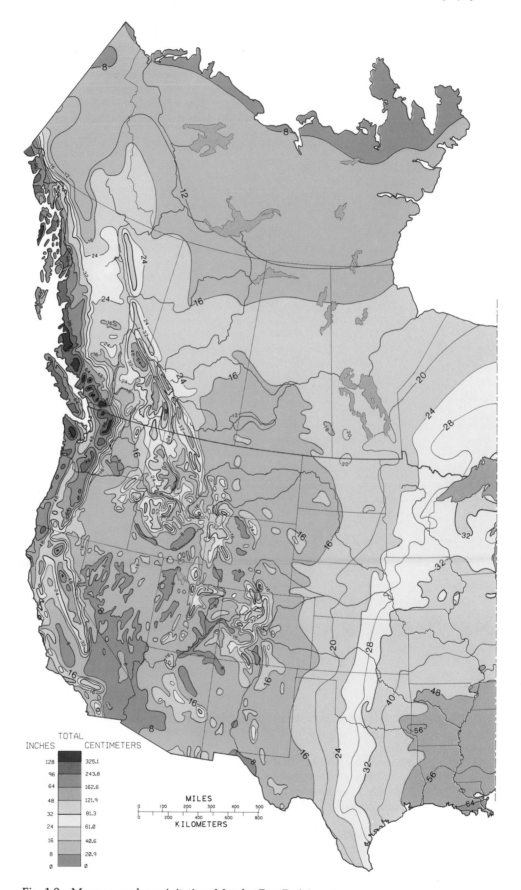

Fig. 1.9   Mean annual precipitation. Map by Ray Radebaugh

intense sunlight, (d) long taproots (as in big-rooted spring beauty, *Claytonia megarhiza*) to utilize moisture deep below ground, and (e) succulent leaves (as in sedums, *Sedum lanceolatum*) to store water for long periods.

Rather than the abundance of the lush foliage plants produced in moister climates, the Rocky Mountains produce a wide range of small plants, each one too busy struggling to maintain itself in the harsh environment to crowd out a neighboring plant. The adaptations are usually genetic, so such plants will often succeed in lower-elevation rock gardens if some of the native climatic conditions can be maintained.

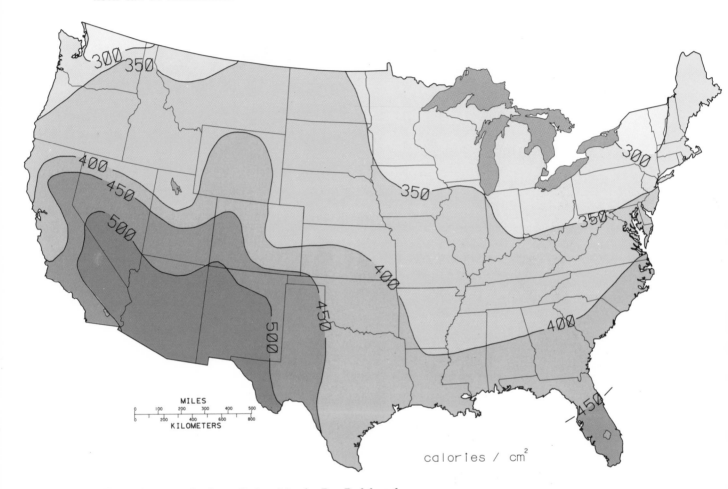

Fig. 1.10   Annual solar radiation. Map by Ray Radebaugh

References

Barry, R. G. 1981. *Mountain weather and climate.* New York: Methuen and Co.

Chapman, J. D., and D. B. Turner, eds. 1956. *British Columbia atlas of resources.* Vancouver, B.C.: Smith Lithograph Co., Ltd.

Cole, David B. 1984. "Rocky Mountains." In *Encyclopedia Americana.* Danbury, Ct.: Grolier, Inc.

Glidden, D. E. 1981. *Summer wind studies near the Alpine Visitors Center, Rocky Mountain National Park.* Denver: Rocky Mountain Nature Assoc.

Hunt, Charles B. 1974. *Natural regions of the United States and Canada.* New York: W. H. Freeman and Co.

Muench, David, and David Sumner. 1975. *Rocky Mountains.* Portland, Ore.: Graphic Arts Center Publ. Co.

Department of Energy, Mines, and Resources Information. 1974. *The national atlas of Canada.* Ottawa: DEMRI.

U.S. Geological Survey. 1970. *The national atlas of the United States of America.* Washington, D.C.

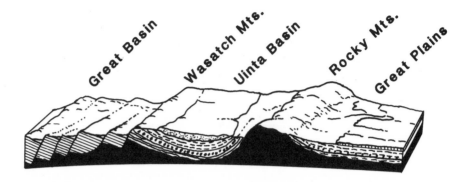

2

Geologic History of the Rockies

by Peter C. Harley

The story of Rocky Mountain alpines is incomplete without some appreciation of the geologic complexity and scenic magnificence of the American Mountain West. The soil on which alpine plants grow is derived from the parent rocks below. Even the relative lack of soil, which influences plant growth in many Rocky Mountain regions, is related to rock structure and glacial events of the recent geologic past. The composition of the rocks, and how and when they obtained the lofty heights they reach today, influenced the evolution and distribution of plant life. It is a complex story the rocks tell; I shall give a brief overview.

In the last 20 years, a theory has emerged which enables geologists to unify their disparate observations in a general notion of causation. This theory of plate tectonics, popularly known as "continental drift," suggests that the earth's crust rests on seven major and perhaps a dozen minor "plates" that are rafting about on the underlying mantle at speeds of an inch or two a year. The core of the continents consists of huge masses of ancient granite, which probably solidified from molten rock when the earth's crust first began to cool, perhaps 4,000 million years ago. The regions between these platforms filled with heavier rock known as basalt, forming oceanic crust. Thus, tectonic plates consist of both continental and oceanic crust. Plate boundaries are found along mid-ocean ridges, where new crust is created as molten lava wells up and hardens into basalt, forcing adjacent plates apart. Other plate boundaries occur where plates moving in opposite directions collide, with unimaginable force. If continental masses collide, the continents may be sutured together as the crust folds and buckles, driving up mountain ranges. The Himalayas have been rising ever since the Indian Plate collided with Eurasia about 40 million years ago. When oceanic crust collides with a continental portion of a plate, the heavier basalt is forced down below the continental crust, a process known as subduction, where it is melted. Thus, crustal material is created at mid-ocean ridges or spreading centers and destroyed at subduction zones. When oceanic crust is subducted, it may cause crustal uplift and volcanism in the overriding continental crust (Fig. 2.1). The Andes Mountains in South America and the islands of Japan are both results of plate subduction, and as we shall see, a collision of this type is responsible for much of the mountain building activity in the North American Cordillera.

Peter C. Harley graduated from the University of Michigan with a Ph.D. in botany and now studies photosynthetic responses of plants to their environment. A research assistant at the University of Utah where he investigates grain amaranths as a potential new agricultural crop, he has botanized extensively in the Great Lakes region and has a special interest in boreal flora. Learning the Western flora amid the spectacular mountain landscape has encouraged his on-going interest in geology.

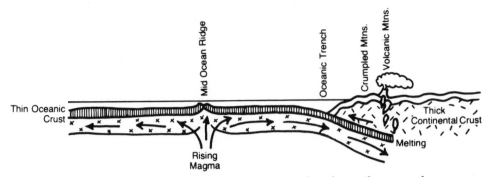

Fig. 2.1 Fueled by atomic reactions deep within the earth, tremendous, powerful, slow-moving convection currents cause upwelling at mid-ocean ridges, where new crust is generated by submarine volcanic action. At the rate of about an inch a year, the oceanic crust is carried toward the continents. Where crustal plates meet, the heavier oceanic crust is pulled downward and remelted. (From *Roadside Geology of Colorado* by Halka Chronic, Mountain Press Publishing Co., 1980.)

Fig. 2.2

GEOLOGICAL TIME SCALE

ERA	PERIOD	AGE (million years)	EVENTS IN ROCKY MOUNTAIN HISTORY
CENOZOIC	Quaternary	3	Glaciation and erosion
CENOZOIC	Tertiary	65	5000 feet (1550 m) of regional uplift Laramide Orogeny continues
MESOZOIC	Cretaceous	135	Mid-Atlantic Ridge forms; beginning of Laramide Orogeny Widespread shallow seas
MESOZOIC	Jurassic	200	Low lying, marshy region; dinosaurs
MESOZOIC	Triassic	240	Pangea supercontinent formed
PALEOZOIC	Permian	280	Erosion of Ancestral Rockies
PALEOZOIC	Pennsylvanian	325	Uplift of Ancestral Rockies
PALEOZOIC	Mississippian	370	Pangea coming together Widespread open seas
PALEOZOIC	Devonian	415	
PALEOZOIC	Silurian	445	Long stable period with shallow seas and deposition of thick sedimentary layers
PALEOZOIC	Ordovician	515	
PALEOZOIC	Cambrian	580	Continental masses widely spaced along equator
PALEOZOIC	Precambrian		Long stable period; mountain erosion Two or more periods of mountain building over 1500 million years ago Earth's origin about 4600 millon years ago

The idea of continents adrift, crashing into one another, of entire mountain ranges being created and destroyed, is mind-boggling. What makes it all possible, of course, is equally unimaginable expanses of time. A plate movement of only an inch a year, less than the current movement of the North American Plate, when projected over 100 million years, represents a movement of almost 1,600 miles. To help us deal with those immense blocks of time, the geological time scale (Fig. 2.2) remains indispensable.

In light of plate tectonics, the geology of our region is largely explicable as the result of interactions between what is now the North American Plate and adjacent plates during the last 2,500 million years. The relative positions of the continents since the beginning of the Mesozoic Era is well understood, and the geologic record relatively intact. All the continental masses were grouped together 240 million years ago in a "supercontinent" known as Pangaea. The subsequent breakup of Pangaea and the movement of the plates into their present positions is of crucial importance to the geologic structure of the western third of North America.

The granitic core of the North American continent is known as the Precambrian Shield. These ancient rocks, along with horizontal layers of sediment which have accumulated over the eons, form a stable platform, or craton, which has been relatively unaffected by the turbulent tectonic events of the last few 1,000 million years. Along the continental margin, however, outside the craton, plate interactions have had profound geologic consequences. The oldest rocks present in our region occur in northwest Wyoming and southwest Montana. These rocks, between 2,500 and 3,000 million years old, once formed part of the Shield, but were deformed and altered by high pressure and temperatures, suggesting an intense period of mountain building at that time. Similar rocks in the southern Rockies, dating from 1,700 million years, such as those forming the core of Mount Evans near Denver, provide evidence of another period of mountain building, and there may well have been others. By the end of the Precambrian Era, however, the forces of erosion had worn those ancient ranges down to a monotonous plain, covered by shallow seas.

Thus, at the beginning of the Paleozoic Era, 570 million years ago, North America consisted of a huge lowland area centered in what is now the Canadian Arctic, surrounded by shallow seas. Over the eons, successive layers of sediment were deposited in these seas and compressed into rock. The major continental masses, scarcely recognizable as today's continents, encircled the world in equatorial latitudes. The ensuing 300 million years, encompassing much of Paleozoic time, saw the various continental masses gradually move into position to form Pangaea. By 420 million years ago, a small continent known as Baltica had collided with northeastern North America, giving rise to mountain building in what is now eastern Canada. Seas receded somewhat in the western portions of the continent, but vast areas remained largely under water. Finally, about 300 million years ago, as Pangaea took final shape, another plate collided with North America, giving rise to mountain building in central Europe and the rise of the Appalachians. This plate collision also lifted mountains in western North America, giving rise to a range known as the Ancestral Rockies, and lifting parts of the area above the seas which had dominated the scene for several hundred million years. The massive supercontinent of Pangaea remained more or less intact for over 100 million years, during which time erosion wore the Ancestral Rockies down to a plain, depositing thick beds of sediment in the surrounding seas.

In late Jurassic time, Pangaea began to break up. The present Mid-Atlantic Ridge formed. creating new oceanic crust and forcing North America and Europe/Africa apart at a rate of an inch or two a year. As the North American Plate moved west, the continental crust composing the western part of North America collided with oceanic crust of another plate. The lighter continental crust of the North American Plate began to ride over the oceanic plate, which was forced down thousands of feet into the earth's interior.

The consequences of this collision were many. Molten rock welled up, forming the granite core of the Sierra Nevada, beginning perhaps 135 million years ago. Later, massive faulting caused formation of the mountains of Nevada and western Utah. And, beginning about 75 million years ago, in Late Cretaceous time, as activity along the mid-Atlantic Ridge apparently accelerated, the resulting forces created along the western margin of the North American Plate were sufficient to force the ancient Precambrian rock upwards, bending the thick layers of sedimentary rock covering our region, and lifting them above the shallow Cretaceous seas. This uplifting was often accompanied by faulting, as great blocks, unable to stand the stress, ruptured along lines of weakness.

These events, over a period of 40 million years, constitute the birth of the present-day Rocky Mountains, a process known as the Laramide (for the Laramie Mountains in Wyoming) Orogeny. The forces created as the North American Plate overrides the adjacent oceanic plate continue to the present day, and have led to periodic volcanism over the last 40 million years, evidence of which is apparent in many areas. Finally, between 26 and 5 million years ago, a vast area of western North

America, centered in the Colorado Rockies but extending from Mexico to Canada and Nevada to the Mississippi, was gradually uplifted, but without the large scale faulting which had accompanied the Laramide Orogeny. At the center of this large dome, in Colorado, uplift was a much as 6,000 ft., lifting the Rockies and the surrounding plains and plateaus to near their present heights.

Occasional and widely dispersed episodes of volcanism aside, the last 5 million years have seen the processes of erosion dominate in western North America. Large and vigorous river drainage systems, fed by the snow and rain falling in the mountains, have had ample time to carve well-defined channels on their way to the sea, carrying away massive amounts of sediment from the mountainsides. Much of this sediment accumulated in intermountain valleys and basins, partially burying the mountains in their own debris. About 3 million years ago, the climate throughout the Northern Hemisphere became wetter and slightly cooler, leading to several episodes of glaciation. In the Northeast and the Great Lakes region, massive continental ice sheets, thousands of miles in extent and thousands of feet thick, moved out of Canada as far south as the Ohio River. In the Rocky Mountain region, much smaller alpine glaciers formed and moved downslope, scouring out large U-shaped valleys and greatly modifying the mountain landscape. So important were these glacial events in establishing the present appearance of the Rockies that they will be dealt with in detail later.

In summary, the geological evidence suggests several periods of mountain building along the western edge of the stable craton underlying North America. Mountain ranges formed at least twice during Precambrian time, leaving ancient contorted rocks as evidence of their creation and ancient sedimentary rocks as evidence of their erosion. Another period of mountain building occurred in Pennsylvanian time as Pangaea formed, but these mountains also eroded to a plain, leaving only sedimentary rock in their wake. In Late Cretaceous and Tertiary time, the Laramide Orogeny led to the formation of the present Rockies, and a subsequent period of general uplift throughout North America west of the Mississippi raised the mountains to their present height. The geologic evidence for these events is seen in many of the spectacular land forms with which western North America is blessed, including many of our national parks and monuments.

Were we able to take a vertical cross section through the stable craton of North America, largely undeformed by the cataclysmic events we have been describing, we would see thousands of feet of horizontal strata, layer upon layer of sedimentary rock laid down during the hundreds of millions of years during which this area was lying under shallow seas. Fortunately, as the Colorado Plateau was uplifted in the last 25 million years, the developing Colorado River drainage cut deep and spectacular canyons into the arid landscape, providing us with just such a cross section of geologic time. Taken as a unit, the Grand Canyon, Zion Canyon and Bryce Canyon expose to view rock strata laid down throughout virtually all of Paleozoic and Mesozoic time. Granite Gorge, in the bottom of the Grand Canyon, is cut into Precambrian basement rock, 1,700 million years old, similar to the rock in the heart of much of the Rockies. The rock layer lying immediately above Granite Gorge is dated at 570 million years, meaning that over 1,100 million years of the geologic record is missing in the Grand Canyon. From this point upwards, however, the record is nearly complete, until the canyon rim, limestone formed about 240 million years ago as Pangaea took final shape, is reached. More recent layers have all been lost to erosion. The lowest layers of Zion Canyon, however, date from about 225 million years ago and the rocks on the canyon rim from about 100 million years later. Finally, the rocks exposed at Bryce Canyon and nearby Brian Head, the highest point on the Colorado Plateau, date from 130 million to about 37 million years ago, the period encompassing both the initial breakup of Pangaea and the Laramide Orogeny. To be sure, a few gaps in the record exist, since certain layers eroded completely away before subsequent layers were formed, but generally speaking, the rocks exposed in these three magnificent parks document the existence of those vast, generally shallow seas, which ebbed and flowed across most of western North America for hundreds of millions of years, and in which sandstones, limestones, shales and other sedimentary rocks were deposited in turn.

For most of this time, the area now occupied by the Rocky Mountains was also flooded with shallow seas, save for the 100 million years or so during which the Ancestral Rockies created large islands in that great sea, and the time since the Laramide Orogeny. What of the sediments laid down there?

Wells drilled on the high plains near Denver reveal the presence of 12,000 ft. of sedimentary rock. Near the town of Morrison, Colorado, just east of the Front Range of the Rockies, some of these sedimentary layers are exposed, layers geologists have named the Morrison Formation. These rocks were laid down between 130 and 160 million years ago. They indicate a low-lying, swampy environment and contain a great many fossils, including those of some of the largest of the dinosaurs. Interestingly enough, this same formation is found 280 miles away in large areas west of the Rockies, including Dinosaur National Park. The inescapable conclusion is that these rock layers were once continuously distributed over what is now the southern Rocky Mountains, and that their present discontinuity is the result of the Laramide Orogeny, which thrust ancient Precambrian rock up in between. (See figure 2.3.)

Indeed, the layers of the Morrison Formation, laid down horizontally, are now upturned, those found east of the mountains sloping sharply down to the east and those on the west side sloping to the west; one can almost imagine the entire sedimentary platform bulging upward. Most of the rock forming the middle of the bulge has been lost to erosion, and we are left only with the two upturned end points. When upturned layers of sediment like these erode unevenly, they often form prominent ridges, called hogbacks, along the edge of mountain ranges. Hogback ridges occur all

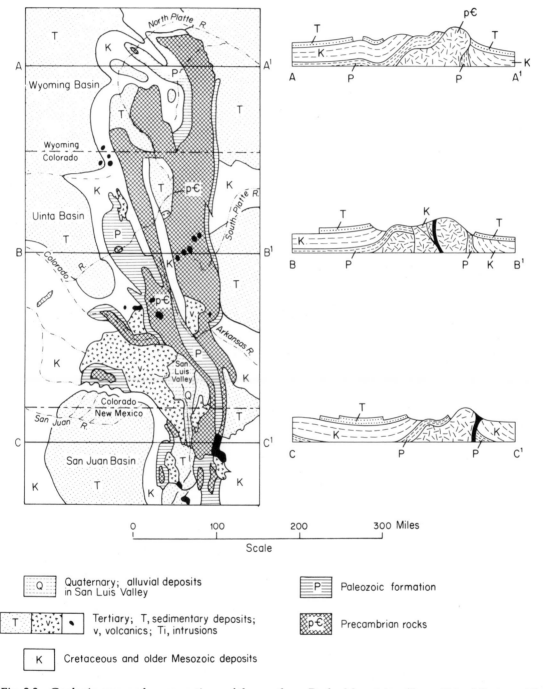

Fig. 2.3 Geologic map and cross sections of the southern Rocky Mountains. (From *Natural Regions of the United States and Canada* by Charles B. Hunt, W. H. Freeman and Co., 1974.)

along both the east and west side of the Rockies, especially in the southern portion; a particularly dramatic example occurs just west of Denver, where Interstate-70 cuts through such a hogback, exposing dozens of almost vertical layers of sedimentary rock, deposited horizontally over a period of perhaps 100 million years and later tilted upwards during the birth of the mountains.

Other well-known landmarks illustrating the way in which overlying sediments were bent upwards during the Laramide Orogeny are the Flatirons, near Boulder, and Red Rocks Park near Denver, both of which represent upturned layers of Pennsylvanian age red sandstone, deposited along the edge of the Ancestral Rockies; and the Garden of the Gods, near Colorado Springs, the rocks of which date from about the same time.

Driving west on Interstate-70 into the heart of the Front Range, one cannot help but be impressed by the towering mountains, cloaked by vegetation at lower elevations. Above timberline, on Mount Evans, Longs Peak and dozens of other high peaks where rocks are exposed, we no longer see stratified sedimentary rocks but crystalline rocks, part of the ancient Precambrian core of the craton which still underlies the adjacent high plains. Today, as the result of the Laramide Orogeny, 22,000 vertical ft. separate these once contiguous rock formations.

The southern Rockies represent a series of north-south trending arches, known as anticlines. Erosion has exposed crystalline Precambrian rock in the centers of the arches, and upturned Paleozoic and Mesozoic sedimentary layers are exposed along their flanks. The basins in between the mountain ranges have been partially filled with relatively recent sediments of Tertiary and Quaternary age. Superimposed on this general pattern is a patchwork of detailed geologic phenomena, including volcanism, large-scale faulting, and intrusions of molten rock which forced its way into cracks created by the forces of mountain building. The major area of volcanism in the southern Rockies is the San Juan Mountains on the southwest margin of the region, formed as the result of large-scale volcanic activity between 40 and 10 million years ago. Of particular geologic and historic interest is the Colorado Mineral Belt, containing most of the major gold and silver deposits that attracted Colorado's first settlers in the second half of the 19th century, as well as huge deposits of less romantic minerals. This belt occupies a 50-mile wide zone stretching from the mountains above Boulder to the southwest corner of the state, and was formed during the Laramide Orogeny, adjacent to areas where molten rock was intruded, as hot solutions containing dissolved minerals forced their way into cracks and fissures and solidified, forming mineralized veins.

The generalizations made above apply to the southern and middle Rockies, particularly those in Colorado and southern Wyoming. The situation in the northern Rockies, located in Idaho, Montana, and adjacent Canada, is somewhat different. Throughout much of Precambrain time, all of the Paleozoic and half of the Mesozoic, the region was geologically quiet (the Ancestral Rockies of 300 million years ago were located farther south) and generally consisted of a flat plain flooded by shallow seas, in which layers of sediment thousands of feet thick were deposited. As oceanic crust was subducted below the North American Plate, the situation changed drastically. Rather than being bent into the granite-cored arches of the southern Rockies, the northern Rockies formed as the layers of sedimentary rocks were crumpled and stacked one on top of the other by broad, almost flat faults called thrust faults. The varied topography of the northern Rockies is the result of differential resistance to erosion of the folded and faulted limestones, shales and sandstones. Unlike the granite-cored Laramide uplift region of Colorado and Wyoming, the northern Rockies contain little Precambrian crystalline rock. In addition, throughout a large part of Idaho, heat within the crust melted huge volumes of rock, forming magma which rose towards the surface. Some of the magma solidified before reaching the surface, forming huge masses of granite. Where it reached the surface, however, the magma erupted as volcanoes, blanketing enormous areas with lava and volcanic rocks.

Thus, there are three major kinds of mountains in the northern Rockies. Folded and faulted sedimentary rocks form the majority of the mountains, but others are the remains of once active volcanoes and some have a central core of granite. Widespread volcanism in the Tertiary Period formed two distinctive areas, the vast Columbia Plateau in western Idaho and adjacent Washington and Oregon, and the Snake River Plain, in southern Idaho, both of which are composed of extensive basaltic lava flows. Active volcanoes in recent geologic time and frequent earthquakes in the area provide evidence that the faulting and uplift are not yet over. (See figure 2.4.)

If the Columbia Plateau and Snake River Plain provide ample evidence of volcanic activity in the previous 50 million years, the marvelous geothermal features in Yellowstone National Park serve notice that similar geologic activity continues in the present. Molten magma may well exist only a few thousand feet below the Yellowstone Plateau.

A noteworthy example of mountains formed by faulting is the Grand Tetons, the magnificent east face of which was formed as large blocks of crust were raised along faults while the adjacent

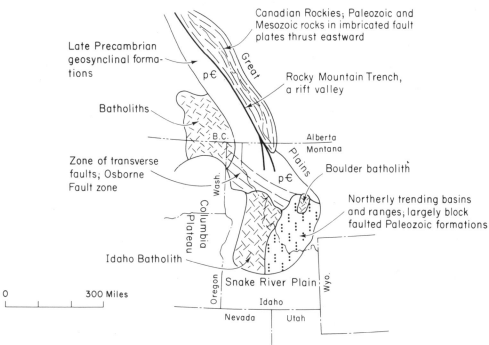

Fig. 2.4 Structural elements in the northern Rocky Mountains. The Rocky Mountain Trench separates the Canadian Rockies from mountains of folded and faulted Precambrian rocks to the west. These three structures end southward at a zone of transverse faults north of the Idaho batholith. In the southwest is an area of block-faulted basins and ranges. (From *Natural Regions of the United States and Canada* by Charles B. Hunt, W. H. Freeman and Co., 1974.)

Jackson Hole block was lowered. There is now a 7,000 ft. vertical difference between layers of crust that were once contiguous. Similar block faulting formed the abrupt west face of the Wasatch Range, east of Salt Lake City.

Although we have now discussed the forces responsible for uplifting the Rocky Mountains to their present lofty heights, we have touched only briefly on those events most responsible for the topography of today's montane and alpine landscapes, the glaciations of the past 3 million years.

We tend to think of the ice ages as times of intense cold, but apparently that was not the case. The average temperature may have been a few degrees cooler, but more importantly, the climate was much wetter. If more precipitation falls as snow in the winter than melts in the following summer, snow accumulates. If this happens year after year, the snowpack reaches great depths, and pressure transforms the underlying snow into glacial ice, which slowly spreads out and flows downhill. We know there have be at least four major advances of glacial ice in our region in the last 3 million years, but most of the glacial features we see in our alpine areas are the result of the last one, which receded in some areas less than 10,000 years ago.

Alpine glaciers generally form at the head of existing stream valleys and then move downstream, scouring rock from the bottom and sides of the valley and carrying it away, transforming typical V-shaped stream valleys into the U-shaped valleys characteristic of glaciated areas. Evidence of glacial movement is everywhere in alpine and montane regions today. Containing sand and other debris, the glaciers acted like giant sandpaper, polishing rock over which they moved. Where large boulders became embedded in the ice and were dragged across rocks, deep scratches or grooves were worn in the rock, parallel to the direction of glacial movement. At the head of the glacier, the action of the ice plucked rock from the headwalls of the valley, forming large amphitheatre-shaped basins. These basins, visible at the head of U-shaped valleys throughout the Rockies, are called cirques, the bottoms of which are often filled with water, forming picturesque alpine lakes or tarns.

As a glacier flows slowly down the valley, it picks up and carries along tremendous amounts of rock and soil. At a lower elevation, or if the climate warms, the glacial advance stops as the ice at the leading edge melts. In so doing, it drops its accumulated mass of rock, forming a ridge of glacial debris marking the termination of the glacier. Such a ridge, often hundreds of feet high, and generally heavily forested, is called a terminal or end moraine. Other ridges, recessional moraines, form as the glacier melts back up the valley and comes to a temporary halt; and lateral moraines develop along the sides of the advancing glacier, forming long ridges along the margins of today's U-shaped valleys. Morainal debris often dams streams, producing the beautiful lakes so common in the Rockies. The most recent glaciers in the southern Rockies came down only to about the 8,000 ft. level, so it is common at that elevation to find morainal lakes. Farther north, however, glaciers reached lower elevations, sometimes extending out into the adjacent plains. Many lakes along the edge of the northern Rockies, including Jackson Lake, were formed by the damming of streams with glacial debris.

Though the glaciers temporarily receded about 10,000 years ago, and temperatures are now warming slightly, the numerous small glaciers occupying cirques throughout the Rockies serve notice that a small change in our climate could trigger new glacial advances. And although the glaciers are gone, the action of ice and snow continues to erode our mountain tops, breaking down rock faces into boulder fields, and boulder fields to talus slopes, and helping to form the thin soils of alpine meadows. Alternate freezing and thawing forces rocks to the surface, in strange polygonal patterns or as rock streams, and is instrumental in causing alpine soils to creep slowly downhill, a process known as solifluction. Thus, geological processes, from the movements of gigantic crustal plates to the erosive force of a single ice crystal, continue to shape our mountains and alter the habitats to which our unique alpine flora is so well adapted.

References

Alt, David D. and Donald W. Hyndman. 1972. *Roadside geology of the northern Rockies.* Missoula, Mont.: Mountain Press.

Chronic, Halka. 1984. *Pages of stone: geology of western national parks and monuments. Vol. 1: Rocky Mountains and western Great Plains.* Seattle, Wash.: The Mountaineers.

Chronic, Halka. 1980. *Roadside geology of Colorado.* Missoula, Mont.: Mountain Press.

Larkin, Robert P., Paul K. Grogger, and Gary L. Peters. 1980. *The southern Rocky Mountains.* Dubuque, Iowa: Kendall/Hunt.

Redfern, Ron. 1983. *The making of a continent.* New York: Times Books.

Rigby, J. Keith. 1976. *Northern Colorado Plateau.* Dubuque, Iowa: Kendall/Hunt.

Skinner, Brian J., ed. 1981. *Paleontology and paleoenvironments.* Los Altos, Calif.: William Kaufmann, Inc.

3

The Botanical Discovery of the Rockies

by Panayoti Kelaidis

There are many reasons why a gardener should know something about the botanical exploration of the Rocky Mountains. Most of the early accounts read like high adventure, for the Rockies were inhospitable wilderness throughout much of the nineteenth century. Knowing something about the principal explorers will suddenly make the task of learning the many honorific epithets far more pleasant and worthwhile. Above all, by viewing Western botany in a historical perspective, one understands more clearly why so much uncertainty and controversy still surround many of the names of plants that grow in this region.

Lewis and Clark Expedition (1804–1806)

The first specimens of plants taken in the Rockies were those collected by Meriwether Lewis and William Clark on the famous transcontinental journey inspired and mandated by Thomas Jefferson. There is something magical about this grandest of American expeditions: so little was known of the West, and so great were the dangers that lay in their path, it is indeed remarkable that the party of a few dozen explorers survived at all. Not only did they survive, but both Lewis and Clark made extensive notes on the lands they traversed. These have been edited and published in many versions, on many occasions, and they comprise the earliest detailed account of the northern Rocky Mountains. In addition to almost 200 plant specimens that have survived from this expedition, seed of various plants was collected along the way. This was subsequently grown by Bernard McMahon—a well-known Philadelphia nurseryman of the period—and included *Toxylon* (now *Maclura*) *pomiferum*, the Osage orange; *Ribes odoratum*, the buffalo currant; *Ribes sanguineum*, the winter currant; and *Mahonia aquifolium*, Oregon grape. The latter was named for McMahon by Thomas Nuttall.

Most of the herbarium specimens collected by the Lewis and Clark expedition were lost when the Belt Mountains Creek rose in flood and destroyed the cache where they were stored. Even so, Frederick Pursh was to describe 123 new species on the basis of the few sheets that did survive. Pursh was a student of Benjamin Barton, Thomas Jefferson's friend who had given Lewis and Clark

Panayoti Kelaidis, curator of Denver Botanic Gardens Rock Alpine Garden, has been interested in botanical history since, as a youth, he discovered and read widely about the adventures of early plant explorers. His search for the cultural "roots" of botany and horticulture in the Rocky Mountains is ongoing.

instruction on how to collect and preserve plant specimens. It is not known to this day how Pursh managed to supplant Barton as author of these western collections.

Although neither Lewis nor Clark was trained in the sciences, they were both highly cultured people with great powers of observation. As it is, their collections comprise some of the most treasured possessions of the Philadelphia Academy of Natural Sciences. If all of their collections had reached Philadelphia safely, the course of Western botany would have been very different.

Four new genera of plants were described from this expedition: the most famous of these (from the point of view of rock gardeners) is *Lewisia,* named for Meriwether Lewis. William Clark was commemorated in *Clarkia pulchella* which Pursh spelled "*Clarckia.*" *Calochortus elegans* was described from this expedition as well, the first species of the genus to be named. The ubiquitous western shrub *Purshia tridentata* was originally called *Tigaurea tridentata* by Pursh. The generic name was already applied to an altogether different plant by Aublet, and De Candolle renamed the genus in Pursh's honor.

The indefatigable Thomas Nuttall was to make his first foray west of the Mississippi River from 1810 to 1812 in the company of John Bradbury. They managed to travel up the Missouri as far as eastern Montana, gathering a wealth of plant specimens. Bradbury today is best known for *Penstemon bradburyi,* the giant-flowered penstemon of the tall-grass prairie long known by the name *P. grandiflorus.* As with the Lewis and Clark expeditions before this, Frederick Pursh managed to obtain access to Bradbury's collection prior to the owner's return, naming many new species of western plants. Although these two collectors didn't reach the Rockies, their collections constituted the first extensive sampling of the Great Plains flora, which includes so many plants with western affinities. Both collectors wrote books that influenced subsequent investigations.

Meriwether Lewis
Courtesy of Denver Public Library
Western Collection

Dr. Edwin James
Courtesy of Library, State Historical Society
of Colorado

Stephen Long Expedition (1821)

The first botanist to climb to the alpine zone in the Rocky Mountains was Edwin James, scientist with the Stephen Harriman Long expedition, which set forth in 1820 to explore the sources of the Platte River and returned to the Mississippi by way of the Arkansas River. Only 23 years of age, James was widely read and an astute observer of natural phenomena. His *Account of an expedition from Pittsburgh to the Rocky Mountains* is a classic of Western exploration. Even at this early date, James

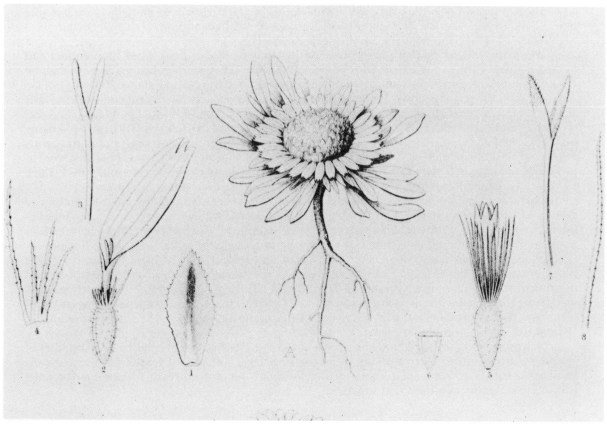

Townsendia rothrockii from the report of the Whipple expedition.
Helen Fowler Library, Denver Botanic Gardens

knew the need for "some law for the preservation of game . . . rigidly enforced in the country, where the bison is still met with: that wanton destruction of these valuable animals, by the white hunters, might be checked or prevented."

This same sort of lively intelligence imbues much of his *Account,* which is filled with numerous descriptions of the austere landscape he was the first scientist to visit: "Every step of our progress to the west brought us upon a less fertile soil. . . . Notwithstanding the barrenness of the soil, and the aspect of desolation which so widely prevails, we are often surprised by the occurrence of splendid and interesting productions springing up under our feet . . ."

James mentions hundreds of plants in the course of his exciting narrative: so vividly does he describe them and their setting that it is possible to follow the course of his expedition quite closely from his descriptions. The expedition arrived at the foot of the Rockies by the Fourth of July. The next few weeks were passed from the vicinity of Longs Peak (which they referred to as Pikes Peak) to the present day Pikes Peak, which was actually ascended by James and a few members of the party.

James mentions the "Castle rock," which still goes by that name. Nearby, James records that he "collected a large species of columbine, somewhat resembling the common one of the gardens. It is heretofore unknown to the flora of the United States, to which it forms a splendid acquisition. If it should appear not to be described, it may receive the name of *Aquilegia caerulea.*"

This has since been named the state flower of Colorado, and is surely one of the loveliest wildflowers in the West. He was impressed with many of the flowers on this expedition, and wrote most eloquently that "A deep blue is the prevailing colour among these flowers, and the *Penstemon erianthera* (sic) [either *P. alpinus,* or *P. virgatus*], the mountain Columbine (*Aquilegia caerulea*) and other plants common to less elevated districts, were here much more intensely coloured, than in ordinary situations . . . May the deep coerulean tint of the sky, be supposed to have an influence in producing the corresponding color, so prevalent in the flowers of these plants?"

James goes on to describe how "we met, as we proceeded, such numbers of unknown and interesting plants, as to occasion much delay in collecting, and we were under the disagreeable necessity of passing by numbers which we saw in situations difficult of access."

The tundra on Pikes Peak was "filled with clouds of grasshoppers, as partially to obscure the day ..." As they arrived late in the afternoon, they spent less than an hour above timberline. That night (July 15, 1821), the temperature dropped to 38°F.

The many collections that James made on his ascent of Pikes Peak were later studied and named by John Torrey of the New York Botanical Garden. They were published in a "Catalog of Plants" by the American Philosophical Society. They include such famous alpines as *Trifolium nanum, T. dasyphyllum, Primula angustifolia, Penstemon alpinus, Mertensia alpina* [which Torrey called *Pulmonaria alpina*], *Androsace chamaejasme* var. *carinata* [which Torrey first named *Androsace carinata*], *Castilleja occidentalis* and even *Pinus flexilis*. These were all named by Torrey. Torrey was also to give the name *Saxifraga jamesii* to the plant now known as *Telesonix jamesii*, which has also been put in the genus *Boykinia*. This is one of many plants, including *Chionophila jamesii* and *Jamesia americana*, that were to be named in honor of Colorado's first botanist. Pikes Peak was not climbed again until July 1, 1862, by Charles Christopher Parry who wrote of his experience to the same John Torrey.

David Douglas was to travel up the Columbia River Gorge, through the Palouse country of eastern Washington across the 49th Parallel in 1826 and 1827 in his first extensive foray into the interior of the Pacific Northwest. This was an extremely productive expedition, although the bulk of the plants he encountered were from lower elevations, technically to the west of the Rockies.

In 1825 Thomas Drummond, a Scottish botanical explorer, was assistant naturalist to John Franklin's second expedition to the Northwest. At the Saskatchewan River the party turned northward toward the Arctic Ocean and Drummond left them to go west. He spent two years wandering through the northern Rockies in search of plants. He returned to the Saskatchewan with many new species of plants and an intimate knowledge of the high country. He is commemorated in *Dryas drummondii* among other plants.

Nathaniel Jarvis Wyeth, commemorated in the genus *Wyethia*, was to collect a small number of specimens from the Northern Rockies while crossing the Continental Divide from the Missouri Drainage to the Columbia in 1832. It was not until the following year, however, that a trained botanist was to cross the Rockies from east to west.

Gilia watsonii
from the report
of the King expedition.
Helen Fowler Library,
Denver Botanic Gardens

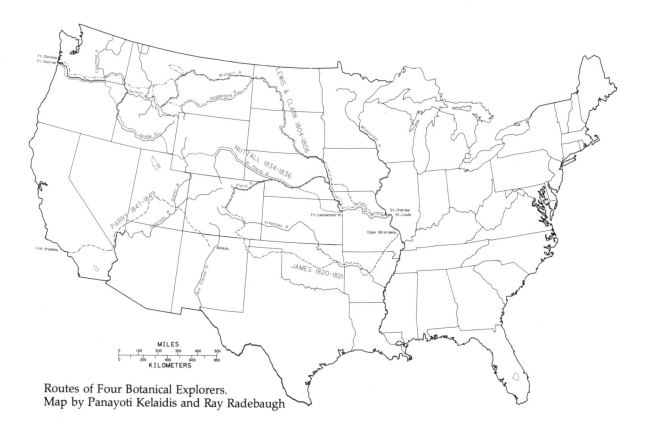

Routes of Four Botanical Explorers.
Map by Panayoti Kelaidis and Ray Radebaugh

Thomas Nuttall's Transcontinental Expedition (1834)

Thomas Nuttall launched his third expedition across the Mississippi in company with Nathaniel Wyeth and John Kirk Townsend. It was his most ambitious trip yet and the greatest exploration of the Rockies in that decade. Although Nuttall was both a meticulous correspondent and voluminous writer, he either neglected to keep a journal of this momentous expedition, or else it has been lost. Most of the information concerning his travels is derived from herbarium labels and the journals of Townsend, which were later published as a *Narrative of a journey across the Rocky Mountains, to the Columbia River, and a visit to the Sandwich Islands, Chili &c. with a scientific appendix.* Nuttall appears obliquely as "Old Curious" in Richard Henry Dana's *Two Years Before the Mast,* for he is the model for the naturalist aboard the Alert, which he boarded in his return trip to Boston in 1836.

It is the overland trip that concerns us here, and this is certainly the most productive expedition ever mounted through the Rockies. Townsend delights in describing how "The birds thus far have been very abundant. There is a considerable variety, and many of them have not before been seen by naturalists. As to the plants, there seems to be no end to them, and Mr. N. [Nuttall] is finding dozens of new species daily . . ."

This expedition crossed the Great Plains through southern Nebraska and southeastern Wyoming along the North Fork of the Platte River as far as Casper, Wyoming. Proceeding westward south of the Wind River Mountains through southern Idaho, they arrived at Walla Walla, Washington, on the Columbia River, down which they descended to the Pacific.

The greater portion of this journey took place during the summer of 1836, and almost the entire trip was spent on Great Plains grasslands east of the Divide and in the sagebrush desert to the west. These regions might be thought of as barren and unproductive; however, they yielded hundreds of new species of plants that feature prominently in any flora of the Rocky Mountain region, either bearing the epithet *"nuttallii"* or named by Nuttall himself.

The bulk of his collections was deposited in the British Museum, although many isotypes were also placed in the Academy of Natural Sciences in Philadelphia. It is estimated that Nuttall collected over 4,000 species of plants in his travels throughout the United States, many of which constituted the first collections of these plants ever made. In speaking of Nuttall, Asa Gray notes that ". . . no botanist has visited so large a portion of the United States, or made such an amount of observations in the field and forest. Probably few naturalists have ever excelled him in aptitude for such observations, in quickness of eye, tact in discrimination, and tenacity of memory."

Since relatively few of Nuttall's collections come from higher elevations in the Rockies, his contributions may not be as glamorous as those of other botanists. Yet, it is these plants of lower elevations which constitute many of the most dramatic and easily grown Western wildflowers. Surely no flower surpasses the sego lily (*Calochortus nuttallii*) in purity of form or color, and *Linanthastrum nuttallii* remains to this day one of the loveliest of Western phlox relatives. It is amusing to note how many plants well known to Nuttall (such as *Tanacetum capitatum*—now usually referred to as *Sphaeromeria capitata*) are only now gaining a toe hold in cultivation.

Indeed, many of Nuttall's discoveries were to fall into a sort of botanical limbo for over a century, until a new era of intensive botanical exploration commenced. *Parthenium alpinum* (now usually referred to as *Bolophyta alpina*) was only rediscovered in the 1940s, although it grows in vast numbers over its limited range. Nuttall was indeed a man far ahead of his time.

The Golden Age of Exploration

The acquisition of California and the southwestern states in the course of the war with Mexico in the 1840s sparked a new era of travel and exploration throughout the West. The doctrine of Manifest Destiny blossomed, and the wave of western migration began to swell. James, Douglas and Nuttall represent the loneliest and bravest sort of botanical explorer who truly ventures into *terra incognita*. It is a measure of the worth of these explorers that they accomplished so much in the face of such adversity, and then returned for more!

Henceforward, although exploration was still dangerous, botanists now had the experience of these pioneers to guide the way. Although numerous botanists were to explore the West in succeeding decades, none were to dominate the scene as did the first generation of explorers.

One of the most productive expeditions to be mounted in this later period was led by William D. Brackenridge with the express purpose of collecting plants of horticultural merit as well as botanical specimens. This expedition traveled throughout much of California, Oregon and Washington, as well as extensive portions of the Idaho Panhandle. About 10,000 collection numbers of plants, and over 50,000 individual specimens were said to have been collected by this expedition, surely unprecedented in its scope.

It is interesting to compare this earlier expedition with the highly publicized and enormously popular travels of John Charles Frémont. Frémont mounted five major expeditions in the West, although he only collected plants on the first three trips. Due to the wide coverage of his travels in the newspapers of the time, and his books describing his travels, Frémont created tremendous interest in the subject of western exploration. It is easy to debunk his accomplishments from a current vantage point, but a cursory view of his travels shows that he possessed remarkable energy and courage to cover literally thousands of miles of little-known and dangerous territory. Much of this was in the Rocky Mountain province.

On his first expedition, Frémont collected 352 species of plants, of which 16 were new to science. He possessed virtually no scientific training and traveled over regions previously botanized by James and Nuttall, so it might be said that he did quite well. His second expedition was incomparably more ambitious—extending throughout practically the entire West from the Rockies to the Sierra and back again. Unfortunately, most of the 1,400 species collected were damaged over the many thousands of miles that were traversed over uncharted territory. John Torrey and Asa Gray nevertheless managed to describe dozens of new species and even a few new genera on the basis of the imperfect collections of this second expedition.

Frémont's third expedition of the decade crossed much of the southern border of the country. Due to the historical upheaval of the Mexican War, much of his energy was expended in political and military maneuvering in California. It was from that state that most of the botanical specimens were taken in this expedition.

His subsequent expeditions (including the disastrous attempt to cross the San Juan Mountains of southwestern Colorado in midwinter) bore virtually no botanical fruit. Frémont remains a colorful and ubiquitous figure in the history of Western exploration. Surely no explorer covered more territory, or capitalized more effectively on his travels. His work cannot begin to compare with that of serious scientists, but then his primary accomplishment was to be the trailblazer and publicist of the West. This role he executed with flair.

Meanwhile, more and more serious botanists were to explore wider and wider areas throughout the West. Karl Theodor Hartweg, Ferdinand Jakob Lindheimer, William H. Emory and

Friedrich Adolph Wislizenus all conducted separate expeditions into the Southwest during the 1840s, harvesting an abundance of new plants in this rich botanical region.

Two other expeditions first tapped the wealth of plants that grow in the Southern Rockies: William Gambel in 1841, and August Fendler, from 1846 to 1849, concentrated on the mountains of northern New Mexico, where they were to find numerous undescribed taxa, many of which now commemorate their names.

Searching the Higher Mountains

Thorough collection of plants in the higher mountains of the southern and central Rocky Mountains did not take place until the 1850s and 1860s, when many botanists accompanied the early wave of miners and settlers to the Rocky Mountain region. Chief among these was Charles Christopher Parry. Parry practiced medicine in Davenport, Iowa, but must have spent most of his summers and spare time exploring the West (and writing extensively on his discoveries for 74 newspapers). His interest in botany was apparently sparked by John Torrey, with whom he studied at Columbia College in New York City. It was to Asa Gray, however, that Parry sent most of his specimens, although he carried on voluminous correspondence with most of the eminent botanists of his day. Parry had a cabin in Grizzly Gulch, a few miles south of Clear Creek Canyon thirty miles or so to the west of Denver. From his cabin he was to climb many of the peaks of the Colorado Front Range, which he subsequently named for his botanical friends: Torreys and Grays Peak, along with James Peak and Mount Flora (named for its flowery meadows) date from the time of Parry's explorations. He is commemorated in numerous honorific epithets from the entire West, notably *Primula parryi* and *Gentiana parryi (Pneumonanthe calycosa)*—two of the loveliest wildflowers in the Southern Rockies.

Dr. Charles Christopher Parry
Courtesy of Denver Public Library
Western Collection

In 1862 Parry was joined by Elihu Hall and J. P. Harbour—professional collectors of botanical *exsiccatae*—and Asa Gray was to describe a wealth of new species from their collections including the alpine penstemons, *Penstemon hallii* and *P. harbourii* named for these energetic explorers.

In 1870 an Episcopalian minister was to begin his career as a botanist in the same region: Edward Lee Greene began collecting plants in the high country of Colorado. Greene accompanied Parry and Asa Gray and his wife to the summit of Gray's Peak in August of 1872. In 1876 he departed for California where he was to live most of his life, although he returned to Colorado on several occasions to do fieldwork. He became the first professor of botany at the University of California, as well as editor and publisher of several botanical publications and leading antagonist to the predominant, East Coast school of botany led by Asa Gray. Greene was an inveterate "splitter" who resurrected numerous pre-Linnaean genera of plants, as well as inventing hundreds of new ones and naming literally thousands of species of Western plants. He is perhaps the most controversial figure in Western botany.

Another botanist was to begin her career in Denver as an amateur: Alice Eastwood arrived in Denver in 1880 where she taught a variety of subjects at East Denver High School. She collected extensively in the vicinity of Denver and in the mountains nearby. She published the first local flora for the Rocky Mountains: *A Popular Flora of Denver, Colorado,* issued in 1893. She moved to San Francisco shortly thereafter, and was to spend the next six decades exploring the West extensively, publishing widely and establishing a career as the leading botanist of the California Academy of Sciences.

Meanwhile, the United States Government continued to sponsor expeditions to assess the values of the extensive Western lands, and later to seek possible routes for transcontinental railroads. Most of these governmental surveys included botanical reports, and each of these reports contains a wealth of species new to science. These include the Whipple expeditions (1853 to 1854), which included J. M. Bigelow as botanist (determinations were done with assistance from George Englemann), that ranged widely through New Mexico and Arizona. *Penstemon whippleanus* is a noteworthy discovery of this expedition.

A party under Captain John W. Gunnison and Lieutenant Edwin Beckwith crossed what is now Colorado, climbing La Veta and Cochetopa Passes and many high mountains in the southwestern part of the state. Plants collected by F. Creutzfelt and later by J. A. Snyder added much to the knowledge of Western plants, particularly alpines. The Gunnison party (including the leader and Creutzfelt) were waylaid and massacred by Indians in Utah, and the mission was completed by Lieut. Beckwith with Snyder as botanist. In spite of the tragic ending of the first part of the expedition, notes and specimens gathered by Creutzfelt were saved and incorporated in the journals of the expedition. Leaders of this exploration are remembered by *Calochortus gunnisonii*—the incomparable mariposa lily of the Rockies—as well as the vivid sagebrush violet, *Viola beckwithii.*

Viola beckwithii from report on the Gunnison and Beckwith expedition. Helen Fowler Library, Denver Botanic Gardens

Clarence King conducted the "U.S. Geological Exploration of the 40th Parallel" from 1867 to 1871. Sereno Watson and Daniel C. Eaton accompanied him as botanists. Volume Five of the report of this expedition contained the account of the plants found on that expedition. It includes descriptions, together with exquisite line drawings, of such notable Great Basin endemics as the ultimate cushion plant, *Lepidium nanum.* Sereno Watson subsequently joined the staff at Harvard University, where he eventually succeeded Asa Gray as curator of the herbarium. D. C. Eaton became the leading student of American ferns, publishing the first comprehensive monograph on them.

The Hayden Surveys in 1853–1854 of the Bighorns were followed by Ferdinand Hayden's collections as part of the Raynold's Expedition to the headwaters of the Missouri and Yellowstone Rivers in 1859–1860. Later, in 1872–73, Hayden was accompanied by John Merle Coulter through the hitherto unbotanized mountains of central Colorado in explorations that yielded a wealth of new plants. Coulter was to become professor of botany at the University of Chicago where he authored the *Manual of Botany of the Rocky Mountains* in 1885. This was the standard fieldbook for the region for many decades, written along the conservative botanical lines of Asa Gray.

In 1909 Coulter's *Manual* was revised and thoroughly updated by Aven Nelson, professor of botany at the University of Wyoming at Laramie. Nelson was to found the Rocky Mountain Herbarium at that University, which has become the principal repository of the Rocky Mountain Region. Nelson was the dean of Rocky Mountain botany for sixty years, exploring widely throughout the region and encouraging an army of students, first as professor, later as president of the University of Wyoming.

Two other botanists rival Nelson as doyens of Western botany in the first half of the twentieth century. Per Axel Rydberg, a native of Sweden, came to America in 1882 and spent the next fifty years researching the flora of the American West. He began his career teaching a variety of subjects at the Luther Academy in Wahoo, Nebraska. From 1891–1896 he collected widely throughout the West as field agent for the U.S. Dept. of Agriculture. In 1896 he collected extensively throughout Montana, forming the basis for his *Flora of Montana and Yellowstone National Park* in 1900. In 1899 he began his work with the New York Botanical Garden. The following year he began collecting throughout Colorado; these collections formed the basis for the *Flora of Colorado* published in 1906. Together with Edward Greene, Rydberg represents the "splitter" extreme of Western botany, a heterodox tradition that maintains itself to this day. He is remembered in *Penstemon rydbergii,* a widespread montane species, which appropriately is quite similar to a number of other penstemons in its section.

The other giant of this period was Marcus Jones, who likewise began his botanical career as a Latin teacher in Colorado in 1878. During much of the same period as Rydberg, Jones collected throughout the Great Basin, discovering hundreds of new species of plants and selling *exsiccatae* to herbaria throughout the world. He authored a long series of analyses of Western plants under the title "Contributions to Western Botany."

The Renaissance of Western Floristics

With the passing of Jones and Rydberg in the early 1930s, the broad outlines of the Rocky Mountain flora were clearly emerging. It was no longer easy to discover dozens of new taxa on a single field trip. Roads and travel had opened up whole new regions for careful observation, and suddenly dozens of specialists began to scour the western countryside in the study of specific groups of plants. In the last fifty years, more and more of the principal groups of Western plants have been studied in detail, and the groundwork is being laid for a comprehensive flora of the Rocky Mountain region.

Increasingly, modern scholars tended to specialize in specific groups. Reed Rollins, for instance, has selected the Brassicaceae for special study, producing a series of monographic studies of *Lesquerella* and *Physaria*. Edgar Wherry spent years in monographing *Phlox*, while *Penstemon* has occupied the energies of Francis Pennell, David Keck, Frank Crosswhite and Noel Holmgren. The epitome of recent research is represented by Rupert Barneby.

Barneby emigrated to America from England in the early 1940s, commencing a series of monumental explorations throughout the West with his friend and associate Dwight Ripley. Ripley was well known in England as a connoisseur of alpines and grower of difficult plants. In a long series of articles for the Alpine Garden Society, Ripley documented the early travels of these witty and astute explorers who criss-crossed the American West as thoroughly as Humbert-Humbert and Dolores Haze.

In addition to locating a wealth of new species, Barneby relocated numerous "lost" localities of early explorers such as Nuttall. Increasingly, his attention was focused on *Oxytropis* and *Astragalus*. He wrote his first monograph on the former genus in 1952, and completed an extensive and intensive monograph on the North American species of *Astragalus* in 1964 which occupies 1,181 pages of print.

With the increased exploration for oil and minerals throughout the West in the 1960s and 1970s, a new era of intensive exploration has been launched, leading to an even more thorough analysis of the plants of the Rocky Mountains and Great Basin. The monumental *Intermountain Flora* published by New York Botanical Gardens offers testimony to this renaissance of Western floristics. However, no comprehensive modern flora has yet been written covering the Rocky Mountain region: this may not appear until we reach a third century of exploration.

References

Bartlett, Richard. 1962. *Great surveys of the American West.* Norman, Okla.: University of Oklahoma Press.

Coues, Elliott. 1965. *History of the expedition under the command of Lewis and Clark.* 3 vols. New York: Dover Press.

Ewan, Joseph. 1950. *Rocky Mountain naturalists.* Denver: University of Denver Press.

James, Edwin. 1823. *Account of an expedition from Pittsburgh to the Rocky Mountains, performed in the years 1819 and '20.* Philadelphia: Transactions of the American Philosophical Society, New Series.

McKelvey, Susan Delano. 1955. *Botanical exploration of the Trans-Mississippi West, 1790–1850.* Jamaica Plain: The Arnold Arboretum.

A rock garden with 19 errors. From the M. Walter Pesman Collection.

4

Early Rock Gardening in the Rockies

by Gwen Kelaidis

Where the mountains dominate the western skyline, and the foothills descend to the plains, it is only natural that there should be interest in the plants of the highlands. When summer heat leaves the plains shimmering, and water evaporates as quickly as it can be applied to lawns, it should come as no surprise that the gardener thinks of growing the native plants, which require so much less attention than their traditional garden counterparts.

Many of the early homesites in cities such as Colorado Springs and Boulder had rocks, and certainly many mountain homes of the early 1900s did also, and so many early landscapes quite naturally incorporated rocks. Plants were certainly grown in and among rocks from very early settlement. But who made the native plants available, and who influenced and encouraged naturalistic garden design and the development of the rock garden in this region?

In 1892 Darwin M. Andrews came to Colorado. He had an interest in both horticulture and botany, and had already successfully made a living from selling plants: he put himself through college by selling herbarium specimens. He soon started a nursery, and began selling a line of plant material which included shrubs, trees, an array of hybrid phloxes, irises, peonies, and lilacs, and soon expanded to include wildflowers. Andrews was the first to offer many of the native shrubs, such as New Mexican privet (*Forestiera*), jamesia, cercocarpus, and *Amorpha nana*. His 1924 catalog includes many of the hardy cacti, as well as *Mirabilis multiflora*, the sand lily (*Leucocrinum*) at $6.00 for 100, three species of *Penstemon*, and *Townsendia grandiflora*, among many others. The listing of "A Few Choice Alpines" includes *Primula angustifolia*, *Gentiana parryi*, and *Dodecatheon radicatum* (now *D. pulchellum*). In the 1934–35 catalog there are nine species of *Penstemon*, seven varieties of *Iris spuria*, three species of native *Oenothera*, and four of the choice, dwarf native phloxes. Many of the plants, are, alas, not offered by any nursery in the Rockies today.

D. M. Andrews explored and collected widely in the West, and his catalog was renowned in the parts of the world where rock gardening was most popular. He was a correspondent of Reginald

Gwen Kelaidis began gardening as a child in upstate New York. The daughter of west Texans, she knew her destiny lay in the West: she migrated as far as Wisconsin in her college years, settling there to teach high school and later to serve as curator of the Herbarium at the University of Wisconsin. She built several small rock gardens, served as president of the Wisconsin-Illinois chapter of ARGS, and became an active member of the American Penstemon Society. In 1984 she decided to pursue a career in horticulture and field botany in partnership with Denver rock gardener Panayoti Kelaidis. She now has a small business in landscape design and construction, and she currently serves as secretary of the ARGS Rocky Mountain Chapter.

Farrer, and is mentioned in *The English Rock Garden.* It was said that travelers from Colorado to England frequently were greeted with a query whether they knew the visionary nurseryman. That he was a man ahead of his time, and one who contributed greatly to Colorado horticulture cannot be doubted. In Boulder on the site of his nursery, which was subdivided some years after his death in 1938, there are still today marvelous specimens of wavy-leaf oak, shingle oak, Ohio buckeye, and a variety of lilacs, which have survived beautifully despite neglect and lack of water. They stand as testimony to the wisdom of his selection of hardy materials. Andrews left behind a large manuscript, including sections on both alpines and native plants, which we hope may someday be published.

Early Rocky Mountain nursery catalogs. Helen Fowler Library, Denver Botanic Gardens

In 1912 another devoted horticulturist had arrived in Colorado. Kathleen Marriage had studied horticulture and garden design at the University of London. She opened a nursery in Colorado Springs in 1916. The undated catalog which I saw contained a list of 140 genera, and many more species; of *Penstemon,* she lists seventeen! Mrs. Marriage states that all were grown in her nursery, and that although collected plants might be had on special order, they were not recommended. She does include a description of the snow melt which waters mountain plants, and recommends an underground moraine-type watering system and a lath house shade for high alpines. Beyond that she gives no cultural instructions for the plants other than to describe their native habitat. For, she says, "moist for Colorado is usually dry for England." Her list included such impressively ungrowable species as *Stanleya bipinnata, Phlox bryoides, Calochortus gunnisonii,* and *Boykinia (Telesonix) jamesii.* The latter she sent to the Chelsea Flower Show, where it took an Aware of Merit. This woman was surely one of the first great growers of western American alpines. Marriage also wrote very perceptive articles for *The Green Thumb,* the magazine of the former Colorado Forestry and Horticultural Association. She designed home gardens, and oversaw their installation and maintenance. Reputed to be a strong-willed and rather intimidating woman, it is surprising that little has been recorded about her life and work. Whether she built many rock gardens for customers, whether these successfully included the alpines of the connoisseur, whether any of her work is extant today, I do not know. She closed her nursery about 1948, and died in 1958.

The market for many of the rock garden plants offered by these two great nurseries was primarily European. But as early as 1916 there had begun to be some local interest. That year S. R. DeBoer, brilliant landscape architect and designer of so many of Denver's city parks and neighborhoods, built what he says was the first rock garden in the city. In his very readable and charming book, *Around the Seasons in Denver Parks and Gardens* (Denver, 1948), he tells us that he and his workers used whatever stone was available, because the trouble of hauling rock from the mountains by horse-drawn cart was too great an undertaking. The garden, complete with small stream, was part of the great Sunken Gardens on Eighth Avenue and Speer Boulevard. Unfortunately this rock garden was let go, DeBoer tell us, due to the necessity of maintaining it with trained, knowledgeable hand-labor. The garden was clothed with such traditional plants as wallflowers, sedums, pinks, armerias, nepetas, soapwort, pussytoes, sandworts, aubrietias, campanulas, and snow-in-summer. By 1948 several great private rock gardens had been constructed by DeBoer,

The Reed garden in Denver designed by DeBoer. Helen Fowler Library, Denver Botanic Gardens

including the garden of C. C. Gates, the John Gates estate, and the garden of the late Mrs. Verner Reed. The Reed garden, including the rock garden and its pool, which reflects the mansion, underwent a 35-year period of neglect after the death of Mrs. Reed. The present owners uncovered the rockwork, which had been buried under soil and junipers, by prodding with poles to find the rocks, then carefully excavating.

The first rock garden of Denver Botanic Gardens was also designed by DeBoer. It was a great canyon constructed at City Park in 1951, with funds donated by the Gates family. Due to increased recreational use of City Park, and accompanying damage to plantings, the entire herbaceous section of the Botanic Gardens was moved to its present York Street location, and the Gates Canyon, as a rock garden, was abandoned in 1959. The rock work is now planted to turf, and can be seen to the southwest of the Natural History Museum.

M. Walter Pesman was a partner of DeBoer for seven very fertile years. Pesman's emphasis was on naturalistic landscaping, and on the use of native plants. He used the plants of western North America extensively in his designs, and also incorporated lots of rock work, especially rock walls. There's a story that he once had a customer in Boulder with a very rocky yard. He was excited about the possibilities of designing something unique, but when he arrived, the homeowners had had the lot bulldozed. Pesman refused the job, saying that any landscaper could now fit a standard plan to the lot. Pesman taught rock garden design, and wrote an article on that topic in the first Brooklyn Botanic Garden's *Handbook on Rock Gardening*. A few of his old lantern slides on the subject are now in the Denver Botanic Gardens Helen C. Fowler Library. They are not labelled, but it isn't hard to guess which represent "good", and which "bad" design. Perhaps as great a contribution as his landscapes was Pesman's book *Meet the Natives,* which is an introduction to the plants of Colorado for the non-botanist. Many Coloradans still learn about native plants through this book. Pesman also wrote many articles in praise of wild landscapes, and of their preservation, and was, with DeBoer and Kelly, instrumental in the establishment of the Denver Botanic Gardens.

Possibly the best known of all Colorado horticulturists is George Kelly. Author of *Rocky Mountain Horticulture* (Boulder, 1958), and *How to Have Good Gardens in the Sunshine States* (Boulder,

PLATE 1

Glacier National Park, Montana
Photo: Glacier National Park

Aquilegia jonesii
Photo by Ned Lowry

Townsendia montana
Photo by Elizabeth Neese

Collomia debilis
Photo by Elizabeth Neese

PLATE 2

Caltha leptosepala
Photo by Ted Kipping

Cassiope mertensiana
Photo by Sharon Sutton

Erythronium grandiflorum
Photo by Ned Lowry

Phyllodoce empetriformis
Photo by Ned Lowry

Dryas octopetala subsp. *hookerana*
Photo by Ted Kipping

Ranunculus sp.
Photo by Sharon Sutton

1958), and long-time editor of *The Green Thumb,* the magazine of the Colorado Forestry and Horticulture Association, and now of the Denver Botanic Gardens, Kelly has vigorously promoted the use of native plants in naturalistic gardens. Although not so much a rock gardener himself as a spokesman, Kelly kept the natives in everyone's consciousness. He ran a nursery which made these plants available, and he offered a landscape design service which encouraged thousands of people to plant Colorado plants. He built a long, freestanding rock wall in front of his nursery, and designed many home rock gardens. He contributed the chapter on Rocky Mountain alpines to the Brooklyn Botanic Gardens *Handbook on Rock Gardening.* In 1959 he said, "I know of no place where there is a better blending of art and science than in designing, building, and maintaining a good rock garden." (*The Green Thumb,* Vol. 16(6):192.).

Many others contributed to the art of rock gardening in Colorado. There were many who built rock gardens and grew the Rocky Mountain alpines, and there were nurserymen who carried on the growing, especially of the woody natives. There was Bernice Petersen, now honorary editor of *The Green Thumb,* who promoted rock gardening not only through her writing and editing, but by organizing the rock garden booth at Denver Botanic Gardens' annual plant sale for many years, thus making a wider variety of these plants available to an ever-growing public. By the mid-1960s Colorado could boast of T. Paul Maslin, who was perhaps the first since Andrews and Marriage to grow the choicer alpines here in Colorado. He contributed articles to the American Rock Garden Society bulletins, and brought into cultivation, from his plant explorations, the brilliant Mexican phloxes.

Elsewhere in the Rockies the rock garden art was practiced by Montana's Clare Regan. Starting from a magazine-inspired "wedding cake" construction in 1925, Regan had become one of the great rock gardeners of the country by the late forties. She writes of exchanging seed with many Europeans, of growing dozens of members of the Campanulaceae, of the response of the rock garden to a summer more like winter. Her writings may be found in those rare early issues of the ARGS bulletins, the last appearing in 1954. A picture of her garden is included in Vol. 5:15 (1947).

Another Montanan active in ARGS circles was Frank Rose, who offered a catalog full of western American rock plants. These he collected all over the West, taking orders also for specific desired plants not listed. Since the likelihood of actually finding all the requested plants or seeds in a season was low, he billed his customers only when he shipped the order, asking that money not be sent in advance! He also contributed to the ARGS bulletin in the early years, including an article discussing the still-confused taxonomy of the genus *Dodecatheon.* This was at the time when the society was choosing its plant emblem, and despite his obvious interest in shooting stars, he casts his vote for *Lewisia rediviva,* surely a Montana loyalist.

The early pioneers of this field stood almost alone in their efforts, working over the decades to create a gardening community who could appreciate their work and study. That so many years are required to popularize a style of gardening so natural and adaptive for the climate and conditions here can only be considered a comment on the conservative nature of gardening itself, and the consequent unwillingness of the gardening public to try new plants and regimes of soil and watering. In 1976 a Rocky Mountain chapter of the American Rock Garden Society was founded, and its increasing membership and activity demonstrate the rising interest in this form of garden artistry. With the construction of the Rock Alpine garden at the Denver Botanic Gardens in 1979, and the continuing support of the Gardens for the testing of new plant materials and cultural methods, it seems that the work of these early lovers of plants and nature may indeed be forged into a new and enduring naturalistic gardening tradition.

References

Ash, Suzanne, and Bernice Petersen. 1973. "A catalog of rock plants and ground covers." *The Green Thumb.* 29(1):15–22.

Brooklyn Botanic Gardens. 1952. *Handbook on Rock Gardens.* Special printing of *Plants and Gardens,* Vol. 8:3. New York: Brooklyn Botanic Gardens.

DeBoer, S. R. 1958. *Around the seasons in Denver parks and gardens.* Denver: Smith-Brooks Press.

———. 1964. "In memoriam M. Walter Pesman." *The Green Thumb.* 20(1):6–7.

Johnson, Frederick R. 1969. "In retrospect (M. Walter Pesman)." *The Green Thumb.* 20(1):7–8.

More, Robert. 1959 "Mrs. G. R. (Kathleen O'Neil) Marriage." *The Green Thumb.* 15(3):109.

Petersen, Bernice E. 1976. "Colorado's horticultural pioneers." *The Green Thumb.* 33(3):66–75.

Regan, Clare W. 1947. "A beginner's rock garden in the misty past." *Bull. Am. Rock Garden Soc.* 5:48–50.

PART TWO
Wild Rock Gardens of the Rockies

Section I

Northern Rockies: Glacier and Muskeg

Courtesy of Travel Alberta

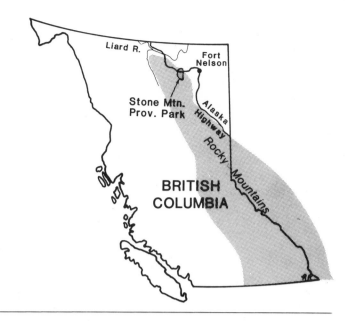

5

The End of the Rockies: Northern British Columbia

by Bodil Leamy

The province of British Columbia (B.C.) is large, with many mountain ranges marching across it. The Canadian part of the Rockies forms much of the border between B.C. and Alberta, and when people talk about the Canadian Rockies, they usually mean the areas around Banff and Jasper, both justly famous for their beautiful and spectacular scenery.

But in reality, the Canadian Rockies stretch farther north, all the way up to the 59th parallel, ending just south of the central part of the B.C.-Yukon border. The Alaska Highway, which runs almost due east and west in this area, crosses the northern end of the range, and it is here that Stone Mountain Park is situated. The Highway reaches its highest elevation, 4,250 ft., inside the Park at Summit Pass, which is on the Continental Divide. There is also a small lake, Summit Lake, and beside it a gas station, a four-room motel and a restaurant.

The list of plant species found in Stone Mountain Park is lengthy. It is a limestone area and the home of many choice plants with ten species of the genus *Salix,* nine of the genus *Potentilla,* and five of the genus *Draba.* Many northern American species new to me, such as *Potentilla biflora* and *Rhododendron lapponicum,* reach their southernmost location here, but there are also many old friends to be found, including *Silene acaulis* and *Draba densifolia.*

While picnicking alongside Summit Lake we found several interesting plants growing on the gravel banks supporting the road above the lake. There were mats of *Cornus canadensis* growing almost into the wheel-tracks, including one plant with rose-stained bracts. It would be a choice plant to grow in your garden, if the color remains true.

In the bare, graveled areas around the gas station were clumps of the familiar, annual foxtail grass, *Hordeum jubatum.* Blowing in the wind along the highways, it is well known to all of us. What made these particular plants so special was the color of the stems and awns. They were suffused with purple, darker in the stems with lighter rose-pink awns. It should be tried in cultivation to learn whether the color persists.

We found the tiny annual *Gentiana (Ciminalis) prostrata* growing in moist soil around the edge of the lake. The small, clear blue flowers are square in shape, and they act as a weather indicator,

Bodil Leamy helped develop and plant the E. H. Lohbrunner Alpine Garden at the University of British Columbia Botanical Garden where she now works as propagator of alpine and hardy herbaceous plants. She is a past secretary and president of the Alpine Garden Club of British Columbia, and has written and lectured extensively about plants. Her life-long interest in gardening began in her grandmother's garden in Denmark when she was four or five years old. She immigrated to Canada with her family when she was 17.

opening only when the sun shines. In the same area we found a charming dwarf sedge, *Carex aurea.* It is a slender plant, 4–6 in. high, with a golden yellow inflorescence. It looks like a yellow grape hyacinth and contrasts beautifully with the blue gentian. Both plants are ideally suited for growing in a trough.

A rough, four-wheel drive road leaves the highway on the south side of Summit Pass and winds its way up to a long ridge. The road was built to install and service a microwave station, and at the top, about 5,500 ft., it levels out into acres of alpine meadows and scree slopes.

The plants growing at the lower end of the road just above the pass are typical subalpine plants. Here we found no fewer than four different blue-flowered perennials: *Delphinium glaucum, Polemonium acutiflorum, Aconitum delphinifolium* ssp. *chamissonianum* and the lovely *Mertensia paniculata.* This species of *Mertensia* ranges all the way south to Wyoming and west to Oregon in the United States. It was in full flower in early July, the glaucous leaves contrasting beautifully with hanging croziers of vivid blue.

Higher up we found a form of *Mertensia paniculata* with two-tone flowers. They are pure white with a band of pale blue around the edge of the corolla. The effect was lovely close-up, but a bit "wishy-washy" from a distance.

Aconitum delphinifolium is a widespread species whose range extends into northwestern Siberia. The species is highly variable so it has been divided into three subspecies. The tallest form, *A. delphinifolium* ssp. *chamissonianum,* is a forest-edge species with rather coarse foliage. On the ridge, the subspecies *A. d.* ssp. *delphinifolium* took over. This form grows only 6–8 in. high in the wild and has much better leaves. The flowers are large, of the typical helmet shape and dark blue with no trace of purple. The stem is always rigidly erect, even on the windy ridge where it finds shelter in the *Betula nana* thickets. In cultivation, this subspecies grew and flowered well over a long period. The flower stalks eventually reached a height of 12 in. when grown in a 4 in. pot.

The third subspecies, *A. delphinifolium* ssp. *paradoxum,* has so far not been found in Stone Mountain Park. This is a highly desirable plant I first saw in the wild in Mount Edziza Park, which is situated far west of here and is not part of the Rockies. *Aconitum delphinifolium* ssp. *paradoxum* is the high alpine form that grows on bare windswept screes over 6,000 ft. It is a small plant about 3 in. high with 2 to 5 enormous dark blue flowers and a couple of small leaves lying flush with the ground. It is hoped seed will be available one day so that it can be tried in an alpine house.

The vegetation became lower and more sparse as we walked up to the ridge, which was covered with a thick growth of mosses and lichens in a wide range of colors. There were miniature forests of a waist-high species of *Salix* and knee-high clumps of *Betula nana,* both of which sheltered many plants. Here we found *Campanula lasiocarpa,* always as a single plant with only one flower stalk growing through the pale gray reindeer moss. *Campanula aurita* chose a more conventional habitat

Lake where *Arnica lessingii* grows. Photo by Bodil Leamy

for an alpine. It grew on stony soil between large rocks and looked superficially like *Campanula piperi*. This is not surprising as they are closely related. *Campanula aurita* has dark blue, flattish star-shaped flowers on 4–8 in. stems. It can only be called a second class campanula because the flowers are too small in proportion to its height. It would be interesting to cross it with *C. piperi* to see what kind of offspring would be produced.

Three different species of *Arnica* grow on the ridge. Each has chosen its own microclimate, and in spite of growing fairly close to each other, there is no sign of hybrids. All three are small 4–6 in. plants with nodding yellow flowers.

Arnica alpina var. *attenuata* grew alongside *Dodecatheon frigidum* in thick turf close to seeping moisture on a rather steep slope facing north or northwest. *Arnica lessingii,* the most beautiful of the three species, has soft yellow flowers highlighted by a dark red calyx. It grew singly and in drifts in the gently sloping alpine meadow along the shore of a small shallow lake where it was well protected from the wind—a charming plant in a delightful setting.

Arnica louisiana is the smallest of the species, growing only about 4 in. high. It chooses to grow right on top of a small ridge, where it is constantly buffeted by the wind. The leaves form a small rosette, and the plants grow thickly embedded in moss and lichen. This species has been grown successfully in Vancouver without any protection, and it keeps its dwarf habit in cultivation.

Just a few feet below the ridge, on the quiet side out of the wind, grow some small thickets of stunted *Betula nana* in which we found *Pyrola grandiflora*. The thickets are such a successful shelter that the pyrolas scarcely move in the wind, in sharp contrast to the arnicas above. It is a surprising place to find pyrolas. They grow as single rosettes in moss and lichen with 1 or 2 flower stalks per plant, each carrying up to 12 flowers. They are large, up to 0.5 in. across, and the color is a soft lime green. They fully live up to their specific name. This is one of the most beautiful pyrolas I have seen.

We especially wanted to find plants of *Corydalis pauciflora*. I have seen it in flower on Mount Edziza where I found only three plants in two locations a good mile apart. There they were growing in level alpine turf with such plants as *Dryas integrifolia* and grasses such as the dwarf *Luzula wahlenbergii*. Luck was with us in Stone Mountain Park, for we found about a dozen small, nonflowering plants in an area approximately 10 ft. square on the same slope where the *Arnica alpina* var. *attenuata* and *Dodecatheon frigidum* were growing. The corydalis appears to be as rare in nature as in cultivation, but it is no great loss since it, too, lives up to its name and has only a few, insignificant mauve flowers on a 6–8 in. stem.

Dryas integrifolia was the most common plant on the ridge. Close to the little lake where the *Arnica lessingii* was found, we came across one plant of this *Dryas* with semidouble flowers. It was very lovely and would be a most desirable plant to grow in our gardens. The extra petals gave the flowers more substance, which set them apart from the single ones. Unfortunately, the one small

Arnica lessingii, left, and *Pyrola grandiflora*
Photos by Bodil Leamy

cutting we brought back failed to root.

Since it was early July, we were just too late to see *Rhododendron lapponicum* in full flower, although there were still a few late ones—enough to give us an idea of what the ridge looked like when all the plants were flowering. The flowers are a vivid reddish magenta, and the multitude of plants in bloom must provide a spectacular display. The rhododendrons grow everywhere; every situation and exposure seems to suit them. They grow in a mixture of moss and lichens on top of and between tumbled rocks where the soil is often a foot below the surface, providing faultless drainage.

Rhododendron lapponicum has a bad reputation as a garden plant. Collected plants are almost impossible to establish in the garden, and cuttings are difficult to root. One of the plants, grown from seed collected in this area and planted in a garden situation beside a tufa rock, has survived for the last two years. Other specimens planted in other gardens have also survived, although all have grown somewhat reluctantly and none has flowered. It would certainly be a mistake to say that they have settled down in cultivation.

Personally, I think one of the most interesting plants found along the ridge was *Potentilla biflora*. I had read about it years ago in Sampson Clay's book *The Present Day Rock Garden*. He describes it as a tight, choice, cushion plant found in China and also ranging across Siberia into Alaska and northern B.C. He says the North American form is larger and looser than its Asian counterpart and has paler flowers. On the ridge it grew beside *Rhododendron lapponicum*, but it seemed to prefer the north slope just above the track. *Potentilla biflora* forms loose domes of small gray-green leaves, each slashed into 2 to 5 linear segments. The leaves are deciduous, colored a beautiful dark red in the fall. The flowers are large with soft, yellow petals carried on short 1–1.5 in. stalks. Unfortunately, they are sparsely produced, and *P. biflora* is only a second-rate plant for this reason. A search for a many-flowered plant would be well worth the effort. The species can be propagated by cuttings, though it is much easier to grow from seed. It has survived outside in Vancouver, planted on its side in a rock crevice. It should be strictly guarded from attacks by root weevils, to which it is rather susceptible.

There was a wet scree facing north just below the microwave station. We found some small cushion plants in the moist gravel on this slope. They looked like a large-leaved form of *Silene acaulis*, but the large, white daisies gave the game away. We were looking at *Chrysanthemum integrifolium*. It is a choice plant. The flowers stayed cool and crisp-looking in spite of exposure to a strong wind that kept them in constant motion. *Chrysanthemum integrifolium* would be well worth growing in our gardens, but so far two different batches of seed have not germinated.

There were many plants of the tiny *Tofieldia pusilla* growing in the same scree. The whole plant is less than 2 in. high. A small fan-shaped tuft of linear leaves is crowned with off-white flowers carried by a thread-like stem. The delicate proportions make it a perfect choice for growing in a trough. Plants in my garden have grown well for two years. They were planted in a scree mix and given half shade plus some protection from winter rain.

In the disturbed soil of the track itself grew no less than three species of *Saxifraga*. *Saxifraga aizoides* and *S. flagellaris* formed rather small plants 3–4 in. across. *Saxifraga oppositifolia* grew into large, perfectly round, dense cushions, some up to a foot wide—a far better plant than any I have seen in cultivation. It was obvious from the number of green seed pods that every shoot had flowered. The plants must have been a stunning sight in full flower.

The plants described are just a few of the many interesting ones to be seen in Stone Mountain Park. It is an area to be visited again and again, for Stone Mountain Park has everything: spectacular scenery as well as beautiful plants. Standing on the top of the ridge and looking north, the view is breathtaking. You can see for miles. The air is fragrant, and the light is so clear and bright you almost feel weightless. Looking down toward the Alaska Highway and Summit Pass, one can see the Tetsa River flowing east and the McDonald River flowing west toward the Pacific Ocean. This vast, panoramic view confirms the impression that this is, indeed, the top of the Rocky Mountains and you are, in all reality, standing on the backbone of a continent.

References

Alaska Magazine, ed. staff. 1974. *The Alaska-Yukon wildflower guide.* Anchorage: Alaska Northwest Publishing Co.

Hardy, George A., and V. Winnifred. 1949. *Wild flowers in the Rockies.* Saskatoon: H. R. Larson Publishing Co.

Hulten, Eric. 1968. *Flora of Alaska and its neighboring territories.* Stanford, Calif.: Stanford University Press.

Taylor, Roy L., and Bruce MacBryde. 1976. *Vascular plants of British Columbia: a descriptive resource inventory.* Vancouver: University of British Columbia Press.

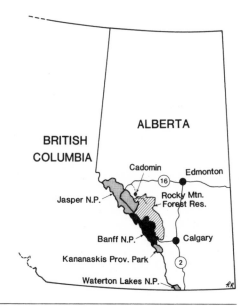

6

Alpines of the Canadian Rockies

by Patrick D. Seymour

The geologically complex Canadian Rockies (Continental Ranges) rise as high as 3,700 m and extend from 49 to 54 degrees north latitude, trending northwest to southeast along the Continental Divide. Much of the area was extensively glaciated during the Pleistocene Ice Age, but parts of the eastern front of the range, among other areas, escaped severe glaciation, leaving intact ancestors of the fascinating flora we find here today.

Ease of access to alpines in the area varies greatly: from six-hour hikes to driving directly onto the tundra, and even to trips by helicopter. I have selected several typical areas, moving from south to north: two in Waterton Lakes National Park (Rowe Lake and Carthew Pass); two in Banff National Park (Larch Valley and Peyto Lake); one in Kananaskis Provincial Park (Ptarmigan Cirque); two in Jasper National Park (Mount Edith Cavell Meadows and Whistler's Mountain); and one in the Rocky Mountain Forest Reserve (Cardinal Divide). Some of these I have visited many times. Specific areas will be mentioned for viewing specific plants. The most recent information was gathered during the first week of July 1985 when I walked all the trails below.

Rowe Lakes

Access is from the Cameron Lake road. The trail climbs gently through pines. In aspen areas are found large clumps of brilliant blue upright *Penstemon albertinus* and pale purple upright *Penstemon lyallii* mixed with *Hedysarum sulphurescens*. *Xerophyllum tenax*, 1 m tall, appears low on the trail, gradually becoming more numerous higher up. Cream-colored *Calochortus apiculatus* spangles the dry, open areas along with *Sedum lanceolatum* and large mats of different species of *Antennaria*. A light red species of *Castilleja* is frequent. Cream *Pyrola (Ramiscia) secunda* is in the shade.

A shrub smelling of skunk when touched is pale, reddish, cream-flowered *Menziesia ferruginea*. At the trail switchback appears a sea of blue *Penstemon albertinus* along with white *Rubus parviflorus*. Beside a fast-flowing stream *Delphinum bicolor* glows darkly on a red shale slope. *Erythronium*

Patrick D. Seymour, graduate of the Royal Botanic Garden in Edinburgh, brought his love of rock gardening from that institution to the Canadian West where he serves as director of the Devonian Botanic Garden of the University of Alberta in Edmonton. He has explored for alpines throughout the United States, Canada and New Zealand as well as Europe. Living near the Canadian Rockies, he has had fertile ground for plant exploration near at hand.

Mimulus lewisii. Photo by Loraine Yeatts

grandiflorum appears early on the trail. It must have bloomed in June; higher up it is still in bloom. Growing in deep shade under conifers is *Clintonia uniflora* with its white chalices followed by blue berries in the fall. Next to appear are the wonderfully sculptured leaves of *Veratrum viride,* not yet in flower. Airy *Aquilegia flavescens,* yellow occasionally tinged with pink, brightens the shady areas. I found a plant of *Calypso bulbosa* going to seed on a rotting log. On the shady side of the trail, blue *Clematis columbiana* sprawls over surrounding plants.

An old, open slide area is covered with 60 cm high shrubs of *Prunus virginiana* with white flowers, *Rhamnus alnifolia* and white *Amelanchier alnifolia.* Damp areas have beautiful, bright sky-blue *Hackelia micrantha* resembling a giant forget-me-not. Next to appear are powder-purple spikes of *Phacelia sericea,* the envy of any grower of alpines. Yellow *Viola glabella* grows in damp areas at higher elevations. A charming dwarf shrub is yellow-flowered *Lonicera utahensis.* Another notable dwarf shrub is *Ledum glandulosum* with large white pincushion heads. There is an open meadow just before upper Rowe Lake. From here the trail climbs steeply. Near the start of it dark blue *Gentiana (Pneumonanthe) calycosa* blooms in August. Stupendous views of surrounding mountains are all along the trail. It is a round trip of 9.6 km from the beginning of the trail to the meadow.

Carthew Pass

This hike starts at Cameron Lake. It is a 6 hour (with time for photographs) 16 km round trip with a vertical rise of 830 m. The first 3.2 km follow a forested switchback trail. On the lower part are *Ledum glandulosum; Actaea rubra,* with white flowers followed later by red berries; and sheets of the delicate oak fern *Gymnocarpium dryopteris.* As on the Rowe Lakes trail, *Menziesia ferruginea* and *Veratrum viride* are found. *Viola glabella* is quite spectacular in damp places. Unlike Rowe Lakes, there are no calochortus or penstemons. *Xerophyllum tenax* increase gradually, particularly at the 3.2 km point, which is on a saddle. All along are the ubiquitous yellow umbels of *Angelica dawsoniana* with a quaint green collar, not unlike a giant hacquetia. In August, pink *Mimulus lewisii* is on the trail. In shady places, delicate *Stenanthium occidentale,* in the Liliaceae, also blooms later with its miniature bronze-yellow bells.

Erythronium grandiflorum
Photo by Loraine Yeatts

Xerophyllum replaces grass in open areas. The trail now climbs steeply through open trees, levels out to emerge from the trees and then—a magnificent sight! It looks like a couple of acres of *Xerophyllum tenax,* a sea of creamy spikes in August. From there the trail crosses a steep scree with scattered plants. *Viola nuttallii,* a yellow lanceolate-leaved species with odd distribution from prairies to mountains, is growing in quantity. Growing with it is the rather dingy white *Phacelia leptosepala.* Next come scattered, neat 15 cm high clumps of blue *Polemonium pulcherrimum* with occasional cushions of nameless white saxifrages.

The trail now zigzags up what appears from below to be an empty scree slope. Next to appear are *Polemonium viscosum* with large blue flowers and ribbed foliage that smells of skunk; scattered misty purple spikes of *Phacelia sericea;* brilliant blue *Myosotis alpestris;* creamy, scented buds of *Smelowskia calycina.* Then comes the gem of a weedy genus—*Crepis nana*—a bright little bunch of yellow hummock flowers with a collar of blue-green leaves like a Victorian posy. Alas, when brought down to Edmonton it goes leggy! Then come fat silvery cushions of *Potentilla ledebouriana* with almost-stemless, brilliant yellow flowers, and then buns of *Silene acaulis* with a variety of flower sizes in pinks and reds, but no white.

Carthew Pass is at 2,311 m. To the left it rises to the summit. Not easily seen against the dark scree are delightful 10 cm delphiniums, possibly *Delphinium bicolor,* in two color forms, one dark blue and the other blue with white spots on the lower lip. Nearby is *Lomatium sandbergii,* of the Umbelliferae, with tightly appressed, lemon yellow flowers. Creamy *Oxytropis cusickii* (*O. campestris* var. *cusickii*) is almost prostrate. On the ridge are grayish, flat cushions of *Eriogonum androsaceum.* Later, under a snowbank in July, appears dwarf, orange *Papaver alpinum,* which is hard to see against the red rock.

Ptarmigan Cirque Trail

This is in the 2,253 m Highwood Pass area of Kananaskis Provincial Park. It is a 2.5 km looped trail, that rises to 2,430 m. The trail crosses the highway at the parking lot and immediately plunges into a dark subalpine forest of *Abies lasiocarpa* and *Picea engelmannii* with undercover of *Phyllodoce glanduliflora* highlighted by an occasional *Erythonium grandiflorum*. The trail climbs steeply and emerges just below timberline where there are many dwarfed trees. In the open areas are forms of white, pink-tinged *Valeriana sitchensis*, together with *Myosotis alpestris* and a brilliant pink castilleja. A greenish yellow *Pedicularis bracteosa* is just opening.

Above the tree line are sheets of *Erythronium grandiflorum* glistening in the sun, smaller here than among the trees. *Pulsatilla (Anemone) occidentalis* is in damp patches where snow has just melted; *Potentilla diversifolia* and myosotis dot the ground together with pinkish white claytonias. Higher up is occasional krummholz of *Larix lyallii*, spruce and fir.

Higher still, in a tundralike area above any trees, are numerous alpines: *Erigeron aureus* with its 3 cm wide, deep yellow flowers on 2 cm stalks; cream *Smelowskia calycina*; wide areas covered with *Dryas octopetala*, soon to open; *Astragalus alpinus* with small, pale mauve pea flowers (weedy in the alpine garden); cream *Hedysarum sulphurescens*, much shorter than lower down; *Hedysarum boreale* var. *mackenzii*, just opening its brilliant rose-carmine flowers; and cushions of *Silene acaulis*.

At the top of the trail is a sign indicating where fossils are located. A plant that eluded me is *Claytonia megarhiza* which is found in the rocks above the fossils. *Saxifraga oppositifolia* here has quite small plants with large ruby flowers. High on the rocks is *Saussurea nuda* var. *densa*. On the edge of a scree is a good bronze-red form of *Sedum (Rhodiola) roseum*.

Moraine Lake, Larch Valley, and Sentinel Pass

After an hour of steep, forested switchbacks, a fork in the trail is reached. Bear right for Sentinel Pass. Shortly, there is an abrupt transition from alpine fir and spruce to *Larix lyallii*. Here the path levels slightly. The first color is bright rosy purple *Phyllodoce empetriformis*, with an occasional creamy *Pulsatilla occidentalis* and *Claytonia lanceolata*. The trail emerges onto a conglomerate moraine below Sentinel Pass. In early July there is a still-frozen lake. At this time of year I saw a limited number of alpines: *Erigeron aureus*; *Sibbaldia procumbens*; *Dryas octopetala*; *Silene acaulis*; *Potentilla uniflora*; *Potentilla diversifolia*. I have seen this area only in early July or early fall when the larix are golden. I am sure there are more alpines to be seen here at other times. The scenery is stupendous with a fantastic view of the Valley of the Ten Peaks. It is 4.3 km to the moraine and 5.8 km to Sentinel Pass, a 3-hour round trip.

Peyto Lake

Along the Banff Parkway on the way to Peyto Lake, magenta *Oxytropis splendens* and creamy white *Oxytropis monticola* (*O. campestris* var. *gracilis*) have hybridized with a range of shades, from a light bluish green to a beautiful lavender. White *Spiranthes romanzoffiana* and a greenish habenaria are colonizing the damp banks. Here we find a colorful contrast between the green habenaria, a bright red castilleja, purplish red dodecatheon and glistening 20 cm purple spikes of *Pedicularis groenlandicum*.

Peyto Lake Nature Trail leads to an overlook of the blue-green lake. Along the trail are general interpretive signs. Individual species are not labelled. *Phyllodoce empetriformis*, and *P. glanduliflora* are the two main ground covers, along with some *Trollius albiflorus* (*T. laxus* var. *albiflorus*), *Erigeron aureus*, and later on, many mauve erigerons. This is a sadly overused area.

There is no sign of *Erythronium grandiflorum* along the trail, but it is abundant in the light forest 100 m away. *Dryas drummondii*, with nodding lemon yellow flowers on 10 cm stems, is a prime colonizer along road banks and gravel flats from here northward. The flowers never turn upward despite an erroneous account published some years ago that called it a yellow *D. octopetala* and has been repeated *ad nauseum*.

Mount Edith Cavell Meadows

The trail starts with a short, steep walk up and over a lateral moraine, then proceeds for a while between the moraine and a steep, forested slope. On this rather damp slope, rosy purple *Phyllodoce empetriformis* is at its best, together with patches of yellow *P. glanduliflora*. These two species have hybridized producing *P.* × *intermedia* with reddish sepals over pale pink petals. It is seen here beside both parents. Next to be sighted is rosy pink *Kalmia microphylla* in wet moss. *Cassiope mertensiana* (with no groove on the back of the leaf) forms sheets of solid white; higher up the trail it makes a fantastic ground cover in the open meadows.

The path zigzags quite steeply and emerges onto open meadows. In the lower meadows are masses of *Trollius albiflorus*, which has been described as having "dirty white flowers." When they first open they are a delightful delicate shade of cream; they do, I admit, fade later. Usually it is seen as individuals, but sometimes it forms large clumps. Along and in the streams in the meadows is *Caltha leptosepala* with blue-white, narrow-petaled flowers; it needs water in cultivation.

In the upper meadows pinkish white *Claytonia lanceolata* spangles the ground. Yellow *Viola orbiculata* is sparse. Above the meadows the path leads through gravelly, rocky slopes covered with mats of *Dryas octopetala,* rosy pink *Pedicularis arctica* and *Silene acaulis* in a variety of shades and flower sizes—but no white. Also found are a few plants of *Saxifraga oppositifolia,* not in flower, and likewise *Gentiana glauca,* a most disappointing plant with hard-to-see, blue-green, upright flowers. Dwarf, tight, hairy-gray cushions of *Potentilla nivea* and *P. uniflora;* and bluish purple *Oxytropis podocarpa* are also seen. Higher up appears *Cassiope tetragona* var. *saximontana,* a smaller, less straggly plant than the *C. mertensiana* found lower.

Later in the year many different colored castillejas and erigerons are found. If you are very energetic, you can get beyond the trail to the top of the ridge for a stupendous view of the surrounding mountains. A good viewpoint for the Angel Glacier on Mount Edith Cavell is found about 3.2 km up the trail.

Whistlers, Jasper

Access is by the Jasper Aerial Tram. A short half-hour walk leads to the top of Whistlers at 2,425 m. Just outside the upper terminal much of the original vegetation has vanished, but we see many interesting alpines along the path. The most colorful in early July are many species of *Potentilla*. *Potentilla nivea* and *P. uniflora* are found, together with what appear to be intermediates. All are

Peyto Lake, Banff National Park. Courtesy of Travel Alberta

Phyllodoce glanduliflora. Photo by Loraine Yeatts

dwarfed silky cushions of soft grayish green and of varying looseness. All are covered with bright yellow flowers with orange spots at the base of each petal. Flower stalks are 1–2 cm high.

Assorted pink shades of *Silene acaulis* abound. On south-facing slopes are many neat clumps of *Cassiope tetragona* var. *saximontana. Cassiope mertensiana* is not present here. *Saussurea nuda* var. *densa* has lovely silvery foliage that shows great promise; then come miserable, purple, rayless flowers. *Erysimum pallasii,* a short-lived perennial, has compact heads of bright purple, wallflowerlike flower heads nestled in a collar of green leaves; after flowering, erect seed pods up to 10 cm long are produced. Sulphur yellow *Papaver kluanense,* 6–9 cm tall, with neat hairy leaves, occurs sporadically on scree slopes.

On the top of Whistlers *Oxytropis podocarpa,* with its purplish blue flowers in pairs, is almost prostrate; its beautifully inflated reddish seed pods come later. *Oxytropis cusickii* has few-flowered cream clusters, again on almost prostrate silvery plants.

I have never been early enough to see *Saxifraga oppositifolia* in flower, but its green cushions with seed pods are here. A neat dwarf dandelion, *Taraxacum ceratophorum,* appears occasionally. *Pedicularis arctica* dots the summit with its 5 cm high domes of rosy purple. *Crepis nana,* forming a Victorian posy, is also here. *Sedum lanceolatum* (formerly *S. stenopetalum*), with bright yellow heads, is frequent.

Lower down on the saddle, where it is quite wet, *Pulsatilla occidentalis* is in quantity. It is here in two color forms; one is tinged with blue, the other cream. Also here is *Caltha leptosepala, Trollius albiflorus* (*T. laxus* var. *albiflorus*) and *Kalmia microphylla*. On Indian Ridge in late July are several high-altitude *Erigeron* species including charming *E. lanatus* with solitary white buds, sometimes pink or blue, with a very wooly involucre.

Along the Althabaca River near the Jasper townsite grow *Cypripedium calceolus, C. passerinium* and *Orchis rotundifolia.*

The Cardinal Divide in the Forest Reserve

This is south of the town of Cadomin on the Forestry Trunk Road south of Hinton. One kilometer north of Cadomin in early July are sheets of purple spotted with white—a hybrid population of *Oxytropis splendens* and *O. jordalii,* together with *O. cusickii.*

Next appears brilliant blue *Penstemon procerus.* Later in the summer along the road are clumps of *Delphinium glaucum, Phacelia sericea* and *Polemonium acutiflorum.*

About 19.7 km from Cadomin we reach the Cardinal Divide. At 2,000 m, it is the highest point outside the national parks that is possible to reach readily by car. The divide is a saddle of arctic tundra that harbors a great variety of plants according to the time and the season. Early in the year (late June) *Pedicularis lanata* has wooly spikes with pink flowers. This is followed by *P. arctica,* very similar but without the wool. *Pedicularis capitata* with a few 5–10 cm yellow flowers is here, as is *P. flammea* with small yellow and purple flowers and *P. contorta* with large yellow flowers. Later is found *Gentiana (Ciminalis) prostrata,* a biennial with small sky blue flowers. *Campanula uniflora* is frequent in August. *Hedysarum boreale* var. *mackenzii* is here with its carmine flowers, as is pinkish purple *Hedysarum alpinum* var. *americanum,* which appears to be an intermediate form here. *Androsace chamaejasme* with its cream flowers and orange eye is common on rocky ground. *Dryas integrifolia,* similar to *D. octopetala* except for its linear leaves, is present in large mats and is quite striking when in seed.

In north-running depressions on the saddle grow both *Cassiope mertensiana,* which faces east, and *C. tetragona* var. *saximontana,* which faces west. This is the only place I have seen these two species almost side by side. Normally, they are separated vertically.

Later, *Zigadenus elegans* raises its creamy spikes. Prostrate *Betula glandulosa* creeps over the surface. *Aquilegia flavescens* is common on south slopes. *Gentiana glauca* forms 10 cm wide clumps in damp moss. *Arctostaphylos rubra* is stunning in late August with its brilliant red foliage and occasional red berries. All over the area are numerous dwarf *Salix* species.

Over the edge of the escarpment to the east are some brilliant forms of *Silene acaulis;* also, purplish *Erigeron humilis* and smelowskia, *Polemonium viscosum* are reported here. Going up to the escarpment we find several species of *Arnica.* Here is also the highest, in altitude, of the orchid family, *Habenaria viridis* var. *bracteata,* in many-stemmed clumps about 10 cm high.

To the west are moist alpine meadows that are very colorful in August. Pink-purple *Oxytropis jordalii* is found on the drier banks. *Aconitum delphinifolium* with its dark blue hoods is common as is the dingy purple-flowered *Delphinium glaucum.* The meadows are brightened by senecios, several species of *Erigeron,* and *Trollius albiflorus* (*T. laxus* var. *albiflorus*). This is a charming area; unfortunately, it has been badly damaged by trail bikes and four-wheel drive vehicles.

In my wanderings in the Canadian Rockies, some plants have eluded me: *Rhododendron lapponicum* (though a piece was left on my doorstep by a climbing friend!), *Aquilegia jonesii* (of the limestone screes) and *Lewisia pygmaea.*

It is obvious from the above that certain plants have curious distribution—from high alpine screes to the prairies. For one, *Physaria didymocarpa,* the bladderpod with a rosette of yellow crucifer flowers, is found on the prairie outside Waterton and in the mountains. Alberta is a meeting place for species from the north, south, east and west, and sightings in new localities are still being recorded. Our goal at the Devonian Botanic Garden in Edmonton is to introduce as many native alpines as possible. Each spring, to the delight of visitors, they flower here at our lower elevation one to two months earlier than they occur in nature, a welcome preview of the later show in the mountains.

References

Cormack, Robert G. S. 1977. *Wild flowers of Alberta.* Edmonton: Hurtig Publishers.

Currah, Randy S., A. Smreciu, and M. Van Dyke. 1983. *Prairie wildflowers.* Alberta: Friends of the Devonian Botanic Garden.

Kujit, Job. 1982. *Flora of Waterton Lakes National Park.* Edmonton: University of Alberta Press.

Moss, E. H. 1983. *Flora of Alberta.* 2nd ed. Revised by J. A. Packer. Toronto, Buffalo and Alberta: University of Toronto Press.

Porsild, A. E. 1979. *Rocky Mountain wild flowers.* 2nd ed. Ottawa: National Museum of Sciences.

Shaw, Richard and Danny Or. 1979. *Plants of Waterton Glacier National Lakes and the northern Rockies.* Missoula, Mont.: Mountain Press Publishers.

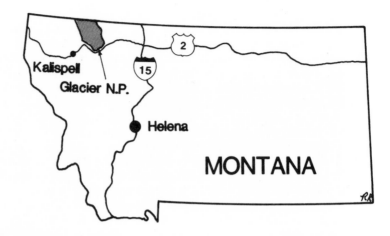

7

Alpine Plants of Glacier National Park

by Ann DeBolt and Peter Lesica

Throughout the Rocky Mountains, some of the most beautiful and rugged alpine country is protected in national parks. Glacier National Park is the northernmost of the U.S. parks and one of the largest. It straddles the Continental Divide and is bounded on the north by its Canadian sister, Waterton Lakes National Park, and on the south by the newly created Great Bear Wilderness. Glacier National Park encompasses 1,538 square miles, nearly all of which is mountainous. Two mountain ranges occur in the Park: the Lewis Range straddles the Continental Divide, and the Livingston Range lies west of it in the northwest corner. Both ranges trend northwest to southeast. Elevations are low by southern Rocky Mountain standards, ranging from near 3,000 ft. at the West Entrance to 10,466 ft. Mount Cleveland, the highest peak in the Park; however, upper timberline is also relatively low, generally 7,000 ft. and even lower in windswept areas along the east front of the Lewis Range. Nearly one-quarter of the Park is alpine terrain.

The Lewis Range acts as a barrier, partially confining Arctic air masses and dry continental air east of the Continental Divide, while moist, temperate maritime air is generally restricted to the west side. Powerful desiccating winds are frequent along the east slope. A strong Pacific storm track occurring along the Canadian border from western Washington to northwestern Montana brings relatively large amounts of precipitation to the Park, particularly to the area along the Continental Divide and the Livingston Range. At low elevations on either side of the Park, the average annual temperature is approximately 40°F, and average annual precipitation is approximately 28 in. Higher elevations average 10–20°F cooler, and average annual precipitation in the higher mountain areas is surprisingly high: 100–150 in. During summer months, daytime temperatures are generally around 80°F at low elevations and in the 60s in the alpine zone. In the high country, precipitation occurs as rainfall from June through August and as snowfall during the remainder of the year. Although summer days in the alpine zone are usually warm and without precipitation, average relative humidity is a high 74 percent, and cool and rainy or snowy days are frequent enough to support the glacial activity found throughout the Park.

Ann DeBolt is a graduate of the University of Montana where she worked two years in the herbarium. She works for Glacier National Park, and has compiled a preliminary species list of Glacier National Park lichens.

Peter Lesica completed a checklist of vascular plants for Glacier National Park in 1984, and has researched rare and endangered plants in Montana, while conducting Natural Heritage Inventories for the Nature Conservancy.

Both authors enjoy mountain climbing above tree line whenever possible.

PLATE 3

Wyethia in Custer Co., Idaho
Photo by Sharon Sutton

Moraine Lake, Alberta
Photo by Joel Spingarn

PLATE 6

Douglasia montana
Photo by Ned Lowry

Astragalus kentrophyta var. *implexus*
Photo by Ned Lowry

Gentiana algida
Photo by Ned Lowry

Kelseya uniflora
Photo by Sharon Sutton

Lewisia rediviva
Photo by Ted Kipping

The most striking geological features of Glacier National Park are the result of glaciation. At the height of the Pleistocene period, only the summits of the highest peaks remained free of ice. The effects of this glaciation are everywhere in evidence. At lower elevations, broad U-shaped valleys dissect the backbones of the main mountain ranges. Many of these valleys have been dammed by terminal moraines which created the finger lakes that are such a conspicuous feature of the Park. With the exception of the relatively gentle summits found along the drier east slope, the mountains of Glacier Park are characterized by precipitous slopes and knife-edged ridges carved by glacial activity. Rocky cirques formed by the scouring action of glacial ice can be found at the head of almost every drainage. These cirques usually harbor fresh moraines and often contain lakes. Fifty to sixty of them still contain active glaciers. These glaciers are not the remains of their Pleistocene ancestors but have formed anew since the warm dry period which followed the last glacial retreat.

The mountains of Glacier National Park are composed almost entirely of sedimentary rock. The Park is basically an enormous slab of Precambrian rocks, several thousand feet thick, which slid eastward across younger underlying Cretaceous rock. One of the striking features of the area is the evident layering of different colored strata which can easily be seen on the steep bare cliffs, especially above timberline. Almost all of these strata are limestones, mudstones, sandstones, and shales. The mudstones and sandstones form silty or coarse-textured, slightly acidic soil, while the limestones and shales generally weather to fine-textured neutral to alkaline soils. The differences between soil parent materials may or may not affect the vegetation, depending on the age and development of the soil. However, many alpine plants in Glacier National Park are restricted to calcareous soils formed from limestone or shale.

The Rocky Mountains form an almost continuous chain of alpine habitat extending from circumpolar arctic regions to Arizona and New Mexico, and many alpine species found in Glacier Park can be found throughout the Rockies. Due to its position in the northern part of the cordillera, floristic affinities of the Park's alpine zone are more similar to those of arctic regions and the Canadian Rockies. Many genera typical of alpine regions in the southern Rockies, such as *Hymenoxys, Trifolium, Primula,* and *Pedicularis,* are absent or poorly represented in Glacier's alpine flora. On the other hand, many arctic and Canadian species such as *Tofieldia pusilla, Euphrasia arctica, Pinguicula vulgaris, Draba macounii, Lycopodium alpinum, Juncus albescens* (*J. triglumis* var. *a.*), *Carex petricosa* and *C. eleusinoides* reach the southern limit of their range in the Park's alpine zone. As a result of the almost complete glaciation of the region, endemism in Glacier Park's flora is low when compared with areas farther south. Nevertheless, the region does have a few alpine endemics, such as *Papaver pygmaeum, Erigeron lanatus, Eriogonum androsaceum* and *Aquilegia jonesii.* These species are among the favorites of Glacier Park's dedicated alpine botanists.

Eriogonum androsaceum. Photo by Desanto

Although Glacier National Park has roads along its boundaries on three sides and access roads penetrating short distances into the interior, only the Going-to-the-Sun Road crosses the Park and allows easy access to alpine areas along the Continental Divide. Glacier is truly a hiker's park, and even from Logan Pass on the Going-to-the-Sun Road, one must hike in order to see the full array of alpine plant communities present in the area. Terrain along the Continental Divide is generally very rugged, and thus there are few large expanses of alpine vegetation. Most of the area above timberline is sheer cliffs, relatively barren talus slopes and snowfields. The Logan Pass area is an exception to this rule as it has large expanses of meadows and many small alpine bogs. Plant diversity is high in this area, and it is a good place to find alpine treasures.

At an elevation of 6,650 ft., Logan Pass is actually below the Park's average timberline; however, because of fierce winds and heavy snow accumulation, the trees found there are stunted krummholz. The meadows that dominate the area are lush and showy and similar in composition to those found in subalpine zones, yet to many park visitors they are nonetheless alpine meadows. Due to the late snow melt, the growing season for these meadows is short, and consequently almost everything blooms at once. Glacier lilies (*Erythronium grandiflorum*), buttercups (*Ranunculus eschscholtzii*), and spring beauty (*Claytonia lanceolata*) bloom almost immediately following snow release, showering the still-brown turf with yellow and white. Very quickly the soil warms, and the meadows become truly luxuriant. Fields of fleabane (*Erigeron peregrinus*), arnica (*Arnica* spp.), speedwell (*Veronica wormskjoldii*), paintbrush (*Castilleja* spp.), bistort (*Polygonum bistortoides*), valerian (*Valeriana sitchensis*) and sedges such as showy sedge (*Carex spectabilis*) come into bloom and continue to bloom as long as soil moisture is sufficient. The meadows abound with the pollinating activity of bumblebees, butterflies, and hummingbirds; white-tailed ptarmigan may also be observed feeding on dwarf willows (*Salix* spp.), insects, and a variety of forbs.

Along some of the creeks and in areas underlain by bedrock where soil drainage is impeded, there are small alpine bogs. Cool temperatures and poor soil drainage inhibit decomposition of organic matter by soil microbes resulting in a build-up of fibrous water-soaked peat. This habitat is home for some of the Park's rarest alpine plants. Four-angled mountain-heather (*Cassiope tetragona*), northern eyebright (*Euphrasia arctica*), small bog asphodel (*Tofieldia pusilla*), and alpine rush (*Juncus albescens*) are all arctic species at the southern limit of their range in Glacier's cold alpine bogs.

Perhaps the most interesting plant found in these bogs is butterwort (*Pinguicula vulgaris*). It is North America's only alpine carnivorous plant. Its basal rosette of yellowish-colored leaves lies flat on the ground, and small insects, usually flies, are caught and "digested" on the sticky surface. The butterwort's insectivorous habit is thought to be a means of securing additional nitrogen and phosphorus in a nutrient-deficient environment. Its single, showy, lavender-colored flower is held at the end of a short scape and can be seen for only a brief period around late July and early August. Other species common in the alpine bog habitat are the common bog asphodel (*Tofieldia glutinosa*), yellow mountain-heather (*Phyllodoce glanduliflora*), snow willow (*Salix nivalis*), explorer's and moss gentians (*Gentiana (Pneumonanthe) calycosa* and *G. (Ciminalis) prostrata*, respectively) chestnut rush (*Juncus castaneus*), and hair sedge (*Carex capillaris*).

A habitat in many ways similar to the bogs is the wet rock ledge. These charming communities are very common in Glacier National Park, but a little bit of rock climbing may be required to view them. Wet ledges seem to be a favorite haunt of members of the saxifrage family. Leatherleaf saxifrage (*Leptarrhena pyrolifolia*) is a Northern Pacific Slope species and the only member of its genus. It has attractive, thick, dark green basal leaves, a tall scape with a single clasping leaf, and a tight cluster of white flowers. Leatherleaf saxifrage is reported to do well in cultivation, although extra moisture and a humid environment may be necessary. Another coastal species that finds a home on the wet ledges in Glacier National Park is the rusty saxifrage (*Saxifraga ferruginea*). This species is often found growing in wet moss, perhaps because of its unusual method of reproduction. Approximately half of the pedicels of the rusty saxifrage's open inflorescence bear small white flowers; the other half bear tiny plantlets, miniature rosettes of leaves which sometimes grow to one-half inch in length before dropping from the parent plant. The tiny plantlets seem to survive best in moist moss. This species can also be cultivated. One potted specimen is known to have found a home in a bathroom window where it fruitlessly dropped its plantlets on the tile floor.

Northern suksdorfia (*Suksdorfia ranunculifolia*) and Sitka mistmaiden (*Romanzoffia sitchensis*) are two more species commonly found on wet alpine ledges. Although these two plants belong to completely unrelated families (Saxifragaceae and Hydrophyllaceae), their appearance is strikingly similar. Both have a basal rosette of reniform-orbicular lobed leaves and an open inflorescence of regular white flowers. Both species propagate themselves by producing bulbils in the axils of basal leaves, as well as by seed. The similarity between these species occurring in the same habitat might appear to be a case of convergent evolution, but the reason for the convergence is unknown. Western

Saxifraga ferruginea. Photo by Desanto

saxifrage (*Saxifraga occidentalis*), pygmy saxifrage (*S. debilis*), Merten's saxifrage (*S. mertensiana*), and grass-of-Parnassus (*Parnassia fimbriata* and *P. kotzebuei*) are other members of the Saxifrage Family common to wet rock ledges in the Park.

Examples of wet ledge species other than members of the saxifrage family are purple monkeyflower (*Mimulus lewisii*), butterwort, and the tiny alpine pearlwort (*Sagina saginoides*), which can all be found both above and below timberline. Macoun's draba (*Draba macounii*), a Canadian Rockies species, has recently been collected for the first time in the United States on wet limestone cliffs in the Logan Pass area.

Perhaps the most interesting and distinctive alpine plant assemblages in Glacier National Park are found on talus slopes, stabilized moraines and shingle derived from calcareous rock. The few alpine species endemic to the Glacier National Park region, such as the pygmy poppy (*Papaver pygmaeum*), wooly daisy (*Erigeron lanatus,* disjunct in Colorado), and limestone columbine (*Aquilegia jonesii,* also known to occur in the Bighorn Mountains in Wyoming), are all found in this habitat. Limestone columbine is an exceedingly attractive plant with small, crowded leaves and large flowers with deep blue sepals and light blue-to-almost-white petals. The whole plant is usually less than six inches tall. The pygmy poppy is another small plant, never found in abundance. It has delicate salmon-colored petals that fall from the plant shortly after opening.

Dwarf hawksbeard (*Crepis nana*), alpine spring beauty (*Claytonia megarhiza*), and modest buttercup (*Ranunculus verecundus*) are all specialists on shifting·talus. Over the years, as the talus moves slowly downhill, the roots of these plants elongate so that they are able to move with the talus. One can find individuals flowering many feet down slope from where they are actually rooted in the soil. Alpine spring beauty is a fairly large plant with thick fleshy leaves that can be successfully cultivated. Its large, starchy roots are a favorite of grizzly bears. Another favored bear food of these rocky habitats is alpine fireweed (*Epilobium latifolium*). Its flowers, large and deeper in color than common fireweed (*E. angustifolium*), will often blanket an area where this rhizomatous species is growing. Alpine fireweed can also be found at lower elevations on riparian gravel bars. Other attractive plants found in the Park's rocky alpine areas are sky pilot (*Polemonium viscosum*), known for its large, bell-shaped, blue flowers and skunky odor; alpine campion (*Lychnis apetala,* or *Silene uralensis*), which is found on stabilized moraine and has nodding flowers with an inflated calyx resembling a Japanese lantern; and northern rock jasmine (*Androsace lehmanniana, A. chamaejasme* var. *l.*), with its tight cluster of white flowers, each with a bright yellow eye.

In areas of relatively level terrain where wind velocities prevent large snow accumulations, and soil development remains minimal, the dominant vegetation is dry meadow or fellfield. Although these plant communities can be found on ridges and in passes throughout the Park, they reach their best development on the broad windswept peaks along the east front of the Lewis Range. Relatively short but steep hikes from the Many Glacier or Two Medicine areas offer quick access to alpine fellfield country. The most conspicuous feature of Glacier's calcareous fellfields are the mats of mountain avens (*Dryas octopetala*) which can be over 3 ft. in diameter and often seem to be evenly spaced on level wind-blown terrain. Other cushion plants which form smaller mats are moss campion (*Silene acaulis*), rock jasmine buckwheat (*Eriogonum androsaceum*), arctic sandwort (*Arenaria [Minuartia] obtusiloba*), bearberry (*Arctostaphylos uva-ursi*), Payson's draba (*Draba paysonii*), and tufted saxifrage (*Saxifraga caespitosa*). Many taller, single-stemmed species are often found growing in cushion plant mats, where germination and early growth may be easier than on the bare soil. The arctic rock sedge (*Carex petricosa*) is disjunct in Glacier Park where it has been found growing in mats of mountain avens. Bird's-foot buttercup (*Ranunculus pedatifidus*) and alpine bistort (*Polygonum (Bistorta) bistortoides*) are also commonly found growing in cushion plants.

Along the east front of the mountains, the forest zone occupies only a small area between the high plains and the alpine zone, and many species common to windswept rocky areas on the plains can also be found above timberline. Among these are douglasia (*Douglasia montana*), kittentails (*Besseya wyomingensis*), slender crazyweed (*Oxytropis campestris*), and yellow sweetvetch (*Hedysarum sulphurescens*). Many other common species have an arctic-alpine distribution, such as alpine arnica (*Arnica alpina*), arctic aster (*Aster sibiricus*), candytuft (*Smelowskia calycina*), and single-spike sedge (*Carex scirpoidea*). Fellfields on these drier peaks come into bloom early, long before the snow has retreated from the mountains to the west. Douglasia, kittentails, and Payson's draba may begin to bloom in May, and most species are in full bloom by late June. While the rugged peaks along the Divide are still accessible only to the trained alpinist equipped with an ice axe, the gentler peaks along the east front are at their floral best.

A view of the jagged peaks, colorful cliffs, and snow-covered slopes is reason enough to climb above tree line in Glacier National Park. There it is not hard to imagine that the thousands of feet of Pleistocene ice have just recently departed. The ice and snow that carved this magnificent landscape now nourish the diminutive plants that are so pleasing to our eyes. Discovering a slope covered with limestone columbine or a pygmy poppy that has just opened heightens the feeling that this is a very special place.

Silene uralensis
Photo by Desanto

References

Bamberg, S. A., & J. Major. 1968. *Ecology of the vegetation and soils associated with calcareous parent materials in three alpine regions of Montana.* Ecol. Monogr. 42:417–450.

Choate, C. M. 1967. *Alpine plant communities at Logan Pass, Glacier National Park.* Mont. Acad. Sci. 27:36–54.

Lesica, P. C. 1985. *Annotated checklist of vascular plants for Glacier National Park, Montana.* Proc. Mont. Acad. Sci.

Standley, P. C. 1921. *Flora of Glacier National Park, Montana.* Washington, D.C.: Contrib. from the U.S. Natl. Herb., Vol. 22(5):235–438.

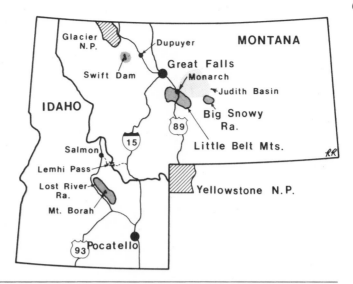

8

Some "Idamont" Limestones

by B. LeRoy Davidson

There are some special places I'd like to show you. The first is on the east face of the Front Range of the northern Rocky Mountains, just south of Glacier National Park in Montana. As we come down off Rogers Pass (not the one in British Columbia of course), we cannot help reflecting on the easier time Lewis and Clark might have enjoyed had they known of this gentle route over the Continental Divide. Rogers was to make his discovery only on his return trip in 1806, and we now wend along ridgetops as he must have done on the way north to Blackfoot country that year. All has been glacier-plowed and contoured by wind and water to resemble nothing so much as a great golf course—until we suddenly encounter a remarkable towering wall of white limestone, now our western backdrop. Highway 89 is easily one of the most scenic of Western drives. It has been called the Park-to-Park Route: Glacier to Yellowstone.

This part of the Rockies consists of a series of unrelated geological corrugations uplifted, the highest and easternmost an ancient seabed now smoothed by ice and weathered to reveal a variety of fossils such as ammonites and sea-worms. At one summit of about 9,000 ft., there is only a shallow cleft separating the limestone and the adjacent granite. A dramatic place facing northwest, it looks to the peaks of Glacier, with the reddest of *Silene acaulis* to the west nodding to *Androsace lehmanniana* on the limestone. Far below on the plains this same bedded limestone appears in unexpected little rock gardens that seem to have been magically dropped there on the prairie, plants intact, the creamy androsace along with wee drabas and others known usually only from the summits. But this particular summit also holds such treasures as the tiny *Papaver alpinum* and the ashen-leaved, white-flowered *Draba lonchocarpa* in a very fine form, along with *Penstemon ellipticus,* and just below in the saddle, huge, old, parsnip-rooted *Aquilegia flavescens* watches over the descent with stoic patience, surely a very long-lived species. *Calochortus apiculatus* is in the grass too, and long before *Erythronium grandiflorum* (the bland form, with no tint of red to the stalk or stamens) must have flowered just as the snow melted.

Between Rogers Pass and Glacier (Marias Pass), three of the Missouri River tributaries have carved their escapes into this rock, narrow almost secret chasms of the Sun, the Teton and the Marias Rivers, each with several branches. So well-suited are these cool places to *Cypripedium montanum* that it is found here in vast colonies in the deep detritus under the pines, and it is to one of these places we are headed—beyond the dam on Birch Creek, a branch of Two Medicine, fork of the Marias, in the northwesternmost part of the Missouri drainage just short of the Hudson Bay Divide. Here high

An amateur botanist, plant collector and proponent of North American plants, **B. LeRoy Davidson** is a retired florist and landscape designer who maintains a large garden of native plant material as well as a collection of exotics at his home in Bellevue, Washington. He is a contributor to iris, penstemon and rock garden society publications and *Pacific Horticulture.* He is also author of the forthcoming *North American Mountain Plants.*

Aquilegia flavescens
Photo by Gwen Kelaidis

ridges hold tightly to sprawls of *Dryas drummondii.*

From my cousin's place I've admired this scene for years. The Reef, as he calls it, rises starkly from a base on the plains at about 5,000 ft., to tower in successive cliff formations to almost 9,000 ft., its faces so steep that even the game trails are possible only along the stream-cuts. It all seems so close in the clear mountain air that you could hike right out to the base after breakfast. Well of course you could—but take along a lunch. It is twenty miles, one way.

This is a country of special places and special plants.

Juniperus horizontalis

This expanse was open range, still unfenced, when I first knew it. We could drive anywhere we liked, and did, in studying the ground cedar, as this juniper is known locally. In these basins are some of the largest and westernmost of its occurrences and, as is so often the case with plant populations on the margins of their ranges, there is free expression. No two individuals are identical, and many seem to duplicate or even surpass the selections propagated commercially. Here they patch the soft coloring of the prairie landscape with somber greens, often bluish, sometimes brownish, lending a certain stability to the scene. I once found a 60 ft. individual below Swift Dam, sprawled there on the banks of Birch Creek. I brought back one, calling it 'Big Sky', a fine, close-growing form, bluish green in color, that promises to be a tidy lawn subject.

Upon this incredibly green steppe is spread in the high spring of May and June an intricate tapestry of miniature wildflowers, continuing through summer into fall when *Liatris punctata* and solidagos finish off the short season. *Pinus banksiana* is found occasionally in dark patches, either individuals or widely dispersed groups. Ubiquitous cottonwoods and willows mark the bottoms. A few shrubs are conspicuous on the prairie, the true *Rosa arkansana* in dry places, *Potentilla fruticosa* (*Pentaphylloides floribunda*) in wet swales, often with *Iris missouriensis* near at hand; silvery buffalo berry, *Shepherdia argentea,* consorting with the willows, is hung with scarlet jelly-fruits in the crisp days of autumn. Everywhere are quakers (aspen) in groves that always offer the best campsites, and everywhere, contributing to the soft verdancy of this gargantuan landscape, is the tiny, tough and tufty *Selaginella wallacei* with its uncanny ability to rise from the dead. When the land is cool and moist it forms a silver-green warp binding the tapestry together, tight to the earth. When the land is parched, it folds up into furry little dead-nothings, yet still it is attractive. On ledges it can form lovely mats.

Dupuyer, in the words of contemporary Montana author Ivan Doig, who lived here next-door in his high school years, is a little town that just "sprigged up along the trail." It hasn't changed much, looks homey and prosperous in its spectacular setting. From town, there are three separate roads west, out toward the Reef, keeping to themselves on the ridges to stay clear of the mire of bottoms. We are headed to Swift Dam which stores the Birch Creek waters for crops farther to the east. About twenty years ago the original 1910 dam gave way, releasing hellish forces, and my record juniper was

The Marias River from the report of the Stevens expedition.
Helen Fowler Library, Denver Botanic Gardens

among the minor casualties. Many people drowned. As the dam was rebuilt so also was the road, now improved but still wisely following the old route deviously from ranch to ranch on higher ground.

Eritrichium howardii

It was out toward Birch Creek I first found the silvery *Eritrichium howardii* one October. A crew, improving the road while destroying the prairie, had stopped the season's operations just inches short of a huge plant of it, a silvery filigree pancake about a foot across. It came home with me, and Bob Putnam of Kirkland, Washington, kept it for several years in his alpine house, double-potted in its natural limestone rubble with just a trace of the black prairie soil. Though it was never happy away from Montana, it did manage a few flowers, evidence that the plant can, with care, be moved. A few small plants I had put into the arid rock garden in eastern Washington were budded up in promise when caught in a warm June rain that did them in overnight. In late June last year I was able to gather quite a lot of seed on the ridge out past the village cemetery toward the Reef. Though it was hardly dry, the seed was quite mature and, planted in early winter, gave a good crop of seedlings. When everything is exactly right the flowers of this most exquisite of little borages can spread to a full quarter-inch, with a dozen or so on unfurling thready stems. On the chasm to which Swift Dam is anchored, it flowers right at the Fourth of July; and south of the dam on limestone pavement formations, craggy old plants looking like miniature bonsai tumble from a miniature eroded cliff. This species is limited to this seabed steppe of the upper Missouri drainages. It succeeds best with no competition whatsoever, and second-best plants are to be found flowering a bit earlier in blowouts of the ridgetops where the persistent winds have whisked away all traces of soil to leave a scree that surely qualifies as a barren. *Phlox muscoides* will inevitably be found nearby, as will *Douglasia montana* and *Paronychia sessiliflora,* all precious little huddled buns.

Many plants common to similar foothill-plains as far away as Colorado find their northern limits hereabouts, and one of the greatest interest is the sole member of its genus outside Eurasia: *Bupleurum americanum,* a 2 in. umbellifer unusual for simple leaves that early-on look like dense clumps of coarse grass. Only when the little violet-purple umbels appear do they reveal their identity. It is said to be sometimes yellow; here all are purple.

Some June I would like to go back to the place where Charlie Thurman of Spokane, Washington, and I once found this blue jewel, the eritrichium, another October, while in quest of a little pellaea. This is much to the east, at the south base of the Big Snowy Range, a huge block of this same seabed formation, cleft almost in two by glaciation. Swimming Woman Creek charges forth from the maw of the cirque; it also serves as the narrow access roadbed into it. The pellaea was here. To the west from this point, we opened barbed-wire gates from pasture to pasture across the base of the alluvial plain off the west shoulder of the massif. Here we found the *Eritrichium howardii,* by the thousands and by the acre, the major plant of the entire area, and very nearly the only one, except for a scraggle of willow along a dry stream bottom, apparently the sole plant in acres and acres of pasture. Can it be cattle fodder?

Eritrichium howardii
Drawing by Margaret Alice Smith

Cheilanthes feei
From 1879 *Ferns of North America* by D. C. Eaton

Rock Ferns: *Pellaea* and *Cheilanthes*

When I was just a wee tad (June 1926), the family drove this Park-to-Park Route visiting aunts and cousins as well as parks. It was still a dirt road, and we were caught in a downpour as we approached the little village of Monarch, tucked in the Belt River Valley. There we found a warm, dry cabin—an available summer home lent by a compassionate caretaker who took pity on a weary mom with three squalling-tired little boys. Fifty years later I found Monarch again, still a cool and pleasant little mountain retreat away from the summer heat of the prairie. Along both forks of the Belt River the eroded cliff faces are furred with wisps of the tiny *Pellaea glabella* var. *occidentalis,* often quite densely so; and though it is only about an inch high, it is easily seen, the same as that at Swimming Woman. This is likely the most elfin of rock ferns, and it is not any easier than are the most difficult— but it is not impossible. Aridity and limestone are prerequisite to any thought of even trying. This is of wide distribution, but I have only seen it on eroded vertical faces. Quaint and cunning, the foliage bathes in sunshine while the rootstock is safe in cool crevices, scarcely seen, and surviving surely on dewdrops. *Cheilanthes feei* is also of wide distribution. Once in southeast Wyoming I picked out a remote but likely crag and then hiked to see if the plant was there. It was. Although said to keep strictly to lime, I know a small colony in the Snake River Canyon of eastern Washington, on basalt of course. It seeks low light conditions, such as beneath a rock overhang or just inside the mouth of a cave—on the ceiling! It will make a lovely, lacy but sturdy tussock of 8 in. or so, colored a sort of mealy gray-green with the reverses felted in rich rusty red. It holds much fascination and little easy promise in cultivation—though not quite impossible.

Aquilegia jonesii

Another autumn visit to cousins took me again to Monarch, and farther in the Little Belt Range where Rae Berry, the great Portland gardener, once went with Clara Regan, the remarkable rock garden pioneer of Montana, to find her "Jonesy." (*Eritrichium* was her "Tricky.") The road up onto the mountain from King's Hill (now a ski site, off Highway 89) is so eroded as to be impossible if not actually impassable, though easier as a descent. I found that the basin of the South Fork of the Belt River above Niehart was being logged, so I drove in as far as was safe on the new snowfall, scanning the slopes above the timber across the way in a south exposure, and then hiked to find if that barren place toward the grassy summit might be hiding "Jonesy."

I hiked down and then up with the plan to reach the bald-looking patch high up, and when I got there, there it was, by the thousands, pale withered leafage all but hidden in a light powdering of snow, yet still showing fat buds of promise at the crowns.

In later years in this place I've found the logging roads progressively higher until one has looped up to join the old road on the ridge top, winding away in all directions amid all sorts of lovely flowers, pulsatillas and the finest *Delphinium bicolor,* calochortus and more. Maps promise it is possible to drive clear across the range, past Big Baldy—at just 9 ft. short of 10,000, it is the sleepy-looking patriarch to the north on this vast, broad-shouldered range—and down into Judith Basin.

It is always a jolt to find that the most cherished and coveted, the rarest and grandest, are totally common at home. *Aquilegia jonesii* grows right in the roadway of the first saddle; one must run it over and ruin it to find it. Another modest calcicole that only seeks to avoid any competition, it subsists best where little else can make it at all. Some years there are precious few flowers, but when such snow as has not been blown away gives sufficient moisture, this ridge is ethereal with the cupped violet flowers over the froth of blue gauze that is the foliage in the first days of a spring that, here, may come in July. Along with it are a few pinkish alliums, some wee yellow drabas and a smattering of *Eritrichium nanum* (often known as *E. aretioides,* "of the summits"), which is always above the trees.

Kelseya and Petrophytum

Frequently my returns from Montana outings have taken the Lewis and Clark route over Lemhi Pass in the Beaverhead Range into what is now Idaho. On the east side, still in Montana, one plant that always catches the eye for the very blueness of its matted leafage is *Petrophytum caespitosum,* usually on limestone, but sometimes on granite. At its best this is almost mirror blue, but I've never seen it approach this in cultivation. In flower this is, of course, one of the great Rocky Mountain treasures, and it is also to be found in Great Basin ranges. To some eyes, such as mine, it is quite preferable to its patrician Olympic sister, *P. hendersonii.* This is of course one of the great Western treasures, a slow and stealthy shrub scarcely of any stature at all, the tiny white plumes of flowers suggesting miniature astilbe.

It is only in this part of the "Idamont" limestone world one may search out the elusive *Primula incana* frequenting such places as are, in the wet season, quite charitably called marshy floodplains or limy seeps when in reality they are but mine dumps or smelly backwaters to mineral springs. Although this has not the unmatched violet beauty of *P. cusickiana* farther west in Snake River territory, nor of the rather similar pastel *P. nevadensis* of Great Basin summits, there is considerable appeal to the extreme mealiness of this entire plant. Only the petals escape; they are usually lavender. The white form, said to occur only in Idaho, has recently been described as a species in its own right, *P. alcalina* (Cholewa & Henderson 1984).

In this general province, too, the large purple bugles of *Penstemon montanus* poke up from plants submerged in coarse talus, their roots creeping beneath rocks that have frost-heaved just enough to allow them under.

Idaho's Lost River Range, scene of such devastating earthquake damage just a few seasons ago, is on the way home. Its crowning Mount Borah, 12,662 ft., is the state's highest peak. This calcareous north-south uplift is like a magnet to all plant-minded people for its population of the fabulous *Kelseya uniflora.* Though known from at least two other stations, one in Montana and one just to the south in Wyoming, I have found it only here in Bluebird Canyon where a cooling stream bisects the range. It may well be quite common throughout the range at higher elevations. It seems to continue much higher in sheltered places when I've investigated above the narrow canyon, but it is far from easy climbing, and I've soon come down. Here, too, is the petrophytum, and from afar the two look superficially alike when not in flower, although the kelseya has not so blue a look. When they are flowering, this is indeed a splendid place to be, petrophytum studded with elegant little white

Kelseya uniflora. Photo by Allan Taylor

plumes and kelseya with a single tiny rosy crescendo at each branch-tip. In passing this way we always hold a symbolic meeting of the Kelsey-moss Society of the Universe. This is a pair of equally fine, equally slow, and perhaps equally lovely Rocky Mountain polster shrublets, both party to Rosaceae.

The floor of Big Lost River Valley hereabouts is a marvel of Nature's tapestry-work, here done all in silvers. I have never been so fortunate as to pass this way in flower season nor have I been able to puzzle out what all those little things can be, other than an obvious phlox and pediocactus, but even so, it is fascinating to see, as is every limestone flora.

References

Cholewa, A., and D. M. Henderson. 1984. "*Primula alcalina* (Primulaceae): a new species from Idaho." *Brittonia* 36:59–62.

Ryberg, Per Axel. 1922. *Flora of Rocky Mountains and the Great Plains.* New York: the author.

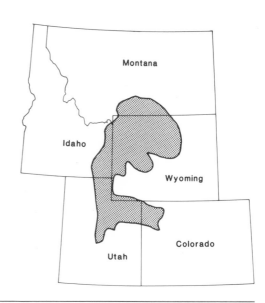

Section II

Middle Rockies: Sagebrush and Scree

Standard Oil (New Jersey) Collection, University of Louisville Photographic Archives

9

The Beartooth Plateau:
A Wealth of Alpines

by Frederick W. Case, Jr., and Roberta B. Case

The alpine tundra of the Beartooth Plateau is legendary among alpine plant and wilderness enthusiasts. The Plateau, or Beartooth Range, lies east of the Absaroka Range along the Wyoming-Montana border just northeast of Yellowstone National Park. Much of the area is a wilderness within the Custer and the Gallatin National Forests. Access roads extend into the area mainly from the east, following major stream drainages upward toward their sources, but a large part of the Beartooth-Absaroka wilderness remains inaccessible by road.

A notable exception is U.S. Highway 212 out of Billings, Montana. Known as the Beartooth Highway, it ascends the plateau a few miles out of Red Lodge, Montana, travels west for many miles along the treeless tundra, and crosses the Beartooth Pass at an elevation of 10,940 ft. It then descends again into the forests, continues to Cooke City and to the Silver Gate entrance (northeast) into Yellowstone National Park.

To our knowledge, no other North American mountain road traverses so much alpine tundra containing such a variety of plant species. But it is not the alpines alone that draw us to this region. It is also the breathtaking beauty of the Plateau, the vast landscapes, the scope of the glacial geology, and the changing moods of the Big Sky Country. The Beartooth has been called the most scenic highway in the United States. We agree.

A true plateau, the area was abraded and eroded by ice age glaciers, leaving a relatively flat top with precipitous U-shaped valleys, typical of glaciated regions. Here and there blunt-topped, or occasionally sharp, peaks extend skyward.

Most of the mountains along the Beartooth Highway consist of igneous or metamorphic rocks, and much of the flora reflects the somewhat acidic nature of the parent rock. Behind Beartooth Lake lies a light-colored, stratified, sedimentary mountain with rocks quite unlike those surrounding it. Though we have not botanized this mountain, it is reported to harbor rare plants partial to limestone that do not occur elsewhere in the area.

The Beartooth Highway usually opens in mid-June and closes in late September. In our expe-

Frederick W. Case, Jr., and his wife Roberta have developed an extensive garden in Saginaw, Michigan, featuring a wide variety of microclimates accommodating high alpine cushion plants as well as woodlanders and bog-lovers. An award-winning high school biology teacher and lecturer on alpines and native plants, he is also an acknowledged authority on *Sarracenia, Trillium* and native orchids; his *Orchids of the Great Lakes Region* is a classic now being reprinted by Cranbrook Institute. The Cases are enthusiastic field botanists who have spent summers exploring throughout the United States, Canada and Alaska.

rience, the best time to travel it is between July 4 and July 20. Both the nature of a particular season and the distribution of winter snow affect the abundance of bloom on a given date, but for overwhelming masses of color and exciting discoveries, mid-July always pays high dividends. For gentians and late-flowering plants, early August is a good time.

The Beartooth Highway travels along above timberline. It ascends quickly from the east in a series of breathtaking, even alarming, switchbacks and, because the flora is so extensive, almost any stop may provide exciting finds. One could not chronicle all the plants and places to see here. We will describe a few of our favorite places where, over the years, we have located especially interesting plants.

Starting from the east on the high prairie, at the foothills town of Red Lodge, we'll work up onto the plateau, cross it, and descend again into timber beyond the pass through the high country.

Pulsatilla patens
Photo by Vernon Tomppert

Red Lodge

An old ranching and mining town, Red Lodge has been revitalized by a thriving summer tourist industry that grows even larger during the ski season. The area is much less crowded than Yellowstone, however.

One approaches across dry and desolate sagebrush plains and foothills, and comes upon Red Lodge nestled in Rock Creek's ice age valley. The old town in the valley is quaint, with a typical "pioneer village" appearance.

Plant hunting near the town provides many desirable items. Almost any highway, byway, or farm service road leads through pastures and subdivisions to open range, sagebrush-filled grasslands, aspen and spruce groves, or meadows. Along these roads, often in heavily pastured areas, *Lewisia rediviva* in a very fine form can be seen in flower from a moving car.

Other desirable plants of these meadows are the mat eriogonums. *Plants of Yellowstone National Park*, McDougall and Babble, lists ten species. *Eriogonum umbellatum*, *E. ovalifolium*, and *E. flavum* grow in the Beartooth country at higher elevations; other species occur in the foothills. Most species grow in pastures, scablands, along roadsides and even on the floor of gravel pits. In areas of recent disturbance small mats often abound. We have had good success growing eriogonums in Michigan. One of our plants is about 20 years old.

The dry, grassy sagebrush fields produce other fine plants: several arnicas including *Arnica cordifolia*, which we find difficult to grow; penstemons, including both the mint-headed species of section *Proceri* and large, showy members of the *Habroanthus* section.

Various species of *Calochortus*, the mariposa tulips of the West, grow in sloping meadows, blooming until mid-July, often while grasses and other plants in their vicinity are bone-dry and the soil a dusty powder. McDougall and Baggley list three species from the vicinity. Probably the one most likely to be encountered without considerable search is the purple eye mariposa, *Calochortus eurycarpus (C. nitidus)*.

Other plants to look for here: several low-growing, showy, yellow composites, bushy or almost mat-forming, which occur in the genera *Senecio* and *Chrysopsis* (*C. villosa* is growable in Michigan); *Eriophyllum;* and one of the larger, truly spectacular plants of the Rockies, *Balsamorhiza sagittata,* balsamroot. Too large for the rock garden, and with a root like a fencepost, it can dominate whole hillsides with its large clusters of arrow-shaped leaves.

Several small cacti grow in the drier meadows and the common prickly pear, *Opuntia polyacantha,* can be abundant. Many cacti now carry special national protection, but the prickly pear can be a destructive pest in pasture lands.

On the dry sagelands grows a small, pale, sky-blue-flowered mertensia with silvery, blue-green leaves, probably McDougall's and Baggley's *Mertensia coronata.* Not showy, and not as tiny as the alpine species, it is, nevertheless, a satisfactory and growable plant in Eastern scree gardens. A search among flower clusters will usually reveal a few large, green nutlets which germinate well and provide an easy way to obtain this plant. Digging is rarely satisfactory on the dry prairie. Transporting roots without rot or desiccation is difficult.

The scarlet mallow, *Sphaeralcea coccinea,* often grows in company with the mertensia. It will grow and spread, sometimes too much, in a rich, sunny scree in Michigan.

The banks of small brooks, trickles and seeps harbor dodecatheons, *Dodecatheon pauciflorum* or *D. radicatum.* (Authorities do not agree or distinguish dodecatheon species clearly and with consistency.) The shooting stars bloom early, and are on the decline by July except at high altitudes. Green seed, collected from the large pods, frequently ripens and will germinate.

Some roadside ditches and seepages have large colonies of yellow monkeyflower, *Mimulus guttatus.* Although rampant in cultivation, and not actually perennial if the plant freezes solidly, it is a characteristic and appropriate rock garden plant, with the advantage that it flowers all season. We have not seen the deep pink-purple *M. lewisii* along the Beartooth Highway, although it grows in Yellowstone Park.

Leaving these interesting and worthwhile plants of the dry fields and scablands, we start our trek to even more exciting places.

USDA Campgrounds, Rock Creek

From the mountains to the southwest Rock Creek descends into and through Red Lodge. The Beartooth Highway follows Rock Creek Canyon for 15–20 miles before ascending abruptly, in switchbacks, up over the plateau rim and onto the alpine tundra. A few miles out of town, on national forest land, are several USDA campgrounds located in clearings placed back a bit from the stream. Sheltered there in the canyon, at higher elevations than the meadows at Red Lodge, these clearings make good flower hunting in late summer.

Of special interest to alpine gardeners are mat-forming *Penstemon procerus* or *P. rydbergii* with good showy heads of violet-blue and clear blue; the yellow daisies of *Arnica cordifolia;* and the soft rose-red globular blooms of *Geum (Erythrocoma) triflorum,* an easy plant with feathery foliage and showy fluffy seed heads in smoke pink (hence the name, prairie smoke). A small-leaved, green-flowered heuchera forms clumps along roadsides and on rocky outcrops—not showy, but possessing character. *Clematis columbiana,* in a lovely, soft blue-lavender, clambers over shrubbery in shady, moist spots. It reaches its peak of luxuriance a bit higher on the mountains.

The choicest plant we have found in these campgrounds, where it is very rare and hard to locate, is the leopard lily or purple fritillary, *Fritillaria atropurpurea.* With its several hanging, dull purple and greenish spotted flowers, it is long past its bloom by the time we reach Beartooth country each year. We find only the erect, lilylike, seed pods on dry stalks among sagebrush thickets. We have never attempted to grow it.

Upper Rock Creek

In the upper Rock Creek area, about 13 miles from the junction of U.S. Highways 212 and 308, we find steep slopes clothed in pine and fir. Nearby, in recently burned-over spots, a younger growth of lodgepole pine descends to the road. Outcroppings of rocks and piles of massive boulders, which seem barren at first, lie above the road. Roadside pullouts offer views of the creek, the forests below,

Cryptogramma crispa var. *acrostichoides*
Photo by Gwen Kelaidis

Penstemon eriantherus
Photo by Panayoti Kelaidis

and the impressive beauty of the head of Rock Creek Canyon. Do stop, and climb above the road. Upward, as far as one can see into the dense spruce and pine forest, cascades of the blue *Clematis columbiana* drape shrubs and small trees. It is a magnificent sight when the plants are in full bloom.

A common shrub here is the dioecious Canada buffaloberry, *Shepherdia canadensis*, with punctate, rusty dots on its oval blue-green leaves. Always a modest-sized shrub, it would make a good background plant for a larger rock garden, but it is difficult to move. In season, it is covered with inconspicuous, fragrant, creamy yellow flowers and later, with showy, translucent red berries, if female.

In deep, mossy pockets in the woods, pipsissewa (*Chimaphila umbellata*) and various species of *Pyrola* grow. But the real prize here is a substantial colony of the lovely orchid, *Calypso bulbosa*. Although it is widespread in the Western mountains and can occur in large colonies at some localities, it is not a common plant. It is not frequent along the Beartooth Highway, but it does occur there, and again on the approach to Sylvan Pass, always as scattered plants. It blooms on this slope about mid-July, indicating that the snow must lie long here, for calypso is one of the earliest flowers to bloom after the snow melts.

On the open rock outcrops and boulders in this section of the highway, and sometimes in the gravel of the roadside, one can find clumps of a large, shrubby, evergreen penstemon. This is *Penstemon fruticosus* ssp. *fruticosus*. A large plant, the local form here is generally of pale lavender coloring, not the finest shrubby penstemon by far, but always worthwhile and interesting. It occurs along the highway at this elevation and again, as one drops below the level of Beartooth Lake to the west.

Below the road on rocks and in crevices, grows a very worthwhile heuchera. I have been unable to determine exactly what species it represents. It is somewhat hairy throughout, and has moderate-sized palmate leaves with puberulent, showy, creamy white flowers on rather tall stems. This garden-worthy plant grows well in our rock scree in Michigan with no special attention.

In sunny rock crevices and on boulder-talus piles along the road, grow two attractive rock ferns. One, Rocky Mountain woodsia, *Woodsia scopulina*, grows abundantly in loose rock slides and piles, often in full sun and in rather dry sites. It transplants well and stays many years where it is happy. We have had plants which grew well for over 20 years. A less frequently seen plant in the Beartooth, but an outstanding rock garden subject, is the parsley-fern, *Cryptogramma crispa* var. *acrostichoides*. This interesting fern ranges from Alaska to the Rockies and sporadically eastward to the Isle Royale region of Michigan and the north shore of Lake Superior. Two features make this an outstanding garden plant. First, its color is a light apple green, lighter or with more yellow in it than is common to most rock ferns; and secondly, its fronds are dimorphic. The sterile, photosynthetic fronds grow

PLATE 7

Physaria didymocarpa in seed
Photo by Sharon Sutton

Eriogonum umbellatum
Photo by Elizabeth Neese

Gentianopsis thermalis
Photo by Ned Lowry

Mimulus guttatus
Photo by Allan Taylor

Castilleja miniata
Photo by Ted Kipping

PLATE 10

Astragalus sericoleucus
Photo: Grand Ridge

Calochortus gunnisonii
Photo by Ted Kipping

Oenothera caespitosa
Photo by Pat Pachuta

Erigeron poliospermus
Photo by Sharon Sutton

Linanthastrum nuttallii
Photo by Ted Cochrane

fairly low, triangular, and flattish, although much divided. The fertile fronds grow taller, with more numerous and narrower segments; they are highly divided and more erect than the sterile ones. It is these spore-bearing fronds that so much resemble parsley and give the fern its name. It flourishes for us in a soil mix of sand and peat in a rock crevice in partial shade. We have had one plant for over 15 years.

At about this same location in Rock Creek Canyon, a road turns off to the right into Rock Creek Valley to reach several campgrounds and, eventually, to climb the opposite valley wall up to Glacier Lake. At this junction, there is an open meadow with sagebrush. Here grow calochortus, *Lewisia rediviva* and *L. pygmaea*, arnicas, and in July, one can find dried-up heads of dodecatheon—each with a single fat seed pod on a 5 in. stem—among the grasses. I have never been able to obtain solid information on just what constitutes the concept *Dodecatheon uniflorum*. The late Carl Worth used to write intriguingly about it. At this location, at the very summit of the highway in one wet trickle, and at Storm Lake, out of Anaconda, Montana, I have found large populations of dwarf, single-flowered, large and showy shooting stars. All were exceptional. Just what species they were I cannot say.

Not far past this location, the pace quickens. Highway 212 begins to ascend the Rock Creek Canyon wall in a series of steep, dangerous switchbacks. All the usual plants we have seen along the road are present, but now higher alpines descend in patches to join them. At each switchback bend a roaring creek drops under the road. Along these streams grow some fine alpine and subalpine plants. *Aquilegia flavescens*—soft rich yellow with short, almost hooklike spurs—leans out over the waters. Clumps of the larger, soft gray-blue *Mertensia paniculata* serve as a foil for the bright columbines. If the exposure is drier and more prairielike, the pasque flower, *Pulsatilla (Anemone) patens,* may cover the bank. By July, it is usually in fluffy seed. In roadside gravels along here, large plants of a viscous-hairy lavender penstemon can be seen. This is *Penstemon eriantherus*. This handsome plant, with its large, sticky-glandular flowers, is related to the giant-flowered *P. cobaea*. It is a short-lived plant but well worth the trouble necessary to keep it coming from seed. Very rarely, pure white forms occur.

Several senecios begin to appear, and the land now quickly becomes more open and alpine in aspect. Timber, where present along streams and in sheltered coves, is mostly fir and more dense than before. There is little plant variety in the shade. Under the trees the ground is mossy or carpeted in vast dense beds of the subalpine vaccinium, *Vaccinium scoparium*. The little vaccinium makes a most garden-worthy ground cover for dark, peaty, cool spots in the rock garden. The plant is so green in stem and leaf as to look somewhat artificial, or slightly parasitic, but it is not difficult to cultivate.

Not reassuring along this section are the occasional glimpses of wrecked autos below the road. Indeed, this road is not for the faint of heart, and if you do not enjoy heights, curves, drop-offs and grand views, it is not for you. We have always heard from friends how frightening and steep Colorado's Mount Evans road is. We avoided it for years. But compared to spots on the Beartooth, the Mount Evans road is a "pussycat."

As one nears the top of the Rock Creek Canyon wall, there is, on one of the switchbacks, a rest area and parking lot. The short walk out to the valley overlook deserves a few minutes of your time. Along the walk grow clumps of a loosely mounded, smallish, short-stemmed, golden yellow senecio that is a very nice plant. A fleshy herb, it does not transplant well; one ought to collect a pinch of seed. As with many composites, its quite green seed will often germinate fairly well.

About a quarter-mile up the highway, the road rounds a curve and mammoth, very steep screes and talus slopes come into view across the valley; there is a pullout on the right against a wooded cove. Years ago in this grove of trees, let us record, we had our first alpine picnic and saw nearby our first eritrichiums. It was a lovely spot. Though construction and camping (illegal here) have marred it somewhat, the spot is still lovely. On the floor of the grove grow mint-headed penstemons, some arnicas, and little else; up the steep wooded slope beyond the flat, however, is a wonderland. The trees, twisted and warped by the severity of winter weather, are beautiful to behold, clothed in masses of brilliant yellow lichens, almost unreal in color. At the very crest of the ridge above the cove, the forest stops abruptly. One literally steps from huge trees to dwarf alpine scree plants in a single step. The view of Rock Creek is awesome.

On this scree grow *Eritrichium nanum, Mertensia alpina, Dryas octopetala, Smelowskia calycina* (with silvery, dissected leaves and white heads of crucifer flowers), sedum, *Silene acaulis,* dwarf *Salix* species forming ground-hugging mats and—best plant at this spot—the alpine bladderpod, *Lesquerella alpina*. Here, too, grows the tightest, tiniest bun or polster we have seen, *Trifolium nanum,* a tiny clover with single purple blooms. On another slope here, with a less exposed aspect, grow pulsatilla, *Geum triflorum, G. (Acomastylis) rossii,* and *Potentilla fruticosa (Pentaphylloides floribunda)*.

Soon after leaving this delightful spot, the road ascends beyond the steep scree-slides to break

Eritrichium nanum. Photo by Bob Heapes

out onto the plateau proper. On the left are natural and blasted cliffs and great rocks along the road. These contain many fine plants and demand exploration. At the head of these bluffs, the road heaves up over the canyon rim onto the plateau. On the left, in season, are lupines as far as the eye can see: *Lupinus argenteus* var. *depressus.* Their base color is a dark purple-blue, but salmon pink and white plants occur, too. The ground is turfy and studded with boulders, an obscure fellfield, perhap , but not so severe and somber as some. On this windswept field grow many dwarfed buns of the shrubby cinquefoil, *Potentilla fruticosa (Pentaphylloides floribunda).* We have collected a number of the dwarfest of these and brought them back to Saginaw. Interestingly, many were not true dwarfs and, in our climate, resumed upright growth too large for the rock garden. A few, however, have become genetically fixed for dwarfness, and while they grow larger here than in the exposed Beartooth environment, they have remained hand-sized buns.

Beyond this point the wall of the canyon becomes a series of steps up onto the plateau, with a moderate-sized creek cascading down from the meadows above, over the steplike rocks into Rock Creek Valley below. This is Quad's Creek, and it was at one time so marked. Beside an abandoned road section on the right grow some fine plants. In the gravelly turf *Dryas octopetala* var. *hookeriana* grows abundantly. Dwarf willows, resembling *Salix reticulata* in leaf, but smaller, form marvelous mats. Eritrichium, douglasia, oxytropis in purple and in pale yellow, violets, polemonium, penstemon, dodecatheon, all desirable and spectacular, mingle here with abandon.

Lower down, the stream bed flattens out into a turfy, peaty, boggy meadow filled with wonders. The dwarfest form of the alpine bog laurel, *Kalmia microphylla,* grows almost prostrate against the moss. Here, too, grow *Phyllodoce empetriformis* and *P. glanduliflora.* Careful search will usually produce the hybrid between the two, *P.* × *intermedia,* as well, but this hybrid is easier to find farther west as the road descends.

Alpine globeflower, *Trollius laxus,* and alpine marsh marigold, *Caltha leptosepala,* dot the mossy mounds. Later in the season the fantastic elephant head, *Pedicularis groenlandica,* rears its pink-lavender spikes of little elephants. Later in the season in the same area, on the drier edges, the much rarer arctic disjunct Oeder's Lousewort, *P. oederi,* raises its dwarfed bright yellow blooms. The genus *Pedicularis* is said to be partially parasitic and hence, not transplantable. Seed cast near other plants in a peat bed may be the only hope for growing these—if they will tolerate the higher lowland temperatures.

Kalmia polifolia ssp. *microphylla*. Photo by Loraine Yeatts

Other plants, which appear at this spot in season, are the one-flowered bellflower, *Campanula uniflora,* so tiny one usually tramples it without notice, and the fantastic greenish white, purple-spotted *Gentiana algida.* The large, blue *G. (Pneumonanthe) calycosa* grows on the Beartooth, but we have not seen it there.

It is difficult to leave the many alpine treasures here, but leave we must; we have barely reached the high plateau.

The High Plateau

For several miles now the road has crept upward, in so gradual an incline it seems level. Grassy sod-meadows alternate with grotesque fellfields where frost action heaves giant rocks, first upward like tombstones, then topples them on their sides in eerie heaps and clusters, ultimately moving them along in giant "rock rivers" until they plunge over the edge of the plateau in rock slides and talus slopes. Poking around among the boulders reveals a variety of fine plants, but the grassy meadows have such dense turf that most of the interesting ones are excluded by the competition. Only around animal tunnels or against a boulder, where disturbance destroys the grass turf, can the showier plants survive.

Just beyond Beartooth Pass, the road itself becomes suddenly very interesting. Switchbacks alternate with precipitous drop-offs where, without much of a barrier, a thousand-foot cliff is just a foot from the right front wheel of the car. The passenger beside the driver may now become quite agitated, checking the door locks, taking considerable interest in the driver's technical skill, often uttering half-stifled comments or gasps. Two thousand feet below—or it *seems* like two thousand feet—lie two jewel lakes set in green meadows and dark evergreen groves. At the head of the cirque, vertical walls ascend to higher levels, towards ponds, meadows, or snowbanks. Above all this is a horizon-to-horizon panorama of mountains. Because of the severe glacial scouring, one has the impression of being above the area looking down into it. The effect is spectacular, the coloring superb, the mood—euphoric.

Now the road makes several more short, sharp switchbacks. On the inside of each curve is a parking pullout. Do stop and get out on one of these. The gravelly floor of the area is itself a rock garden. The loose rock and perpetual disturbance lends itself to invasion by choice alpine seedlings: *Saxifraga oppositifolia* (very rare here), *S. chrysantha* (*S. serpyllifolia*), eritrichiums, *Polemonium viscosum,* phlox cushions in white and blue, senecios, dryas, *Lewisia pygmaea,* various species of *Draba, Douglasia montana, Saxifraga flagellaris,* wooly-leaved, orange-flowered composites, and many other fine plants.

For a real thrill, cross the switchback curve, and climb up over the roadcut onto the natural slope. Be careful! A slip here could mean a thousand-foot fall. The steep, open meadow, punctuated with rock slides and outcroppings is now truly alpine scree, fabulously decorated with the choicest plants. Crevices and niches in the outcrops which face north or northeast have great mounds of purple saxifrage, *Saxifraga oppositifolia,* some in rich, dark colors. Dryas covers the ground, and raw spots are blue and pink with eritrichium and douglasia. The variety of species here is spectacular. Of course, slope, exposure and soil type all affect the plant composition of the particular spot. A partial list of plants here includes:

Androsace lehmanniana	*Dryas octopetala*	*Polygonum (Bistorta) bistortoides*
Antennaria spp.	*Erigeron caespitosus*	*Potentilla nivea*
Arenaria spp.	*E. compositus*	*Rumex paucifolius*
Arnica spp.	*Erigeron* spp.	*Salix arctica*
Aster spp.	*Eritrichium nanum*	*S. nivalis*
Astragalus spp.	*Gentiana algida*	*Saxifraga chrysantha*
Besseya wyomingensis	*G. prostrata*	*S. oppositifolia*
Campanula uniflora	*Geum rossii* var. *turbinatum*	*S. rhomboidea*
Castilleja spp.	*Lloydia serotina*	*Senecio* spp.
Cerastium beeringianum	*Lomatium cous*	*Sibbaldia procumbens*
Chaenactis alpina	*Mertensia alpina*	*Silene acaulis*
Claytonia lanceolata	*Myosotis alpestris*	*Smelowskia calycina*
Dodecatheon pulchellum	*Oxytropis* spp.	*Stellaria* spp.
Douglasia montana	*Pedicularis* spp.	*Thlaspi fendleri*
Draba aurea	*Phacelia sericea*	*Townsendia* spp.
D. incerta	*Phlox pulvinata*	*Trifolium* spp.
D. oligosperma	*Polemonium pulcherrimum*	*Veronica wormskjoldii*
Draba spp.	*P. viscosum*	

All across the summit of the pass these and many other alpine plants abound—there is so much of this tundra-scree along this highway! Moreover, at Beartooth Pass the scenery is so spectacular one is apt to forget the alpines. But don't.

Continuing along the road floors of gravel pits yield *Saxifraga flagellaris,* the whiplash saxifrage with its bright red runners and little "hen and chick" offsets. Alpine shooting star, some years, covers the wetter, turfy meadows in rich purple. Some very dark forms occur. I have had trouble, however, flowering this species in Michigan. This year, using more peat and less gravel scree, I finally got the plant to bloom. It is super!

Westward along the roadway, wetter screes, old snowfields, stream banks and bogs glow with the rich gold of a spectacular buttercup, *Ranunculus eschscholtzii.* This spectacular plant seems to emerge from the ground in full bloom, the quarter-size flowers appearing and bursting while still sitting on the ground. As the plant matures the stems reach about 6 in., and the stems flop a bit, but what a beautiful flower! It will grow in Michigan, and it is lovely, but it does not keep its compact, commanding character. Not long-lived, it comes easily from fresh, never-dried seed.

Descent to Beartooth Lake

About a half-mile below this summit area, the road begins to dip into dwarfed trees. On large granitic outcrops, somewhat rounded but ledgelike, the trees have a krummholz aspect and form extremely dense, impenetrable thickets. Here on peaty ledges grow beds of matted, foot-tall willows. Under the ledges a variety of fine species of *Draba,* dwarf alpine mertensia, and other excellent plants grow. They are not exclusive to this area, but here in the shelter of the rocks, they form excellent, showy clumps.

After a few long, gradual switchbacks, the road flattens out onto a boggy plateau with several ponds or small lakes on the left. This side of the mountain is wetter, more subject to midday thunderstorms or rains. Hence, the area is mossier, peatier, and the flora is essentially alpine-bog flora. Around the lakes fine beds of alpine red heather, *Phyllodoce empetriformis,* bloom long into the summer. Much rarer, *P. glanduliflora* grows here too, and the soft pink of hybrid *P. × intermedia* is not

Gentiana algida
Photo by Vernon Tomppert

rare. Near snowbanks, rafts of the white alpine cowslip, *Caltha leptosepala,* dot the peaty bog. In places, especially around brushy thickets, *Trollius laxus* var. *albiflorus* in soft, transparent yellow, colors the meadow. We have been unable to keep either of these plants long in Michigan. We suspect there is a temperature requirement we cannot meet. The eastern form of *T. laxus,* however, grows well for us and seeds about the peat beds prolifically. *Rhodiola (Sedum) roseum* or *R. rhodanthum* form clumps at poolside. Though not spectacular, they do please the eye.

Boulders along the roadside in this series of boggy, pond-studded meadows may bear numerous bright pink *Lewisia pygmaea* plants in their crevices. Off the main road about a quarter-mile, and well worth the time, is beautiful Beartooth Lake with its backdrop of the limestone Beartooth Butte.

Beartooth Lake Area

A side road takes you to the site of an old camping area and store that have been demolished. Here, meadows between road and lake yield a fine dark blue tuberous delphinium (probably *D. bicolor*), *Ranunculus eschscholtzii,* numerous and excellent arnicas, *Aquilegia flavescens,* matted penstemons, occasional glacier lilies, *Erythronium grandiflorum,* and in boggy willow and birch thickets around the lakeshore, a weird, lurid, blue-green, starry-flowered gentian relative, *Swertia perennis.* Here, too, grows the lovely fringe-petaled *Parnassia fimbriata.* The bog birch is *Betula glandulosa,* a fine, dwarf shrub. All these plants are garden-worthy and desirable. A day spent at Beartooth Lake could not exhaust the floral finds.

Clay Butte Area

One last area on this road deserves special mention. A few miles past Beartooth Lake a road ascends to the right (it was closed by earth slides during the 1983 season) to Clay Butte Fire Lookout. In a small pond across the road from the junction, in wet moose meadows, grows the largest flowered spatterdock or cowlily (yellow waterlily) species, *Nuphar polysepalum.* Rhizomes thick as fence posts and huge yellow-cupped blooms characterize this arctic-alpine waterlily. We grow it and like it very much.

Just at the junction to Clay Butte, in an area where, in winter, rodents tunnel the soil and work it almost raw, grows one of the jewels of the highway: the tiny, golden lily with nodding flowers,

Fritillaria pudica. One-to-several flowered, this 5 in. plant is truly beautiful and very difficult to grow.

From this point down the mountain, one descends into groves of aspen and fir and sagebrush fields. There are spectacular subalpine meadows with larger plants—*Aquilegia flavescens, Geranium viscosisimum,* meadow rues, delphiniums, penstemons and the like. A good plant here, too, especially on the road to Lily Lake, is the shrubby clematis, *Clematis hirsutissima,* with its blue-black "old maid's bonnets." It becomes more common as one descends.

The Beartooth Highway is a wondrous road for scenery and for native plants. We know no other single drive that will produce such variety in its flora and also provide such glorious views.

In the long run, seed remains the most satisfactory method of obtaining the growing native Beartooth species, and it offers an added bonus. In seed flats, a degree of natural selection occurs, and some seedlings may actually thrive under your conditions, while a given plant, uprooted in the wild, no matter how spectacular its blooms, may lack the genes for tolerance of your lowland climate.

We must make sure that Rocky Mountain alpines are brought into cultivation, made available through seed exchanges, selected and developed for horticulture, and distributed to the rock gardeners of the world. We expect Beartooth plants to contribute greatly to this American alpine treasure. We have seen most of the accessible mountain tundra areas and alpine roads from Colorado through Alaska. All are wonderful and interesting, but the Beartooth Highway merits your special attention.

References

Anderson, Bob. 1984. *Beartooth country, Montana's Absaroka and Beartooth Mountains.* Montana Geographic Series, no. 7. Helena, Mont.: Montana Magazine Inc.

McDougall, W. B., and Herman A. Baggley. 1956. *Plants of Yellowstone National Park.* Yellowstone Interpretive Series, no. 8. Yellowstone Park, Wyo.: Yellowstone Library and Museum Assoc.

Rydberg, Per Axel. 1954. *Flora of the Rocky Mountains and the adjacent plains.* 2nd ed. New York: Hafner Publishing Co.

10

The Yellowstone Region: Endemics and Other Interesting Plants

by Erwin F. Evert

The Yellowstone region, comprising northwestern Wyoming, southwestern Montana, and adjacent eastern Idaho, is an area of considerable botanical interest. It harbors over four dozen endemic species, making it a notable center of plant speciation, boasts a varied assemblage of widespread species, and offers an interesting juxtaposition of northern and southern floristic elements. Finally, much of the region, particularly southwestern Montana, is virtually unexplored botanically.

I have spent the last 10 summers exploring primarily one drainage basin in the Absaroka Mountains adjacent to Yellowstone National Park. This relatively small, unexplored area of about 1,000 square miles has already yielded much of botanical interest, including at least four new species. The botanical surface of this exciting Greater Yellowstone Region has barely been scratched; many botanical surprises await the explorer. I shall examine here a number of the little-known regional endemics; some of the more interesting peripherals (species occurring at the limits of their ranges); a few interesting widespread species; and last, a few remarkable disjunct species—all of which occur in the remarkable Yellowstone region.

Basically the area includes three altitudinally controlled vegetation zones: the lower grass and shrub zone, a middle forested one, and the upper alpine zone. The lower zone is usually dominated by sagebrush, *Artemisia* species, and grasses with species of *Agropyron, Stipa,* and *Festuca* most prominent. Usually found in the intermountain basins, it sometimes reaches considerable elevations so that occasionally no intervening forest belt is found. Usually, however, artemisia-steppe gives way to forest at 5,000–6,000 ft. in the north and 7,000–8,000 ft. in the south. The lower reaches of the forest zone are often dominated by Douglas fir, *Pseudotsuga menziesii,* and occasionally by lodgepole pine, *Pinus contorta.* Yellow pine, *P. ponderosa,* a dominant at lower tree line to the east and

Erwin F. Evert is a former biology teacher, now an active field botanist. He has published a number of new species of vascular plants and a new genus, *Shoshonea,* which promises to be a fine rock garden plant. He started his first garden at the age of four and discovered the magic of the North Woods about the same time. Later he fell under the spell of Rocky Mountain plants and natural wonders. When not found in his naturalistic garden in Park Ridge, Illinois, he can be traced to rich deciduous woods, bogs, fens, alpine tundras, or to his cabin near Yellowstone National Park.

west of the region, is conspicuously absent from almost the entire Yellowstone region, a fascinating and unexplained distributional hiatus for this widespread species. With increasing elevation, Engelmann spruce, *Picea engelmannii*, and subalpine fir, *Abies lasiocarpa*, become dominant in the upper reaches of the forest zone. Frequently near upper tree line, we encounter extensive stands of white bark pine, *Pinus albicaulis*. Upper tree line is reached at about 9,300 ft. in the north and at about 10,500 ft. in the south, and the alpine zone begins. Here vegetation is dominated by low-growing graminoids with species of *Carex, Poa, Festuca,* and *Deschampsia* occurring often. A heterogeneous assemblage of low-growing nongraminoids, often very showy species, occur less frequently. Many of the region's numerous endemics are found at these higher elevations.

The Yellowstone region has a vascular flora of about 2,500 species that fall into several readily apparent geographical groups: species with boreal affinities, species with western American cordilleran correspondencies, a group of non-natives, a cosmopolitan group, and finally a group that might be called "plains" or "Great Basin." The great majority, about 75 percent, fall into the first two major floristic groups: the boreal and the western American cordilleran. Species belonging to the widespread boreal contingent range around the whole Northern Hemisphere with some southern extensions into the mountains of Eurasia and America. Some boreal species that occur in the forest belt of the Yellowstone region are: *Actaea rubra, Adoxa moschatellina, Arctostaphylos uva-ursi, Calypso bulbosa, Cornus canadensis, Equisetum sylvaticum, Linnaea borealis, Lycopodium annotinum, Pyrola secunda,* and *Trautvetteria caroliniensis.* Representing this group in the alpine zone would be such well-known arctic alpine species as: *Dryas octopetala, Carex bipartita, C. rupestris, Eritrichium nanum, Juncus biglumis, Kobresia bellardii, Lloydia serotina, Saxifraga oppositifolia,* and *Silene acaulis.*

Calypso bulbosa
Photo by Gwen Kelaidis

Species of the western American cordilleran group are restricted mostly to the Rockies and coastal ranges of western North America. Some are wide-ranging, extending from southern Alaska south through the mountains of western Canada, the Cascades of Washington and Oregon, and occasionally as far south as the Sierra Nevadas. In the Rockies they extend south to Colorado, Arizona, and New Mexico. Examples of such wide-ranging cordilleran species in the forest zone of the Yellowstone region would include such woody dominants as *Abies lasiocarpa, Picea engelmannii, Pinus contorta, Pseudotsuga menziesii,* and such prominent herbaceous members of the understory as *Anemone multifida, Arnica cordifolia, Calamagrostis rubescens,* and *Erigeron peregrinus;* while *Antennaria media, Arabis lemmonii, Carex albonigra, C. phaecephala, C. scopulorum, Draba lonchocarpa, D. oligosperma, Hieracium gracile, Juncus drummondii, J. mertensianus, Kalmia microphylla, Minuartia (Arenaria) obtusiloba, Poa rupicola, Ranunculus eschscholtzii,* and *Senecio fremontii* are common representatives of this group in the alpine and subalpine zones of the region.

Most of the species in the western cordilleran group do not range as far north or south as the former and an interesting group that might be called a Pacific Northwest subelement reaches its southeasternmost limits in the Yellowstone region. *Alnus viridis, Crataegus columbiana, Cassiope mertensiana, Ledum glandulosum, Menziesia ferruginea, Phyllodoce empetriformis, Lysichiton americanum* (if old reports from Yellowstone National Park are substantiated) and *Xerophyllum tenax* are a few of the most conspicuous species of this group. Most of these have horticultural possibilities. The Yellowstone region also contains a number of mostly subalpine and alpine species with more southern affinities—southern Rocky Mountain endemics—that reach their northernmost range limits in our area. Such showy garden-worthy species as *Aquilegia caerulea, Artemisia scopulorum, Carex elynoides, Draba crassa, Erigeron leiomerus, E. simplex, E. ursinus, Haplopappus acaulis, Hymenoxys grandiflora, Oxytropis parryi, Phlox caespitosa, Primula parryi, Senecio amplectens, S. dimorphophyllus, Trifolium dasyphyllum, T. nanum,* and *T. parryi* belong to this group. Five species of Great Plains or Great Basin affinities would be welcome additions to most gardens and also, interestingly, reach their northernmost range limits in the region. Two showy composites, *Platyschkuhria integrifolia* and *Xylorhiza glabriuscula;* the charming shrub *Cercocarpus ledifolius;* the brilliant *Zauschneria (Epilobium) garrettii* and *Astragalus gilviflorus,* a cushion plant, are of interest in this regard.

Thus, the region's flora is composed almost entirely of rather wide-ranging species, most of which we could probably say did not originate in the region but have migrated there from northern and other western North American regions.

The Yellowstone region is thus an interesting meeting ground for northern, southern, and wide-ranging species. It is an even more interesting meeting ground for species that are more or less restricted to the region: the endemics, those species that probably originated in the Yellowstone region. These are the true natives.

Endemics

The Yellowstone region contains 50 or more species (see plant list) that are apparently more or less restricted to this area. Thus, about two percent of the region's flora can be considered endemic. Whether or not these species originated in the area (since we lack a fossil record for all these species) is a difficult question to answer. It appears that the majority probably did. However, if they did originate in the region, what prevented them from leaving? Did they all originate so recently that there has not been enough time for migration, or were there other factors operating to prevent dispersal out of the area?

The Yellowstone region at present appears to be something of a large semi-isolated, montane ecological island. The region is surrounded on the east, south, and southwest by the different, more arid, moisture regimes of the Great Plains, Red Desert, and Snake River lava plains respectively and on the northwest by a region of generally greater moisture, more extensive forest, less continentality (more maritime), along with a different edaphic milieu (more acidic soil and less edaphic variety) in the uplands of the granitic Idaho batholith. It is possible that these surrounding ecological barriers, except perhaps to the north, were more or less instrumental in preventing migration out of the area. It is possibly significant that a number of these presumably autochthonous taxa do occur to the north of the Yellowstone region in apparently isolated stations (perhaps due to lack of collecting in the intervening areas) in the Glacier Park area adjacent to southern Alberta and southern British Columbia. It is precisely in this direction that ecological barriers appear to be significantly less pronounced, or seemingly nonexistent, and thus apparently were and are less effective in preventing dispersal out of the region. A few of the region's endemics have reached apparently isolated stations in the Wasatch and Uinta Mountains of northeastern Utah as well as in the Wallowa Mountains of eastern Oregon. This is as would be expected given the differing dispersal abilities of the species involved, the varying lengths of time available for dispersal (since it is improbable that all these species originated simultaneously), and the probable relaxation of barriers to dispersal during the many glacial periods of the Quaternary period.

All of the region's endemics that I am aware of are adapted for growth in open situations or in open woodlands. None is really shade-tolerant. A few are plants of wet, open situations such as *Juncus tweedyii* and *Castilleja gracillima.* Most of these natives are plants of higher elevations. However, most appear not to be obligate alpines. Indeed, one is impressed with the altitudinal amplitude of many of the species. They range from the bottoms of basins to the tops of mountains (*Kelseya uniflora* is instructive in this regard), if the requisite edaphic conditions and openness are present. A good number of these natives are specialists of unstable shifting substrates such as talus and scree; *Erigeron flabellifolius* and *Penstemon montanus* are good examples. Some, such as *Shoshonea pulvinata* and

Shoshonea pulvinata. Photo by Erwin Evert

Aquilegia jonesii, are restricted to calcareous cliffs or calcareous substrates. In short, they specialize in the open, usually unstable habitats that abound in the region—habitats that were probably even more abundant in the past than at present.

Kelseya uniflora, Shoshonea pulvinata, Aquilegia jonesii, Antennaria aromatica, and occasionally *Castilleja nivea* are five endemic calcareous cliff specialists that grow on Rattlesnake Mountain west of Cody, Wyoming. I vividly remember seeing the first three for the first time on Rattlesnake Mountain in 1979. I had rushed up there looking for *Petrophytum caespitosum,* a plant I had been looking for unsuccessfully for a number of years in the North Fork Shoshone River drainage area in the Absaroka Mountains of northwestern Wyoming. A friend told me he had seen some just a few days before while botanizing on Rattlesnake. As it turned out, I never did find the petrophytum (maybe it migrated) but as my friend later expressed it with some chagrin, I did "manage to find all the good stuff." This place was amazing! It was one of those high, free places with 50 mph winds that make your eyes water and your nose run—a high buckled limestone anticlinal welt sticking up in the sky and dropping precipitously to the west. And there it was, that fantastic little shrub, not petrophytum but *Kelseya uniflora* plastered all over the cliffs and ledges. The stuff was all over the place in mats, cushions, and in weird protuberances of all dimensions. Furthermore, this stuff wasn't supposed to be there at all, at least not on this side of the Bighorn Basin in Park County. Kelsey's rock rose, a plant not unlike some of those vegetable lambs from New Zealand, I had never seen in the field before. I had seen photographs of kelseya and a nice little specimen growing in a piece of tufa in a garden a few months before in, of all places, Wisconsin. But what a surprise to find it growing there on Rattlesnake. Some of the cushions were as much as a yard across, but of course only a few inches high, with the remains of the year's rose flowers right down on the tiny gray foliage. It is an early bloomer, late May to early June here at 8,600 ft. and even earlier, probably April, in the basins. And it was already mid-August. This amazing shrub had been known for a long time from the Bighorns and for an even longer time from Montana where it was discovered by the Rev. Frank Kelsey in 1888. It is known apparently from only three counties in Montana, two in Idaho, and now from five counties in northwestern Wyoming. Kelseya is very discontinuously distributed and is absent from large stretches of seemingly suitable habitat. *Kelseya uniflora* is certainly one of the great rock plants of western North America. It is normally a plant of limestone ledges, crevices, and soaring cliff faces. Occasionally, as in the Shoshone Canyon where Precambrian granite is faulted into the Paleozoic limestone, kelseya, the calciphile, grows where it's not supposed to grow, in the crevices of the adjacent granite! Here on Rattlesnake it was growing on limestone with *Cheilanthes feei* and *Telesonix (Boykinia) jamesii* on the cliff faces, and on the more horizontal ledges and pavements in the company of *Aquilegia jonesii, Carex rupestris, Eritrichium howardii,* and an odd little umbellifer that turned out to be a new genus, *Shoshonea.*

Aquilegia jonesii was another of many surprises that day on Rattlesnake. It, too, had never been reported from the western side of the Bighorn Basin, though it had been collected initially over a century ago by C. C. Parry with the 1873 Jones expedition on Phlox Mountain in the Owl Creeks at the southern end of the basin. This most coveted of alpines ranges from the northern end of the Wind Rivers east to the Bighorns and north, sporadically, to Glacier Park and southern Alberta. *Aquilegia jonesii* is one of those endemics that apparently hasn't been able to disperse to the west in Idaho where seemingly suitable habitat for it exists, but it has had no trouble making it up north along the eastern front of the Rockies. This is a great plant of tufted habit, interesting gray-green foliage and large royal purple-blue flowers. What more could you ask? Except, perhaps, that it could be more easily grown! This is a plant of limestone crevices, screes, and taluses, not a plant of the vertical cliff faces like the fantastic kelseya. Here on Rattlesnake on the eastern flanks of the Absarokas this subalpine charmer was growing abundantly among the limy rubble, its stature, including the seed capsules, less than two inches! The elevation was about 8,600 ft., over 1,000 ft. below timberline, but you would never know this from the looks of the associates. Typical arctic-alpines were in evidence here, including *Eritrichium nanum, Carex rupestris,* and *Saxifraga caespitosa,* indicative of the harsh windswept site that this certainly is. Experience has taught me that harsh, open sites such as these, particularly if they are of limestone parent rock, are often an indication that the place may harbor rare, local, and occasionally undescribed species. Such was the case on top of Rattlesnake that day in August.

However, you need not stray far from the roads in this region to find just as much. Such was the case with *Shoshonea pulvinata.* After discovering and describing this delightful little cushion-forming umbel from the top of Rattlesnake Mountain, and after collecting it in a number of other equally unfrequented places, I noticed, somewhat to my chagrin, while showing a botanist some plants in the Shoshone Canyon, not more than 20 ft. from the Cody-Yellowstone highway, that *Shoshonea pulvinata,* unlike the scarlet pimpernel, was perhaps not so "damned elusive" after all! How it escaped detection all these years—along with kelseya which was also here right along the roadway in such a patently obvious spot—is hard to imagine.

Shoshonea pulvinata is a herbaceous cushion-forming plant, somewhat woody at the base, of open limestone cliff crevices and ledges. It is a true dwarf, never more than 6 in. high even when in fruit and even at a low elevation. Indeed, the dryer the situation the smaller the vertical scale, but not so with the horizontal, since this plant may be as much as 2 ft. across. The lemon yellow flowers are held on short peduncles above the tight, intricately incised green foliage mats. The whole plant is delightfully aromatic. Its cushions, frequently located on vertical cliff faces, can be found over a wide range of altitudes from around 5,000 ft. at the bottom of the Shoshone Canyon to 9,000 ft. on top of Rattlesnake Mountain. This is as far as the limestone goes in the Cody region. This plant was initially thought to be restricted to the Shoshone River drainage in Park County, Wyoming, but has recently been found in Fremont County in the Owl Creeks and in Montana near the Wyoming border in the Pryors.

This is an elegant little plant that seems to be more amenable to cultivation than either kelseya or *Aquilegia jonesii,* its miffy sometime associates. A small transplant has done well despite complete neglect over the last five years in a rather shady spot in slightly acid soil at my cabin near Yellowstone National Park. If this plant were given optimal conditions, it would probably do quite well in the garden or trough.

Antennaria aromatica is another of those calciphiles that grow on Rattlesnake Mountain, although I didn't see it on that first trip in 1979. It is also another one of those plants that I first discovered in out-of-the-way places (that's where new species are supposed to be) but later found growing right along the road. This time, it was on the Beartooth Highway just over the line in Montana near the head of Quad Creek. This same situation had been visited by A. Cronquist in 1955 when he picked up the plant in a mixed collection with *A. media* and by G. L. Stebbins and R. Bayer just a month before I stopped there! Stebbins and Bayer knew of the Cronquist collection; I didn't. They had obviously done their herbarium homework, admittedly an easier way of finding new species than mine; but I was learning! *Antennaria aromatica* was apparently first collected in Cascade county, Montana, in 1887 and much later from the Bridger Range by F. W. Pennell in 1938, the same year he found *Castilleja nivea* on the Beartooth Plateau. This fragrant, perennial, mat-forming dwarf pussytoes, has now been found in Glacier Park, the Madison Range in Montana, and as far away as

Antennaria aromatica. Photo by Erwin Evert

the Wallowas of Oregon.

I first stumbled upon this densely white tomentose orophyte, barely distinguishable from the Madison limestone, while collecting cytological material of *Shoshonea pulvinata* on Sheep Mountain west of Cody in 1980. My first reaction on seeing this highly distinctive glandular and fragrant (the fragrance is citronellalike) antennaria was that it must be new. Subsequent investigations indicated that such was the case.

This plant also has a wide altitudinal range, from less than 5,000 ft. on the eastern flanks of the Beartooths to over 10,000 ft. on Beartooth Butte. It is always dwarf, however, as most antennarias are, the foliage never more than 1 in., and the flowers scapes never more than 4 in. *Antennaria aromatica* occurs abundantly on top of Heart Mountain north of Cody with typical calciphiles such as kelseya, shoshonea, *Telesonix jamesii,* and *Clematis columbiana* var. *tenuiloba.* It grows on limestone ledges, crevices, and talus, avoiding the vertical cliff faces. It also grows well, as all antennarias do, at my cabin near Yellowstone.

I first became acquainted with the yellow-flowered *Castilleja nivea,* with its snowy tomentose inflorescence and shaggy villous galea, on Clayton Mountain in the Absarokas. It was here that I also first saw the elegant mat-forming endemic clover *Trifolium haydenii.* Both occur here in some abundance. The castilleja is found in isolated clumps above timberline in the screes and loose volcanic soils that abound here and throughout the Absarokas. (Someone said the Absarokas are the most magnificent slag piles on earth.) The clover occurs lower, near timberline, in extensive swards in the picturesque whitebark pine parkland. Of the two, the clover is the more impressive since it occurs in much greater abundance, carpeting large expanses with its beige-pink to salmon flowers, hard to miss when in bloom and difficult to forget.

Both of these endemics apparently do not reach Idaho, and were both first collected in the 19th century. Both *Trifolium haydenii* and *Castilleja nivea* are fine plants that deserve to be more widely known and cultivated.

The genus *Pedicularis*—with about 30 species in North America, a total of about 500 species worldwide, appears to be the largest genus of the Scrophulariaceae. Although I have certainly not seen all 500, or even seen all those from North America, I have never seen one I didn't like! So with considerable effort, I will restrain myself and limit my remarks to two here and one later on, lest this become a lousewort exegesis! *Pedicularis cystopteridifolia* and *P. pulchella* both have basically the same flower color, a deep ambrosial wine red, not the ubiquitous magenta of which the Creator appeared to be so inordinately fond. Here the similarity ends. *Pedicularis cystopteridifolia* is three to four times the size of *P. pulchella* and is usually a plant of subalpine meadows, where it is not overwhelmed by such stalwarts as *Arnica fulgens, Heydysarum sulphurescens, Valeriana edulis,* and *Polygonum bistortoides*. *Pedicularis pulchella* is an altogether more condensed plant, thus appearing more woolly, and it is a plant of fellfields and dry alpine meadows, occurring with typical alpine cushion plants. Both plants have the dissected foliage which is so common in this handsome genus. Both of these species are restricted to southwestern Montana and northwestern Wyoming and deserve to be better known.

Unstable, open substrates such as talus and scree abound in the higher elevations in the rigorous mountainous environments of the region. A number of the region's endemics are restricted to these substrates. There are also a number of widespread species that are restricted to these same unstable, open habitats. Seven nonendemics stand out as being particularly noteworthy with regard to form, flowers, and/or fragrance: *Chaenactis alpina, Collomia debilis, Crepis nana, Draba ventosa, Hulsea algida, Ipomopsis spicata* var. *capitata* and *Townsendia condensata*. These seven are frequently found in delightful combination with the region's endemic specialists of scree and talus. Of the endemic scree and talus specialists, I am most familiar with three: *Erigeron flabellifolius, Penstemon absarokensis,* and *P. montanus.*

All three occasionally occur together in the Absaroka Mountains, and all three are extremely handsome perennial plants. *Penstemon montanus* is the most wide-ranging of the trio. It has been found as far south as central Utah as well as central Idaho, southwestern Montana, and of course, northwestern Wyoming. *Erigeron flabellifolius* and *Penstemon absarokensis* are more restricted, the former to southwestern Montana and northwestern Wyoming, and the penstemon, which I have recently described, thus far to only northwestern Wyoming. *Erigeron flabellifolius,* a prostrate, open, mat-former with interesting flabelliform lobed leaves, is highly distinctive and unlike any other erigeron in the region. The flower color in this species varies from white to pink to purple-lavender with all three colors occurring intermixed, festively, in one population. This erigeron is certainly an interesting little plant and not at all common. It is usually found on the highest alpine screes, but occasionally it descends lower. The two beardtongues frequently occur together but usually at lower elevations than the erigeron, though both also frequently ascend to the lower alpine zone. Of the two, *Penstemon absarokensis* is certainly the more showy, with its large secund inflorescences of brilliant deep blue flowers, over an inch, on tufted plants usually no more than 6–8 in. tall. The entire deep green leaves are thick and somewhat succulent.

Penstemon montanus is more of a mat-former; it has smaller but very attractive lavender flowers, and the leaves, at least in *P. montanus* var. *montanus,* are glandular and grayish-hairy. Both of these penstemons are plants of montane and subalpine scree slopes with *P. absarokensis* occasionally found at rather low elevations on river gravels.

Finally, *Erigeron rydbergii,* while not a plant of the screes and taluses, is nevertheless a Yellowstone region endemic that is well worth knowing. It is a very compact, elegant little plant with entire, finely hairy oblanceolate leaves from a branching, somewhat woody caudex. The heads are solitary, and the ray flowers are usually violet-lavender though occasionally, as on Trout Peak in the northern Absarokas, extensive very beautiful white-flowered populations occur. This perennial, along with *Pedicularis pulchella* and *Erigeron flabellifolius,* seems to be one of the few obligate endemic alpines of the region; it is seldom found at lower altitudes. However, *Erigeron rydbergii,* unlike the other two, is one of the commonest alpine plants of the Yellowstone region, where it decorates the fellfields and dry alpine meadows.

Peripherals and Disjuncts

Among the more interesting and unusual nonendemic species of the Yellowstone region are: 1) some of those species that reach the limits of their often widespread ranges in the region, and 2) those species of highly disjunct distributions that are also found in the region. Among the former, the peripherals (excluding the Pacific Northwest group mentioned earlier), is an interesting group that includes *Hulsea algida, Senecio fuscatus, Antennaria lanata,* and *Pedicularis oederi*. The last three species occur in the region at their southernmost range limits. However, *Hulsea algida,* which ranges from California across the northern Great Basin in Nevada to the Wallowa and Blue Mountains in Oregon and Washington in a somewhat unique and peculiar distribution pattern, reaches its northeasternmost range limits in the region.

Senecio fuscatus and *Antennaria lanata* frequently grow together in the mesic alpine meadows of the region. Both have gray foliage; the antennaria, somewhat unusual in these parts, is not

Hulsea algida
Photo by Erwin Evert

stoloniferous, and both plants ultimately reach the same height of 4–8 in. A good place to see both of these fine plants, if you or your vehicle can make the steep grade, is Daisy Pass in the Beartooths. The senecio is very showy, with solitary heads of orange-yellow ray flowers, the entire mostly basal leaves arachnoid-tomentose. It is a great little plant not at all common in the region, except in the Beartooths and Absarokas, where it reaches the southernmost limits of a circumboreal alpine distribution. *Antennaria lanata* is not showy, but its tufted, silvery tomentose leaves and scapes of compact cymes of heads subtended by greenish black phyllaries make this an extremely handsome plant. It is a western American alpine endemic ranging from Alaska to Oregon and northwestern Wyoming, and it is apparently closely related to the Eurasian alpine *A. carpatica*.

Pedicularis oederi is another of those engaging louseworts found in the region. It is a circumboreal arctic-alpine plant reaching the southernmost limits of its range in North America on the Beartooth Plateau. Here it grows in abundance with an exceptionally rich assemblage of arctic-alpine species. It is a tufted plant usually less than 6 in. tall, has clear light yellow corollas with wry little bananalike galeas. The abundant pinnatifid leaves are quite handsome. In *Pedicularis oederi* we have another plant well worth knowing, admiring, and perhaps cultivating.

Those species that have very disjunct distributions are particularly interesting and fascinating, numbering, as they often do, among the rarest plants of the region. No discussion of the region's flora would be complete without mentioning some of these rare plants. Several of these species are found on adjacent Beartooth and Clay Buttes in the Beartooth Mountains of northwestern Wyoming. Beartooth and Clay Buttes consist of calcareous sedimentary rocks and are apparently erosional remnants of strata that once covered the granitic rocks of the Beartooth uplift. These two over 10,000 ft. calcareous mountains, surrounded now by a sea of granite, are famous for the unusual plants, particularly drabas, that reside among their crags and screes. In fact, over a dozen alpine *Draba* species are in residence here. One of these is *Draba pectinipila*, described by R. Rollins from the Buttes in 1953. It is a little mat-forming plant superficially resembling the ubiquitous *D. oligosperma* with which it occurs here. *Draba pectinipila*, unlike *D. oligosperma*, is known only from Beartooth and Clay Buttes and from two other localities—one in British Columbia, the other in Colorado. Another unusual draba is *D. nivalis* var. *brevicula*, which was also described by Rollins. This endemic variety is known from only Beartooth and Clay Buttes and from a recent collection in the Absarokas.

Two other plants of interest that occur on Beartooth Butte and have very fragmented ranges are

Erigeron humilis and *Parrya nudicaulis.* Parrya, a neat, purple-flowered crucifer, is known only from the region from Beartooth Butte and the Wind River Range. It also occurs disjunct on limestone in the mountains of northeastern Utah and is apparently absent from the rest of the contiguous U.S. as well as much of the Canadian Rockies. *Parrya nudicaulis* is primarily a circumpolar arctic-alpine species with southern range extensions primarily in the Asiatic mountains and a few isolated stations in the American Rockies.

Usually *Erigeron humilis* is less than a quarter of an inch high when it begins to flower. Later in the season the scapes of this American arctic-alpine fleabane reach a somewhat untidy 4 in. Its flowers, in monocephalus heads with erect, white, tiny but numerous rays set off by purplish black phyllaries, give this plant considerable elfin charm. This erigeron occurs in the Colorado alpine zone. *Erigeron humilis* has been, until quite recently, known only from the Bighorns in Wyoming. It has now been found at a number of stations in the Absarokas and was recently rediscovered on Beartooth Butte, where it occurs among the crags in the company of other distinguished orophytes.

Within view of Beartooth Butte are the Cathedral Cliffs to the south. These conspicuous limestone bluffs capped with volcanic rocks harbor at their base an unusual complex of wetland habitats in which are found an extraordinary assemblage of recently discovered rare and disjunct plant species. In the Cathedral Cliffs' wetland complex, we find habitats ranging from swamp forest and muskeg to marl flats and open water, a veritable refuge for plants that were undoubtedly more abundant in the region at one time and have since retreated or disappeared. In this unusual mosaic of wet calcareous substrates, which provide summer air conditioning, are to be found at least half a dozen boreal species known from nowhere else in the region, some that are unknown elsewhere in the lower 48 states and dozens of other species that have very localized distributions.

Of the many remarkable plant species in the Cathedral Cliffs wetland, *Arctostaphylos rubra,* *Orchis rotundifolia,* and *Primula egaliksensis* stand out as being particularly remarkable in occurring here in extensive, vigorous populations far removed from their main centers of population to the north. The prostrate, deciduous shrub *Arctostaphylos rubra* is known in the lower 48 states only from here. This red-berried shrub of the far north, with its attractive rugulose leaves that turn scarlet at the end of the growing season, is disjunct from central British Columbia. In the Cathedral Cliffs wetland *A. rubra* occurs in swamp forest and muskeg, isolated here with other northern plants such as *Petasites sagittatus, Picea glauca, Juniperus horizontalis,* and *Orchis rotundifolia.* The beautiful little *O. rotundifolia* occurs here by the thousands; its tiny, purple-spotted white lips brighten the somber spruce forest. This is the orchid's only location in Wyoming, and as far as is known, the only location in the region. This is also its most southerly station in the U.S.

Occurring also by the thousands on the open marl flats of this unusual wetland along with *Carex limosa* and *Kobresia simpliciuscula* is *Primula egaliksensis,* the Greenland primrose. This plant is disjunct from southern British Columbia and was previously known in the contiguous U.S. only from Colorado. This delicate primrose brightens, as it doubtless has for centuries, the open areas of this most extraordinary natural area. Certainly, the Cathedral Cliffs wetland with its unusual habitats and plants represents one of the most outstanding and exciting natural areas in the Yellowstone region.

Indeed, this remarkable place is symbolic, a microcosm of the beauty, the surprises, the delights, and above all the considerable botanical wealth of that part of the Rocky Mountains with which I am most familiar, the Yellowstone Region.

References

Cholewa, A., and D. M. Henderson. 1984. *"Primula alcalina* (Primulaceae): a new species from Idaho." *Brittonia* 36:59–62.

Davis, R. J. 1952. *Flora of Idaho.* Provo, Utah: Brigham Young University Press.

Dorn, R. D. 1977. *Manual of the vascular plants of Wyoming.* New York: Garland Publishing Co.

Dorn, R. D. 1979. *"Townsendia nuttallii."* In *Rare and endangered vascular plants and vertebrates of Wyoming,* edited by T. Clark and R. D. Dorn. 15–17.

Dorn, R. D. 1984. *Vascular plants of Montana.* Cheyenne: Mountain West Publishing.

Dorn, R. D., and R. W. Lichvar. 1981. "A new species of *Cryptantha* (Boraginaceae) from Wyoming." *Madroño* 28(3):159–162.

Dorn, R. D., and R. W. Lichvar. 1981. "Specific status for *Trifolium barnebyi." Madroño* 28(3):188–190.

Evert, E. F. 1983. "A new species of *Lomatium* (Umbelliferae) from Wyoming." *Madroño* 30(3):143–146.

Evert, E. F. 1984. "A new species of *Antennaria* (Asteraceae) from Montana and Wyoming." *Madroño* 31(2):109–112.

Evert, E. F. 1984. *"Penstemon absarokensis,* a new species of Scrophulariaceae from Wyoming." *Madroño* 31(3):140–143.

Evert, F., and L. Constance. 1982. *"Shoshonea pulvinata,* a new genus and species of Umbelliferae from Wyoming." *Syst. Bot.* 7(4):471–475.

Hartman, R. L., and L. Constance. 1985. "Two new species of *Cymopterus* (Umbelliferae) from western North America." *Brittonia* 37(1):88–95.

Henderson, D. M. 1981. "A new *Douglasia* (Primulaceae) from Idaho." *Brittonia* 33:52–56.

Hulten, E. 1964 & 1970. *The circumpolar plants.* 2 Vol. Stockholm: Almquist and Wiksell.

Hulten, E. 1968. *Flora of Alaska.* Stanford, California: Stanford University Press.

Lichvar, R. W. 1983. "Evaluation of *Draba oligosperma, D. pectinipila* and *D. juniperina* complex (Cruciferae)." *Great Basin Nat.* 43(3):441–444.

Pemble, R. H. 1965. *A survey of the distribution patterns in the Montana alpine flora.* Missoula: University of Montana (unpublished master's thesis).

Rollins, R. C. 1953. *"Draba* on Clay Butte Wyoming." *Rhodora* 55:229–235.

Scott, R. W. 1966. *The alpine flora of northwestern Wyoming.* Laramie: University of Wyoming (unpublished master's thesis).

Wright, H. E., ed. 1983. *Late quaternary environments of the United States.* 2 vols. Minneapolis; University of Minnesota Press.

Smelowskia calycina. Photo by Gwen Kelaidis

PLATE 11

View to the Gore Range, Colorado
Photo by Louise Roloff

Mertensia alpina
Photo by Ned Lowry

Penstemon harbourii
Photo by Loraine Yeatts

Paronychia pulvinata
Photo by Loraine Yeatts

PLATE 14

Eriogonum flavum var. *xanthum*
Photo by Bob Heapes

Lewisia pygmaea
Photo by Loraine Yeatts

Primula angustifolia
Photo by Loraine Yeatts

Oreoxis alpina
Photo: Grand Ridge

Draba streptocarpa
Photo by Sharon Sutton

PLANT LIST
Endemics of NW Wyoming, SW Montana, and EC Idaho

ASTERACEAE
Antennaria arcuata Cronq.–W, I, N*
A. aromatica Evert–W, M, O
Cirsium subniveum Rydb.–W, M, I
C. tweedyi (Rydb.) Petr.–W, M, A
Erigeron allocotus Blake–W, M
E. flabellifolius Rydb.–W, M
E. gracilis Rydb.–W, M, I
E. rydbergii Cronq.–W, M, I
E. tweedyi Canby–W, M, I
Machaeranthera conmixta Greene–W, M
Nothocalis nigrescens (Henderson) Heller–W, M, I
Townsendia alpigena Piper–W, M, I, O, U
T. condensata Parry ex Gray–W, M, Ca
T. nuttallii Dorn–W
T. spathulata Nutt.–W, M, A

APIACEAE
Cymopterus douglasii Hartman & Constance–I
C. williamsii Hartman & Constance–W
Lomatium attenuatum Evert–W
L. idahoensis Math. & Const.–I
Musineon vaginatum Rydb.–W, M.
Shoshonea pulvinata Evert & Constance–W, M

BORAGINACEAE
Cryptantha caespitosa (A. Nels.) Payson–W
C. spiculifera (Piper) Payson–W, M, I
C. subcapitata Dorn & Lichvar–W
Eritrichium howardii (Gray) Rydb.–W, M

BRASSICACEAE
Arabis fructicosa A. Nels.–W
Draba nivalis Liljeb. var. *brevicula* Rollins–W
Thlaspi parviflorum A. Nels.–W, M

FABACEAE
Astragalus drabelliformis Barneby–W
A. paysonii (Rydb.) Barneby–W, I
Trifolium barnebyi (Isley) Dorn & Lichvar–W
T. haydenii Porter–W, M

JUNCACEAE
Juncus tweedyi Rydb.–W, M, I, U

ONAGRACEAE
Epilobium suffruticosum Nutt.–W, M, I

POACEAE
Agrostis rossiae Vasey–W

POLYGONACEAE
Erigonum brevicaule Nutt. ssp. *canum* (Stokes)
Dorn–W, M

PRIMULACEAE
Douglasia idahoensis Henderson–I
D. montana Gray–W, M, I
Primula alcalina Cholewa & Henderson–I

RANUNCULACEAE
Aquilegia jonesii
Delphinium glaucum Wats.–W, M, I

ROSACEAE
Kelseya uniflora (Wats.) Rydb.–W, M, I

SAXIFRAGACEAE
Commitella williamsii (Eaton) Rydb.–W, M, I, Co

SCROPHULARIACEAE
Castilleja crista-galli Rydb.–W, M
C. gracillima Rydb.–W, M, I
C. nivea Pennell & Ownbey–W, M
C. pallescens (Gray) Greenm.–W, M, I
C. pulchella Rydb.–W, M, U
C. rustica Piper–M, I, O
Chionophila tweedyi (Canby & Rose ex Rose)
Henderson–M, I
Pedicularis cystopteridifolia Rydb.–W, M
P. pulchella Pennell–W, M
Penstemon absarokensis Evert–W
P. caryi Pennell–W, M
P. cyaneus Pennell–W, M, I
P. lemhiensis (Keck) Keck & Cronq.–M, I
P. montanus Greene–W, M, I, U
P. pumilus Nutt.–I
Synthyris pinnatifida Wats.–W, M

* KEY
W --------NW Wyoming
M --------SW Montana
I ----------EC Idaho
A ---------S Alberta-British Columbia
N---------N Nevada
O---------E Oregon, Wallowa Mtns.
U---------NE Utah
Ca -------California, White Mtns.
Co -------Colorado

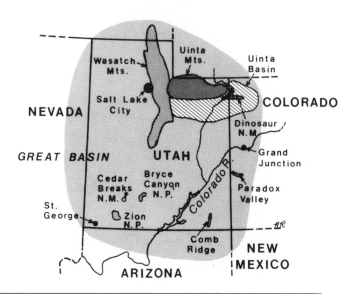

11

Plants of the Great Basin and the Western Slopes

by Elizabeth Neese

Between the crests of the Rocky Mountains and the Sierra Mountains—those two great ranges that dominate the geography and geology of western North America—lies a vast land of cool deserts, intricately dissected plateaus, and isolated lesser mountain ranges. Here grows a diverse assemblage of plant life that includes outliers of the flora of those eastern and western barrier mountains, as well as boreal and plains species from the north and east, heat-loving plants more at home in the warm deserts to the south, and endemics known only from within this phytogeographic area. Much of the land is relatively arid. Rains, when they come, fall often as localized torrential downpours that remove great quantities of rock. Through sheet erosion of barren slopes and headwall-cutting in stream channels, water carries its burden pell-mell downward, to deposit its load of sediments in nearby lowlands or to carry it seaward.

Microhabitats and Plant Endemism in the Intermountain Area

Two basic, very different, erosional patterns are evident: one of accumulation, one of attrition. In the Great Basin (the western portion of the Intermountain Region, which includes most of Nevada and roughly the western third of Utah), no drainage to the sea exists; erosional products accumulate in the valleys. The streams, arising in the numerous small mountain ranges, carry their burden of gravels, sands, silts, suspended clays, and dissolved salts downward, slowing as they reach the gentler slopes at the base of each range, dropping first the rocks and gravels in great fan-shaped bajadas, then successively the sands, the silts, and finally the fines in the shallow land-locked lakes and level valley floors. In these arid areas of deposition, the water evaporates, leaving behind the clays and concentrations of previously dissolved salts. The chemical composition of the deposits

Elizabeth Neese obtained her doctorate in botany from Brigham Young University, writing a flora of the Henry Mountains for her dissertation. Since graduation, she has explored extensively throughout the Intermountain Region, often studying little-known plants for the Natural Heritage Inventories of the Nature Conservancy and for federal land management agencies. In the course of her extensive researches she has not only added numerous new locations for little-known plants, she has also been party to the discovery of several new species of plants including *Penstemon flowersii* and *Hymenoxys lapidicola* in the Uinta Basin. She is currently completing, as co-author, a flora of that rich floristic region. She loves exploring the Intermountain West, and regrets only that it leaves little time to grow the native alpines and dryland plants she loves so much.

varies from valley to valley according to that of the eroding strata from which the materials were derived. White, gray, or tan, variously alkaline, saline, gypsiferous, or seleniferous, these deposits are each unique in chemistry and texture.

Between the Great Basin and the Rocky Mountains proper (in the eastern portion of the Intermountain Region, consisting in large part of eastern Utah) lie numerous smaller mountain ranges and the high Colorado Plateau. Here the erosional pattern is one of attrition, not accumulation. The deeply entrenched and ancient Colorado River and its tributaries carve piecemeal at the mile-and-a-half-deep sediments through which they cut; in these lands Mother Nature is busily sweeping clean the canyons of the rock particles removed by wind and water, carrying them seaward to deposit them finally in the distant Gulf of California. At flanks of mountains, at margins of great monoclines, and along cliffs of the drainage systems, tilted ancient sedimentary strata of chemically differing shales, sandstones, and siltstones are exposed. Eventually, erosionally resistant cliffs and remnants of truncated strata remain, often separated by strike valleys cut into the softer rock layers. The result is a complex series of differing edaphic regimes that occur in close proximity.

Thus, the climatic regime in conjunction with a geologic history of deposition, uplift, and volcanism has produced vast regions of apparently desolate wasteland where highly varied soils are exposed. Often limited in extent and separated spatially and elevationally from similar soils, these microhabitats have given rise to the endemism of the Intermountain Area. Wanting a plentiful moisture supply, much of the land is destitute of substantial vegetative covering and devoid of any accompanying layer of organic soil that might buffer the chemical effects of the raw substrates. Various sedimentary deposits and rock outcrops, each unique in chemistry, texture, and water relations and often of poor or toxic quality, provide, when newly exposed for colonization, a testing ground for deviant forms of the surrounding vegetation. It seems that evolutionary processes have worked rapidly here. New plant forms, perhaps differing only slightly from nearby parental types, have arisen, have proven more perfectly adapted or better able to compete in the harsh environments than ancestral ones, have stabilized, and have multiplied.

Scores of species of these plants of narrow distribution and arid habitat are worthy of investigation for horticultural use. In this harsh and broken land settled by a practical people immersed in wresting a livelihood from a land deemed hostile, it is not surprising that botanical exploration in search of horticultural ornamentals has been afforded low priority. To a large extent the wealth of handsome species is unknown and untested by gardeners, having been observed only superficially by those passing through, on their way to somewhere else, along the few direct routes of transportation.

The Intermountain Region has apparently served as an evolutionary cradle for a number of plant genera. Four in particular come to mind: *Astragalus, Cryptantha, Eriogonum,* and *Penstemon.* Each of these four has as its center of distribution the Intermountain West; each consists of a large number of species differing in small degrees; each is characterized by a high proportion of narrow endemics; and each contains members of exquisite beauty. Horticultural potential of plants of these groups and of many other species of the Intermountain Area has been barely tapped.

The plants discussed in the following paragraphs are some of my favorite candidates for consideration by gardeners for utilization in wildflower, rock, or alpine gardens. These are plants mostly endemic, some very narrowly so, to the Intermountain Area. As far as I know, none is well known to gardeners. A great many grow in poor-quality soils with low organic content. Some of them may find a garden environment not to their liking or may prove difficult to establish, subject to disease, or reluctant to flower. Others, in the relatively lush environment of cultivation, may respond so exuberantly that they lose the dwarf and compact characteristics that make them so appealing in their natural habitat. Of course, species in the wild are variable, and one may see some populations or individuals of even choice species that are not particularly attractive—too coarse or scraggly, not highly floriferous, the flowers pale or small. Still needed is selection of favorable wild stock and development of successful horticultural techniques for these dryland specialists.

Most of the species discussed below have very narrow distributions. Several of them are protected by rare plant conservation programs. It should be stressed emphatically that transplant of sensitive species should not be attempted, and that special permits are required for even seed collection of those protected under Endangered Species legislation. Investigation of such rare taxa for horticultural purposes can contribute to conservation goals, but should be conducted only in cooperation and compliance with agencies responsible for their protection.

Astragalus utahensis. Photo by Elizabeth Neese

Great Basin and Western Slope Plants for Rock and Alpine Gardens

Astragalus utahensis

 Astragalus is a staggeringly large genus in the legume family with species of worldwide distribution. In North America, the greatest concentration of species is in the West, where most are narrowly restricted to some specific edaphic situation. *Astragalus* is the largest genus in Utah, its North American center of distribution. Members of the genus are of diverse habit, but are usually marked by the presence of pinnately compound leaves and rather uniform, often showy, sweetpealike flowers. The pods, however, are amazingly and apparently endlessly diverse. Many species of *Astragalus* are rather unattractive horticulturally, but a sizeable number have much to recommend them for wildflower or rock gardens. In fact, there are so many to choose from, of such diverse habitat and such novel habit and morphology, that I half expect to see formed in the future an Astragalus Society to accommodate the interest of those gardeners who discover in the genus entrancing horticultural possibilities.

 Surely, one of the species with the most to recommend it for the dry rock garden is *Astragalus utahensis*. This milkvetch has everything: low, compact habit; furry white-tomentose leaflets; plentiful, large, shocking pink, pealike flowers; and delightful novelty pods that look like little balls of cotton. Occasionally maintained by Utah gardeners in semiwild gardens on gravelly foothill slopes of the Wasatch Range in the Salt Lake Valley, where it is native, this charmer promises to be of easy culture since it freely self-sows on road shoulders. It is one of the earliest of our wildflowers, usually in full bloom at 5,000 ft. elevation by mid-April.

Astragalus chloodes

 The horticultural merit for this charming little anomaly lies in its decidedly unastragaluslike leaves as well as in its attractive pink-purple, miniature sweetpealike flowers and preference for rock crevice habitats. First collected in the Uinta Basin of northeastern Utah in 1912, it remained unnamed until 1947. The name *chloodes*, derived from a Greek word for grass, refers to the grasslike appearance of the simple, linear leaves. The species is known only from an area of a few dozen square miles in eastern Uintah County, Utah, near Dinosaur National Monument, where it

Astragalus lutosus. Photo by Elizabeth Neese

grows in sand-filled crevices and depressions of soft, crumbling, exposed and barren sandstone strata. Although once considered for inclusion on the federal list of endangered species because of its narrow distribution, it is now known to be locally abundant and with no apparent threats to its specialized habitat. Well-established plants form clumps that catch sand grains loosened by wind and rainfall, and serve as soil stabilizers. Seedlings establish readily in nature in adjacent sand pockets. The closest relative of the grass milkvetch is *Astragalus spatulatus,* which is another good candidate for rock gardeners; it is more dwarf, sometimes even mat-forming, with fewer flowers and less elongate leaves.

Astragalus lutosus

This distinguished little specialist, which is at home on inhospitable, steep shaly slopes, has several things to recommend it: it has a dwarf and refined habit, it has novel, inflated, red-tinged, sprawling sausagelike pods, and it has delightful folded little boat-shaped leaflets. First described in 1910 from material taken near the Colorado-Utah line at the White River, the plant remained obscure for many years. Because it was presumed very rare, and because it is habitat-specific for a narrow band of oil-rich shale of great interest to the petroleum industry, federal agencies have funded exhaustive studies to document its distribution. Now known to be common on its specialized shale-barren habitat in Utah and Colorado, it could again be jeopardized if wholesale processing of the oil-shale strata should occur.

The plant is soboliferous in its native habitat, with leafless frail subterranean branches emanating from the caudex which is buried in cracks of solid shale. The branches elongate sufficiently to accommodate shifting surface fragments on the steep slopes. A tuft of pinnately compound leaves with finely strigose, folded leaflets, is produced at the shaly surface, looking at first glance like a cluster of trilobite fossils. The small, white flowers appear very early, soon replaced by the more showy, large, reddish pods.

Cryptantha breviflora

Members of the perennial cryptanthas occupy for the most part dry habitats at middle elevations, where they often grow in the harsh environment of raw, recently exposed strata. The flowers are white, or less commonly yellow, and like their blue-flowered cousins the forget-me-nots are usually marked with a yellow central eye. Although most of the 200 or more species are too coarse and bristly or too small-flowered for inclusion in gardens, several are very showy and have habits suitable for rock or desert wildflower gardens. *Cryptantha breviflora,* endemic to poor quality, fine-textured substrates in the lower parts of the Uinta Basin, forms rounded mounds of sleek, silvery-haired leaves. The clustered stems, mostly 20–30 cm tall, arise above the mound of basal leaves and bear numerous white flowers in compact inflorescences. The corollas have a flat, five-lobed limb; the tube is exceptionally short for the genus, as indicated by the specific name. Included in early lists of species considered for federal designation as threatened or endangered, the plant is now known to be relatively common on appropriate habitat across two counties. If brought into cultivation it would probably be best-suited for inclusion as a novelty in a badlands portion of a wildflower garden, perhaps keeping company with numerous others of the showy inhabitants of dry spare soils in the Intermountain Area.

Cryptantha paradoxa

This is a delicate little species distinguished by its relatively large, bright white flowers, small leaves and caespitose habit. Growing on clay, sandy, or sometime gypsiferous soil, it occurs locally in eastern Utah and western Colorado, usually on old terrace gravels along tributaries of the Colorado River. The source of the specific epithet, the location where it was first collected, is Paradox Valley in Colorado. Unlike the preceding species, the stems are short, so that the flowers are borne close to the low clump of leaves. In nature it often grows with *Sclerocactus glaucus,* an attractive species of ball cactus which has been federally listed as threatened. If included in a cool desert wildflower garden, it might respond well to elevated, clay-impregnated gravels.

Penstemon uintahensis

The genus *Penstemon,* predominantly of western North America, includes such a great number of handsome and pleasing species that it is well-known to rock gardeners. The American Penstemon Society includes dozens of species on its seed exchange list. Nonetheless, the many penstemons of the Great Basin and the Western Slope of the Rockies are under-represented or unknown in gardens, perhaps because so many are narrowly restricted to out-of-the-way places. Of the hundred-plus species known for the Intermountain Region (almost all sufficiently attractive to warrant cultivation), about 70 occur in Utah. *Penstemon uintahensis* is a high-elevation dwarf that grows only on the rocky quartzite crests of the Uinta Mountains. Although the stems are only a decimeter or so tall, the flowers are as large as those of many of the more robust, lower elevation species. Rich blue in color, the 2 to 5 flowers are held jauntily just above the neat tuft of basal leaves. The refined habit and lovely flowers of the Uinta Mountain beardtongue should make it a favorite with alpine rock gardeners should it prove amenable to cultivation. This may well be the case, since *P. subglaber,* a tall, robust near-relative of lower elevations, thrives on roadcuts and is easily cultivated.

Penstemon acaulis and *P. yampaensis*

These, according to penstemon specialist Noel Holmgren, may be the most peculiar of all penstemons. The most reduced in size of any of the genus, the diminutive acaulescent plants form mats to 30 cm in diameter. The linear leaves are mostly about 1 cm long and are so densely crowded that the stems are not evident to casual observation. The up-facing flowers are subsessile, relatively large, solitary, and tubular-campanulate. The corollas are clear blue, the palate yellow-bearded, and the staminode bearded with short golden hairs. *Penstemon yampaensis,* from near the northern Utah-Colorado border, is slightly more robust in all its parts. It might be better treated at varietal level within *P. acaulis.*

Penstemon grahamii

This species was moved into the limelight because of the Endangered Species Act, which stimulated intensive study of its distribution. Not so rare as first thought, it is a sharply marked species known only from oil-bearing shales of the Green River Formation in the Uinta Basin. The tiny basal rosette of leaves is overshadowed by the striking ventricose-ampliate, markedly bilabiate corollas, which are lavender-pink and are usually prominently marked with wine red guidelines in the throat. The distinctive character which has appealed to beardtongue fanciers is the staminode—densely bearded, old gold in color, prominently exserted, and curled downward at the tip like a saucy tongue. As far as I know, it is still largely uncultivated. What a shame—a single blooming plant would probably cause the grower to feel well-rewarded for all the season's effort.

Penstemon grahamii. Photo by Elizabeth Neese

Eriogonum thymoides

Eriogonum, variously known as wild buckwheat, St. Catherine's lace and California buckwheat, is an enormous genus in the Polygonaceae whose 200+ members are almost exclusively Western. It is perhaps better known and more frequently grown in California than in the Intermountain Area, where the greatest assemblage of species occurs. The diversity of form, attractive foliage, and beauty of its graceful flower clusters have made *Eriogonum* a favorite with those few who have grown it extensively. The genus includes a diverse array of plants, including tall shrubs, semiwoody mat-formers, perennial herbs, and annuals. Most of those few that are occasionally cultivated are shrubby, rather robust, and often little-suited to the inclination of rock gardeners. But a myriad of untried handsome species of low and compact habit grows in the dry rocky lands of the Intermountain Area.

One of my favorites is *Eriogonum thymoides,* known from sagebrush flats and ridges in drier parts of Idaho, Washington, and Oregon. It is a densely matted, rather variable, miniature shrub with small, heatherlike, tightly involute leaves. The flowering stems are usually about 5 cm tall and are leafless except for a whorl of linear bracts near the middle. Cream-colored or pink flowers are borne in numerous small heads clustered at the stem summit. Plants from one population I've seen, uniformly dwarf and laden with brilliant, rose-red flower clusters, would be enchanting growing in gravelly pockets of a dry rock garden.

Eriogonum ovalifolium

Another candidate with excellent potential for the dry rock garden is *Eriogonum ovalifolium.* Grown to a limited extent by botanic gardens, it is a cushion plant which includes several geographic races. The leaves, petioled and with silvery spatulate or ovate blades, are crowded into basal tufts. The flowers are clustered in dense, globose heads like fluffy balls and are borne on slender scapes mostly 10 to 15 cm long. Flower color varies from creamy white to pink, or sometimes brick red, bright yellow, or some combination or blend of white, pink, red, and yellow. The yellow form and the white or pink form have been recognized as different geographic varieties, but in some populations in the Uinta Basin the two grow intermixed with all the intermediates, making a tremendous show on dry clayey hillsides. There is also a much-dwarfed matted alpine variety which has tiny, white-lanate, orbicular leaves and scapes generally less than 5 cm long.

Taxonomically, *Eriogonum* is a bit of a mess, since specialists disagree about where species lines should be drawn. There are few genetic barriers between many of the species, and it is common to find, on isolated, unusual, poor-quality substrates, distinctive phases which defy identification. Apparently, locally adapted phases arise readily from what must be a very rich genetic pool.

Hymenoxys lapidicola

Many who grow alpines are probably familiar with the Rocky Mountain species *Hymenoxys grandiflora* and *H. acaulis*. There are several less well-known members of the genus in the Intermountain Area that might prove rewarding for dry rock garden enthusiasts. Of particular promise may be *H. lapidicola*, a recently described rock crevice plant from near Dinosaur National Monument in Utah. The plant's habit, reminiscent of some of the densely tufted saxifrages, is impeccable, the crowded leaf rosettes forming tight rounded mounds on rock faces and cliff margins. The flower heads are golden yellow, and are scattered starlike across the dark green mounds. Known currently from a half-dozen collections, the species has been found only on sandstone cliffs of the Weber Formation near the east end of the Uinta Mountains. The habitat is largely inaccessible (except by helicopter), and only the individuals which occur at the margins of the cliffs can be reached.

Talinum breviflorum

For those rock gardeners fortunate enough to have a sandstone outcrop in their garden, the Intermountain Area offers several good experimental candidates for cultivation. One of these is *Talinum brevifolium*, a member (along with one of the favorites of alpines gardeners, *Lewisia*) of the Portulacaceae. Like most members of its family, *T. brevifolium* is a fleshy plant; it occurs in dry environments of the three-corners area of Utah, New Mexico, and Arizona. The sausage-shaped little leaves, reminiscent of those of *Sedum*, are about 1 to 1.5 cm long and are crowded on numerous, clustered short stems. The mossroselike pink flowers, centered with clusters of golden anthers, are usually about 2–3 cm across. I have seen, though, growing in southern Utah in crevices of sandstone and in sandy pockets on top of the bedrock, a population with flowers fully 4 cm across.

Houstonia (Hedyotis) rubra

Growing in the sand-crevice habitat with the large-flowered *Talinum* mentioned above is another choice candidate for the sandstone rock garden, *Houstonia rubra*; this member of the Rubiaceae can be found occasionally on dry sandy mesas from southern Utah to Mexico. Perhaps better treated within the genus *Hedyotis*, the houstonias include within their eastern membership the well-known and delightful bluets, or Quaker ladies. The leaves of this small, caespitose desert-dweller are opposite, fleshy, linear, and clustered in erect, short tufts. The up-facing white to pale pink flowers, borne in more abundance than are those of the *Talinum* and about 1.5 to 2 cm across, have a long, slender tube and four flat-spreading lobes. During flowering, the effect is that of little, four-pointed stars studded across the tiny, leafy clumps which emerge from the crevices of the barren sandstone. The whole plant is neat and inconspicuous when it is not flowering.

Astragalus chloodes, discussed earlier, grows on the same general geologic series of sandstone strata as do *Talinum breviflorum* and *Houstonia rubra*, but where the strata resurface far to the north in the Uinta Basin. Other colorful, attractive, often dwarf or matted plants of sandstone crevices and nearby sand come to mind: *Heterotheca jonesii, Hymenoxys lapidicola, Petradoria pumila, Cryptantha flava, Sclerocactus parviflorus, Astragalus humillimus, Castilleja scabrida, Asclepias ruthiae, Astragalus desperatus, Sophora stenophylla, Petrophytum caespitosum,* and *Tripterocalyx carnea* to name a few. What fun it would be to try to establish a rock garden to illustrate the assemblage of sandstone-lovers from the Intermountain Area, and to discover which of these rock plants might grow together under cultivation!

My selection of the species discussed above is arbitrary, since many others are equally promising. An additional list of species for possible investigation, with a thumbnail sketch of each, follows.

APIACEAE (UMBELLIFERAE)

Cymopterus bulbosus. Most of the three dozen or so species of this genus (which has been almost totally neglected by gardeners) grow in Utah and Nevada. Best suited to be grown as novelties, most kinds are acaulescent or nearly so and have one or a few pinnately dissected, hairless, rather thick leaves which arise from a swollen caudex. The flowers are small, inconspicuous, usually white or yellow and, as is usual in the family, are borne in compound umbels. In *C. bulbosus* the clustered purplish flowers of each involucel are subtended by several broad, papery, bright white bracts. In bud and early flower, each inflorescence looks like a little nosegay with each flower cluster wrapped in a collar of white paper.

Cymopterus megacephalus—This intriguing novelty has a cluster of thick and glaucous much-divided leaves arising directly from the ground. The scapes, which overtop the reclining leaves, are terminated by a dense, greenish, almost rayless umbel of tiny flowers. As the fruits mature, the flower heads assume the size, and nearly the weight, of golf balls; because the scapes cannot bear the weight, the heads come to lie in a circle around the tuft of leaves.

ASCLEPIADACEAE

Asclepias cryptoceras. Unusual among the milkweeds because of its glaucous, orbicular leaves, this is a low species with sprawling stems and huge (for *Asclepias*) cream and purple flowers. It grows in cool salt-desert communities of southeastern Utah on clay-impregnated badlands.

Asclepias ruthiae. This is a miniature milkweed of subtle charm. Known from sandy soils of south central Utah, it was included on early lists of candidates for threatened or endangered species, but is no longer considered sufficiently rare to warrant federal protection. The ovate leaves are softly pubescent, especially so on the wavy margins, giving the leaves a frost-rimmed appearance. Flower color is dusky rose.

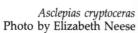
Asclepias cryptoceras
Photo by Elizabeth Neese

ASTERACEAE (COMPOSITAE)

Chamaechaenactis scaposa. This is a dwarf plant of neat habit that should be ideal for the small scale rock garden. The only member of its genus, it occurs on limy or shaly semibarrens and badlands in eastern Utah and adjacent portions of Colorado and Arizona. The tiny oval leaves appear early in the spring in small tufts. Leaves, scapes and involucres are softly long-villous. The solitary heads of white or pale pink flowers are carried like jaunty little pompoms a few centimeters above the tiny mound of leaves.

Chaenactis alpina. A caespitose mound-former, this plant has been called false yarrow because of its much dissected leaves. The heads are scapose and discoid, containing about a dozen miniature starry florets. The pink stamens and styles protruding from the flower head account for the other common name of pincushion.

Erigeron pumilus ssp. *concinnoides*. Photo by Elizabeth Neese

Erigeron pumilus. High-elevation fleabanes are already well-known to alpine gardeners, but there are many others of these small daisies of compact habit that grow in dry, midelevation habitats in the Intermountain West. Most are similar in appearance, with numerous narrow white or pink ray flowers and yellow disks, the different kinds separated by small, technical differences. One of the most widely distributed and variable is *E. pumilus*. Early and prolifically blooming, and happy in many habitats, it warrants investigation by gardeners. Other dwarf or caespitose kinds, some of recent discovery and all from Utah, include *E. carringtonae, E. compactus, E. goodrichii, E. untermannii, E. caespitosus, E. compositus,* and *E. ursinus.*

Haplopappus acaulis. One wonders why this showy mound-former of apparently exemplary rock garden habit has not been widely cultivated. The tight, bright green mounds are formed from dozens of crowded, compact stems terminated by tiny leaf tufts, and bear dozens of solitary golden flower heads atop short scapes. The closely similar and equally floriferous *H. armerioides* has somewhat taller, sometimes branched flower stalks, broader involucres, and larger flower heads.

Heterotheca jonesii. This is a golden aster of refined and charming mien. The crowded, hairy leaves form small, loose mats in the sand of crevices and pockets in Zion National Park. The bright yellow daisies nestled against a background of gray-green leaves and red-ochre sand is a sight not soon to be forgotten. Its slightly less-restrained first cousin, *H. villosa,* is a freely flowering beauty of wider distribution.

Psathyrotes pilifera. Annuals are seldom grown by rock gardeners, but perhaps an exception should be made for this strange-looking desert-dweller. A summer and fall-blooming annual forming hemispherical cushions mainly 5–15 cm across, it has gray-pilose ovate leaves about 1 cm wide. The name *"pilifera"* refers to the long, white setae which fringe the leaf margins. The rather sparsely borne, few-flowered, little, yellow heads are discoid. The plant inhabits gypsiferous substrates near the Utah-Arizona border.

Townsendia incana. The Easter daisies, so named because of their habit of blooming very early in the season, include about a score of species of western North America; over half of these occur in Utah. Because of their low, neat habit and relatively large flower heads they represent choice selections for alpine or rock gardens. *Townsendia incana,* of the Colorado drainage system, is one of the most widely distributed and variable, differing from most of the other perennial kinds

Psathyrotes pilifera. Photo by Elizabeth Neese

by its evident, above-ground, white strigose stems. The white ray flowers are often dorsally suffused with pink. Not particular about the soils or communities in which it grows, it may respond readily to cultivation.

Townsendia jonesii. This exceptionally beautiful species grows in salt desert shrub and juniper communities of midelevation in western Utah. The little rosettes of hoary narrow leaves 1 to 3 cm long are borne on a sparingly branched caudex. The short-stalked flower heads are often larger than the tuft of leaves upon which they are borne. The rays are pink or reddish on the lower surface and white or pale pink on the upper. *Townsendia j.* var. *lutea*, which grows among volcanic gravels on gypsiferous clays of the Arapien Shale Formation in Sevier and Piute Counties, Utah, has exquisite pale yellow or apricot yellow ray flowers.

Townsendia montana. A handsome Easter-daisy of mountains of Idaho, Montana, Wyoming, and Utah, *T. montana* has nearly hairless green leaves and blue to lavender or sometimes white ray-flowers. Two particularly dwarf and compact varieties grow on montane badlands in Utah: *T.m.* variety *minima*, of white and pink limestones of Cedar Breaks and Bryce Canyon in Kane and Garfield counties, Utah, has smaller-than-typical leaves and sessile heads; *T.m.* variety *caelilinensis* forms dense mats on limy shales in Duchesne, Wasatch, and Sanpete Counties.

BRASSICACEAE

Physaria and *Lesquerella*. The mustard family contributes numerous species to the early color on mountain ridges and spare desert soils in the West. Members of *Alyssum, Arabis, Cardamine, Draba, Erysimum, Lepidium,* and *Smelowskia* are already familiar to alpine gardeners. Perhaps less well-known are members of *Lesquerella* and *Physaria*, variously known as twinpod or bladderpod. The leaves, characteristically abruptly petiolate from spatulate blades, are borne chiefly in basal rosettes, and are usually gray in color because of a covering of stellate hairs. Alyssumlike yellow flowers are borne in slender-stemmed, racemose clusters. In *Physaria,* the fruits are didymous and bladdery-inflated. The common Colorado drainage species, *P. acutifolia* is replaced in the Great Basin with its close counterpart, *P. chambersii.* Either would make a worthy addition to a sunny well-drained rock garden.

Lesquerella wardii is a free-blooming montane or subalpine species of the plateaus of central and southern Utah. The flowering stems recline, allowing clusters of lemon yellow flowers to form a halo around the pretty gray-green leaf rosette. *Lesquerella tumulosa* and *L. rubicundula* are rare and tiny pulvinate-caespitose species from limy barrens of Iron, Garfield, and Kane Counties, Utah. *Lesquerella subumbellata,* which has a freely branched caudex, covers itself with mounds of tiny flowers in early May. It grows on white shales and rocky badlands at low elevations in the Uinta Basin. On barren outcrops in pinyon-juniper or grassland communities near the Arizona-Utah border, one may find low mounds and mats of *L. arizonica* hidden beneath golden yellow flowers.

Lesquerella wardii
Photo by Elizabeth Neese

CAMPANULACEAE

Campanula is a large, mostly European genus whose members are highly treasured by alpine gardeners. Relatively few species grow in the Intermountain Area, but there is one, *C. parryi,* that has been generally overlooked by gardeners. Similar to *C. rotundifolia* in size and habit, it differs in its deeper blue color and in having erect rather than nodding flowers. It may be found occasionally in mountain meadows of Colorado, Utah, and northern New Mexico and Arizona.

FABACEAE (LEGUMINOSAE)

Astragalus. Besides *A. lutosus* already discussed, one of the most beautiful and rarest of this genus for rock gardeners is *A. humillimus* from northwestern New Mexico. Its pink-purple flowers cover the circular mats of spine-tipped leaves that grow in rock crevices where sandstone bedrock is exposed on mesas. It is protected by rare species conservation programs. *Astragalus detritalis* has erect racemes of bright magenta-pink flowers which are borne just above neat 8 cm tufts of leaves. *Astragalus megacarpus* has unbelievable papery-walled, red-mottled, giant pods up to nearly 10 cm long. They recline by the dozen in a circle on the barren gravel around the tuft of erect, pinnately compound leaves. *Astragalus ceramicus* has slender rushlike stems and leaflets and beautiful, pendulous, inflated, cream-colored pods marked with red. There are many other low species with pretty flowers and curious pods.

LILIACEAE

Calochortus. Sego or mariposa lilies are bulbiferous plants of western America with marvelously marked, spectacularly beautiful flowers. Rather temperamental in their performance, they are best suited for rock gardens which can be kept relatively dry in summer. The most commonly seen kinds in the Intermountain Area are *C. gunnisonii, C. nuttallii, C. flexuosus,* and *C. aureus,* all of which apparently perform more perfectly in nature than under cultivation. Of these, perhaps the most beautiful and least well known is *C. aureus.* Once treated as a variety of *C. nuttallii,* it clearly deserves specific rank. In favorable years it is locally abundant and so floriferous that one wonders where it has been hiding between times. The flowers are bright yellow, usually with a rich mahogany red band across each petal above the showy basal gland.

PAPAVERACEAE

Arctomecon. This is a genus of three rare and narrowly endemic beauties that reportedly do not take kindly to cultivation. The common name, bearclaw poppy, is in reference to the hair-tipped teeth of the apically tridentate leaves. *Arctomecon humilis,* the smallest of the three species, has achieved celebrity status since it was designated as endangered by the federal government. Known only from a few square miles of gypsiferous barrens near St. George, Utah, much of its habitat has been sacrificed to urban development. In early May the long-lived, perennial clumps are smothered with snowy white flowers, each centered with a powdery puff of yellow stamens; the barren hillsides where they grow then appear dotted with drifts of crumpled tissue paper. Nearly as rare and perhaps as beautiful as *A. humilis* is the white-flowered *A. merriamii,* of loose rocky slopes in the Mojave Desert of California and Nevada, and the more robust, yellow-flowered *A. californica,* known from a small area in southern Nevada and northwest Arizona. If the secret of cultivation of these treasures could be discovered, they would surely become beloved garden plants.

POLEMONIACEAE

Collomia debilis. This is an alpine plant tailor-made for steep scree slopes. The soboliferous, slender stems proliferate in response to shifting limestone gravels. Above the mats of low foliage are many bright pink-lavender, chalice-shaped flowers highlighted by blue anthers.

Gilia (Ipomopsis) aggregata var. *arizonica.* Sky-rocket, or scarlet gilia, is frequently cultivated for its hummingbird-attracting, scarlet, tubular flowers. It is a variable biennial of dryish soils. Perhaps best-suited for cultivation is *G. a.* var. *arizonica.* This desert-dweller differs from other varieties in its lower habit, shorter flower tubes and broader corolla lobes. It has a luminous, coral red coloration unmarked with or diminished by yellowish or whitish overtones.

POLYGONACEAE

Eriogonum. In addition to the wild buckwheats discussed earlier, many others might be worth cultivating. *Eriogonum brevicaule* is a variable species which includes a series of narrowly endemic forms which sometimes have been recognized at specific level. The most attractive variants are acaulescent mat-formers with yellow, white or pink-tinged capitate heads. Some are true alpines, growing in limestone or quartzite crevices; others are from low-elevation barrens. The epithets *desertorum, loganum, nanum, promiscuum, kingii,* and *chrysocephalum,* among others, have been applied.

Eriogonum panguicense is a pulvinate plant with globose white heads endemic to the upper

Eriogonum shockleyi
Photo by Elizabeth Neese

rim of Cedar Breaks in Iron County, Utah. *Eriogonum jamesii* has white-tomentose leaf rosettes and relatively large and showy yellow flowers. *Eriogonum clavellatum* is a beautiful, profusely flowering, small shrub with fluffy, white flower heads. It is known only from near Comb Ridge in San Juan County, Utah. *Eriogonum shockleyi* is a gray-wooly miniature with white, yellow, or red-suffused pilose flowers. Variable *E. umbellatum* has bright green tufts of leaves terminating slender, often prostrate, woody stems. *Eriogonum u.* var. *subaridum,* with yellow flowers and open, compound umbels is of desert areas. The similar *E. u.* var. *umbellatum* has simple umbels and is montane; *E.u.* var. *porteri* is a dwarfed, alpine version with capitate yellow heads.

SCROPHULARIACEAE

Castilleja. Because of their hemi-parasitic nature, the showy paintbrushes of the Western states have not responded well to the attempts of gardeners to cultivate them. Sophisticated modern techniques may eventually provide a means for propagating members of this highly ornamental genus. Many of the paintbrushes of the West are far better-known than *Castilleja scabrida,* one of the more showy and compact of the genus. It has often been confused with the smaller-flowered and more common *C. chromosa. Castilleja scabrida* favors sandstone crevices of the pinyon-juniper zone of southern Utah and adjacent Colorado.

Penstemon. The completion of Volume Four of the Intermountain Flora will surely stimulate horticultural effort as regards many of the Intermountain penstemon endemics. In addition to ones discussed in earlier paragraphs, many others deserve consideration. *Penstemon fremontii* is probably the most common penstemon of the low-elevation, salt desert shrub communities of the Uinta Basin of northeastern Utah. It has partially dehiscent, short-hairy anthers, densely flowered stems mostly 15–30 cm tall, and intensely blue-purple flowers. It is easily distinguished from sympatric similar species by presence on its foliage of a covering of cinereous hairs.

Penstemon petiolatus. A penstemon with densely glandular flowers, not so large nor showy as some, it deserves particular attention on several counts: the flowers are rich magenta, instead of the more common blue, purple, or lavender; unlike most Intermountain penstemons, the ovate to orbicular leaves are gray-glaucous, relatively thick, and sharply toothed; the plant is a mound-former, at home in crevices of limestone cliffs, making it a natural for rock gardens.

Penstemon ambiguus (the non-penstemon penstemon). Most people's reaction when they first see this is "That is *not* a penstemon!" The plant is shrubby, with linear leaves. The white to pink flowers are salverform and phloxlike rather than tubular-companulate, with a flat-spreading oblique limb. The inflorescence is more widely branched than in most penstemons, so that the plants form large, rounded, flower-covered clumps.

Many more species might be proposed that represent equally good candidates for evaluation of horticultural merit. I have seen no place to match the arid barren lands of the Intermountain Area for the frequency of landscapes where one catches one's breath with the perfection of the natural garden and its flowers. May I recommend the plants discussed here to that special class of gardeners who find particular beauty in wild species?

Section III

Southern Rockies: Peaks and Parklands

Photo by Louise Roloff

PLATE 15

Erigeron simplex
Photo by Pat Pachuta

Aquilegia saximontana
Photo by Ted Kipping

Hymenoxys acaulis
Photo by Ted Kipping

Aquilegia saximontana
Photo by Deane Hall

PLATE 18

Phlox condensata
Photo by Ted Kipping

Saxifraga caespitosa, Eritrichium nanum and *Claytonia*
Photo by Merle Moore

Trollius albiflorus
Photo by Pat Pachuta

Phlox pulvinata
Photo by Merle Moore

Silene acaulis, Dryas octopetala and *Erysimum nivale*
Photo by Ted Kipping

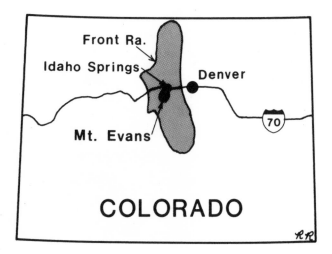

12

A Hike on Mount Evans

by Janet L. Wingate

Mount Evans is located about 35 miles west of Denver in the Front Range of the Colorado Rocky Mountains. It can be reached by State Highway 103 from Bergen Park or Idaho Springs. The Mount Evans Road begins at Echo Lake on Highway 103 and winds to the summit of the mountain, elevation 14,284 ft., for a spectacular view of the Colorado Rockies. On the way to the top you will pass Summit Lake, an important phytogeographic landmark because of the many rare and disjunct alpine plants that occur here.

An excellent place for a hike on the Mount Evans tundra is the Mount Goliath Natural Area, about 5 miles above Echo Lake. Mount Goliath, a lesser peak of the Mount Evans complex, is the site of the Denver Botanic Gardens Alpine Unit, established in 1958 in cooperation with the U.S. Forest Service for the purpose of education and research. It is an area of dry tundra with alpine plants scattered among rocks on a gravelly soil. The upper limit of the M. Walter Pesman Trail, named in honor of the early Denver advocate of the horticultural use of native plants, is located at an elevation of 12,100 ft. It winds downward about 1.5 miles to a lower parking area at 11,500 ft. A shorter trail loops back to the upper parking area and remains entirely on the tundra.

As in other alpine tundra regions, the plants of Mount Evans endure harsh growing conditions, with high winds and subfreezing temperatures lasting most of the year. The continued existence of this fragile flora can be threatened by careless human treatment. The M. Walter Pesman Trail was established to afford ready access to the tundra, while encouraging visitors to refrain from picking, digging, or trampling the fascinating flora. The short growing season of 6 to 12 weeks produces a virtual carpet of beautiful wildflowers, with a striking display of colors that belies the impression of barren, rocky slopes you will get from the inside of an automobile as you navigate the steep, winding road.

As you walk down the trail, you will see many alpines common to most tundra regions of the U.S. Rocky Mountains, as well as some plants with circumpolar distribution throughout the Northern Hemisphere.

This brief discussion of the Mount Goliath Natural Area is concerned primarily with "showy" plants of special interest for their horticultural potential. Although the grasses and sedges are not discussed here, these too, of course, are important alpine plants; over 50 species of *Carex* alone are

Janet L. Wingate received MS and Ph.D degrees in botany from the University of Oklahoma, following a BS in education, specializing in biology, from Kansas State University. She has been associated with Denver Botanic Gardens (DBG) as a volunteer worker and staff member since 1973. She now works in the DBG Kathryn Kalmbach Herbarium, writes for the DBG magazine *The Green Thumb*, and has published guides, illustrated with her own drawings, to the alpine wildflowers of Mount Goliath and the grasses of Denver. She is now preparing guides and keys to Colorado grasses and Rocky Mountain wildflowers.

Pinus aristata. Photo by Cooper & Cooper

found on the Rocky Mountain tundra.

Perhaps the most striking plant that can be seen on the tundra is *Hymenoxys grandiflora,* variously known as rydbergia, old-man-of-the-mountain, or alpine goldflower. The height of this alpine member of the Asteraceae ranges 3–8 in. with its yellow heads often nearly 4 in. wide and always facing east. The foliage is wooly-pubescent with leaves separated into linear divisions. This plant is endemic to Rocky Mountain tundra from Montana and Idaho south to Colorado and Utah.

Another member of the the genus *Hymenoxys,* which is also restricted to the tundra, is *H. (Actinea) acaulis* ssp. *caespitosa.* The yellow heads are similar to *H. grandiflora* but smaller, and the leaves are hairy but not divided. The plant is only 1–3 in. tall and is endemic to the Rocky Mountains, growing in southern Wyoming, Colorado, Utah, and northern New Mexico.

An interesting alpine thistle that grows in disturbed areas is *Cirsium scopulorum,* the wooly thistle. This spiny alpine has nodding, densely cobwebby, cream-colored heads and grows 8–24 in. tall. It is endemic to the Rocky Mountains and is restricted to the alpine tundra from Montana to Colorado and Utah.

Two erigerons found along the trail are *Erigeron pinnatisectus,* the pinnate-leaf daisy, with pinnatifid leaves, and *E. simplex,* one-headed daisy, with simple leaves. Both range from 1–5 in. tall. *Erigeron pinnatisectus* is endemic to the Rocky Mountains and is found in the high ranges from Wyoming to New Mexico. *Erigeron simplex* grows in the high mountains from Montana south to New Mexico and Arizona, as well as in the high ranges of Oregon.

An alpine goldenrod that may be seen on the trail is *Solidago spathulata* var. *nana,* dwarf goldenrod, which has rounded clusters of flowers and ranges from 2–7 in. tall. It is found in high mountains from British Columbia, south to Colorado, Arizona and Oregon.

Tonestus (Happlopappus) pygmaeus, pygmy tonestus, is a tiny yellow composite restricted to the alpine tundra. It is 1–2.5 in. tall and is restricted to the alpine tundra from Wyoming to New Mexico.

Achillea lanulosa, or yarrow, is a white-headed composite with finely dissected, grayish leaves. It grows from the plains to the alpine tundra and is widely distributed in western North America and is also circumpolar.

Two species of *Artemisia* are present along the trail. *Artemisia pattersonii,* Patterson's sage, and *A. scopulorum,* alpine sage, are both small silvery plants with rounded yellowish heads up to 0.3 in. wide. They are restricted to the alpine tundra and are endemic to the Rocky Mountains.

Acomastylis (Geum) rossii, alpine avens, a member of the Rosaceae, is a common alpine plant on the tundra growing in many different communities. The flowers are yellow and leaves pinnatifid or pinnate. Its height ranges from 1.5–12 in., and it is restricted to the alpine tundra from Montana to Nevada, and south to New Mexico and Arizona. *Sibbaldia procumbens,* sibbaldia, another member of the Rosaceae, has inconspicuous yellow flowers and 3-parted leaves. It grows from 1–3 in. tall and is circumpolar. A common potentilla growing on Mount Evans is *Potentilla nivea,* alpine potentilla. This is a hairy plant with 3-parted leaves that grows from 1.5–6 in. tall. It is restricted to the alpine tundra from Greenland through Quebec and Alaska to Eurasia and south to Colorado. *Potentilla diversifolia,* which has palmately compound 5-parted leaves, and *Pentaphylloides floribunda (Potentilla fruticosa),* a shrub with pinnately compound 5-parted leaves, are also found on the trail.

Oxyria digyna, alpine sorrel, is an interesting plant of the Polygonaceae with a panicle of reddish, membranous fruits. It grows from 2–8 in. tall and is often found among rocks. It is circumpolar. The white spikelike inflorescences of *Bistorta (Polygonum) bistortoides,* the American bistort, dot the landscape on the tundra. This member of the Polygonaceae is 4–16 in. tall, and it ranges from Montana to British Columbia, and south to New Mexico and California. *Bistorta (Polygonum) vivipara,* the alpine bistort, can also be found here. The lower flowers of its spikelike raceme are replaced by bulblets. Its height range is 2.5–12 in., and it grows from Greenland to Alaska, south to New Mexico, and is also found in Eurasia.

Another plant with a dense cluster of white flowers is *Saxifraga rhomboidea,* snowball saxifrage, The cluster of flowers is scapose on a slender stem with a basal rosette of toothed leaves. It ranges from 2–8 in. tall and grows from Montana south to New Mexico. Other members of the Saxifragaceae that can be seen along the trail are *S. flagellaris,* whiplash saxifrage, and *S. cernua,* nodding saxifrage. Both are found in the Rocky Mountains and in Eurasia.

Several members of the Brassicaceae are found on the tundra. In this area the fragrant flowers of *Erysimum nivale,* alpine wallflower, range from yellow to rose-purple. Its height is from 2–11 in., and it is endemic to the Rocky Mountains of Colorado and eastern Utah. *Thlaspi montanum,* mountain candytuft, is a small plant of the Brassicaceae growing on the tundra as well as at lower elevations. It is 0.75–5 in. tall and is found from Montana south to New Mexico, and along the Pacific Coast in high ranges of California and Washington. Several tiny drabas can be seen if you look closely. A common species is *Draba streptocarpa,* twisted-pod draba. Twisted fruits are produced on this small plant ranging from 1–3 in. tall. It is endemic to the Rocky Mountains and grows in Colorado and New Mexico. Some other drabas found on Mount Evans are *D. aurea, D. exunguiculata* and *D. grayana.*

Hymenoxys acaulis var. *caespitosa.* Photo by Loraine Yeatts

A fleshy plant found in rock crevices or rock slides on the tundra is *Claytonia megarhiza,* alpine spring beauty. This member of the Portulacaceae has white or pinkish flowers surrounding a rosette of roundish leaves. It grows to 5 in. tall and is found in the higher mountains from Montana and Washington south to Colorado and Utah. Another plant in the Portulacaceae found on Mount Evans is *Lewisia pygmaea,* the pigmy bitterroot. This tiny plant is 0.5–2 in. tall and has a rosette of narrow leaves and pink flowers. It grows from Montana and Washington, south to Arizona and California.

Two interesting members of the Crassulaceae are present on Mount Evans. *Rhodiola integrifolia (Sedum roseum),* the kings crown, has a flat cluster of dark red flowers and ranges from 1.5–9 in. tall. It is circumpolar in distribution, extends south from Alaska through Alberta to Colorado and is also found in California. *Rhodiola (Sedum) rhodantha,* the queens crown, ranges from 3–7 in. tall with a rounded cluster of rose-colored flowers and is endemic to the Rocky Mountains from Montana to Utah, south to New Mexico and Arizona.

Oreoxis alpina, alpine parsley, is a member of the Apiaceae found on the tundra. This small plant ranges from 0.5–3 in. tall with an umbel of tiny yellow flowers. It is endemic to the Rocky Mountains and is found from Wyoming to Utah, south to New Mexico and Arizona.

Allium geyeri, Geyer's onion, is a pink onion that ranges from 1.5–10 in. tall, is found from the plains to the tundra and is widespread in western North America. *Lloydia serotina,* the alp lily, and

Hiking on Mount Evans
Photo by Carolyn Knepp

Rocky Mountain bighorn sheep on Mount Evans. Photo by Carolyn Knepp

Zigadenus elegans, the wand lily, are two white-flowered monocots scattered along the trail. *Lloydia serotina* has perianth segments with purple veins, and the flowers are solitary. The poisonous *Zigadenus elegans* has a raceme of flowers with a green spot on each perianth segment. *Lloydia serotina* ranges from 2–6 in. tall, grows in the mountains from Alaska to Alberta, south to Nevada and New Mexico and also grows in Eurasia. *Zigadenus elegans* is 5–10 in. tall and ranges from Alaska to Saskatchewan, south to New Mexico and Arizona.

Another common white-flowered alpine is *Cerastium beeringianum* ssp. *earlei,* the alpine mouse-ear, of the Caryophyllaceae. It has lobed petals and sticky foliage. It grows from 1.5–8 in. tall and is found only on the alpine tundra in the mountains from Quebec to Alaska, south to New Mexico, as well as in Asia. Another plant in the same family is *Arenaria fendleri,* Fendler's sandwort. The flowers are white with red anthers, and the leaves are linear. Its height range is 1–5 in., and it grows in the mountains and hills of Wyoming and south to New Mexico and Arizona.

Several mat plants can be seen along the trail. Two common mat-forming members of the Caryophyllaceae restricted to the alpine tundra are *Silene acaulis,* moss campion, and *Minuartia (Arenaria) obtusiloba,* the arctic sandwort. *Silene acaulis* has pink flowers that have narrow, notched petals. It is circumpolar and extends southward in the Rocky Mountains as far as New Mexico. *Minuartia obtusiloba* has numerous white flowers and grows in the mountains from Labrador to Alaska, south to New Mexico and California. Another mat plant restricted to the alpine tundra is *Paronychia pulvinata,* the alpine nailwort. This plant is woody with inconspicuous flowers and can be found on high mountains of Wyoming, Colorado and Utah.

Another common mat plant is *Phlox condensata* or alpine phlox. This member of the Polemoniaceae has numerous flowers that can range from white to light blue. It is restricted to the alpine tundra and grows from Montana south to New Mexico, and also in California and Oregon. *Polemonium viscosum,* the sky pilot, is another member of the Polemoniaceae that is frequent along the trail. It has clusters of blue flowers with orange anthers and numerous, tiny leaflets. It grows from 3–8 in. tall and ranges from Alberta and British Columbia south to New Mexico and Arizona, and westward into Oregon.

Three alpine clovers endemic to the Rocky Mountains are common along the trail. *Trifolium nanum,* dwarf clover, is a mat plant with pink flowers in groups of two or three. It grows from Montana south to New Mexico and Utah. *Trifolium parryi,* the alpine clover, has pink flowers with papery bracts and broad leaflets. It reaches a height of 1–5 in. and grows on high mountains of Wyoming, Utah, and Colorado. *Trifolium dasyphyllum,* whiproot clover, has pink bicolored flowers and narrow leaflets. It grows from 1–5 in. tall and is found in the high mountains throughout the southern Rocky mountains.

One of the unforgettable flowers along the trail is *Eritrichum aretioides* (*E. nanum* var. *elongatum*), alpine forget-me-not. Its fragrant blue flowers and silvery foliage are an alpine treat. It grows from 0.5–1 in. tall. Its range is circumpolar, and it extends southward along the Rocky Mountains through Montana to Utah and New Mexico. It is also found in the high mountains of Oregon. Another member of the Boraginaceae on Mount Evans is *Mertensia viridis,* the greenleaf mertensia. This blue alpine has nodding bell-like flowers. It grows from 2–10 in. tall and is found only on the alpine tundra from Montana south to Colorado and Utah.

Two campanulas are present: *Campanula rotundifolia,* harebell, and *C. uniflora,* the alpine harebell. *Campanula rotundifolia* has several nodding flowers while *C. uniflora* has one erect flower. *Campanula rotundifolia* grows from 1–7 in. tall and is widely distributed in the mountains of North America and in Eurasia. *Campanula uniflora* grows from 1–4 in. tall and is found in high mountains from Greenland to Alaska, south to Colorado, as well as in Eurasia.

Two members of the genus *Castilleja* may be seen on the trail. *Castilleja occidentalis,* Western paintbrush, ranges from 2–9 in. tall and has greenish yellow bracts; and *C. rhexifolia,* rosy paintbrush, is 7–15 in. tall and has crimson or rose-colored bracts. *Castilleja occidentalis* grows in the high mountains of Colorado, Utah, and New Mexico, while *C. rhexifolia* can be found in the mountains from Oregon to Montana, and south to Colorado and Utah.

Penstemon whippleanus, Whipple's penstemon, can be seen as you continue along the trail. Its flowers are a dusty purple or white. It grows 3–17 in. tall and is endemic to the Rocky Mountains, growing from Idaho and Wyoming, through Utah and Colorado, to Arizona and New Mexico. *Pedicularis parryi,* Parry's lousewort, is another member of the Scrophulariaceae on the tundra. It has a raceme of whitish or yellowish flowers with a sickle-shaped upper petal. It is from 4–10 in. tall and is endemic to the Rocky Mountains from Montana south to New Mexico and Arizona.

Another plant with a spikelike inflorescence is *Phacelia sericea,* the purple fringe. This member of the Hydrophyllaceae has a purple raceme of flowers with exserted stamens, giving it a fringed appearance. It ranges from 4–10 in. tall and is found on the tundra and at lower elevations in the mountains from Alberta to British Columbia, south to Colorado and Arizona, and also in California.

Two interesting members of the Primulaceae are found on Mount Evans. *Primula angustifolia,* alpine primrose, has rose-colored flowers with yellow centers. It grows from 0.25–2 in. tall and is found only in the south-central Rockies. *Androsace chamaejasme* ssp. *carinata,* alpine rock jasmine, has clusters of white flowers with yellow centers that turn pink with age. It is only 0.25–2 in. tall and is circumpolar, extending southward along the Rocky Mountains.

Gentiana algida, the arctic gentian, may be found along the trail. Its large whitish corolla is streaked with dark blue and it grows 2–7 in. tall. It is circumpolar and extends southward in the Rockies from Alaska through Montana to Utah and New Mexico.

Reaching the lower end of the M. Walter Pesman Trail, one's attention is diverted from the colorful display of small alpine wildflowers to a stand of gnarled, weather-beaten conifers marking the boundary between the tundra and the subalpine zones. These bristlecone pines, *Pinus aristata,* represent one of the most ancient living species on earth. Many individual bristlecones have stood against gale winds and winter blizzards for over two thousand years. They provide a fitting coda to a visit to the tundra, offering graphic testimony to the difficulties facing plants in this highly stressed mountain ecosystem.

The continued existence of the alpine tundra in the face of increasing human usage depends on the commitment of all who come here to leave this environment undisturbed and pristine, preserving a delicate balance of nature that has existed through eons of time.

References
Wingate, Janet L. 1982. *Alpine wildflowers of Mt. Goliath.* Denver: World Press.

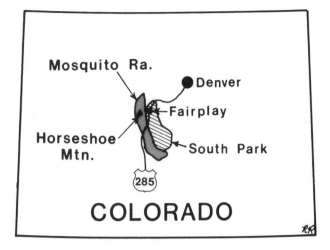

13

A Walk on Horseshoe Mountain in the Mosquito Range

by Pat Thorn

Horseshoe Mountain is one of those rare places we learn about only through the alpine plant-lovers' grapevine. Nestled in the Mosquito Range in the midst of the Colorado Rockies, the area is virtually unknown to the general public, and it is filled with rare and beautiful tundra plants.

Horseshoe Mountain is about 15 miles southwest of the historic town of Fairplay, Colorado, and just under 100 miles southwest of Denver. Highway 285 is the scenic route to take out of the city; it meanders through small mountain towns, canyons and broad meadows. The highest point along the drive is Kenosha Pass at 10,000 ft. It is here that you get your first view of the impressive Mosquito Range, which includes five peaks over 14,000 ft. and about 20 peaks over 13,000 ft.

Located on a relief map, the Mosquitoes are the chain of peaks that lie along the west side of South Park, which is a high alitude meadow that stretches 50 miles in length and 35 miles in width in this part of Colorado. The Park, bordered on all sides by mountains, sits at 8,500 to 10,000 ft. above sea level.

Most of the Mosquito Range was created about 600 million years ago at the beginning of the Paleozoic era. Two peaks, just north of Trout Creek Pass, are volcanic piles created after the Mosquito uplift. The floral abundance in the South Park area is due mainly to rich glacial and volcanic deposits laid down through time. In the late 1800s Western pioneers also discovered the richness of the area, but they were concerned with mining the silver, gold and other mineral deposits, rather than discovering the wildflowers.

With this brief historical perspective of the area, join me as we enter South Park from the north, then find our way up to Horseshoe Mountain on the west, investigating along the way the wealth of flowers found here.

Dropping down Kenosha Pass, the snow-spotted Mosquitoes to the west catch the eye. As we enter the northern end of South Park, fields of blue *Iris missouriensis,* yellow *Thermopsis divaricarpa,* and creamy white *Caltha leptosepala* in full bloom remind us that here nature's color scheme is in full

Pat Thorn is sales coordinator for Little Valley Wholesale Nursery in Brighton, Colorado. She holds a degree in ornamental horticulture from Alfred State College in New York. Like many other Colorado horticulturists, she became interested in rock gardening after meeting and visiting the garden of the late Paul Maslin of Boulder. She is a member of the Rocky Mountain Chapter of ARGS, currently serving as treasurer.

Horseshoe Mountain. Photo by Sandy Snyder

balance. In June the ground is wet from the spring runoff of the mountain snows. Up in the higher, drier areas, various species of *Castilleja, Penstemon teucrioides, Astragalus kentrophyta, Potentilla hippiana, Geranium fremontii, Frasera speciosa,* and the common *Artemisia frigida* fill the grasslands with color.

Fairplay is the first real town you pass through in South Park, and it is just 1.3 miles south of Fairplay to the Fourmile Creek turnoff that leads up a dirt road to the 13,898 ft. peak of Horseshoe Mountain.

Heading west, straight into the wind, you notice the *Populus tremuloides,* dwarfed by the harsh conditions, growing in thick stands. A trip in mid-June would allow you to see *Potentilla fruticosa (Pentaphylloides floribunda), Erigeron compositus, Smilacina stellata,* and *Antennaria parvifolia* in bloom on your right on the dry roadcut. To the left, along the creek banks, several species of *Salix* have just leafed out, and the soft catkins are in bloom. Later, in August, *Ipomopsis (Gilia) aggregata, Epilobium angustifolium* and *Geum (Erythocoma) triflorum* will be in full color.

At the bend in the road, where the abandoned Leavick Mine stands, you find your first slope filled with mounds of *Phlox condensata.* It is in bloom from mid-June through early August. Each white, sometimes bluish, flower, 0.25–0.5 in. wide, is sitting flat on the dense foliage. The buns vary in size up to 8 in. across; more often they are 3–4 in. across. *Fragaria americana, Polemonium viscosum, Anemone multifida* ssp. *globosa, Phacelia sericea,* and *Cerastium arvense* are also found around the old mine.

To get to the base of the mountain itself, take the unmarked road that crosses left over the creek, 11.4 miles from the turnoff at Highway 285. The road is rocky and sometimes steep, but it takes you by car, relatively easily, up to a height of over 11,000 ft. In June, snowdrifts may still block the road, but by July you can drive all the way up to the lower lake just below Horseshoe Mountain. Here, looking up, you see the striking, deeply eroded slopes and upper cirque that gave the mountain its name.

Stepping out of the car, the first plant you observe is *Dryas octopetala* var. *hookeriana,* the tundra's perfect, almost evergreen ground cover. It is the first plant to emerge from the melting snows, almost immediately coming into bloom. It is unmistakable since it is the only flower in the region to have 8 creamy white perianth segments, 1–2 in. above the dark green mat of deeply veined leaves.

In June you would also find *Rhodiola (Sedum) rosea* ssp. *integrifolia,* kings crown and *R. (Sedum) rhodantha,* queens crown, starting to bloom, growing in the runoff areas below the snow drifts. These

Phlox condensata
Photo by Bob Heapes

Eriogonum flavum var. *xanthum*
Photo by Bob Heapes

Penstemon hallii
Photo by Vernon Tomppert

rhodiolas require this extra spring moisture. Other plants found along the snow's edge and above timberline are *Anemone parviflora,* which has white perianth parts backed with purple; *Saxifraga rhomboidea; Lloydia serotina; Ranunculus adoneus; Anemone narcissiflora,* the showier of these two alpine anemones; and *Besseya alpina.*

Keeping a keen eye out for the tiniest of plants is the only way to spot *Primula angustifolia.* It grows alone or in small clumps in harsh, exposed alpine situations, often on rocky slopes. The purple-to-rose colored flowers are 0.5–1 in. across with a bright yellow eye, 2–3 in. above the tiny, narrow leaves.

The drier slopes at the base of Horseshoe Mountain hold such alpines as *Physaria alpina* with its tight rosette of gray leaves ringed by yellow blossoms; *Castilleja occidentalis,* yellow; *C. rhexifolia,* crimson to pink; and *Eriogonum flavum* var. *xanthum. Thlaspi montanum* begins to bloom in June while its flower stalks are only 1–2 in. tall. In August it is still blooming, but on 6–8 in. stalks. *Erysimum nivale* also begins to bloom on short stalks which elongate during the season.

The most exciting part of every trip to Horseshoe is coming upon the hundreds of mounds of *Eritrichium aretioides (E. nanum)* that cover the dry, rocky hills. Each individual bloom is scarcely 0.25 in. across, varying in hue from almost turquoise to vibrant royal blue. The cushions are caespitose, barely mounding and 2–4 in. wide, made of rosettes of hairy silvery-looking leaves. In full bloom, plants at this elevation are barely 1 in. tall. This alpine forget-me-not is found growing only at very high altitudes, on exposed ridges, blooming mid-June to mid-July, setting seed by the first of August.

Scattered among the eritrichium you find *Arenaria (Minuartia) obtusiloba,* a somewhat larger-growing bun plant with tiny, stiff leaves, starred with numerous white flowers. *Paronychia pulvinata* stays tight and low as well, but its inconspicuous flowers are greenish and sessile. *Minuartia (Arenaria) biflora* has fleshier leaves and short-stemmed white blossoms, and it is similar to *Arenaria obtusiloba,* but slightly less compact. *Phlox condensata,* also found here in abundance, is in full bloom along with the eritrichium.

Walking up toward the lake, more alpine species are found. *Astragalus alpinus,* a dainty vetch bearing conspicuously two-toned flowers, grows in the more shaded spots. A solitary *Aster (Machaeranthera) coloradoensis* may still be found blooming in August. *Erigeron pinnatisectus* grows in the gravel of the road, while *Chionophila jamesii* may trick you into believing that it is actually a 4 in. tall, creamy white penstemon.

Penstemon whippleanus and *P. hallii* are in full bloom by the end of July. *Penstemon whippleanus* is such a dark purple that on cloudy days it is hard to spot from a distance. *Penstemon hallii* is a large-flowering species, but it is shorter, 4–8 in. tall, and less floriferous. Its flowers, violet-blue with white markings at the throat, are abruptly inflated. *Penstemon hallii* is a species found only above 10,000 ft.

Heading toward the lake that is the source of Fourmile Creek, you cross what is in June a roaring, sometimes snow-covered stream, a gentler one in August. Growing near the stream are *Polygonum (Bistorta) bistortoides* and *P. (Bistorta) viviparum. Polygonum bistortoides* is the larger of the two species with 2 in. long heads of white or pink flowers held tightly on almost leafless 12 in. stems. *Polygonum viviparum* is less conspicuous, standing no more than 6 in. tall with very narrow 2–4 in. long, spikelike racemes. At the top of the raceme sit small white or pink flowers, which on the lower part are replaced by bulblets.

Two *Salix* species also grow near the water. *Salix arctica* can be easily distinguished from *S. nivalis* by its yellow petioles and taller growth habit of 2–3 in. *Salix reticulata* is prostrate, 1–2 in. tall, with catkins that are a deeper red.

Another prize found up in this tundra is *Caltha leptosepala,* growing almost in midstream. The leaves are basal, almost heart-shaped, and glossy green. Gold-centered, white-sepaled flowers are borne 4–6 in. above the foliage, and they bloom during most of the alpine season. They are also found just below the melting snow banks.

Three gentian family members can be found blooming early in August. The most difficult to find is *Gentiana (Ciminalis) prostrata,* difficult not only because of its tiny size but also because it is so sensitive to light and touch that it closes up immediately if a cloud passes over or if it is touched. The blooms of *G. prostrata* are blue, starlike, and less than 0.3 in. wide when open. Its stems are 1–3 in. long, slender, and they bear tiny, white-margined leaves.

Gentiana (Gentianopsis) barbellata is a larger, fringed gentain with fragrant flowers that vary from a light grayish blue to a dark purplish color. It is also quite rare. The flowers of *G. algida* are greenish white, spotted or streaked with purple on the outside of each lobe. Both *Gentianopsis barbellata* and *Gentiana algida* are very late bloomers, often the last species to bloom before the snows begin to fly. *Frasera speciosa,* a member of the gentian family, is also found here along the road, dwarfed by the extreme tundra conditions.

Just ahead of the upper lake, a rocky, southwest-facing slope is the home of *Claytonia megarhiza* with its fleshy, dark green leaves arranged in a basal rosette. The flowers are pinkish, several to a stem, blooming June through July. Each flower stalk connects to the central stem, and each is arranged quite neatly in a tight circle between the leaves, with flowers surrounding the entire plant. Each plant is less than 2 in. tall and may grow to 6 in. across. They grow beautifully tucked-in among the rocks because of their very long, thick roots which are purple or red.

Related to the claytonia, though hardly as showy, is *Lewisia pygmaea,* a minute species that blooms later in the season. The leaves are only 0.5 in. long, densely rosetted and often tinged with red. The silvery pink or rose-red flowers are 0.5 in. across, solitary and almost caespitose. *Lewisia pygmaea* is found in areas where the snow melt runs off early, leaving drier soil by July.

The upper lake on Horseshoe Mountain is the final destination of this walk. Even in June it is still half-covered with ice at least 6 in. thick. Ptarmigans and marmots are seen and heard across the lake, just below the semicircular mountain above. But the trip back down often leads to new discoveries not made during the uphill climb.

Hiding under a small outcropping is *Hymenoxys grandiflora.* Blooming mid-to-late season, its golden sunflowerlike blossoms are sitting atop stout stems. The heads are 2–3 in. wide, relatively large for the 4–6 in. tall stems. The foliage, buds and stems are woolly, the leaves once- or twice-dissected.

Other composites that can be found here are *Chrysopsis (Heterotheca) fulcrata, Senecio fendleri* and *S. holmii,* with *S. holmii* being the more compact of the two senecios. *Townsendia rothrockii* is a rare plant; it is in bloom by late July.

Three species of *Trifolium* are found, as well: *T. dasyphyllum, T. parryi* and *T. nanum.* All have conspicuously large white-to-rose-to-pink blooms that are held above compact foliage.

As you make your way through the rocks and over the stream, you might now notice the strange raised rows of soil. These were formed by moles as they tunneled through the damp ground. In these areas *Pedicularis groenlandica* is fairly prolific. It is a plant best depicted by its common name, elephant head, that describes the shape of the purplish flowers held on 6–8 in. tall spikes.

If you are taking a July or early August trip, you will be pleased to find *Silene acaulis* in full bloom, a cushiony plant with sessile, vibrant rose-pink blooms. This is one plant that demands you drop to your knees to appreciate its sweet fragrance. Each mound may grow to 6 in. wide, while its height stays below 2 in.

Back to the car, and you are on your way home. The trip has not ended, however. One last new discovery is the *Zigadenus elegans* found growing in the meadows along the road on the way back down to the highway. A trip to Horseshoe Mountain yields a wealth of discovery of Rocky Mountain plants. The trip up Fourmile Creek Road, although rocky and sometimes nerve-racking, is always rewarding.

Reference

Ingwersen, Will. 1978. *Manual of alpine plants.* Eastbourne, England: Will Ingwersen and Dunnsprint Ltd.

Simmons, Virginia McConnell. 1966. *Bayou Salado—the story of South Park.* Colorado Springs: Century One Press.

14

Pikes Peak: America's Mountain

by Stan Metsker

Pikes Peak stands alone at the western edge of the plains of Colorado like an outpost guarding the approach to the Front Range. Located 80 miles east of the Colorado high country, the primary cordilleran system of mountains that forms the Continental Divide, the Peak rises from 6,000 ft. at its base near Colorado Springs to 14,110 ft. at the summit. This is the greatest base-to-summit rise found anywhere in the Colorado Rockies; yet it is only the 31st highest peak in Colorado.

This physical separation from the other peaks perhaps explains the many endemics found here such as the dark purple-flowering *Telesonix (Boykinia) jamesii;* the large alpine parsley, *Oreoxis humilis;* and the white-flowering alumroot, *Heuchera hallii.*

Pikes Peak is in the Pike-San Isabel National Forest in the Colorado Springs watershed area, and there are no private homes on the Peak. The mountain was formed about a billion years ago as igneous rock cooled slowly at a depth of perhaps 20 miles beneath the surface of the earth, forming the characteristic Pikes Peak granite, easily recognizable by its large crystal size and unusual orange-pink color. Most of the rock that originally overlaid the granite has long since been eroded away through the action of wind, water and air. The relatively recent glaciation has also affected the shape of the Peak. Acting like giant cookie cutters, glaciers on the shaded north and east sides of the mountain gouged out the rock, leaving deep, straight-walled basins called cirques. Among these are the "Bottomless Pit," with its sheer drop of 1,700 ft. and the "Crater," which in spite of its name, has nothing to do with volcanic activity. Some of the canyons that lead down from the Peak to the plains show the U-shaped valleys characteristic of streambeds formed by flowing "rivers of ice," although others clearly were formed by more recent streams.

Because of its high visibility from the Great Plains, its convenient location, and its beauty, Pikes Peak long ago became both famous and popular. Sometimes called "America's mountain," it is easily accessible to the public, more so perhaps than any other mountain of the Front Range. The Cog Wheel Route of the Manitou and Pikes Peak Railway is the highest standard-gauge railroad in the world. It runs a distance of 8.9 miles, rising 7,518 ft. with an average grade of 12.5 percent. It was

Stan Metsker grew up in Englewood, Colorado, where he worked summers at George Kelly's nursery, The Green Spot, famous for its native plants. He is president of the Rocky Mountain Chapter of the American Rock Garden Society. He earned a degree in horticulture from Colorado State University and is golf course superintendent at the Country Club of Colorado in Colorado Springs, a course known for its dramatic view of the Pikes Peak Massif and extensive use of native plants. Metsker has also pioneered the cultivation of alpines in troughs in the Rocky Mountain region, inspiring and teaching many people by his example.

Pikes Peak. Photo by Cooper & Cooper

opened in 1891, and it is still a great way to travel! There is a pristine view all along the route because no one is allowed off the train.

There are many hiking trails on the Peak, but the most famous is 13-mile Barr Trail. You can use the Mount Manitou Scenic Incline Railway to take you up the first 2,000 ft. at a maximum grade of 68 percent. This cable car has been operating since 1903, and is very safe. You may then hike up the rest of the way if you wish.

The Pikes Peak Toll Road was opened in 1916. It reaches an altitude only slightly lower than the Mount Evans Road, which is said to be the highest road in the United States. The Pikes Peak Road runs 18.8 miles and rises 6,719 ft. and you are allowed to stop and view the sites and the flowers. It takes only about an hour by car from Colorado Springs to reach the alpine tundra. The road is used each July for a popular auto race "to the top of Pikes Peak." It also gives access to a ski slope and the Glen Cove tourist facilities at 11,427 ft. and to more tourist services provided at Summit House at the top of the mountain. The summit area itself is rather flat and barren of vegetation, the latter possibly due simply to overuse.

My favorite area is called Elk Park, located at the lower edge of the alpine zone at an elevation of 12,000 ft. When you leave the highway to enter the Elk Park Road, you feel as if you are driving into the sky because of the extremely sharp edge. It is always a thrill. In just a few hundred yards you are standing in a rocky pasture with a 360-degree view. Underfoot among the grasses and sedges, the most common flowers are the yellow *Geum (Acomastylis) rossii,* alpine avens; the sky blue of *Eritrichium aretioides (E. nanum),* the alpine forget-me-not; and the white of *Androsace chamaejasme* ssp. *carinata,* rock jasmine. Also present are *Antennaria alpina,* alpine pussytoes; *Castilleja occidentalis,* Western yellow paintbrush; *Lloydia serotina,* alp lily; *Mertensia alpina,* alpine chiming bells; *Minuartia (Arenaria) obtusiloba,* alpine sandwort; *Paronychia pulvinata,* alpine nailwort; *Primula angustifolia,* alpine primrose; *Saxifraga rhomboidea,* snowball saxifrage; *Sedum lanceolatum (S. stenopetalum),* yellow stonecrop; *Sedum (Rhodiola) roseum,* kings crown; *Silene acaulis* ssp. *subcaulescens,* moss campion; *Solidago spathulata* var. *nana,* alpine goldenrod; and *Zigadenus elegans,* wand lily.

The Englemann spruce form many krummholz islands. There is one bristlecone pine playing dead in the pasture, but it is given away by three healthy branches straining to live behind the stump of the tree. The wind here is from the northwest, so only the east and south sides of the mountain have any trees at all. Most of the ridge called Elk Park is usually blown free of snow so it is a dry area most of the year, but there can be dirty snowdrifts caught in between the few trees surviving in protected areas.

Even more exciting is the nearby east-facing scree. This area is so loose it is hard to walk on, and it seems to be in constant movement. *Dryas octopetala* ssp. *hookeriana,* the alpine dryad, seems to be the main stabilizing force. There are also krummholz groups of *Pinus flexilis,* limber pine, and *Picea englemannii,* the Englemann spruce. The *Potentilla fruticosa (Pentaphylloides floribunda),* shrubby cinquefoil, and the *Juniperus communis,* common juniper, are more matlike.

Surprisingly, the view looking down the slope is not nearly as colorful as the view up. The reason, of course: many of the tiny herbaceous plants are snuggled below big rocks or larger

Dryas octopetala
Photo by Panayoti Kelaidis

stabilized plants. This is particularly true of our delightful little *Aquilegia saximontana,* the Rocky Mountain columbine; *Polemonium brandegei,* honey sky pilot; and *Sibbaldia procumbens.* Some of the plants from the turf area occasionally show up in the scree, but in addition, there are: *Achillea lanulosa,* yarrow; *Arenaria fendleri* var. *tweedyi,* Fendler's sandwort; *Artemisia borealis,* alpine sage; *Aster foliaceus* var. *apricus,* sun-loving aster; *Cirsium scopulorum,* alpine thistle; *Erigeron melanocephalus,* black-headed daisy; *Hymenoxys acaulis* var. *caespitosa; Lewisia pygmaea,* pygmy bitterroot; *Minuartia biflora,* Siberian sandwort; *Oreoxis alpina,* alpine parsley; *Oxyria digyna,* alpine sorrel; *Penstemon hallii,* alpine penstemon; *Penstemon whippleanus,* dark bearded tongue; *Polygonum (Bistorta) bistortoides,* American bistort; *Senecio werneriaefolius;* and *Thlaspi montanum,* alpine candytuft. *Telesonix jamesii* is always found in crevices. On this scree, it is found in a horizontal crevice, but higher on the mountain they are usually vertical.

Near the scree is a marshy area packed tight with sedges and rushes. *Caltha leptosepala,* the marsh marigold, is also found here, its white flowers in high contrast against the dark green turf. Just a little higher on the slope two different willows form ground covers. They are *Salix arctica,* which has a leaf with a blue underside, and *S. nivalis* whose leaf is quite rounded. There is quite a mixture here. Many of the turf flowers such as *Trifolium nanum,* dwarf clover, are also present. This one is a true mat; the flowers form right down on the ground. I have often collected seeds of this plant in the late summer. There are many seeds available by Labor Day, but some plants like *Gentiana algida,* the arctic gentian, and *Telesonix jamesii* are so late to set seed that the snow comes before the seed.

Pikes Peak has many different plant communities and is very rich in species. Of the more than 250 higher alpine plants—not including grasses, sedges, or rushes—most are present here. Fortunately, there is no commercial grazing, and the wildlife does not seem to do excessive damage. There is much evidence of man in areas near the highway, but most people do not leave their cars except at the summit. Once you get away from the highway, most of the mountain can be enjoyed in pristine condition.

References

Pearl, Richard M. 1976. *America's mountain: Pikes Peak and the Pikes Peak region.* 4th ed. Colorado Springs: Earth Science Publishing Co.

15

The Montane Zone: Middle Elevation Rock Plants

by Andrew Pierce

From northern Alberta and British Columbia to New Mexico the Rocky Mountains are covered along much of their great length with coniferous forests in their middle-to-upper elevations. Nowhere else in this vast area do trees and shrubs play such a dominant role in the environment. The montane zone, as it is called, ranges in elevation from approximately 8,000 to 10,000 ft. in the Colorado Rocky Mountains. The zone is sometimes subdivided into lower and upper montane levels.

The common coniferous trees are *Pseudotsuga menziesii,* Douglas fir; *Pinus contorta* var. *latifolia,* lodgepole pine; *Picea engelmannii,* Englemann spruce; and *Pinus ponderosa,* ponderosa pine. Each is often dominant in its particular locale. Between these densely forested areas are valleys and meadows with multitudes of floral beauties. The abrupt contrast between a lodgepole pine stand, almost devoid of any understory plants, and a lush meadow—is thrilling. These high open areas are termed parks; in Colorado they are exemplified by South, Middle and North Park; Estes Park; and portions of Golden Gate State Park and the San Luis Valley.

Climate, and especially precipitation, influences what grows where; the montane area is no exception. Both rainfall and snow come from three main climatic systems (see Fig. 15.1). Because of these influences the montane zone may actually receive less precipitation than either the Continental Divide and the higher peaks to the west or the foothills below. These three systems create most of the 20–25 in. of annual precipitation, though this can vary considerably depending on exposure and the shadow of nearby peaks, ridges and mountain ranges. Drier areas are often covered with lodgepole pine, while some of the world's finest flower gardens are found in the moist open areas of the aspen groves. The amount of precipitation is considerably greater west of the Continental Divide (Fig. 15.1) where the montane zone is less easily distinguished. Of course, the runoff from either rain or snow has to work its way to lower levels, and large streamside plants include our famous Colorado blue spruce, *Picea pungens,* and many species of willow, with nearby

Assistant Director of Denver Botanic Gardens and past President of the ARGS Rocky Mountain Chapter, now serving on the ARGS National Board, **Andrew Pierce** is chairman of Alpines '86: Second Interim International Rock Garden Plant Conference. Originally from England, he was trained at Kew Gardens and Kent Horticultural Institute and is a holder of the Kew Certificate and the Royal Horticultural Society's National Diploma. His interest in alpines is sparked by the rock garden he constructed around a natural boulder outcrop at his home on Independence Mountain near Denver, situated at 7,800 ft. elevation. At this cool elevation, *Meconopsis* and Asiatic primroses are easily accommodated, and *Lewisia tweedyi* is indestructible.

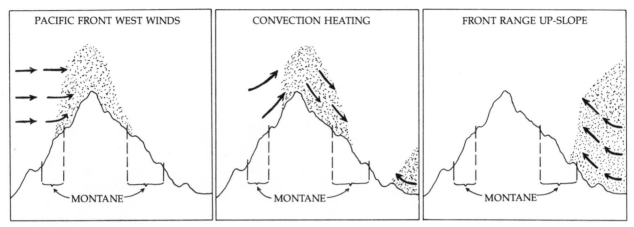

Fig. 15.1A Prevailing westerlies bring moisture to higher elevations.

Fig. 15.1B Thunderstorms from convection heating produce abundant summer moisture.

Fig. 15.1C Main winter precipitation produced by up-slope winds.

moist areas covered with the equally celebrated aspen, *Populus tremuloides.*

A few other deciduous plants such as *Acer glabrum, Lonicera involucrata, Sambucus pubens* and *Prunus melanocarpa* may be present as well. Dry sunny slopes may have *Cercocarpus montanus, Holodiscus dumosus,* various ribes and *Quercus gambelii.* Many of these are upward extensions from lower elevations. A few evergreens from the lower slopes may be found—for example, *Arctostaphylos uva-ursi, Juniperus communis* and *Pachistima (Paxistima) myrsinites*—but in many respects the montane zone is a surprise to the plant lover.

The names of early explorers and adventurers now read like a "Who's Who" of the 19th century: Lewis, Clark, Parry, Gray, Englemann, Lambert, Frémont, Torrey, Nuttall, Rydberg, Bigelow, and the pre-eminent Douglas. How these men must have been amazed at what they found after their trek across the Great Plains! Their excursions often required all the late spring and summer just to make the trip; by the time they arrived, much of the Front Range flora would have already flowered. But as they climbed to the higher elevations of the montane zone, toward those peaks named ultimately in their honor, they would have found blossoms becoming more abundant.

Much of our area is composed of igneous granite and granodiorites, while metamorphic schists and gneisses are abundant in rocky outcrops, cliffs and weathered slopes. On the ridges the boulders are more rounded, but regardless of the type of rock, there are crevices for plants, many useful to the avid rock gardener. As one climbs higher, organic matter, acidity, and nitrogen levels tend to increase, and soil depths vary widely. Glacial weathering helped to create the parks where moraines, with their deep gravel masses, occur frequently. If such moraines occur along with rock faulting, a large dam effect is created as in South Park. This extensive water basin forms one of Colorado's unique floral displays. Many of these plants are not necessarily rock plants, but Mother Nature can be surprisingly adaptive. For example, *Iris missouriensis,* one of South Park's princely inhabitants, is found in low meadows and along streams. It will adapt nicely to a low spot in the rock garden.

Other influences, such as forest fires, are always a part of nature, leaving their mark on all terrains. The valley bottoms, as in other areas, tend to be colder than the surrounding slopes. In fact, some of the open valley areas like Tabernash and Fraser are among Colorado's coldest spots. There is no month, with the possible exception of July, that is frost-free, and the number of frost-free days in an entire year may be as low as 50. Wind is less a factor to plants of the montane zone than to those of the alpine zone, or the lower foothills, where wind speeds from the downdraft chinooks may well reach over 100 mph.

The white man, with his forestry, ranching and farming operations, has caused changes in the environment since the time of his early settlement. Even with only 125 years or so of such activity, much of the zone has lost its pristine character. Cycles of pine beetle, tussock moth and other pests and diseases have also altered nature's balance. More recently, mining, housing, highways, and sporting activities such as skiing are causing great damage to the environment.

To this still remarkable area, however, we will now look for some individual plants for the rock garden, bearing in mind that the true alpine, in the strictest sense of the word, belongs to levels above our altitudinal range.

PLATE 19

Phlox pulvinata
Photo: Grand Ridge

Androsace chamaejasme var. *carinata*
Photo: Grand Ridge

Pinus aristata
Photo by Karen Trout

Lloydia serotina
Photo by Ted Kipping

PLATE 20

Telesonix jamesii
Photo by Panayoti Kelaidis

Primula parryi
Photo by Loraine Yeatts

Castilleja sulphurea and *Castilleja miniata*
Photo by Vernon Tomppert

Gentiana affinis
Photo by Carolyn Crawford

Phlox multiflora
Photo by Karen Trout

Montane Shrubs

Since montane shrubs vary in size from *Arctostaphylos uva-ursi,* or kinnikinnik, which grows just a few inches high on the mildly acid forest floor, to others several feet in height, one might think the area lacking in useful rock garden plants. Not so. *Potentilla fruticosa (Pentaphylloides floribunda)* is a fine example of a plant widely adapted in nature and very useful in the garden. In the past, only yellow forms were available, but plant breeders and selectors can now give us shorter forms in colors down to white. Shrubby in character, potentilla can be used as a design feature, though it may be surpassed by more ornamental conifers of a dwarf nature. Also growing in lower areas of the Rocky Mountain Front Range, rabbit brushes, or *Chrysothamnus nauseosus,* and sagebrush, principally *Artemisia tridentata,* have been selected for improved appearance and garden performance. Though some people would not want them in any rock garden they can be quite spectacular, if treated and selected carefully. Both have relatively low water requirements, a useful attribute.

One plant that creates more interest than many others is *Jamesia americana,* or wax flower. It was named for Dr. Edwin James, who was physician-botanist with the Major Long Expedition. The plant is often assigned to the Saxifragaceae. However, Dr. William A. Weber in his *Rocky Mountain Flora* separates it into the Hydrangeaceae. This ancient shrub, appearing in fossils of the Oligocene beds of Creede, can easily move from its natural habitat in rocky roadcuts, as on Squaw Pass, into the rock garden, where it will form a fairly compact bush if it is carefully pruned. The white flowers in small scented clusters are quite prominent about the new, fresh green leaves, and in the fall, added beauty appears in its colored foliage. Fairly easily raised from seed collected in August before it shatters, the first flowers can be expected in three or four years.

Very different, with its glossy evergreen foliage, is *Arctostaphylos uva-ursi.* Locally propagated plants are being used as a ground cover in shady locations, though I have seen it in direct sun in Colorado Springs; it can sometimes spread as much as three or four feet.

Arctostaphylos uva-ursi
Photo by Vernon Tomppert

More interesting is its very close relative from the Uncompahgre Plateau, *A. patula*, greenleaf manzanita, which can be used as a small feature shrub. Its pink urn-shaped flowers, typical of the Ericaceae, are followed by clusters of small applelike fruits. A very smooth red bark adds to its beauty. Less common, but also from the Western Slope, *A. nevadensis* var. *coloradensis* has hybridized with *A. patula*. Several good-colored or singularly different forms of this plant have been selected by the late Dr. T. Paul Maslin of Boulder, and Panayoti Kelaidis of Denver Botanic Gardens. Further work should be carried out to introduce this group of plants to garden enthusiasts.

The low, clumping shrub *Juniperus communis* comes from various, often quite dry, locations. It can be useful as a feature plant in the rock garden. But if it spreads to almost 15 feet, as it does in my montane garden in Evergreen, Colorado, it is obviously beyond most people's idea of a rock plant! Small plants can be kept compact, however, hardly resembling my large 150-year-old specimen.

From the few shrubs of rock garden potential we move to a much more diverse selection of herbaceous plants from the montane zone. Plants from this 8,000–10,000 ft. elevation do not always perform with the same character at lower levels, however, and each garden has its own intrinsic ecosystem.

Many of the montane plants we attempt to grow in our gardens are from well-drained locales. To put such marvels into the local "plains" soil such as that found in Denver is to court disaster. Taking pussy toes (what a delightfully descriptive name!) as an example, we see a ground-hugging plant of the open forest growing in broken granite. Rainfall or snow disappears almost as rapidly as it falls; consequently, most of the growing season for little pussy toes, *Antennaria parvifolia*, is finished before the real heat of summer. It now goes into dormancy with its fine fluffy seeds scattering abroad—a typical scenario for early flowering plants. Selected forms of this genus should be chosen for color, as in *A. rosea*, or for dwarflike qualities, as in certain selections of *A. parvifolia*, which are found in the Estes Park area. This plant is extremely adaptable to growing between random paving slabs, but remember to remove flower heads as they appear. The plant tends to be monocarpic.

Not reaching much higher is *Arenaria fendleri*, the sandwort, a delightful clumping plant with white flowers that ranges from foothills to tundra. When grown in full sunshine, it retains its tight mat-forming habit. But take care to prevent it from drying out during the heat of summer! As with many of the plants we wish to grow, a deep root run produces success, while one that is too shallow leads to failure. Arenaria is no exception.

One of the first flowers to appear in the montane and in the foothills is the delightful pasqueflower, *Pulsatilla (Anemone) patens*, with its nodding bluish heads followed by clusters of tasseled seeds. So many varieties and species of this plant are available to the rock gardener that our native species is seldom used. Another relative, not always so neglected, is *Anemone multifida* var. *globosa* with its small red flowers and columnar seed heads.

Also producing decorative seeds heads are sundry members of the genus *Eriogonum*, often termed sulphur flowers. Not always the easiest plants to establish in the rock garden (because of their thick root structure), they are well worth growing from seed. The beauty of the eriogonums is in bracts and seed clusters rather than floral parts. As lovely as the common *E. umbellatum*, is *E. subalpinum*, which stretches down into our zone. Its bracts change to a rosy red color, and it is more compact in habit.

The erigerons, or fleabanes, are another interesting group. From the single-headed *Erigeron vetensis* to the trailing stolons of *E. flagellaris* and the twice-divided leaves of *E. compositus*, fleabanes can be adapted to our gardens. Though they may not be long-lived, seedlings often appear in profusion. Most require good drainage with a reasonable depth of soil to succeed.

Also among the composites, gaillardia is well known in the perennial border. Though large for some tastes, *Gaillardia aristata* can be used in the best-drained areas if root depth is adequate. Frequently found on rocky or shale road cuts, it is often biennial in character. Another "daisy" flower, though it lacks the ray florets, is *Chaenactis douglasii*, or pincushion plant. The exserted anthers give it its common name, but some may consider it not showy enough for gardens.

The Rockies are everywhere so well-endowed with penstemons that we sometimes neglect the value of these incredible plants. When one moves up from the foothills in late June, *Penstemon virens* goes along, clothing the hillsides under the ponderosa pines in sheets of blue. Some years are more spectacular than others. However, when they are combined with scattered plants of whisk broom parsley, *Harbouria trachypleura*; golden banner, *Thermopsis divaricarpa*; and the odd senecio—the effect is even more stunning.

In the rock garden a partially shady location is required for *Penstemon virens*, whereas *P. procerus*, a much less common plant, will grow in full sun provided its roots are kept moist. A location along with shooting stars, *Dodecatheon pulchellum*, and *Iris missouriensis* is suitable.

An even more spectacular flower, *Penstemon alpinus* (which should be forgiven its name since it ranges from the foothills to the subalpine zone), is notable wherever it occurs. It requires a less moist situation, and the 15 in. stalks carry showy bright blue flowers. Occasionally they may be tinged with pink or even be completely pink. A less commonly found species, *P. barbatus,* is known as red beardtongue. Found most often on the Western Slope, it is a taller plant, for an open rock garden situation.

Perhaps in greatest contrast to the penstemons is *Pediocactus simpsonii,* the mountain ball cactus. At lower elevations of the montane zone, west of Denver, they grow together in the open ponderosa woodland. The pink of the cactus is a forerunner to the later beauty of *Penstemon virens.* Its 3–4 in. wide ball is often half-hidden amongst the forest floor debris. Treat it more like a garden plant than a cactus-corner speciality, though it must still have excellent drainage. Also from the same locale, the little nodding onion, *Allium cernuum,* is occasionally planted in the rock garden along with pink-flowered *A. geyeri,* another wide-ranging species.

Pediocactus simpsonii. Photo by Vernon Tomppert

An extremely common plant in all zones except the plains is the Colorado state flower, *Aquilegia caerulea.* Perhaps overly large for the rock garden traditionalist or for many of the smaller gardens, it can be used effectively in semiwoodland garden areas. You may find it short-lived, but it generally reproduces itself—though not always where you intended it to grow. Less commonly grown, *A. elegantula,* from the western montane slopes, has a much more delicate appearance. Its red and yellow flowers are carried on very thin stalks, and it should be planted in partial shade unless it is given generous moisture.

Much more diminutive and appealing to lovers of alpine plants are the saxifrages. Unfortunately only two are fairly widespread in the montane zone: *Saxifraga rhomboidea,* the snowball saxifrage, grows randomly in the ponderosa woodland, while *S. bronchialis,* the spotted saxifrage, can be found growing on almost vertical rock faces. But in no way does the latter bear blossoms to surpass many of those already well-known to rock gardeners. One saxifragaceous plant endemic to Colorado, growing only in a few localized areas of the upper montane among large boulders and rocks, is *Telesonix jamesii,* formerly known as *Boykinia* or even *Saxifraga.* This plant is most accessible on the Pikes Peak road above Glen Cove, but it is also found in one location in Rocky Mountain National Park. Such a gem for the rock garden! It can be grown from seed, when obtainable, or divided; and it is not difficult in cultivation if given some protection from extremes of sunlight by being planted in partially shaded crevices. Give it time to mature for flower production.

Also creating beauty in its own right, *Campanula rotundifolia* is widely scattered in the zone. Some years it is prolific, while at other times it is almost absent. Though it is too weedy for many, it makes an interesting addition to the shady or north-facing rough stone wall. Quite different is *C. parryi,* which grows in the moister grassy areas of the upper reaches of our zone. Its blue to purple flowers are borne singly on 5–7 in. stems, but it is not the most cooperative plant in cultivation, and of course, there are many other campanulas already in the alpine book with which it must compete.

Two woodland plants requiring a moist, acid medium are the delicate *Linnaea borealis,* or twin flower, and *Chimaphila umbellata,* or pipsissewa. In Colorado's dry conditions and often extremely low humidity, they are considered difficult.

Another plant, very dissimilar in character, is *Calochortus gunnisonii,* the mariposa lily, which comes from open meadows; this plant again, is not as easy as one would like. Perhaps we try to look after it too well.

At the opposite end of cultivation is the three-flowered avens, or *Erythrocoma (Geum) triflora,* a plant from grassy areas which is also occasionally found among the aspen. The three nodding flowers, very distinctive though not colorful, are held several inches above attractive foliage. They are followed by clusters of seeds quite similar to those of the pasqueflower.

The deep blue of *Delphinium nelsonii* turns up in many places. This small relative of the enormous garden hybrids is found in open areas of ponderosa forests and in some grasslands as well. Named after Dr. Aven Nelson, professor of botany at the University of Wyoming for over 50 years, it can be grown in the wilder areas of the rock garden, though it may behave as an annual.

More primitive, but also growing among and around rocks in the forest region, is the *Woodsia oregana* fern. Along with the lady fern, *Athyrium filix-femina,* and the brittle fern, *Cystopteris fragilis,* it can be used in the rock garden. All of these plants tend to produce their foliage early in the season, then dry up and become dormant as summer progresses. Highly organic soils should be their medium; their location, among the rock crevices.

Two quite spectacular floral displays are offered by *Oenothera caespitosa* and *Sedum lanceolatum (S. stenopetalum). Oenothera caespitosa*'s 3–4 in. flowers are produced early in the day; morning primrose may be a more apt title. At peak times in June it makes a white carpet. *Sedum lanceolatum* relies on large numbers of tiny blossoms for effect, but it is, nevertheless, very colorful. Morning primrose spreads by underground stolons and has the habit of ending up somewhere other than where it was planted. The stonecrop propagates itself by innumerable seeds. This plant may be monocarpic as well.

Mitella pentandra. Photo by Vernon Tomppert

Mimulus guttatus. Photo by Allan Taylor

Flowers of the Parks

Among the distinctions of the parks described earlier are the notable masses of *Dodecatheon pulchellum* and *Iris missouriensis* in their wet locations. These two plants can easily be transferred into the rock garden, but today's commercial selections are a far cry from those naturally occurring types, which are also remarkable. Both these plants require moderate amounts of moisture, but again, nature is adaptive, and the iris can occasionally be found on apparently quite dry hillsides.

One cannot describe South Park without mention of the glorious stands of *Gentianopsis (Gentiana) thermalis,* the fringed gentian. More work needs to be done on its cultivation for the rock garden; it may be that the bog garden is the answer. In North Park, *Gentiana (Pneumonanthe) affinis* is more common, though its almost closed blossoms are less spectacular. Another plant of the North and Middle Parks, but from dry locales, is *Phlox hoodii.* A close relative to *P. bryoides,* it makes large spreading clumps with white flowers. Given good drainage, this fine group, including *P. multiflora,* is highly successful in the rock garden. Again, overculturing may destroy the plant or reduce flower production. After a mild winter, more flowers are produced, though the plants may be perfectly hardy in severe winters. Down in the San Luis Valley is *P. longifolia,* a rather variable plant ranging from white to rose. Good selections should be introduced into the general wealth of rock garden phloxes, though competition with those already established will be severe.

Primula incana, the birds-eye primrose, grows in the wet meadows of North and South Parks, but the small *P. egaliksensis,* which mingles with *P. incana* in South Park, is unusual in that it occurs only there and in the arctic. Again, boggy requirements may be needed to insure these primroses' survival.

More penstemons frequent drained areas of these unique sections of the montane zone. Two of them are creeping in nature, quite different from those discussed earlier. *Penstemon crandallii* forms mats just a few inches high, but the lowest mat is created by *P. caespitosus,* which rarely reaches 2 in. *Penstemon teucrioides* creeps along with gray-foliaged stems, and it will stand drier conditions. It is often found inhabiting stands of sagebrush on gravelly slopes. Now that these penstemons are finding their way into cultivation, we will see them used more often, not only as ground covers, but also as featured rock plants.

The lowly *Lewisia rediviva,* or bitter root, grows in Middle Park near Granby on gravel slopes. This lovely Montana state flower has rose-colored blooms and small rosettes of linear leaves. It was widely used by the Indians, who prepared the roots for food, cooking them a long time to get rid of the bitterness.

Conclusion

We leave the parks with a feeling of wonder. To find these floral kaleidoscopes in the midst of what is predominantly a forested zone makes us marvel at the complexities of nature. Yet for all its wetness, especially South Park, this area supplies a surprising number of plants for the rock garden. Not only does the endangered *Lilium philadelphicum* grow here in the aspen grove and occasionally the lowly *Cornus canadensis,* but the very commonly used erigeron, anemone and aquilegia abound in glorious array. Given water, patience, and an understanding of their root structures, we can grow not only the inhabitants of the parks but many others from drier areas of the montane zone. The "in-between" montane region, neither an alpine nor a foothills area, can be yet another source of beauty to all would-be "alpiners."

References

Graham, Edward H. 1937. *Botanical studies in the Uinta Basin of Utah and Colorado.* Annals of the Carnegie Museum, Vol. 26. Pittsburgh: Carnegie Institute.

Marr, John W. 1961. *Ecosystems of the East Slope of the Front Range in Colorado.* Boulder: University of Colorado Press.

Ramaley, Francis. 1927. *Colorado plant life.* Boulder: University of Colorado Press.

Vankat, John L. 1979. *The natural vegetation of North America.* New York: John Wiley and Sons, Inc.

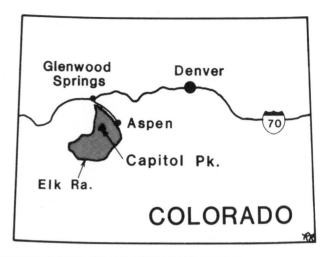

16

A Rock Scrambler's Flora: Special Plants of the Colorado Rockies

by Loraine Yeatts

Imagine the climber, clinging to a bare granite rock face, fingers probing the hidden recesses of a narrow, vertical crevice for a secure hold that will enable her, ultimately, to reach the summit. In this hostile alpine environment, with wind and cold wrenching my being, I gain my greatest respect for the plants that endure here. In this same crevice a tiny draba, fresh with vitality, clings tenaciously to the rock, capable of far more than mere survival. Though my survival may depend on my ability to leave at the appropriate time, these plants are here because of their ability to adapt.

The Colorado Rocky Mountains provide many opportunities to see, study and photograph favorite rock plants in their natural habitat. As I push past timberline on Capitol Peak in the Elk Range of Colorado, the exhilaration of altitude sets my mind free-wheeling, searching for reasons why rock plants hold me under their spell. Is it their toughness, symmetry, brilliant flower color, their fragrance? Sometimes an aura is created, by the isolation of bare rock which surrounds each plant, placing it on center stage for the moment I view it. At other times the tundra becomes ablaze with color as many species compete simultaneously for attention. I want to know each plant's name and why it occupies this special niche in the alpine ecosystem. The many botanists who have preceded me, providing answers to some of my questions, have only sharpened the thrill of discovery. The ultimate Rocky Mountain high is a windswept summit ridge rock garden, unplanned by man, tended by nature.

Paleobotany, Paleogeology, Paleoclimate

Today's Rocky Mountain flora is not here by accident. Plant geneology traces the development of some remarkable family trees. Critical evaluation of fossil floras throughout the area points to

Loraine Yeatts is a well-known Denver nature photographer with an extensive knowledge of native plants, which she seeks out on trips and climbs throughout the western United States. She holds a BS degree in physics from Mundelein College and pursued graduate studies at tne University of Arizona. She lives and gardens in Golden, Colorado, and is a volunteer collector of native plants for the Kathryn Kalmbach Herbarium at Denver Botanic Gardens. She is conducting a plant survey of South Table Mountain in Golden.

origins in the early Paleozoic era over 500 million years ago when plants, other than algae, were rare. By the Pennsylvanian period of the late Paleozoic, about 300 million years ago, the fossil record indicates a swampy lowland area forested by fast-growing, soft-tissued "trees" indicative of a warm, moist climate.

Conifers, with an understory of ferns, flourished during the Triassic and Jurassic periods of the Mesozoic era. Around 190 million years ago the huge flood plain of southern Utah and northern Arizona became a repository for massive conifer-type logs, now silicified and exposed in Petrified National Forest, Arizona. As the Jurassic sea withdrew across Colorado and Utah, late in the period, a vast sheet of mud and clay trapped dinosaurs and plants in what is now known as the Morrison Formation, an easily accessible documentation of the past.

Modern floras began in the Cretaceous period of the Mesozoic era when the dominant conifers were experiencing increasing competition from rapidly developing flowering plants. The North American continent was still extensively covered by sea, but it had assumed its present shape and size by the end of the period, about 65 million years ago. The fossil forests of the Rocky Mountain region confirm the existence of a much wetter, warmer, temperate-to-subtropical climate in the past, with temperature variations minimized due to the proximity of Cretaceous seas. Late Cretaceous flora show the presence of many present-day genera such as *Sequoia, Gingko,* and *Araucaria* (Cronquist et al. 1972). Angiosperms had become more abundant and diverse than non-flowering plants, spreading into every corner of the globe, imparting a modern appearance to the flora (Levin 1978).

During the Tertiary period of the Cenozoic era, climate made a gradual transition from subtropical to warm temperate, with progressive drying as Rocky Mountain range elevations increased. During the Oligocene epoch of this period, 26 to 38 million years ago, flora preserved in Florissant Fossil Beds National Monument west of Colorado Springs, Colo., had become differentiated in moisture and temperature-sensitive vegetational units. Woodland, savanna, chaparral, and thorn shrub were all present, encompassing many present-day genera. *Celtis, Quercus, Rhus, Cercocarpus, Mahonia* are still found in the area while others such as *Prosopis, Bursera, Zizyphus* have migrated south to warmer climates. By the end of the Miocene epoch the Great Basin portion of the Rocky Mountain region had become semiarid, with 15 to 25 in. of annual precipitation and a flora very similar to the present (Cronquist et al. 1972).

The Pleistocene epoch of the Quaternary period saw the advance and recession of four major glaciers and continued crustal uplift in the Colorado Rocky Mountains and most of the globe's major ranges in the Northern Hemisphere. Plants experienced no great innovations during this period, but rather a steady development toward the complex communities of the present (Levin 1978). The 40,000 year periodicity of glaciers caused plant migrations of hundreds of miles north and south and thousands of feet up and down mountainsides. The land bridges connecting continents during the ice ages allowed east-west migration also, giving the present-day alpine flora, isolated on higher peaks, its circumpolar character. Climate was, as it is now, a dominant force in the evolution and development of present-day Colorado Rocky Mountain flora.

Present Climate

Anyone who has lived in this area for any length of time realizes that the most predictable feature of Rocky Mountain weather is its unpredictability. We must, like weather forecasters, talk in terms of statistics and averages. The winter months of November through January tend to be relatively dry and windy, with only occasional storms dusting the high country with dry snow which blows clear of west-facing ridges to settle in the subalpine forest below or form cornices on the east side of the ridges.

The heaviest accumulation of snow occurs during March and April. By May the snow melts faster than it accumulates, providing the moisture necessary to promote rapid growth in alpine plants that have little time to waste before the relatively dry period of June. Solar intensity at high altitudes causes the tundra to dry rapidly, with rocky areas warming first. Plants on exposed ridges and scree slopes experience a peak blooming season from mid-June to the beginning of July, ahead of those in turf communities (Willard 1979). Early blooming allows the plants to set seed or reproduce vegetatively during the warmest part of the summer (Zwinger and Willard 1972). Thunderstorms in July and early August contribute additional moisture to the tundra. Below late-melting snow basins, the season of bloom extends into midsummer in less exposed areas. The storms become much less frequent by the end of August, and the tundra rapidly becomes dormant with relatively few fall-blooming species. July is the only dependably frost-free month above

Valley leading to Capitol Peak. Photo by Deane Hall

treeline. High winds and freezing night temperatures are encountered regularly during September and October. By November the tundra is at rest awaiting its life-renewing snow cover (Willard 1979).

Alpine Plant Adaptations

As with all plants, moisture accessibility is absolutely necessary to the survival of alpines. Over the millennia plants coped with climatic change by evolving in place, by migrating to an appropriate environment or some combination of these strategies (Cronquist et al. 1972). It seems to me that, when the neighborhood is bad, it is easier to move than to accommodate; but the fossil records show evidence of both strategies. Evolution is perhaps the more prevalent response to gradual climatic change, whereas the plant survivors of sudden change may be those with the ability to migrate quickly. One only has to think of how rapidly the dandelion has taken over the world. Evolution probably is responsible for the characteristic forms of alpine rock plants, and past migration has put them in places where they are able to survive, at high altitude in a semiarid climate.

Some of the variables affecting the amount of moisture available to these plants are wind, insolation, and temperature. Plant form is one response to wind, which can be unrelenting at the high altitude of the Rocky Mountain region. Gusts blast across the tundra from the west or north, often in excess of 100 miles per hour, scouring the landscape of anything not pinned down and desiccating all high-profile plants. Many plants form small cushions, circular mounds, which act as airfoils to efficiently shed the high winds, protecting the interior parts of the plants. This form is usually anchored securely to the ground by a long taproot.

The rosette-shaped plant—spreading its leaves flat against the ground in imbricate, spokelike fashion for maximum exposure to the sun—is even less of an obstacle to the wind than a cushion. Some plants grow flat against the ground producing dense mats, rooting at each stem node to stay in place. The boulders of talus slopes sometimes provide protection for larger plants snuggled against their east- or south-facing sides. Single- or few-stemmed plants such as the gentians are usually found on well-developed tundra in the company of taller, matted plants and grasses, rather than in open, exposed, rocky sites.

Aquilegia caerulea. Photo by Loraine Yeatts

The effects of insolation and temperature extremes on plants at high altitude are hard to differentiate, as plant response can be the same for either factor. Since growth occurs only at night in most species, and only at temperatures above 32°F , the active season is short, two months at most, on the tundra. This accounts for the preponderance of perennials above timberline. They are able to flower rapidly and set seed or reproduce vegetatively during the warmest part of summer. The stems and leaves of many tundra plants have a reddish cast, especially early and late in the season. Studies have shown that the red pigments, anthocyanins, impart better tolerance to cold by converting incident light rays to heat more effectively. This gives red-colored plants an early-season advantage over green-leaved plants (Zwinger and Willard 1972). Temperature and sun protection is afforded by variety of surfaces. The fur coats often worn by the earliest bloomers reflect visible light rays while trapping heat rays in a minigreenhouse effect. They also provide insulation from the cold night temperatures. Leaves and stems are sometimes succulent and waxy, minimizing dehydration. One must admire the variety of coping strategies nature provides these high-altitude plants.

Special Plants of the Colorado Rockies

Sheltered by gigantic Engelmann spruce and refreshed by the cool, invigorating morning air, we feel ready to climb. As we move around the krummholz islands of spruce, Capitol Peak's imposing 3,000 ft. north-facing escarpment presents itself. This mountain has been our family's nemesis, eluding our efforts to reach its summit on three previous attempts which span 18 years. This is the last summit my husband needs to complete climbs of all the Colorado 14,000 ft. mountains. Remembering the rich diversity of plants in the area from previous trips, I decide to keep a record of all the blooming plants I see while we are here. Our sons carry a small rocket and launching rod in the hope of firing a salute to our success from the summit.

Although my favorite plants are usually rooted in rock or rocky soil, it is hard to ignore this mosaic of color, displayed in perfect lighting, and beckoning the photographer in me. As I reach for my camera, my family calls from above. I imprint the image on my mind: lupine, paintbrush, columbine, penstemon, marsh marigold, globeflower, anemone, monkshood, sunflower, en masse. I hurry to catch up as the timberline meadow steepens to a well-developed tundra slope with a slippery gravel path worn by those who have gone before us.

Mountain dryad, *Dryas octopetala* ssp. *hookeriana*, blankets the scree soil higher on the slope with dark green leathery leaves almost hidden by the showy 8-petaled, creamy white flowers. Plumose seed heads, typical of the rose family, glow in the low light. The evergreen leaves are protected beneath from sun-heated gravel by a thick felt of white, tomentose hairs. This true pioneer is probably the most successful stabilizer of alpine gravel and scree slopes (Zwinger and Willard 1972). Its tough branches form a thick mat against the ground, catching windblown debris and dirt which gradually builds soil under the plant. The interwoven root system just below the ground's surface anchors the mat in place. This is one of the few plants besides the legumes which contributes nitrogen to the soil. Eventually, as soil and fertility build, other plants invade the dryad mats causing them to die out. Circumpolar in distribution, it is at its prime on Pikes Peak, west of Colorado Springs. Here it seems to flow down the slope, forming terraced steps and risers, unbroken by the invasion of other plants for many feet. This undulating landscape is produced by solifluction, the flow of saturated soil on an impermeable layer of frozen ground or bedrock. One wonders if the specialized circumstance in which dryad grows would make it impossible to cultivate in a lowland rock garden.

Considering the specialized and restricted conditions under which the dryad survives reminds me of another rose family member far removed from the granite of Capitol Peak. One of my favorite rock plants, rock spiraea or rock-mat, *Petrophytum caespitosum*, softens the crevices and cracks of limestone bedrock from South Dakota west to California and south to Arizona. In the canyon country of the Colorado Plateau it often forms huge hanging draperies on the undersides of limestone jumps or pouroffs (dry waterfalls) at elevations under 5,000 ft. In Notch Canyon in the House Range of western Utah, tightly packed rosettes of rock spiraea cascade from the horizontal crevices of a magnificent, steep-walled, limestone rock garden. I have also seen it at timberline in the calcareous portions of the Snake Range of eastern Nevada. Individual rosettes, less than the size of a thumbnail, produce a tiny, compact, oval spike of white flowers late in the summer. Equally attractive in or out of bloom, this is an amazing rock plant. In nature, this plant seems to grow only on limestone. Whether rock gardeners succeed with other soils remains to be seen.

As we cross Daly Pass to follow a route on the south side of the summit ridge, across large talus and boulders, and up a snowfield to the ridge, the first wisps of clouds begin to appear in the crystalline azure sky. Soon after attaining the ridge, a sheer knife edge dropping thousands of feet on each side must be traversed. With care, it is not difficult, but my mind is no longer focused on plants. As the clouds continue to gather, we hurry the last half-mile to the summit, stopping only briefly to record the event on film and fire the rocket. To the west some of the clouds have elevated to the status of thunderheads and rain is starting to fall. Realizing the length of time we must be exposed on the ridge to possible lightning makes us move with urgency. By the time we reach the knife edge, isolated storm clouds are less than a mile away, and I experience the eerie feeling that the hair on my head is standing on end, crawling with static electricity. At the same instant I notice my older son, who has just crossed the knife edge, pull the buzzing metal rocket launching rod from his pack and heave it over the edge. The ability to bound over boulders is directly proportional to the closeness of lightning, and on this day I find that my ability is exceptional as we plummet off the ridge. Glissading down the snowfield to the relative safety of the large boulder field below, we crouch down to await a storm that never arrives. As we grab a bite of lunch I realize that we never heard any thunder and resolve to continue down at a much more leisurely pace.

Plants that blurred by during our hasty retreat come back into focus. Crevices in the smooth rock of the knife ridge are a typical habitat for another pioneer plant, big-rooted spring beauty, *Claytonia megarhiza*, of the portulaca family. Depending on exposure, it is possible to find spring beauty rosettes crowned with delicate, 5-petaled white-to-pinkish flowers from early summer to early fall. The spatulate, fleshy, reddish green leaves are arranged in spokelike fashion around the top of a taproot which can be thicker than a man's thumb and extend 6 ft. into a crevice or the ground. The red pigment so evident in the leaves offers cold protection to this plant, which fills niches and colors ridge top fellfields throughout western North America. The first frost turns the leaves a brilliant, glowing red.

It is easy to describe the habitat of big-rooted spring beauty as an alpine desert when I recall the dudleyas I have seen in similar situations in the Tinajas Altas Mountains of southern Arizona. Only the high altitude is missing, lessening the extent of the cold. Although *Dudleya pulverulenta* is in a different plant family, Crassulaceae, the adaptation of both to cope with the desertlike conditions is the same. Both are taprooted in granite cracks where effective rainfall is very low. They share similar plant forms, succulence, tolerance of extreme temperature ranges, high insolation and evaporation rates, and short growing periods. The southern desert plants become dormant to cope with high summer heat, growing only a short time during the cooler spring months.

Other plants in these two families emphasize the similarities between alpine and lowland deserts. Yellow stonecrop, *Sedum lanceolatum (S. stenopetalum),* of the Crassulaceae, found in almost any well-drained rocky area from crevice to fellfield, spans an 8,000 ft. altitudinal range from foothills to mountaintops. It must be western North America's most adaptable rock plant. Pellet-sized rosettes of tiny beadlike leaves, with a waxy surface and filled with mucilaginous sap, retain water under drought conditions and minimize the amount of surface exposed to the sun. Adjusting its blooming season to the altitude, stonecrop hides its foliage completely under a 1 in. high carpet of yellow flowers and can be found blooming from early summer to early fall. A portulaca family member, fame-flower, *Talinum brevifolium,* seeks shallow slickrock pocket gardens of exposed Navajo and Cedar Mesa sandstone on the Colorado Plateau of southeastern Utah. Its fleshy, terete leaves clothe short, decumbent stems which bear oversized pink flowers reminiscent of garden portulaca. The similar adaptations of all of these plants allow them to flourish in habitats inhospitable to almost any other plant life.

With energy restored by lunch, and spirits lifted by the subsidence of nature's pyrotechnics, we traverse gently upward crossing boulderfield, talus and fellfield en route to Daly Pass. Talus is an accumulation of gravity-sorted rocks, larger than fist-sized, below steep slopes or cliffs. The largest rocks, some house-sized, at the base of the slope, constitute the boulderfield we are crossing; the rocks are gradually reduced in size up the slope. As the steepness of the slope moderates, talus gives way to fellfield, a type of tundra characterized by about 50 percent bare rock with stabilized gravel forming rudimentary soil for the cushion and mat plants interspersed among the rocks. Typical of these is *Senecio (Ligularia) soldanella,* an uncommon, interesting plant worthy of consideration for the rock garden.

Senecio soldanella. Photo by Loraine Yeatts

While on the talus slope I start finding thick-leaved draba, *Draba crassa,* single-stemmed plants tucked in the crevices of large boulders, and multiple-stemmed plants hugging the ground against boulders. *Draba,* one of my pet genera, has become highly diversified as it ranges over western North America. Perhaps they are able to evolve more quickly to adapt to specific site requirements, but for whatever reasons, they belong to a large genus of plants which are difficult to separate taxonomically. The long-petioled, obovate, glabrous leaves make *D. crassa* unmistakable. Its range in Colorado is mostly on the western side of the Continental Divide. My favorite relative of this plant is a Rocky Mountain endemic, twisted-pod draba, *D. streptocarpa,* which occasionally is abundant on the Front Range of Colorado. Tiny clump-forming rosettes of coarsely hairy leaves inhabit fellfields which are free of snow by early June, allowing them to bloom quickly and set seed. In spite of their small size, the intensely yellow flowers are hard to miss against the drab tundra background which is just beginning to green. Following the flowers, pods develop into elongated, miniature corkscrews, a distinctive feature allowing positive identification. Clawless draba (*D. exunguiculata*) is another special Rocky Mountain endemic, much harder to find. It prefers a ridgetop fellfield, with little competition from other plants, where it forms tufted clumps. Although the yellow petals are not especially conspicuous, the sepals fade to yellow and cling to the developing seed pods, an interesting effect. Drabas belong to the mustard family, one of the better represented families on the tundra.

A fairy primrose, *Primula angustifolia,* winks at me from a sheltered, lichen-encrusted, granite boulder crevice, an unusual habitat for this plant. Normally found in fellfields and turf communities, this widespread Rocky Mountain endemic is one of the first tundra plants to bloom. Yellow-eyed, magenta flowers, scarcely one-half inch across, rise singly on short stems above small tufts of obovate leaves. I remember a gravel slope on Pikes Peak where they were blooming so profusely that they colored the tundra magenta. Usually though, they are more widely separated. One cannot talk about fairy primrose without mentioning alpine forget-me-not, *Eritrichium aretioides (E. nanum),* which is usually blooming at the same time and in the same community. The pea-sized rosettes are so tightly packed and densely hairy that the plant looks like a fur cushion against the ground. To capture on film the depth and richness of the yellow-eyed blue that saturates the tiny flowers has been one of life's unmet challenges for me. It is equally impossible to describe the colors, which range from light sky blue to deep, velvety, purple-blue on various cushions. Squaretop Mountain in the Front Range west of Denver, Colorado, puts on an exceptional display of alpine forget-me-not on its eastern summit ridge about the fourth week of June.

Another favorite fellfield resident, which charms me wherever I find it, is rock jasmine, *Androsace chamaejasme* ssp. *carinata.* This diminutive primrose family member also forms furry mats and has yellow-eyed, white to cream colored, fragrant flowers which look a bit like white forget-me-nots. All of these magnificent tundra jewels can be enjoyed only by those willing to brave the wind and cold of an occasional late winter storm, for their blooming period is early and brief. After the show is over the various mats seem to melt into the greens and beiges of the muted tundra tapestry.

There are several aster family members found on the tundra ridges. Pinnate-leaved daisy, *Erigeron pinnatisectus,* which prefers rock ledges, crevices and the driest of fellfield gravels, produces showy heads of blue-violet rayflowers surrounding a yellow disc, and mounds of fernlike, soft-hairy foliage, belying its tough character. It can be found in bloom from early spring through late summer. Alpine goldenweed, *Tonestus (Haplopappus) pygmaeus,* forms gravel-hugging cushions on ridges, and covers itself with bright yellow flowers during late summer.

Near Daly Pass we pause for a drink and I practically sit on a plant I have never seen before. I realize it is an eriogonum but its further identification will have to await our return home, where I can refer to the appropriate plant key (Harrington 1954). The genus *Eriogonum* of the buckwheat family appears to be another taxonomic nightmare, with rapidly evolving plants dispersed throughout western North America. The genus contains many delightful varieties adapted to life in a rocky home. Cushion buckwheat, *Eriogonum ovalifolium,* on the Colorado Plateau of western Colorado and southeastern Utah, has capitate, white-to-pink flowerheads like globular pincushions waving on naked stems above mound-forming mats of hairy gray foliage. On a lava-capped mesa just west of Denver, James' buckwheat, *E. jamesii* var. *flavescens,* colors the bedrock with its lemon yellow flowers for a few weeks in late June. Several weeks later, alpine golden buckwheat, *E. flavum* var. *xanthum,* blooms in the high country fellfields to the west. This is a dwarf version of the former lowland buckwheat. All these Rocky Mountain endemics should be rock gardeners' delights. Upon our return home, my Capitol Peak buckwheat proves to be *E. coloradense (E. multiceps* ssp. *coloradense),* a rare plant, not recorded previously from Pitkin County. The thrill of discovery makes botany ever more exciting.

Chaenactis alpina. Photo by Loraine Yeatts

Crossing Daly Pass, we reach the scree slope above our timberline meadow campsite, and I discover yet another interesting plant overlooked while climbing. Scree, which is smaller than talus, represents an accumulation of unsorted rock fragments, varying from about an inch in diameter to fist-sized, resulting from in-place weathering. Compared to the fellfield, relatively fewer plants are able to cope with its untenable environment. One that does, alpine dusty maiden, *Chaenactis alpina,* anchored in place by a long taproot, builds a 4 in. cushion of tufted fernlike foliage which traps wind-blown soil and stabilizes slope slippage from above. Commonly, members of the aster family have composite flower heads consisting of central tubular disc flowers surrounded by ray flowers. In this case only the central disc flowers are present, with stamens protruding like pinheads. Although the flowers are not showy, the plant as a whole presents very pleasing texture. A close relative, *C. stevioides,* is a desert-dweller of southeastern Utah. The most memorable habitat in which I discovered it was a high bench above the Dirty Devil River. The plants were uniformly spaced over a large area of flat-lying desert pavement. To get an accurate picture of desert pavement, imagine a giant skipping across carefully fitted flagstones cracking them into thousands of small pieces. White pincushion-head flowers on thin branched stems seemed to float above the small rosettes of foliage supporting them, each head highlighted against the dark colored pavement. Except for lack of slope, this habitat is a parallel environment to the scree of the alpine desert.

We slip-slide down the scree, returning to camp, exhilarated by the day's successes. Having allowed ourselves an extra day for climbing, as a hedge against inclement weather, we now have a free day to luxuriate in the Colorado Rockies' most beautiful scenery. It is a day of gentle hiking, fishing, flower watching and reflection. I find that I have become fascinated with the concept of plant response to an impoverished habitat, whether it be rocky alpine substrate or low altitude desert. It seems apparent that plant form is a common element of adaptation and that a short, intense flowering period occurs for both types of flora. Other questions run through my mind and I list them for future research. 1) Why are some families and genera favored over others? The genus *Asclepias*, which occurs commonly in the desert, is one I have never seen above timberline. 2) Why are endemic plants partial to certain genera; are these genera capable of evolving more efficiently than others? What is the percentage of alpine endemics with respect to total alpine flora, compared to the percentage of total endemics with respect to total floral population? 3) Which of these special treasures are most adaptable to cultivation? Are those specific to narrow range or environment more difficult to cultivate? 4) What plants are most likely to survive the next 50 million years, assuming that man does not disrupt the environment faster than nature?

Arriving at the car, I tally my list of blooming plants for the area: 97 species. The Elk Range is certainly a botanist's dreamland. The special plants reviewed here are the opportunists and pioneers of the floral kingdom, true rock scramblers, filling niches where few others dare to go.

References

Kartez, J. T., and R. Kartez. 1980. *A synonymized checklist of the vascular flora of the United States, Canada, and Greenland.* Vol. 2. Chapel Hill, N. C.: University of North Carolina Press.

Kearney, Thomas H., and Robert H. Peebles. 1951. *Arizona flora.* Berkeley: University of California Press.

Levin, H. L. 1978. *The earth through time.* Philadelphia: W. B. Saunders Co.

Welsh, Stanley L. 1984. "Utah flora: Polygonaceae". *The Great Basin Naturalist* 43: 170–357. Provo, Utah: Brigham Young University.

Welsh, Stanley L., and G. Moore. 1973. *Utah plants: Tracheophyta.* 3rd ed. Provo, Utah: Brigham Young University Press.

Willard, B. E. 1979. *Plant sociology of the alpine tundra, Trail Ridge, Rocky Mountain National Park, Colorado. Colorado School of Mines Quarterly* 74(4). Golden, Colo.: Colorado School of Mines.

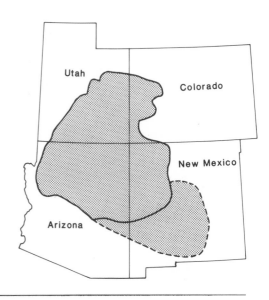

Section IV

Colorado Plateau: Canyons and Color

Photo courtesy Arizona Office of Tourism

Bryce Canyon. Photo courtesy Utah Travel Council

17

Canyonlands

by Karen Trout

On the western edge of the southern Rocky Mountains within the physiographic province known as the Colorado Plateau lie the canyonlands of southeastern Utah, a series of high plateaus and vast tablelands deeply dissected by the Colorado River and its tributaries.

To the south lies Navajo country and the Painted Desert of northern Arizona. To the west are the high forested plateaus: the Aquarius, the Markagunt, the Paunsaugunt, the Fish Lake, and more, nine plateaus in all. On the north the Book Cliffs stretch for miles bordering the great Tavaputs Plateaus.

The structure of the Colorado Plateau consists of layer upon layer of nearly horizontal sedimentary rock formations, only slightly faulted and little deformed over geologic time. As the Rockies were being uplifted to their present elevation, during early Tertiary time, the entire Plateau also rose, as much as three miles, and may still be slowly rising. The general elevation is now higher than 5,000 ft. with some plateaus and mountains rising above 11,000 ft.

The Plateau's extensive layers of sedimentary rock are gently tilted toward the northeast, leaving the oldest layers exposed on the southwest side in the Grand Canyon and on plateau rims overlooking the much lower Basin and Range province. The Plateau's youngest rock layers, of Tertiary and Quaternary age, are exposed in basins in the northeast.

As the Plateau was uplifted, rapid downcutting of already existing rivers produced entrenched meanders and deeply incised canyons. During late Tertiary time several episodes of volcanic activity resulted in numerous cinder cones and lava flows, volcanic necks, dikes, and sills—eroded fragments of igneous activity that can still be seen today.

Isolated dome mountains, such as the La Sals, the Henrys, and the Abajos (or Blue Mountains) are technically laccoliths formed by the intrusion of molten, igneous rock between sedimentary layers, doming up the overlying formations and exposing the granite core.

Over the long expanse of geologic time, erosion and an arid climate have shaped and sculpted this vast land of bare rock into striking forms. The canyonlands' major rivers, the Colorado and its tributaries—the Green, the San Juan, the Dirty Devil and the Escalante—have carved spectacular canyons hundreds of feet deep through the tablelands. Canyons are of every size: there are mazes of canyons, from the huge complex corridors of Glen and Grand Canyons to the tiny, intimate rock

Karen Trout became enchanted with the canyon country of the Southwest as a photography student at Colorado Mountain College in Glenwood Springs, Colorado, when her geology class visited the region almost weekly in spring and early summer. A developing interest in Southwestern plants led to a major in botany at Fort Lewis College in Durango and to further exploration of the canyonlands with her mountain-climbing, geologist husband. Her interest in Western botany continues, and she is now responsible for Denver Botanic Gardens' collections of gesneriads, subtropical and tropical bulbs, and tropical woody plants.

passageways high up in the massive rock layers of the Navajo and Entrada Sandstone.

The sedimentary formations in which most of the canyons of southeast Utah are found are of late Permian to Cretaceous age. They are primarily sandstones, shales, siltstones, mudstones, and conglomerates with some limestone and evaporites. The great cliff-forming layers are made of massive, resistant sandstone. Interspersed with these layers are softer shales that form slopes, sometimes interbedded with small sandstone benches or lenses of resistant rock. They are highly varied and striking in color: buff and tan and yellow layers of solidified sand dunes. There are maroon, mauve and orange sheer rock walls, pinnacles and arches; blue-gray and purple badlands and valleys.

Many of these rock formations can be followed throughout southeast Utah—so distinctive that they can be recognized as the same layer when exposed in sites 100 miles distant from each other.

Spring comes first to the lower canyons of the Colorado River. A riparian ecosystem with its constant supply of moisture prevails along permanent streams and rivers and near springs; here Fremont's cottonwood (*Populus fremontii*) often forms large groves. Willows (*Salix*) and tamarisk line these waterways, forming dense thickets, and along the sandy beaches are communities of cattails (*Typha*), horsetails (*Equisetum*), and various species of rushes (*Juncus*), reeds (*Phragmites*), tules (*Scirpus*) and sedges (*Carex*).

Tamarisk or salt cedar (*Tamarix ramosissima*) is an arborescent shrub with slender, scalelike leaves resembling juniper foliage, and numerous spikes of tiny purple flowers in March and April. It has the appearance of airiness, of laciness, but in reality, tamarisk is a weed out of control. It was introduced from the Old World between 1899 and 1915, for the purpose of controlling erosion along Southwestern riverbanks. The seeds possess a tuft of hairs and are easily dispersed, taking root quickly on the wet, sandy soil. In the ensuing years, tamarisk has spread eastward up the Colorado River drainage to the Colorado Plateau and has, unfortunately, taken over the habitat of many native plants favored by birds and small animals for food and shelter.

Netleaf hackberry (*Celtis reticulata*) with its thick, rough, sandpapery leaves, and single-leaf ash (*Fraxinus anomala*) are often found on the canyon bottoms. Although they are both more abundant along moist stream channels, they are also found widely scattered throughout the dry, rocky canyons and slopes of southeastern Utah.

Townsendia incana. Photo by Elizabeth Neese

The leaves of single-leaf ash are simple and rounded with opposite branching. This tree has the distinction among its many relatives of being the only species with simple leaves. Winged samaras appear in clusters in early summer.

Moving away from the rivers and streams, semiarid country prevails. Desert shrubs are largely dominant in the lower areas. Annual precipitation is generally less than 10 in. with high evaporation rates. Vegetation cover is sparse and liberally spaced to utilize all available water in the form of rainfall and runoff. These plants have devised a variety of adaptations in order to thrive in their dry surroundings.

Some of the most common shrubs found growing on these dry, rugged slopes and desert flats include shadscale (*Atriplex confertifolia*) and 4-wing saltbush (*Atriplex canescens*). Shadscale is a somewhat spiny shrub with silvery gray leaves. It is usually 1–3 ft. tall and produces 2-winged seeds. Distinctive in the late summer, when its thick clusters of papery winged seeds mature, is 4-wing saltbush. It is somewhat taller than shadscale with scurfy, gray foliage. Many of these dryland species can tolerate some degree of alkalinity.

In early autumn, winterfat (*Eurotia (Ceratoides) lanata*) takes on a silvery appearance, its fluffy white seeds covering the upper third of the stems. It is a small shrub, woody only at the base, with densely hairy, gray leaves.

In areas with high concentrations of salts in the soil, greasewood (*Sarcobatus vermiculatus*) can be found. This large shrub has a coarse, scraggly appearance, its narrow, fleshy leaves often feeling greasy to the touch.

Chrysothamnus viscidiflorus, sticky-flowered rabbitbrush, produces golden flower heads in the fall. The entire plant is sticky to the touch. It is a small shrub with narrow, light green, slightly twisted leaves and white bark. Rabbits prefer it for both shelter and food.

In years of ample moisture, when rainfall has been adequate or exceptional, black-brush (*Coelogyne ramosissima*), blooms profusely in May and early June. It is a member of the rose family with yellow, 4-sepaled flowers and many stamens. A low shrub with opposite branching, its dark gray stems become spiny with age. During hot summers, black-brush conserves water by dropping many of its narrow, evergreen leaves. In years of drought it will not bloom at all. It prefers sandy soils, often forming extensive stands along the Colorado River drainage in southeast Utah.

Perennial forbs are sparse and scattered over rocky desert flats and sandy soils. Coppermallow

Physaria acutifolia
Photo by Elizabeth Neese

(*Sphaeralcea grossulariaefolia*), has salmon pink, 5-petaled flowers and many yellow stamens united into a column. It blooms in early spring and summer. Its leaves are similar to gooseberry leaves, deeply 3- to 5-lobed.

Round-leaved eriogonum (*Eriogonum ovalifolium*) is common at these low elevations. Its cream-colored, globose flower heads, often pink-tinged, are borne on scapose stems which arise from compact mats of oval or round basal leaves.

An early bloomer in clay and gravelly soils, Douglas' false yarrow (*Chaenactis douglasii*) is a member of the sunflower family. Its white or pinkish flower heads with exserted stamens and its pinnately divided blue-green leaves give the plant a fine, lacy appearance.

Trailing four o'clock (*Allionia incarnata*) can be found with desert shrubs in sandy soils, its stems often spreading out 2 ft. or more. Its showy blossoms are composed of petallike sepals in magenta and purple with bright yellow stamens. Rough mule's ears (*Wyethia scabra*) grows in very sandy sites and is adapted to life on the changing surface levels of the dunes. Forming large clumps, it has the capacity of rooting along stems that become covered with sand. The plant has large, yellow sunflowerlike blossoms and rough, hispid leaves.

Lepidium fremontii, desert peppergrass, is a bushy subshrub with numerous small white flowers having petals in the form of a cross. Its ovate, ascending seedpods are characteristic of the mustard family, Brassicaceae.

Lepidium perfoliatum. a relative of desert peppergrass, is a weedy annual at lower elevations. Its upper leaves are clasping onto the stem, hence the name *perfoliatum.* Other annuals in this semidesert scrubland include several species of evening primrose (*Oenothera*) and *Eriogonum.*

In the southern reaches of the canyonlands, the Cedar Mesa sandstone has been eroded and carved by water and time to produce a distinctive system of canyons, pinnacles, alcoves and arches. The peach and white banded sandstone has been shaped into towering spires by slow erosion of the vertical joints in the rock. Crossbedding and ripple marks in the sandstone indicate that it was deposited in a shallow sea with a fluctuating shoreline in Permian time, about 250 million years ago.

Down in the canyons of the Cedar Mesa can be found some of the earliest spring bloomers. In March, tiny yellow flowers of Parry's biscuit-root (*Lomatium parryi*) are still hugging the ground. Its finely divided leaves and flowers in umbels are characteristic of the carrot family, Apiaceae. The thick starchy roots of *Lomatium* were ground into flour by early pioneers and Southwestern Indians, hence the common name "biscuit-root." Two species of yellow parsley related to *Lomatium,* and also found in canyonlands, are early-blooming *Cymopteris fendleri* and *C. newberryi.*

Townsendia incana, the Easter daisy, is aptly named, for it is one of the very first flowers to appear each spring. It is a low plant of the sunflower family with white or pink ray flowers and centers of yellow disk flowers. Its gray leaves form matted clumps in sandy soils.

Thompson's woolly locoweed, *Astragalus mollissimus* var. *thompsonae,* occurs throughout eastern and southern Utah. It has silvery, pinnately divided leaves and purple flowers that develop into curved pods, densely covered with tangled, white hairs. It can often be found in flower in April in these canyons. Crescent milkvetch (*A. amphioxys*) is another early blooming purple milkvetch. It prefers clay soils.

Light pink and white flowered umbels of the desert onion (*Allium textile*) appear with slender basal leaves from a subterranean bulb. By late spring, its seedheads are often fully developed.

A common, early-blooming member of the mustard family, *Physaria newberryi,* or twinpod, has bright yellow, 4-petaled flowers and silvery gray, spatulate leaves. In fruit the plant is very distinctive, developing an inflated, papery, double-chambered pod. A very similar species, *P. australis,* is found in Arches National Park in eastern Utah and Colorado National Monument in western Colorado.

Another member of the mustard family with distinctive pods is the white-flowered spectacle pod, *Dithyrea wislezenii.* Its fruit is a flattened, double pod that resembles old-fashioned spectacles. It prefers sandy soils in the canyons, flowering in March.

Dwarf or Hood's phlox (*Phlox hoodii*) is found growing in low, cushionlike mats with its vivid pink-to-white flowers appearing just above sharp, needlelike leaves. It is common in dryland areas in sandy, gravelly and clay soils, and it is widespread in western North America. The range of the desert phlox (*P. austromontana*) overlaps that of Hood's phlox in the southern part of Canyonlands. Both species are often found in the pinyon-juniper woodlands that begin to appear at their lower limits in these canyons.

Pinus edulis, the pinyon pine, and *Juniperus osteosperma,* Utah juniper, are the two characteristic trees of the pinyon-juniper woodland, or pygmy forest, as it is sometimes called. Utah juniper is a broad, rounded, arborescent shrub with coarse, yellowish green, scalelike leaves and gray-brown,

Phlox hoodii
Photo by Loraine Yeatts

shredding bark. It is found on dry, rocky slopes at elevations lower than those of pinyon pine. Moving up the canyons, pinyon pine is observed scattered about with juniper. It is a bushy pine, preferring rocky places. Its needles occur in bundles of two, and it produces small cones that hold edible seeds or "nuts." These trees are found throughout the canyons and often form extensive stands on the mesas above.

Weathering in the Cedar Mesa sandstone characteristically produces overhangs on the vertical cliff faces. These natural shelters in quiet canyons were once the home of a prehistoric people, the earliest of whom made exquisite baskets and were named "Basketmakers" by early settlers. When the Navajos encountered them upon their arrival in the Southwest, probably in the 16th century, they called them the Anasazi, the Ancient Ones. There is evidence for the presence of the Basketmakers as early as the 1st century A.D. in the canyonlands of the Southwest. At this early date, they were seminomadic, growing squash and corn on the canyon bottoms where there was sufficient moisture.

Everywhere in the southern canyonlands there are traces of these enigmatic peoples. The canyons are riddled with their sandstone slab and masonry granaries, manos and metates (grinding stones) and ancient fire rings.

They utilized the plants of the canyons in a great variety of ways. The pinyon pine was a source of roof timbers and firewood, and its seeds and nuts were used as food. The shredding bark of the Utah juniper was woven into mats, thatching for roofs, and bedding.

Serviceberry (*Amelanchier utahensis*), a member of the rose family, is a large shrub with oval, toothed leaves. It produces dense clusters of fragrant 5-petaled blooms in early spring. Indians used the purplish blue berries for food in a variety of ways. This species can be found scattered on moist rocky hillsides in the canyons.

Cowania mexicana, or cliffrose, is found throughout Canyonlands on the rims of mesas and canyonsides. In full bloom the plant is covered with roselike, cream-colored flowers with many yellow stamens. The foliage of cliffrose was used for medicine by the Basketmakers and the stringy bark was braided into sandals, mats and clothing.

Indian women used the strong, pliable branches of 3-leaf sumac or squawbush (*Rhus trilobata*) in making baskets. The sticky, tart, red berries were made into a beverage and used in dyemaking. A very common shrub associated with pinyon and juniper, it is found on dry hillsides and in the canyons. Its shiny, deep green leaves are highly variable in size and indentation. Some individuals have leaves divided deeply into 3 leaflets; others may have only slightly lobed leaves. This woody shrub is a close relative of poison ivy (*Rhus (Toxicodendron) radicans*) which inhabits the shady, more moist canyon bottoms and sandy stream banks.

In the early spring, desert thorn or *tomatillo (Lycium pallidum)* bears showy, light green, trumpet-shaped flowers which develop into small, tomatolike fruits. It is in the same family as tomatoes and potatoes (Solanaceae). This spiny, medium-sized shrub with small, obovate leaves is often found growing close to prehistoric dwellings and is thought to have been used as food by the Indians.

Along the dry washes of the canyons, where ephemeral streams run only occasionally, several species of evening primrose grow on sandy benches beneath the cool groves of Fremont's cottonwood. *Oenothera caespitosa,* the stemless evening primrose, is among the most beautiful of desert flowers, with large, white, delicate petals, fading pink with age, and a tuft of long, toothed basal leaves.

Penstemon utahensis, Utah penstemon, is also fond of sandy soils and at once catches the eye with its elongate thyrse of crimson, tubular corollas with spreading, rounded petal lobes. Its opposite leaves have a bluish, glaucous cast. It can be found blooming as early as April.

Stemless actinea (*Hymenoxys acaulis*) produces bright yellow flowers on tall, leafless stalks arising from a bunch of densely hairy, basal, linear leaves. It prefers sandstone ledges and dry, rocky slopes. Parts of the plant were made into a medicinal beverage by Indians of the area.

Yellow beeplant (*Cleome lutea*) is an annual plant that can grow quite large. It is a member of the caper family closely related to the mustards, and like them it has four clawed, yellow petals, but its stamens are long, exserted from the corolla, and quite showy. Its fruits develop into long, narrow pods and its leaves are palmately compound with 3 to 5 leaflets. The juice of cleome was used by the Anasazi for black paint on pottery.

One of the most beautiful shrubs found growing in all of southern Utah is silver buffaloberry (*Shepherdia rotundifolia*). Its name alludes to attractive, rounded, silvery blue leaves that bear a scurfy pubescence. It is an early bloomer, often as early as March, on canyon slopes in the pinyon-juniper zone and higher.

Along these winding canyons, around the next turn of the wash, and far back in hidden alcoves are many fine rock art paintings and carvings of these ancient peoples. The petroglyphs are pecked into the hard, weathered outer sandstone surface with a stone or other pecking tool. There are strange figures with round shields for bodies, trapezoid-shaped figures with headdresses and antlers, hand prints, circles inside circles, mountain sheep and antelope. As yet there are no adequate explanations for their meaning and purpose: they remain a mystery.

On the canyon walls, in moist caves and alcoves where seeps and springs occur are lush, green hanging-gardens: maidenhair fern (*Adiantum capillus-veneris*), and helleborine orchids (*Epipactis gigantea*) cling to the cool, dripping rock. Helleborine's greenish-purple flowers, the delicate white flowers of *Habenaria sparsiflora,* the pastel shades of *Aquilegia micrantha,* and the bright, crimson blossoms of the Eastwood monkeyflower (*Mimulus eastwoodiae*) dot these green gardens with color. Both the aquilegia and the monkeyflower are endemic to the canyonlands.

These washes hold a wealth of treasures for those with a keen eye; chips of broken pottery with black and white patterns, the potsherds from ancient times, an occasional arrowhead, brightly colored chert, jasper and chalcedony chips and flakes, and rounded pebbles washed down from multicolored rock formations and distant mountains.

Down the Colorado River to the southwest, and up along the old North Wash Trail to the east of the Henry Mountains, sandstone-derived soils stretch for many miles.

Apache plume (*Fallugia paradoxa*) grows in and along edges of sandy washes. It is a medium-sized shrub, with slender, white-barked branches and small, deeply lobed leaves. In June, large white flowers appear, resembling thimbleberry blossoms. Its fruit develops into feathery, plumose styles, giving the Apache plume an airy appearance.

Indigobush (*Dalea thompsonae*) is noticeable at once in bloom. A low shrub with intricate branching, it prefers very sandy soils, and is endemic to Canyonlands. Its fine, pinnately divided leaves are orange-glandular dotted underneath. It produces clusters of pealike purple flowers.

A tiny, pink-flowered borage grows in similar habitats, forming loose mats sometimes a foot or more wide. Matted tiquilia (*Tiquilia latior*) (formerly *Coldenia hispidissima* var. *latior*) has small, linear, hairy leaves with revolute margins, and it blooms in May and throughout the summer.

Out on the desert flats *Yucca angustissima* begins to bloom in May. An erect inflorescence of purple-tinged white, campanulate or globose flowers are held above the compact hemispherical heads of linear leaves.

Below the Henry Mountains on the flat expanse of desert, sego lily (*Calochortus nuttallii*), which is the state flower of Utah, can be found covering many acres when it blooms in June. Appearing as a

Adiantum capillus-veneris
Drawing by Margaret Alice Smith

sea of widely spaced, cream-colored lilies, the flowers are held above the desert floor on slender, leafless stalks. Its three large petals bear crescent-shaped purple markings and long yellow hairs inside at the base. One variety of the species is pink. And a closely related species, *C. aureus*, with yellow petals, can sometimes be found on clay and sandy soils in Utah near Kanab and up into the San Rafael Desert.

Out on the high tableland known as the San Rafael Desert, galleta (*Hilaria jamesii*) and 3-awn grass (*Aristida purpurea*, formerly *A. longiseta*) form a distinctive plant community. This plateau is characterized by large areas of sand dunes constantly shifting and changing.

Poliomintha incana, a very aromatic desert shrub of the mint family (Lamiaceae) forms low mounds in the sand dunes. This is the famous purple sage of the Old West: its pale, blue-lavender flowers bloom throughout May and June and are typically mintlike. Its young twigs, leaves and flowers are covered with white hairs.

Other shrubs growing in association with purpe sage are old man's sage (*Artemisia filifolia*) and rabbitbrush (*Chrysothamnus nauseosus*), both of the composite family; and two species of *Ephedra*, or mormon tea.

Ephedra is a small shrub with green, photosynthetic, jointed stems and scalelike leaves. It is a gymnosperm, related to the conifers. *Ephedra torreyana* has bluish green stems and can be distinguished from the next species by its leaves and bracts in threes at the joints. *Ephedra viridis* has bright green stems with leaves and bracts in twos. Early pioneers made tea of the green stems, hence the name mormon tea. But care must be taken to boil it twice, pouring off the first water, for repeated use will turn the teeth green.

Cryptantha flava, yellow cryptantha, grows interspersed with purple sage on the San Rafael Desert as does coppermallow (*Sphaeralcea leptophylla* and *S. grossulariaefolia*).

Wavy-leaf oak (*Quercus undulata*) is a most attractive, low-spreading oak, forming thickets on the dunes. It has small, blue-green leaves with wavy margins.

A most impressive sight on this vast, flat sandy land is the lone shrub of Fremont's mahonia, *Berberis* (*Mahonia*) *fremontii*, in full bloom, covered with fragrant bright yellow flowers. Its compound, blue-green leaves are spiny and hollylike with 3 to 7 leaflets. In summer, the flowers develop into clusters of dark blue berries.

East of the San Rafael Desert and across and Green River in the northern canyonlands, high mesas of pinyon-juniper woodlands overlook the confluence of the Colorado and Green Rivers and their vast network of tributary canyons. These mesas are topped by Triassic Navajo and Kayenta

Yucca baccata
Photo by Allan Taylor

formations. The Navajo is about 180 million years old, and is composed of aeolian sandstone formed when a huge sea of sand, at least as large as those now found on the Sahara Desert, existed there. It is now exposed as large areas of bare rock, forming many knolls and hills that look very much like petrified sand dunes. This kind of topography has become known as slickrock, and in it delicate rock gardens can be found. Windblown sand and soil slowly fill depressions in bare rock. Cryptogams form on the loose soil. They are composed of several types of fungi, algae and lichens, and they are the first pioneers of soil stabilization. Cryptogamic soil is very fragile: when disturbed, many years are required to reaccumulate only an inch of it. Eventually, higher plants move in, forming miniature communities: annual and perennial herbs, desert shrubs, pinyon and juniper.

Below the Navajo and Kayenta formations, the great orange cliff-forming Wingate sandstone can be found. This rock layer can be traced throughout the desert. A fine-grained, resistant sandstone, it produces steep, vertical walls. Below, the Triassic Chinle and Moenkopi shales, siltstones and conglomerates weather to form dark red benches and slopes. These layers, together with the Wingate formation, produce the classic red mesas and buttes of the old Western films.

In the northern canyonlands from a mesa appropriately called "Island in the Sky," the view is truly unrivaled. Way off to the east the La Sal Mountains loom in the distance, rising to over 12,000 ft. These mountains are oases of coolness in the hot desert summers. Vegetatively, they are closely related to the southern Rocky Mountain flora.

To the south and southwest, the Abajo (Blue) Mountains and the Henrys waver in the bright desert light. The spectacular Shafer Trail leads down, thousands of feet, onto the White Rim sandstone. To the west, across the Green River, the western canyonlands come into view: the Maze, the Land of Standing Rocks, Elaterite Butte, Cleopatra's Chair. To the south, the Needles country: North and South Six-Shooter Peaks, Lavender Canyon and Fable Valley. In this country, the names themselves are evocative: Labryinth Canyon, Gunsight Butte, Waterpocket Fold, Upheaval Dome, and Paradox Valley. More than any other place on earth, this land has the ability to convey the significance, the immensity of those enigmatic qualities of time and space.

Arches National Park is located to the northeast up the Colorado River just above the town of Moab. Here natural stone arches of every size and form have been carved in the Entrada sandstone. The Entrada and its neighboring rock formations are part of the Salt Valley anticline—which has

Canyonlands National Park. Photo courtesy Utah Travel Council

been pushed up over millions of years by the slow upward movement of a ridge of subterranean salt deposits. The Entrada, fractured during upwarping and subsequently exposed to erosion by the action of freezing and thawing water and by the wind, produced thin, vertical rock slabs or fins, which have been subsequently perforated by weathering to produce arches. Other arches are produced by the continued weathering of potholes in the slickrock.

This sandy country supports a sparse pinyon and juniper community with many of the characteristic shrubs mentioned earlier. In years of adequate rainfall, about 7–10 in. annually, there is a wonderful display of wildflowers in spring and early summer.

Fendler bush (*Fendlera rupicola*) is a distinctive shrub of the saxifrage family. It has large 4-petaled flowers with 8 yellow stamens and long, narrow leaves. Its bark is shiny reddish tan when young, eventually becoming shredded and gray. This shrub prefers dry hillsides and rocky canyon ledges.

Utah snowberry (*Symphoricarpos longiflorus*) bears small, numerous, pale to deep pink trumpet-shaped flowers paired in the axils of its elliptic green leaves. It is a small shrub about 4 ft. high. Its smaller twigs become thorny with age. A member of the honeysuckle family, Caprifoliaceae, its flowers are very fragrant. It is often found on sandy washes and benches.

Scattered here and there in these dry washes are several sand-loving forbs. Desert four-o'clock (*Mirabilis multiflora*), in bloom from April to September, has campanulate, rose-pink, petallike sepals with bright yellow anthers on well-exserted stamens. Its stems, with large, dark green, cordate leaves tend to be decumbent, forming spreading clumps. It belongs to the Nyctaginaceae.

Another member of the four-o'clock family, fragrant sand verbena (*Abronia fragrans*), bears loose, globose heads of long, tubular, whitish pink flowers. Each inflorescence is subtended by ovate, papery bracts. The stems are decumbent, with opposite leaves possessing glandular hairs that catch sand particles. Thus, at times, the plant takes on the shade of sand in which it grows.

Yet another plant of sandy desert tracts, sacred datura (*Datura wrightii*, formerly *D. meteloides*) is most striking with its large, pure white, trumpet-shaped flowers and dark green, pubescent leaves. These showy flowers open at dusk and close the following morning. The plant is extremely poisonous, containing the alkaloids atropine, hyoscamine and scopolamine. It forms small clumps at the bases of cliffs.

Big sagebrush (*Artemisia tridentata*) is one of the unforgettable shrubs in the desert. The fragrance on the wind after a rainstorm embodies the essence of the Old West of childhood fantasies.

It has wedge-shaped, silvery blue leaves, and it blooms in early fall.

Desert paintbrush, (*Castilleja chromosa*), grows in association with big sagebrush. It is a partial parasite of the roots of artemisia. The showy red bracts surround an inconspicuous green corolla. Its foliage bears a downy pubescence. It is widely distributed in western North America, from desert shrublands and pinyon-juniper woodlands up into the mountain brush community. It is closely related, and easily confused with, the Eastwood paintbrush (*Castilleja scabrida*). Both prefer rocky, gravelly and sandy soils.

There are three species of mountain mahogany in southeastern Utah. Littleleaf mountain mahogany (*Cercocarpus intricatus*) is a small shrub with rigid, gray branches and small, evergreen leaves that have inrolled margins. Its inconspicuous maroon blossoms appear in April and are often so numerous that they are quite noticeable. This shrub is found growing on solid rock benches in the slickrock. Closely related curl-leaf mountain mahogany (*C. ledifolius*) has leaves that are larger, yet still narrow and inrolled. It grows in more favorable locations at higher altitudes, and may not be found in the Park. It blooms in early spring with abundant yellow flowers. It is a valuable species in the protection of watersheds.

Common mountain mahogany (*Cercocarpus montanus*) has wedge-shaped, deciduous leaves and occurs in the higher reaches of the plateau canyons and lower mountain slopes. Its flowers, like those of its relatives, develop into long, twisted, plumose achenes.

Among the arches and the maze of rock fins, scattered throughout the pinyon-juniper communities, are many common wild flowers of the cold desert. Pollinated by hummingbirds, Eaton's penstemon, *Penstemon eatonii*, bears long, scarlet, tubular flowers that are obscurely 2-lipped. It grows quite erect, usually 2–3 ft. tall with smooth, clasping, heart-shaped leaves. After germination, Eaton's penstemon overwinters as a basal rosette of leaves, growing to flowering size the next season. It can be found on dry slopes growing under pinyon and juniper, on sagebrush flats and up into the mountain brush zones. A somewhat similar species, scarlet bugler (*P. barbatus*) also has red, tubular corollas, but its petal lobes are strongly 2-lipped: the upper lip projecting out, the lower lip reflexed. It can be found in the same habitats as Eaton's penstemon.

Long-leaved phlox (*Phlox longifolia*) is often found growing among woody shrubs. Its 6 in. or longer straggly stems with linear, lanceolate leaves creep around and up through the shrubs' branches. Its salverform corollas in shades of pink to white are slighty scented. It prefers dry rocky sites with pinyon, juniper and sage.

The roots of narrow-leaved puccoon (*Lithospermum incisum*) were used by the Anasazi Indians in making yellow dye. This perennial arises from a stout, woody taproot, its stems up to 20 in. high with hairy, lanceolate leaves. Its bright yellow salverform flowers have flaring, ruffled lobes. It forms loose clumps in dry, sandy ground.

Out on the flat, broad plateau areas near Arches and the northern canyonlands, dry washes wander for miles across arid shrublands. Prince's plume (*Stanleya pinnata*) can often be found growing out in this harsh habitat, blooming even in mid-summer when the desert is at its hottest and driest. It is an attractive perennial with an open habit, sometimes reaching 5 ft. in height. Its showy, yellow flowers with long, exserted stamens develop into long, drooping pods. The plant is an indicator of the element selenium, absorbing it into its tissues from the soil, and grows well in alkaline and gypsum soils.

Desert trumpet (*Eriogonum inflatum*) is a most distinctive and memorable plant growing in these same desert flats. Its yellow involucral flowers are inconspicuous, and its dark green stems are strangely inflated just below each joint. Desert trumpet has a rosette of basal, ovate leaves and can grow to be 1–2 ft. tall. It is common across southern Utah.

The canyonlands of southeastern Utah and the arid plant ecosystems existing there are in many ways a fragile country. A good amount of it is still fairly remote and seldom visited. There is much to explore, to delight in. Traveling there always evokes the desire to know it more intimately.

References

Benson, Lyman and Robert A. Darrow. 1981. *Trees and shrubs of the southwestern deserts.* Tucson: University of Arizona Press.

Hinze, Lehi F. 1973. *Brigham Young University Geological Studies,* Vol. 20:3, *Geological History of Utah.* Provo, Utah: Brigham Young University Press.

Hunt, Charles B. 1974. *Natural regions of the United States and Canada.* San Francisco: W. H. Freeman and Co., Inc.

Welsh, Stanley L., and Glen Moore. 1973. *Utah plants.* Provo, Utah: Brigham Young University Press.

Wormington, H. M. 1973. *Prehistoric Indians of the Southwest.* Popular series, no. 7. Denver: Natural History Museum.

18

A Hike on the San Francisco Peaks

by Jeanette Milne

The Hopi Indian people call the San Francisco Peaks *Nuva tuk ya ovi,* a sacred place. It is the home of their ancestral spirits, the kachinas. During a good snow year the San Francisco Mountain is called "raging" by enthusiastic skiers who delight in the best powder skiing south of Salt Lake City. Travelers in search of a landmark look for "the most perfectly formed mountain." The San Francisco Mountain, or "the Peaks," as the local people call it, is also the highest place in Arizona, and it supports the only alpine tundra in the state.

On a clear day, sitting on top of the Peaks, one can see the North Rim of the Grand Canyon or look over to the northeast and take in the pinks, oranges and purples of the Painted Desert as it meets the endless blue sky. Look hard enough and you will even see the blue roof of the horticultural complex at The Arboretum in Flagstaff. Whichever way you turn, you will find an inspiring view, and you will also begin to understand why the Peaks are so special to people who have had the chance to make their acquaintance.

Presently, we will take several imaginary seasonal hikes on the San Francisco Peaks. Probably we will have most of our attention, and possibly our hands and knees, on the ground in order to see the alpine flora, but we will always take time to savor the spectacular view. Before we get started, however, let us take a look at some of the others who have gone before us and what they have found.

Botanical Explorers

Scattered plant collections on the Peaks were made on expeditions that took place as early as the 1850s. A summary presented in *Arizona Flora,* by Kearney and Peebles, mentions that many collectors well-known in Western plant exploration, such as Captain L. Sitgreaves, S. W. Woodhouse, J. M. Bigelow, F. H. Knowlton, Edward Greene and Marcus Jones, participated in these expeditions.

Probably the best known investigations were made by C. Hart Merriam in 1889. It was here in northern Arizona that he developed the famous "life zone" hypothesis. Driving up from Phoenix to

Jeanette Milne is curator of collections for The Arboretum at Flagstaff, Arizona, where plans are underway for a rock garden. She is interested in the propagation of native plants since suitable plants are now being grown for this collection. The Arboretum (formerly Transition Zone Horticultural Institute) is concerned with ecological horticulture focused on the Colorado Plateau flora.

the Peaks you will see why Merriam chose this area to investigate his idea. As he contended, there are few places in the U.S. where the changes from desert floor to tundra occur so dramatically and within so short a space.

Merriam determined that, as we ascend from the desert to the tundra, we pass through seven distinct life zones. His hypothesis held that distribution of flora and fauna into distinct zones was determined by temperature and climate alone, or what he termed the "laws of temperature control."

Although the hypothesis has since been rejected as too simplistic, it remains an important ecological contribution and serves as a tool for explaining the distribution of plants and animals. During his investigations Merriam reported 20 species of plants occurring above the timberline.

Investigations into the alpine flora were continued by Little (1941), Moore (1965) and most recently by Schaack (1979), among others. The Arizona alpine community now includes 85 taxa of 50 genera in 23 families. New additions were made as recently as April 1985 by Schaack and Morefield.

San Francisco Peaks. Photo courtesy Arizona Office of Tourism

Geology

Scientists have been attracted to the Peaks by the opportunity to study the area geologically as well as botanically. The first person to fully describe the geology of the San Francisco Mountains was Henry Robinson in 1902 and 1913. His work on its volcanic origins can be found in Professional Paper 76 published in 1913 by the U.S. Geological Survey.

Even to the untrained eye, it is evident that the San Francisco Peaks are of volcanic origin. Scattered around the vicinity are approximately 400 cinder cones, making this one of the most extensive volcanic fields in the United States.

The San Francisco Mountain is an extinct volcanic cone that was formed during the Pleistocene Period and at one time reached a height of 15,660 ft. Since extinction it has eroded about 3,000 ft. and no trace of the former crater is evident.

Starting from an elevation of 7,000 ft. on the Colorado Plateau, the three highest peaks projecting above timberline are Humphreys Peak at 12,670 ft., Agassiz Peak at 12,384 ft., and Fremont Peak at 11,984 ft.

The Inner Basin, an interior valley on the northeast side of the Peaks, was carved by a 2 mile long glacier during the Wisconsin glaciation, making it one of the southernmost locations for Pleistocene glaciation in the United States.

Location

The San Francisco Peaks are located about 9 miles north of Flagstaff and 60 miles south of the Grand Canyon. The nearest alpine tundra in the Rocky Mountain range occurs about 250 miles northeast of the Peaks in Colorado's San Juan Mountain Range, making this disjunct area very interesting.

Public access is provided by several State Highways and Forest Service roads. State Highway 180 on the western side of the Peaks heads north out of Flagstaff, and after 8.3 miles, intersects the Snow Bowl Road. This road is followed for 7 miles to the Fairfield Snow Bowl Lodge, located at 9,500 ft. where a chair lift provides access to the 11,600 ft. level on Agassiz Peak.

Should you continue down State Highway 180, about 11 miles farther, you would find a series of Forest Service roads that follow along the north side of the Peaks, and there are several hiking trails available there. A very popular summertime hike is from Lockett Meadow into the Inner Basin. Take State Highway 89 north as it winds around the eastern side of the Peaks. Sixteen miles from Flagstaff, it intercepts Forest Service Road 552 to Lockett Meadow. From a beautiful aspen-ringed meadow at 8,500 ft. a hiking trail leads into the Inner Basin. Here trails lead to several springs including Doyle, Snowslide, Flagstaff, and Raspberry, which provide water for the city of Flagstaff.

Numerous trails on the Peaks are available for the avid hiker and can be found on the Humphrey's Peak Quandrangle Map, U.S.G.S. 1966, Scale 1:24,000.

A Hike in June

It is hard to believe it is already June 24th. A heavy snowpack last winter, accompanied by a few "untypical" early June thunderstorms, predict a colorful alpine display.

It is chilly this morning. A cold snap of 22°F last night in town doomed unsuspecting tender plants, but as we start our hike, the sun shines through with great promise. We take the easy way up today, so that we can spend all of our time above treeline. We will ascend by the Fairfield Snow Bowl Ski Area chairlift, a direct line to Agassiz Peak. As we ride up on the chair, we consider the climate and soils which affect the growth of these alpine plants.

Climate and Soils

In a good year, about three out of five, there will be moderately intense winter storms on the Peaks, dropping up to 150 in. of snow. The greatest snow accumulation typically occurs in late winter, with March being the month of the biggest snows. Snow can linger on into late June, but usually the tundra is free of snow by mid-May.

Moisture is provided by the melt of the snowpack as well as by midsummer thunderstorms. What we call "monsoons" in Arizona are the frequent and intense thunderstorms that start in early

July and last through August. The storms usually begin in early afternoon and are of short duration. It is wise to be below timberline before the storms begin. To be caught on the highest point within 200 miles during a lightning storm can be a hair-raising experience; no time for a siesta after lunch in July!

Soils of the alpine zone are of volcanic origin, derived from andesite and dacite parent material. The primarily sandy and gravelly loams are generally acidic or subacidic. Water storage capacity and fertility are low. The large area of basaltic rock covered slope is very easily dislodged.

As we reach the top and prepare to dismount from the chair, we pull on a windbreaker and a tight fitting cap—it is windy up top. The first plant we see is *Geum (Acomastylis) rossii* var. *turbinatum*, obviously the most abundant plant in the tundra.

Two major plant communities were recognized by Little (1941): the alpine rockfield and the alpine meadow. The peaks have no streams, lakes, or permanent snowfields, so any communities associated with an aquatic habitat are absent. The two square miles of alpine tundra that occur on the San Francisco Peaks form a geologically young, isolated island. Schaack (1970) feels that the primary dispersal corridor for these alpine plants in reaching the San Francisco Peaks is the high elevation areas to the east and north, primarily the main Rocky Mountain chain of Colorado and New Mexico.

A look at the species list reveals that the area is rather poor as far as diversity of species is concerned, as are many other young alpine islands. Little (1941) believed the alpine meadow of Arizona to be a climax community that would continue to provide favorable conditions for further plant growth. Moore (1965) thought that succession on the Peaks is retrogressive and that, as the climate becomes drier and warmer, the vascular flora of the alpine tundra becomes less vigorous and floristically sparse. Schaack (1983) in his study shows that species diversity is greater than previously known, suggesting that plants may be moving in a stepwise, upward dispersal pattern.

All these theories are considered as we hike a well-worn trail up past the splashes of color provided by *Primula parryi* and *Silene acaulis* subsp. *subcaulescens* and on through an area of krummholz that occurs above and below 11,600 ft. This windswept band of trees includes *Picea engelmannii* and *Pinus aristata*.

Plants blooming today in the alpine rockfield include: *Arenaria fendleri*; *Silene acaulis* subsp. *subcaulescens*, which appears to be fading out quite a bit; *Antennaria umbrinella*; *Androsace*

Silene acaulis. Photo by Vernon Tomppert

Primula parryi

septentrionalis; Pseudocymopterus montanus, which displays a wide color range from yellow and orange to deep maroon; *Arenaria (Minuartia) rubella; Thlaspi montanum; Potentilla diversifolia; Draba aurea* var. *leiocarpa;* and *Polemonium viscosum,* which offer a vivid display of bright blue flowers.

We have lunch on the saddle between Agassiz and Humphreys Peak where we find welcome shelter from the wind in a group of rocks. Looking into the Inner Basin, we notice a small pool of snow melt, something that does not often occur in these porous soils. We wonder at the tenacity of a hummingbird which braves the altitude only to find nothing of interest in my red hair.

On the way up to Humphreys Peak we look into the cracks and crevices of large boulders that provide shelter for such plants as a common fern *Cystopteris reevesianus; Heuchera versicolor,* just getting ready to bloom; *Saxifraga debilis; Primula parryi;* and to our delight, a small patch of *Anemone multifida* var. *globosa* and *Oxyria digyna.*

The most interesting part of the alpine hike is observing the combinations of plants in the alpine meadow association. What starts out as small patches of grass such as *Bromus ciliatus, Poa fendleriana* and *Phleum alpinum,* or stands of *Geum rossii* var. *turbinatum,* will soon be replaced by other species that find the environmental conditions conducive to growth. In bloom in the alpine meadow association we find *Mertensia franciscana; Ranunculus inamoenus* var. *subaffinis,* one of two species endemic to the Peaks; *Saxifraga rhomboidea* var. *franciscana; S. flagellaris; Cerastium beeringianum; Pseudocymopterus montanus;* and *Silene acaulis* var. *subcaulescens* which, being opportunistic, grows in many different habitats on the Peaks.

Our descent from Humphreys Peak will follow a new trail developed by the U.S. Forest Service to take some of the pressure off the alpine tundra on Agassiz Peak. The chair lift provides access to the tundra for many people, too many perhaps. The tundra on Agassiz is showing obvious wear. The new trail is steep, and we descend quickly.

A Hike in Early August

Our special purpose today is to observe habitat and populations of *Senecio franciscanus,* a plant endemic to the San Francisco Peaks. On December 22, 1983 (Fed. Reg. 12/22/83), it was listed as a threatened species under the Endangered Species Act of 1973. This species was deemed threatened because of its limited distribution and the pressure caused by hikers during snow-free months. *Senecio franciscanus* is a member of the Compositae; it is often called by its familiar name, San Francisco Peaks groundsel. The species is a perennial with stems 1.2–4 in. tall, and leaves that are pinnately divided. They are less than 0.6 in. long and 0.1–0.8 in. wide. Flowers are yellow, born in clusters of 1 to 6. The plant occurs between 11,300 and 12,400 ft. on talus slopes. It spreads vegetatively by runners.

Today we hike up the Inner Basin. We want to get an early start so we will be down off the mountain before rain begins. Starting at dawn, we see a large gathering of elk in Lockett Meadow feasting on the lush summer growth. On the trail up we encounter large patches of *Dugaldia (Helenium) hoopesii* growing among *Juniperus communis* and *Ribes montigenum.* Once on the alpine tundra, we find that *Senecio franciscanus* is abundant on the talus slopes of both Agassiz and Humphreys Peaks. It is tucked under rocks for extra protection. Walking on the talus makes us realize how precarious the habitat of *Senecio franciscanus* is and why off-trail hiking is not advised. Observations reveal another species, restricted to ridgetops in Arizona tundra, that is threatened by foot traffic: *Potentilla nivea* (a 1983 record for Arizona by Schaak and Morefield).

While observing the habitat of *Senecio franciscanus,* we find other plants of interest that cannot escape notice. In the alpine medow, all in bloom, we find: *Draba crassifolia, Geum rossii* var. *turbinatum, Arenaria rubella, Rhodiola (Sedum) rhodantha, Veronica wormskjoldii, Pedicularis parryi, Ranunculus pedatifidus, Solidago multiradiata, Saxifraga caespitosa* subsp. *exartoides, Penstemon whippleanus,* and *Erigeron simplex.*

We find a beautiful specimen *Gentianella (Comastoma) tenella* in a mat with other plants. With that rare find for the day we head down off the mountain just as the clouds roll in.

A Hike in Late September

Summer has come and gone. A light dusting of snow has already touched the Peaks and gold aspen leaves flutter from the trees.

Starting our hike from the Snow Bowl lodge, we head up the ski trails on our way to the top. Fireweed is still in bloom, and the flowers of sneezeweed droop with the weight of moisture. The snow won't last, and on this bright sunny day it melts quickly.

We consider the "hot spots" on Agassiz Peak that we noticed while driving here from town. These are distinct areas on the mountain where the snow always melts first. We have noticed them before; what makes it happen? Could it be the wind? Why is it warmer in those spots? Somehow the configuration of the Peaks, the angle of the sun, perhaps the prevailing winds, conspire to melt the snow faster here.

Once on the tundra we see the seed heads of *Geum rossii* var. *turbinatum* sticking up above the snow. In melted areas we find a few vestigial flowers of *Senecio franciscanus.* Occasional clumps of *Rhodiola rhodantha* show their red heads along with *Pseudocymopterus montanus.* The flowers of *Gentianella amarella* subsp. *heterosepala* are past, a good reason to come up earlier next fall.

The next time we ascend the Peaks it will be with skis strapped on, but we will remember the alpine flora, well-hidden and protected under the blanket of winter snow.

References

Little, E. L. 1941. "Alpine flora of San Francisco Mountain." *Madroño.* 6:65–81.

Merriam, C. H. 1980. "Results of a biological survey of the San Francisco Mountain region and desert of the Little Colorado in Arizona." *North American Fauna* 3:136.

Moore, Thomas C. 1965. "Origin and disjunction of the alpine tundra flora on San Francisco Peaks, Arizona." *Ecology* 46:862–864.

Schaack, C. G. 1970. *A flora of the arctic-alpine vascular plants of the San Francisco Mountain, Arizona.* Masters thesis, Northern Arizona University.

Schaack, C. G. 1983. "The alpine vascular flora of Arizona." *Madroño.* 30:79–88.

Rhodiola rhodantha. Photo by Roberts

ALPINE FLORA OF SAN FRANCISCO PEAKS
Taken from Schaack (1983, 1985)

APIACEAE
> *Pseudocymopterus montanus*

ASPLENIACEAE
> *Cystopteris reevesiana*

ASTERACEAE
> *Antennaria microphylla*
> *A. parvifolia*
> *A. rosulata*
> *A. umbrinella*
> *Dugaldia (Helenium) hoopesii*
> *Erigeron compositus*
> *E. simplex*
> *Packera franciscana*
> *Solidago multiradiata* var. *scopulorum*
> *Taraxacum lyratum*
> *T. officinale*

BORAGINACEAE
> *Mertensia franciscana*

BRASSICACEAE
> *Draba aurea*
> *D. crassifolia*
> *Thlaspi montanum*

CAPRIFOLIACEAE
> *Lonicera involucrata*

CARYOPHYLLACEAE
> *Arenaria fendleri* var. *fendleri, porteri, tweedyi*

> *A. lanuginosa* subsp. *saxosa*
> *A. (Minuartia) obtusiloba*
> *A. (Minuartia) rubella*
> *Cerastium beeringianum (C. alpinum)*
> *Sagina saginoides*
> *Silene acaulis* ssp. *acaulescens*
> *Stellaria umbellata*

CRASSULACEAE
> *Sedum (Rhodiola) rhodanthum*

CUPRESSACEAE
> *Juniperus communis* ssp. *depressa*

CYPERACEAE
> *Carex albonigra*
> *C. atrata* var. *chalciolepis (C. c.)*
> *C. atrata* var. *erecta*
> *C. bella*
> *C. ebenea*
> *C. elynoides*
> *C. haydeniana*
> *C. petasata*

GENTIANACEAE
> *Gentianella amarella* subsp. *heterosepala*
> *G. (Gentiana, Gentianopsis) barbellata*
> *G. (Comastoma) tenella*

JUNCACEAE
> *Juncus drummondii*
> *Luzula spicata*

ONAGRACEAE
Epilobium (Chamerion) angustifolium

OPHIOGLOSSACEAE
Botrychium reevesiana

PINACEAE
Abies lasiocarpa var. *arizonica*
Picea engelmannii
Pinus aristata
P. flexilis

POACEAE
Agropyron scribneri
A. trachycaulum var. *latiglume*
Agrostis idahoensis
Bromus ciliatus
Festuca ovina var. *brevifolia (F. o.* var. *brachyphylla)*
Phleum alpinum
Poa fendleriana
P. interior
P. pratensis
P. reflexa
P. rupicola
Trisetum spicatum

POLEMONIACEAE
Polemonium pulcherrimum var. *delicatum (P. delicatum)*
P. viscosum

POLYGONACEAE
Oxyria digyna

PRIMULACEAE
Androsace septentrionalis

RANUNCULACEAE
Anemone multifida var. *tetonensis (A. tetonensis)*

ROSACEAE
Fragaria ovalis (F. virginiana)
Geum (Acomastylis) rossii var. *turbinatum*
Potentilla concinna
P. diversifolia
P. nivea
P. subviscosa
Sibbaldia procumbens

SAXIFRAGACEAE
Heuchera versicolor
Ribes montigenum
Saxifraga caespitosa
S. debilis
S. flagellaris
S. rhomboidea var. *franciscana*

SCROPHULARIACEAE
Pedicularis parryi

19

Island in the Sky

by Sonia Lowzow

Thrusting upward from the arid high plateaus of northern Arizona, their summits reaching as much as 12,600 ft. toward the heavens, the mountain ranges north of the Mogollon Escarpment are aptly called "islands in the sky." Look southward from the barren malpais in the north on a summer afternoon: the illusion of an isolated island is immediately apparent as you see the White Mountains silhouetted against the horizon, blanketed by the monsoon clouds above them. The plateau around you is incredibly arid, lighted by a desert sun, and the plants are dryland species. In this country, the rains of July and August and the snows of winter shed their life-giving moisture on the mountains instead, and there the plants are basically a Rocky Mountain flora. The number of species in Arizona that can be included in this characterization is surprisingly high: almost 25 percent of the total number of plant species in the state—ample evidence of the role of water in the ecology of the Southwest.

The White Mountains rise quite precipitously from the malpais to the north, from New Mexico to the east and from the high desert to the south, but far more gradually along the Mogollon Rim, which continues westward almost to the center of the state. On the west, therefore where do the White Mountains begin? Is the town of Show Low the western boundary? (Incidentally, this unusual name has an interesting history: In a long-ago show low poker game the town site exchanged hands when one of the players came up with the Deuce of Clubs; this card has also given its name to the town's main street.) Geographically, perhaps it is, but floristically, probably not. In any case, let's include a few more miles westward so that we can also explore the fascinating limestone country north of Pinedale, with its interesting flora. The White Mountains comprise, then, an area of about 90 miles east to west and 60 miles north to south—not an extensive range—only a little splinter off the massive Rockies, only an "island in the sky." But the shores of the island are at an elevation of well over 5,000 ft. and its highest point, Mount Baldy, reaches up to a true alpine height of 11,600 ft.

Good and not-so-good roads traverse this island. Route 260 begins at Payson, west of the range and just below the Mogollon Rim, ascends the rim 30 miles eastward and follows it, through tall pines, mountain meadows and high-country grassland, until it reaches Show Low. Then, as White Mountain Road, it proceeds through the mountains at elevations of from 6,000 to 8,500 ft., until it intersects Route 666 near Eagar. This is the famed Coronado Trail, which wends its way southward

Sonia Lowzow spent so much time exploring in the White Mountains of Arizona that she moved there a few years ago to enjoy their cool, moist climate, and lovely mountain plants year-around. She has done much to popularize the distinctive flora of the region in a series of articles for the Bulletin of the American Rock Garden Society. Professionally, she was formerly a medical technologist but now operates Fjellgarden, a mail order nursery specializing in native Arizona mountain plants. Drawings for this chapter were done by Janet Fell, a professional wildlife artist and neighbor of Mrs. Lowzow.

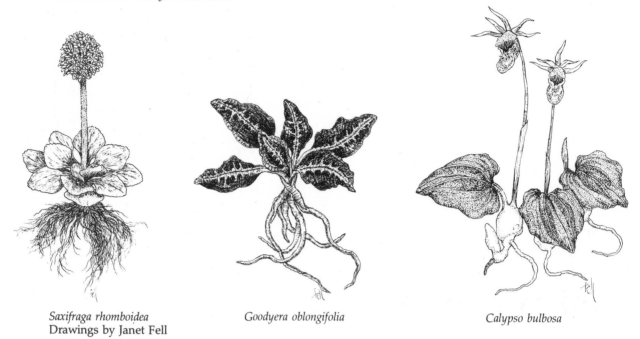

Saxifraga rhomboidea
Drawings by Janet Fell

Goodyera oblongifolia

Calypso bulbosa

through Alpine and Hannagan Meadow, skirting the Blue Range Primitive Area, and thence to the desert. Route 60 is the main north-south road from the desert cities of Phoenix and Tucson. It reaches the White Mountain area by way of the Salt River Canyon, then goes through Show Low and eastward along the northern edge of the range, through floristically interesting grasslands, to Springerville. There are a few other minor paved roads as well as the U.S. Forest Service roads, all of which are unpaved, but even most of these are well-surfaced and easily negotiable, except in winter or during an exceptionally heavy monsoon season.

Approximately half the area is within the boundaries of the Apache-Sitgreaves National Forest; the other half is White Mountain Apache Indian Reservation land. Private land is limited to little pockets around the towns and along the major highways. So most of these mountains are undeveloped and almost undisturbed, except for the hordes of vacationers each summer, who flock to the cool forests and lakes and rivers to escape the desert heat. But there are still many byways that are unfrequented, many areas known only to hikers and naturalists—many, many places where an untold wealth of plants can still be found.

The White Mountains are the watershed of Arizona. The Little Colorado River, the Colorado's main tributary, has its source on Mount Baldy. The White and Black Rivers join in these mountains to form the Salt, Arizona's second largest river. Innumerable creeks and streams and ponds and lakes dot the high country. These, together with the often dense forest cover of pine, spruce, fir, oak and aspen combine to create a mountain wonderland—places of peace and coolth and solitude, far removed from the dry heat of the surrounding deserts and plateaus.

Moisture is the byword, and it comes from the many feet of snow deposited each winter on the peaks; it comes from the monsoons, the predictable, almost daily rains of July and August, refreshing the parched forests, which have lost so much of their moisture during the dry months of May and June. These monsoons, which have their origin in the Gulf of Baja California, skip blithely over the southern half of the state, disdaining to deposit more than an occasional thundershower over the desert, building up, instead, a cloud cover over these mountains late each morning. The rains usually follow within an hour or two. Then the sun appears again, and the dry, clear air of the mountains contributes to a relatively low humiditiy once more. There are no August "muggs" in the White Mountains! There is no excessive heat, either. Rarely does the temperature reach 90°F, and then only in June. Even more rarely does it reach 65°F at night.

Because of the range of elevations and variance in amounts of moisture, there is a wide spectrum of plant life here. On the heights of Mount Baldy, a few species of true alpine plants are found. In the fir-spruce forests, highlighted magnificently with stands of white-trunked aspens, the moist humus supports many Ericaceae and Orchidaceae. This forest is interspersed with innumerable mountain meadows where untold numbers of subalpine species grow in riotous profusion. In the ponderosa pine-Gambel's oak belt, slightly more xerophytic plants begin to appear, including many species of *Penstemon*. The sandy soil regions to the west give rise to an entirely

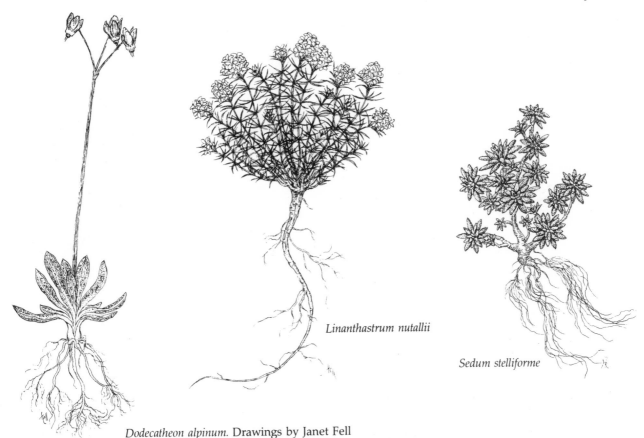

Linanthastrum nutallii

Sedum stelliforme

Dodecatheon alpinum. Drawings by Janet Fell

different set of plants, those adapted to the monsoon fringes, almost xerophytic, with deep-delving roots for the dryer summers and the sand to keep them from becoming waterlogged in the wetter ones. Soil types make a difference, too. Generally, the central and eastern sections have either a clayey or humusy soil (depending on elevation and forest type), mainly volcanic in origin and acid in reaction. To the west, roughly between Lakeside and Show Low, the acid sand area begins, with the accompanying rock, a red sandstone. At Show Low, bits and pieces of limestone come into evidence, culminating to the north and west in an area of pure "Swiss cheese" tufa; this is the home of yet another distinct flora.

On Mount Baldy, at or near its summit, above the tree line, *Primula parryi* is found, an interesting but certainly not particularly attractive plant, being rather large and coarse with red-purple flowers, and even these with a distinct odor of carrion. *Rhodiola (Sedum) rhodantha* is also found here, and *Selaginella densa* grows in Arizona only on this summit, as does *Hymenoxys brandegei*. There are a few other alpine species but none that has as yet proved garden-worthy. *Moneses uniflora* is reputed to be here, but I believe I've searched in every moist cranny on Mount Baldy, and I haven't yet found it.

Down on the trail from the summit, as one descends to the fir-spruce belt, the most important element of the ground cover is *Vaccinium oreophilum*. This is a disputed name, some authors referring the plant to *V. myrtillus*, others to *V. myrtillus* ssp. *oreophilum*. By any name, it is a very delicious blueberry on a very small plant. In moist spots or where additional humus has accumulated, there is a wealth of other Ericaceae: *Pyrola picta*, with thick white-mottled leaves, *Pyrola virens*, *Chimaphila umbellata* and *Ramischia (Pyrola) secunda*, the side-bells pyrola. The latter is easy to grow in pine duff or sandy peat, and the chimaphila, while not quite so amenable, should still be attempted more widely, as one of the more attractive small ericaceous plants. In these moist, mossy environs, the Orchidaceae are also well represented. I saw *one* plant of *Cypripedium calceolus* var. *pubescens* many years ago at Reservation Lake, southwest of Mount Baldy, and I have seen a few reminiscent leaves in inaccessible places along the Baldy Trail since, so it *is* here but is certainly *very* rare. Three habenarias occur here, all in wet places: *Habenaria saccata*, *H. hyperborea* and *H. sparsiflora*. None of these, however, is particularly striking, all having rather insignificant flowers. Two goodyeras are found in these forests, *Goodyera oblongifolia* ard *G. repens*, the latter only rarely seen. Both make very attractive ground covers in the peat bed, and both seem relatively easy to grow. A few other incidental species round out the range of Orchidaceae, including a couple of saprophytic members of the clan and

Lewisia brachycalyx. Drawings by Janet Fell   *Draba asprella*   *Thlaspi fendleri*

culminating in the exquisite little fairy slipper, *Calypso bulbosa.* This is a plant that is alternately praised and damned by gardeners for its recalcitrance in cultivation. It may appear to do well for a while in a peaty situation, but I have found that the surest road to success, defined as multiplying plants, is to establish it in a bed of its native woods duff and let it maintain itself within the vagaries of the climate, giving little or no additional moisture during its dormant period in late spring and early summer. This is never an abundant species, although it can be found here and there in the White Mountains. A really large colony may have 40 or 50 plants. Usually far fewer are found.

Throughout this mesic evergreen forest—where the elevations are 8,000 to 11,000 ft. and where moisture is almost ever-present even in the dry seasons because of the deep layer of humus, the mulch that insulates the soil from the drying effects of the low mountain humidity, and where the dense tree cover further retards evaporation from the intense mountain insolation—many more choice plant species can be found. Here grow occasional small colonies of *Linnaea borealis* var. *americana,* that elfin charmer with its twin pink bells, hauntingly fragrant of almonds. Our Western white marsh marigold, *Caltha leptosepala,* ranges far and wide wherever there are boggy conditions along the streams or in wet meadows. Deep in the forest, in moist rock crevices, the particularly lovely *Heuchera versicolor* grows. I have never found it in other conditions. It is as much a true rock plant as its dryland counterpart, *Petrophytum caespitosum.* In aspen groves, here and there, are patches of a nice little woodland violet, *Viola nephrophylla,* and of *Aquilegia triternata,* shorter, more compact and as as lovely in flower as *A. canadensis.* The pteridophytes are represented by the ubiquitous bracken, two little woodsias, the delicate *Cystopteris fragilis* and that fine rock fern, *Asplenium trichomanes,* among others. *Pedicularis racemosa* and *P. groenlandica* grow on or near Mount Baldy, but at the woods' edges or into the meadows, their only habitat in Arizona.

In these mountains, the insolation factor can be intense. In the thin air, there is little to impede it. So the plants that grow in open meadows are of two types: those that require continuous moisture at the roots and are found in areas with underground water at the root zone or in a soil clayey enough so that the evaporative effect of the sun is mitigated—and those that can handle somewhat drier conditions. In the former category, some of our forest plants will venture out into the open: the calthas and aquilegias and violas. But the sun produces a dividend, for here grow also those plants that can be found only in unshaded places, and their name is legion.

At the Three Forks of the Black River, several miles east of Big Lake, one such meadow supports an astonishing variety of plants. Two of the forks splay outward around this spit of land, so that it is in effect an island. At any time, even in the driest months, the myopic plant enthusiast who must kneel in order to view the miniature treasures of this place, will rise with very wet knees! Here grow two of our native sisyrinchiums, the blue *Sisyrinchium demissum* var. *amethystinum* and *S. longipes (S. elmeri)*, with flowers of a lovely creamy yellow. Clumps of their close relative, *Iris missouriensis*, in many gradations and striations of color from white to blue to lavender, dot the meadow. Along the river's edge, in the wettest portions, hundreds of plants of *Dodecatheon alpinum* display their lovely cyclamenlike blooms of magenta and yellow. The white *D. ellisiae* or, if you will, *D. dentatum* ssp. *ellisiae,* is reputed to grow in a similar habitat in Hannagan Meadow, but I've not yet found it there. Perhaps this year? At ground level, many drifts of *Mimulus primuloides* brighten the grassy hollows with butter yellow monkey flowers on miniscule, threadlike stems. Yellow, too, with a pretty orange eye, are the blooms of *Potentilla plattensis*—on a plant as superficially unlike a potentilla as one can imagine until close examination of the ferny leaves discloses the unmistakable leaflets of the genus. This is a low plant, almost flat to the ground. It is very widespread in other meadow habitats from Big Lake to Alpine. The wettest areas support vigorous patches of *Viola nephrophylla* and, the perhaps less desirable *V. adunca*. Along the very edge of the river grows the lovely *Oxalis alpina, (O. metcalfei)* a tiny plant with large pink blooms, green-centered. In one really boggy stretch of soil *Caltha leptosepala* occurs again, along with a very large yellow ranunculus that I've never keyed out precisely. The meadow mounds up slightly toward its center (never more than 2 or 3 ft. above the water level, but providing a little more drainage, perhaps?), and here grow *Potentilla fruticosa (Pentaphylloides floribunda)*, true blue *Linum lewisii (L. perenne* spp. *l.)*, the beautiful white *Linanthastrum (Linanthus) nuttallii* and tiny blue *Lobelia anatina*. There are equisetums and rushes at the water's edge, and a gravelly spit that almost bisects the "island" sports mounds of brilliant yellow *Corydalis aurea* var. *occidentalis,* more compact and more floriferous than can be imagined. There is a slightly drier meadow across the road where the terrain slopes more sharply upward from the river. Here grow *Geum (Erythrocoma) triflorum,* the prairie smoke, *Potentilla thurberi,* with its lovely blooms of a true wine red, and the almost ubiquitous *Hedyotis pygmaea* is underfoot everywhere. The latter has a wide scope, from this subalpine setting at 9,000 ft. to the hot, dry tufa barrens at 6,000 ft. at the western edge of the White Mountains. Soil acidity or the lack thereof, clay or sand, wet or dry—nothing seems to faze this little plant. Only the hand of man can interfere with its exuberant growth, but that rather easily. It is certainly not particularly amenable to cultivation. It dislikes pots, resents disturbance, hates to be propagated asexually—in short, a rather difficult plant—but a choice little mat of succulent rubiaceous leaves, smothered in tiny four-petalled flowers of white to pink to lavender.

In September, the gentians, moisture-lovers all, begin to bloom, and the White Mountains are rich in species of the genus *Gentiana* and the related *Gentianella*. The most attractive are *Gentiana (Pneumonanthe) affinis* and *G. parryi*. These color the wet meadows between Lee Valley and Greer a deep glorious blue in early autumn.

One can wander indefinitely through these mountains, on almost any little byway that seems to lead nowhere, and find more and more meadow species. Add to the foregoing a long list of additional plants, many of them familiar to the alpine plant enthusiast: alliums, *Allium geyeri* being one of the nicer pink species; *Arenaria fendleri* in its dwarfer forms; sheets of *Campanula rotundifolia* in the meadows near Big Lake; *Commelina dianthifolia* in its lovely, clear blue dwarf form; *Erysimum wheeleri,* with its orange to maroon flower heads on compact plants; *Lewisia pygmaea,* in a few favored spots, here with deep pink flowers; *Mertensia franciscana; Oxalis decaphylla (O. grayi)* with its pleated leaves and large pink flowers; *Saxifraga rhomboidea,* in the half-shade of aspen groves, the full sun of the high meadows or the deep shade of the Little Colorado's banks at Greer; *Sedum cockerellii* wherever it can find a moist crevice or mossy bank; *S. stelliforme* in dryer, sunnier rocky places; and *Silene laciniata,* the clear scarlet species so similar to *S. californica*. Potentillas are here and there in endless variety and penstemons, of course. On the Coronado Trail, between Nutrioso and Alpine, an especially fine form of *Penstemon strictus* occurs, the plant bushy and compact and the flowers a startlingly deep blue purple. A few of the penstemons at these altitudes are deciduous species, and these are among the smallest plants. One such is *P. oliganthus,* found in the moist meadows at Porter Springs, near Lake Mountain.

The composites are so well represented that I will only list some of the genera: *Achillea, Agoseris, Antennaria, Arnica, Artemisia, Aster, Erigeron, Helenium, Helianthella, Hymenoxys, Rudbeckia, Senecio, Stevia, Townsendia* and *Wyethia*. They are all here in endless number and variety, their whites and golds and lavenders a mosaic of color in every open meadow.

Below the 8,000 ft. level, the predominant forest tree is *Pinus ponderosa*, interspersed with groves of *Quercus gambelii* and, at the upper altitude limits of this zone, *Populus tremuloides*. Because of the lower elevation, the temperatures are now a little higher than in the true subalpine zone. Also, by the time they have progressed so far from their sources on the peaks of Baldy and Ord and Warren, the many creeks, rivulets and streams have coalesced into fewer but broader rivers. The pines tend also to absorb large amounts of moisture from the soil while, concurrently, their fallen needles and the leaves of oaks decay rather slowly, so that a deep layer of soft, moist humus is not built up.

All of these conditions contribute to a more xerophytic flora, although many of the higher altitude species will still be found near sources of water. This floristic area, while not as rich in species, is not without interest. Here the penstemons become a more predominant element, including such species as *Penstemon barbatus, P. bridgesii (P. rostriflorus), P. eatonii, P. linarioides, P. pachyphyllus, P. strictus* and *P. virgatus.* The Lilaceae are represented by various additional alliums, *Anthericum torreyi* various species of *Calochortus* and *Triteleia lemmonae. Tradescantia pinetorum* is frequently seen, a most unusual commelinaceous plant with long, thin leaves. In spring, *Phlox woodhousei (P. speciosa* ssp. *w.)* produces its sheets of pinks along the roadsides. This is not a microphlox for the alpine purist, but it is one of our best and most reliable Arizona species, with the sort of wide range that sometimes characterizes the easier rock plants. *Townsendia exscapa* makes its first appearance here in openings among the pines, the so-called parks. Here it is found in incredibly stiff clay. The biennial *Ipomopsis (Gilia) aggregata* is a ferny rosette in its first year, blooming the next on foot-high stems—a fire engine red. At higher elevations, there is sometimes a remarkable color range in a colony, from the typical red of the species to palest flesh pink.

Antennarias come into their own here; the park areas are sometimes carpeted with their silver gray mats. Among the smallest and grayest is *Antennaria arida (A. rosea, A. microphylla). Arenaria fendleri* is found still, now usually a taller form, although this seems to be a genetic, rather than a cultural, characteristic. Erigerons and asters abound, as well as many other composites. Here and there, the gray foliage of eriogonums stands out against the green of the forest and the volcanic red-brown of the soil. Scattered plants of *Hedyotis pygmaea* appear again. Any number of small potentillas can be found, with such a long blooming season range that their sunny yellow flowers seem almost continuous from spring to fall. The shrubby *Ceanothus fendleri* is no more than one foot high, on one of the forest roads going into Greer, and is a cloud of white in June each year. The very earliest spring flowers in this life zone are those of *Thlaspi fendleri,* only a few inches high, its blooms usually white but often a soft lavender pink.

As the soil loses its stiff clayey texture and the lower sandy area toward the western end of the mountains is reached, new and exciting species are found, among them a few really fine rock plants. *Lewisia brachycalyx,* one of the loveliest of its genus, grows in sand and pine duff in part shade. Normally, the flowers are white or sometimes lined with pink. Rarely, a solid pink form is found. Blooming concurrently is *Claytonia rosea,* one of the tuberous Portulacaceae, with deeper pink blossoms. *Delphinium nelsonii* often occupies the same habitat, its clear blue a striking contrast. All of these are summer dormant, but little *Draba asprella's* furry green rosettes are evergreen. Its many bright yellow blooms are on stems only about 3–4 in. high. Nearby may be seen the delicately cut pink flowers of that fleeting saxifrage relative, *Lithophragma tenellum.* It, too, goes dormant after flowering, its only legacy the tiny pink tubers left in the sand and perhaps a few miniscule seeds. *Pedicularis centranthera* grows here—ground-hugging rosettes with 5 in. stems of purple and white flowers. It would be a striking rock garden plant but, like all its clan, it poses some very difficult problems in cultivation. *Townsendia exscapa* reappears, this time in pure sand, seemingly more suited to its needs. Tucked into this galaxy of color, a few plants of *Phlox stansburyi* proclaim their slight difference from the more frequent *P. woodhousei* by a more wheellike arrangement of the petals, and stamens that protrude beyond the tube. Later in the year, after the summer monsoons have started, *Talinum parviflorum* blooms, its pink flowers really not so very "parvi" at all. Then, too, the penstemons begin. The species here are different, reflecting the altitude change and the increased porosity of the soil. Here they are *Penstemon ambiguus, P. angustifolius* and *P. jamesii,* while *P. linarioides* is as wide-ranging as *Hedyotis pygmaea;* it or one of its subspecies can be found in the whole altitude range from 9,000 ft. down.

To the west of Show Low, after a little limestone has been added, the same sandy soil supports two additional fine phloxes. *Phlox austromontana* is here in some of its best forms, a perfectly flat mat of rigid needle leaves topped by almost acaulescent flowers of deep glowing pink. There is a startling resemblance to *Silene acaulis* as it grows in the tundra, when every stem bears a bloom and no foliage can be seen. Little *Phlox grayi* is of a different ilk. It is a "long-leaved" phlox, although these are rough, hard, and somewhat furry; and the stature is small, befitting its lean habitat. The flowers are soft pink, sometimes almost salmon. This one creeps a little, the rhizomatous stems increasing its spread by a few inches.

Now we approach the malpais, where the monsoon sometimes barely reaches, snow cover is light and infrequent, and the sun is again a desert sun. The Polemoniaceae are well-represented here. *Gilia (Ipomopsis) multiflora* can be a dome of soft blue. *Gilia rigidula* is here somewhere, but I've not found it. Its blooms are larger and bright blue. The borages range through all the area below 7,500 ft. A couple of yellow and cream-colored lithospermums and the beautiful white-flowered *Cryptantha jamesii* that is found in the tufa canyons north of Pinedale. A few not quite so verdant plants of *Phlox austromontana* appear again, their flowers bleached to almost white, as if to match the stark white of the limestone. *Hedyotis pygmaea*, incredibly enough, is here again, looking perhaps a little smaller and more succulent in these surroundings, and it is joined now by its sister species, *H. rubra*. This is an even tinier plant, and its blooms are a deeper pink, but I do believe it is going to prove even more intractable in cultivation, if it will condescend to be tamed at all. There are crucifers here, particularly *Lesquerella intermedia*, very gray, with golden yellow flowers in spring. Yellow, too, is lovely *Zinnia grandiflora*, with a deep orange center. This is another fine small dryland rock plant. There is an eriogonum here that is truly unique. It forms a little gnarled, twiggy bush, bonsailike, with evergreen revolute leaves and deep pink flowers—*Eriogonum ericifolium* var. *pulchrum*.

But the plant for which these tufa outcroppings must have been arranged is surely *Petrophytum caespitosum*. Without the tufa, it can certainly not have been here, for not a single plant escapes the rock; not a seedling is to be seen beyond the tufa. Each plant is rooted deepy into the crevices and weaves its way along them on incredibly thick, stout stems for such small rosettes. Indeed, it seems a part of the rock itself.

Our island is certainly as floristically rich as any area this size can be, embracing, as it does, so many habitat areas and microclimates, so many variations in soil type, moisture and altitude. I feel it illustrates very well what must be a maxim of the rock gardener's craft. Nature, the master gardener, has put the right plant in the right place (even *Hedyotis pygmaea*!). We would do well to emulate her, on our own much tinier islands in the sky.

References

Kearney, Thomas H., and Robert H. Peebles. 1951. *Arizona Flora*. Berkeley: University of California Press.

Lehr, J. Harry. 1978. *A catalogue of the flora of Arizona*. Phoenix: Desert Botanical Gardens.

McDougall, W. B. 1973. *Seed plants of northern Arizona*. Flagstaff: Museum of Northern Arizona.

Niehaus, Theo. F. 1984. *A field guide to southwestern and Texas wildflowers*. Boston: Houghton Mifflin.

20

Rocky Mountain Alpines: Southern Limits

by Robert DeWitt Ivey

Southward, the diminishing Rocky Mountains—represented at least by the Continental Divide—extend as peninsulas, archipelagos and scattered islands into a sea of hot, semiarboreal deserts. Fingers of subtropical flora and fauna reach up the canyons from the south, interdigitating with ridges and mesas of cool desert, grassland or lower montane forests. A curious meeting of East and West, North and South occurs here. Great Plains meet the Basin Province. Alpine tundra or taiga reminiscent of southern Alaska approaches to within a few miles of Mexican agave, ocotillo and barrel cactus. South-facing slopes hold a bewildering assortment of chaparral shrubs, while opposite slopes support conifer woodlands. Scattered here and there by capricious geologic events are malpais, gypsum sands and alkali flats.

Coronado's expedition of 1541 was the first to publish a written account of this area. Partly an environmental study, the expedition chronicler noted the reliance of various Indians on the prickly pear (*Opuntia*), organ pipe cactus, acorns, pinon nuts (*Pinus edulis*) and mesquite beans (*Prosopis*). Indians, for whose survival all edible species must be recognized, knew both useful and poisonous plants well. Early Spanish settlers developed a folk medicine based on native plants and practiced by specialists known as *curanderas*. Now, we are discovering for ourselves the advantages of Southwestern shrubs and plantings. These blend our yards and gardens tastefully into the environment, are water-thrifty, and whether beautiful or exotic, call to mind our favorite natural places.

The following descriptions, prepared from recent field notes, are representative of many similar areas. They show the variety and dramatic contrast between the many environments of the southernmost tip of the Rocky Mountain region.

After winning state and regional awards as an outstanding biology teacher in the Albuquerque public schools, **Robert DeWitt Ivey** collaborated on a biology textbook. He has BA and MS degrees from the University of Florida, and he has published his own book, *Flowering Plants of New Mexico*. He is now working on a second edition and illustrating a book on wildflowers for another author. His botanical field work is ongoing, as is his participation in the New Mexico Mountain Club. Native wildflowers, especially water lilies, are his garden favorites.

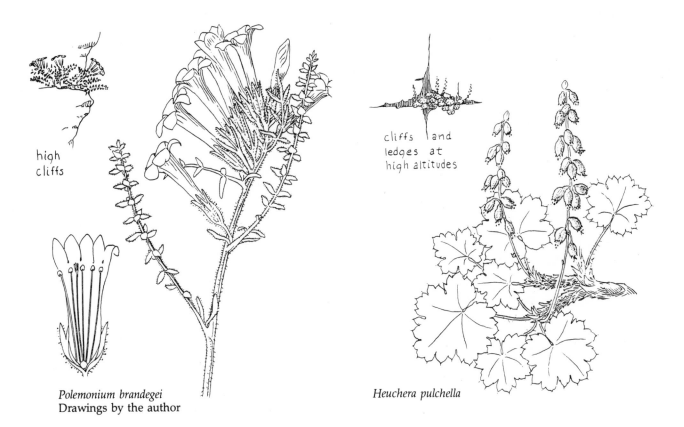

cliffs

cliffs and
ledges at
high altitudes

Polemonium brandegei
Drawings by the author

Heuchera pulchella

A Sandia Crest Loop

The Sandia Mountains resemble a book with one edge propped up on a buried partner. A steep, high, western escarpment of limestone steps and ledges supports marvelous natural rock gardens that are both pruned and nurtured by the raw but warm exposure. The more gentle east slope is covered with cool, coniferous forests.

On a late June morning we are taking a trail north along one of the middle ledges, planning to climb and then return by the highest rim. Our trail is wide enough for sure footing, but shears off so abruptly on the left that the height is dizzying. Far across the Rio Grande Valley and distant mesas, are the mountains of Zuni and Navajo lands. On the right is a limestone wall decorated with orange lichens and fossil sea lilies. Wedged into cracks are the true cliff dwellers: yellow sky pilot (*Polemonium brandegei*), coral bells (*Heuchera*), and cliffbush (*Jamesia americana*). Occupying the merest of ledges is a charmer of the rock face, the cliff primrose (*Primula ellisiae*).

The early morning air, heavy with an unaccustomed humidity, bears a skunkish odor. A few yards ahead, the cause is found to be a stand of Jacob's ladder (*Polemonium*). Shafts of sunlight skim the dewy tops of snowberry (*Symphoricarpos*) and gooseberry (*Ribes*) shrubs on the right, aspen and fir trees on the left. From a thicket ahead, the ominous hum of bees and a flutter of butterflies bespeak a floral bonanza. It is a shoulder-high grove of chokecherries (*Prunus virginiana*), with hundreds of pendant clusters of white flowers. Other trailside plants include mountain parsley (*Cymopteris montanus*), valerian (*Valeriana*), bladderpod (*Lesquerella*), and monkshood (*Aconitum*). Shrubs include Gambel oak (*Quercus gamgelii*), New Mexico locust (*Robinia neomexicana*), ninebark (*Physocarpus monogynus*), and Rocky Mountain maple (*Acer glabrum*).

The chemistry of limestone and its derived soil produces an abundant flora. In some cases, flowers are richer in color, but in others less so. Wallflowers, usually yellow, reach a deep copper or maroon here. Clematis, pale-to-white in some areas, is a strong lavender-to-purple here. On the other hand, monkshoods (*Aconitum*) are of a pale or brownish color.

Now and again, the rock wall has crumbled into a series of small steps, with flowers arranged to fill corners, round edges, or drape from one step to another. Tufts of coral bell (*Heuchera*), mounds of parsley, puffs of yellow sky pilot, and cascades of purple clematis (*Clematis columbiana*) seem so professionally tiered and cultured that it would be an act of vandalism to step off the trail. Up one such staircase, we climb to the summit.

Doubling back along the crest, our trail is at first laid out upon the bedrock of which the mountain is built. Valiantly inhabiting every fracture are perky Sue and purple loco. Occasionally, the trail descends into the forest with a dramatic change of vegetation. Baneberry (*Actaea*), red columbine (*Aquilegia elegantula*), dusky penstemon (*Penstemon whippleanus*), Canada violet (*Viola canadensis*) and creeping mahonia (*Mahonia (Berberis) repens*) are in full flower, while geranium (*Geranium caespitosum*), bedstraw (*Galium*), figwort (*Scrophularia*), and wintergreen (*Pyrola*) are still vegetative or in bud.

Now and again, the trail crosses small meadows. One is a harmonious mass of golden pea (*Thermopsis*) and iris. Others are gardens of mixed flowers including harebell (*Campanula rotundifolia*), paintbrush (*Castilleja*), gentians, pincushion cactus (*Coryphantha vivipara*), groundsels (*Senecio*), asters, fleabane (*Erigeron*), orange agoseris (*Agoseris aurantiaca*) and both meadow and shrub cinquefoil (*Potentilla* sp. and *P. fruticosa* (*Pentaphylloides floribunda*)).

As we continue along the crest rim, we are nearing our starting point. If the downward view is awesome, remember that we are as high as the Grand Canyon rim stands above its valley. Aspens and firs slope away from the prevailing wind. Limber pines (*Pinus flexilis*) have grown into twisted flags. Falcons cruise the updrafts; ravens soar in place; swifts swoop precipitously down the rock faces and as easily up again. A boy leaps off the crest in a hang glider. The rest of us will take the tram.

The Malpais

From a distance, the malpais seems to be only the shadow of a cloud on sunny ground, but look up. There are no clouds! Closer, it is a sinister turmoil of black foam and floe, like a spring thaw in hell. Lava plates are in places collapsed into conical sinks, and elsewhere, upthrust into jagged ridges. Unbroken surfaces are smooth and shiny, but fractured edges are sharp as glass. We enter by a trail between the ridges. Ponderosa (*Pinus ponderosa*) and pinons (*P. edulis*) lightly shade a blue grama (*Bouteloua gracilis*) glade. Phlox, skyrocket and harebells nod in the light breeze. The splash of scarlet against a lava wall is a claret cup cactus (*Echinocereus triglochidiatus*). Our glade ends, and we have to mount into the malpais proper. Careful not to roll a boulder or step into a crevasse while glancing up, we gradually gain skill and confidence. Still, a foot may roll on snaky extrusions of lava that look like black toothpaste squeezed from a long-vanished tube.

The beauty of the malpais is in its contrasts. Black rock and blacker shadows set off a sunlit drapery of virgin's bower (*Clematis ligusticifolia*). A mound of four-o'clocks (*Mirabilis multiflora*) fills the angular spaces between jumbled boulders. The entrance to a bat cave is screened by a spray of taperleaf (*Pericome caudata*). Spring green shrubs of squawberry (*Lycium*), wax currant (*Ribes cereum*), and olive (*Forestiera neomexicana*) cheer a somber alley. A canopy of grape leaves softens the rim of a cliff.

The malpais has many stories to tell. Indians used the caves and holes as safes for pottery and other treasures, also for personal safety during attacks by raiding tribes. "Malpais Joe" Spamberger sought the famed Adams Diggings gold cache here. Skulls show the former presence of desert bighorns and grizzlies. Ice caves gave the children of homesteaders the makings for the rarest of treats—ice cream.

Black rock absorbs solar energy and creates a special microclimate. In oven-warm crevices, many plants get a jump on the season, while others are growing farther north than would otherwise be possible. Even some warm-climate animals seem to prosper here. Certain small mammals and lizards, by becoming dark, have found safety in the rocks. Others have paid for their refuge with broken legs. The malpais is unique, but visit it in cool weather, and wear shoes you can afford to throw away.

The Organ Mountains

As morning light invades the emerald folds of the Organ Mountains, another desert night surrenders to daytime warmth. Our trail toward the mountain slants upward across a plain quilted with light green fluffs of mesquite (*Prosopis juliflora*) and heavier, olive mounds of creosote bush (*Larrea tridentata*). Here and there, arroyo banks are fringed with pink Apache plume (*Fallugia paradoxa*), or sparkle with red and yellow bird-of-paradise (*Caesalpinia gilliesii*).

Our approach to the mountain seems guarded, first by an armament of cat claw mimosas (*Mimosa borealis*), then by legions of soaptree yuccas (*Yucca elata*) with plumed heads and bristling bayonets. Sotols (*Dasylirion wheeleri*) are scattered widely in a flanking maneuver, while the field

Yucca elata. Drawings by the author   *Cowania mexicana*

above is generalled by a few giant agaves (*Agave neomexicana*). Occasionally, a warning is sounded as rock slabs, dislodged by temperature changes, clatter ominously down the domes and pinnacles for which the mountain is named.

As we enter the foothills, the flora attains its greatest variety. Knolls and saddles bear dramatic formations of boulders with exotic shrubs molded to them. Silktassel (*Garrya*), hackberry (*Celtis reticulata*), wolfberry (*Lycium*), Mexican buckeye (*Aesculus*), shrub salvia (*Salvia pinguifolia*), and mountain mahogany (*Cercocarpus montanus*) give refuge to white-winged doves and Gambel's quail. Here, prickly pear (*Opuntia phaeacantha*) reaches an unusual peach shade, while desert willow (*Chilopsis linearis*) achieves its deepest orchid hue. Of fruits, the orange-red berries of limita (*Rhus trilobata*) are at their showiest peak of ripeness. Fendlerbush (*Fendlera rupicola*), white with flowers earlier, now has full, green capsules. Manzanita's (*Arctostaphylos pungens*) little "apples" have already turned black.

Beyond the mountain's billowing skirts, our trail enters a formation of steeply ascending rills and ridges. Some of these are long jetties of boulders, strewn by gargantuan torrents so recently that succession has not yet filled the voids with soil and plants. The trail leads between ridges, through grassy glades with scattered paintbrush (*Castilleja*), blue toadflax (*Linaria canadensis* var. *texana*), and golden smoke (*Corydalis aurea*). It then crosses an older ridge holding a narrow stand of ponderosa pine. In some places we enter deep ravines, overreached and shaded by jungles of shrub live-oak (*Quercus undulata*) and alligator juniper (*Juniperus deppeana*). Grapevines (*Vitis vulpina*) festoon the trees with a semblance of tropical lianas. In clearings, green mounds of turpentine bush (*Haplopappus laricifolius*) alternately fracture and mend in the breeze.

Above this zone of narrow wrinkles, we enter a transverse belt of woodland and forest occupying the uppermost talus. Here, as at the bottom, vegetation is simpler, conforming to the condition found at this altitude on most other southwestern mountains. Pinon and ponderosa pine occupy the higher ground, while wetter canyons are occupied by bigtooth maple (*Acer grandidentatum*), which makes a show of red in autumn. Above this level, except for valiant pioneers in cracks and crevices, the mountain consists only of its exposed skeleton of vertical, bare rock.

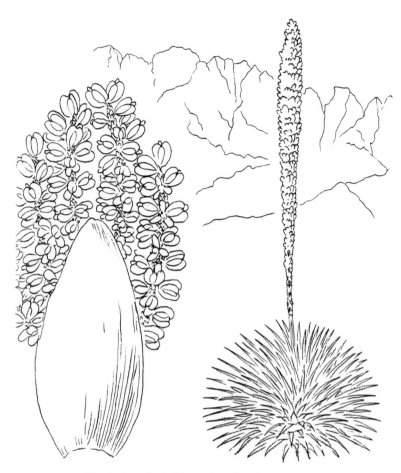

Dasylirion wheeleri. Drawings by the author

Species Recommended for Use or Trial in the Rock Garden

Hymenoxys argentea, H. acaulis, and *H. scaposa:* perky Sue and the stemless bitterweeds. Cheerful, yellow composites rising from a nest of silver leaves, perky Sue grows bravely in the cracks of exposed bedrock on windy ledges, or among cobblestones. Stemless bitterweed grows in shallow soil as high as alpine tundra. At lower or more southerly levels the scapose bitterweed's slender stems sway in desert breezes. All three are heroic but unpretentious and garden-worthy.

Zinnia grandiflora: wild zinnia. This zinnia makes a compact mound about 6 in. high by 8 in. wide. Its deep, yellow rays and orange centers become paperflowers after blooming. There is a larger white zinnia in southern New Mexico.

Talinum pulchellum: talinum. In natural rock gardens and beds of gravel the "fame flower" grows from a stubble of narrow, fleshy leaves. It bears clusters of quarter-sized, rose-pink flowers intermittently throughout the season.

Phlox spp.: various species of phlox. Cheerful, pink windmills related to popular domestic species, several of the wild phloxes should be welcome garden plants.

Cryptantha fulvocanescens or *C. flavoculata:* white hiddenflower or popcorn. These plants of banks or roadsides make a mound or spray of stems all about 8 in. tall and topped with fluffy spikes or balls of white flowers.

Ipomopsis longiflora and *I. multiflora* (*Gilia*): trumpet gilias. Bluish relatives of the skyrockets, these plants are about a foot tall. *Ipomopsis multiflora* is a dense mass of short, blue-violet trumpets. *Ipomopsis longiflora* is spindly of growth with scattered but interesting long, pale trumpets.

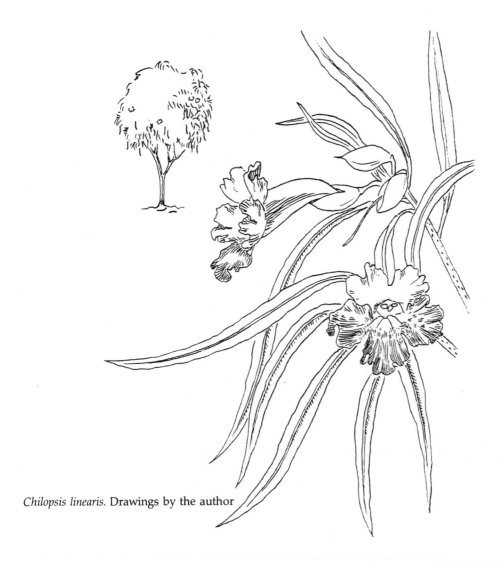

Chilopsis linearis. Drawings by the author

Opuntia erinacea: red-flowered prickly pear. A small, ordinary prickly pear when not in bloom, this plant produces a luxurious show of early summer pink-to-red flowers.

Coryphantha spp.: pincushion and related cacti. Miniature barrels or petite, gray balls, these plants are easily overlooked amid the cobblestones or rock slides where they grow, except when they burst into bloom. Pink or lavender flowers are followed, in some species, by sweet, spineless fruits that may be safely plucked with the fingers and eaten.

Echinocereus spp.: claret cup and strawberry cacti. It is a sight to take your breath away, this great mound of brilliant red clinging to the most unlikely cliffside ledge. Scarcely less surprising are the giant pink blossoms of strawberry and similar cacti amid the stubble of short-grass plains and mesas. Easily cultivated, they give generously for the little space they require.

Cowania mexicana: cliffrose. This shrubby member of the rose family has small leaves with minute, fingerlike lobes. The plant is covered with fragrant, cream-colored blossoms that resemble small, single roses. After the flowers, elongate pistils persist as curly plumes. Its cousin, Apache plume, *Fallugia paradoxa,* is similar, with white flowers and showy pistils but little fragrance.

Chilopsis linearis: desert willow. Widespread and easily grown, this small tree resembles a narrow-leaved willow, although it is really a catalpa relative. It produces somewhat orchidlike flowers over a long season, followed by slender, hanging pods.

Fendlera rupicola and *Philadelphus microphyllus:* fendlerbush (false mockorange) and mockorange. Similar but not closely related, these two shrubs are covered with white, 4-petaled flowers. Fendlerbush blooms in April and mockorange in June, sometimes slightly overlapping in May. The bloom is spectacular, although the shrubs are mediocre in the off-season. Both species grow on canyon sides and chaparral slopes, but mockorange often grows in shadier areas. It also has a nice fragrance.

Dalea formosa: indigobush. A small shrub, gray-hairy, with red-violet pea blossoms nestled in its branches over a long season, indigobush inhabits gravelly slopes and ledges.

Arctostaphylos pungens: manzanita. Growing mainly on steep, volcanic ash slopes, this plant may require special treatment. It has glossy, red branches and a trunk, with an undulating, decorative form. In spring, it has masses of white heather blossoms. The little fruits look and taste like green apples.

Choysia dumosa: Mexican orange. This is an attractive shrub of the desert mountains, with distinctive leaves. Bright green with narrow, palmate lobes, they resemble a mass of little umbrellas. Orange-blossom-sized flowers are showy in season.

Forestiera neomexicana: New Mexico olive. A neat, white-barked tree with small, oval leaves, this attractive little tree is already widely planted in landscape applications in New Mexico. In spring, the male flowers make small, globular sprays of yellow stamens. Its fruits are tiny, purplish olives.

Physocarpus monogynus: ninebark. Ninebark is a bush resembling the currants though it is in the rose family. It has small but attractive maplelike leaves. In summer its branches have terminal clusters of small, white or salmon-colored flowers. The groups of flowers may be round, as with the snowball bush, or more elongate. The bark shreds easily, but hardly has nine layers.

Pinus edulis (*P. cembroides*): pinon. Perhaps the most popular small tree used in landscape plantings in New Mexico, this tree would grow to a symmetrical pine shape were it not for a borer that kills a branch at a time, leaving it picturesquely deformed like a Japanese bonsai. The borer can be detected by the blob of resin oozing out of its tunnel. It can then be traced and gouged out with a piece of wire. Then you can deform the tree to your own taste.

Salvia pinguifolia: shrub salvia. This is a shrub with distinctive character, well-suited to its desert hill and canyon habitat. In late season it is covered with flowers characteristic of the sage genus.

Symphoricarpos spp.: various species of snowberry. The various species in this in this genus mostly have small, oval leaves. In early summer, they have pairs of small, pink honeysuckle flowers. Later, grape-sized white fruits appear, often in pairs.

Rhus trilobata: squawberry, lemonade berry. Known in Spanish as *limitas,* or little limes, this shrubby sumac is 3–4 ft. high, with 3-parted leaves. Its early spring flowers are tiny but numerous along spikelike branches. Its clusters of red, hairy fruits are conspicuous and attractive. It is still used by Indians to make a lemonadelike drink or to flavor other foods. The plant makes a brilliant autumn show, in the orange-red range.

Yucca elata: soaptree yucca. When mature, this yucca bears one or more side limbs with narrow, daggerlike leaves. Annually, each branch develops a gigantic stalk of white flowers. Perhaps the most impressive of all our yuccas, it is the state flower of New Mexico. It has been used for fiber, for food and for the soapy lather obtainable from its roots.

Dasylirion wheeleri: sotol. A symmetrical fountain of narrow, sawtoothed leaves, the plant body itself is attractive. At flowering time, a 10 ft. stalk produces a gracefully tapered mass of rust-colored flowers. A leaf, with its rounded base, is sometimes called a desert spoon.

References

Benson, Lyman, and Robert A. Darrow. 1981. *Trees and shrubs of the Southwestern deserts.* 3rd. ed. Tucson: University of Arizona Press.

Elmore, Francis, and Jeanne R. Janish. 1976. *Shrubs and trees of the Southwest uplands.* Globe, Arizona: The Southwest Parks and Monuments Association.

Ivey, Robert DeWitt. 1983. *Flowering plants of New Mexico.* Albuquerque: the author.

Martin, William C., and Charles R. Hutchins. 1980. *The flora of New Mexico.* Germany: A. R. Gantner Verlag.

Niehaus, Theodore F. 1984. *A field guide to Southwestern and Texas wildflowers.* Boston: Houghton Mifflin Co.

Spellenberg, Richard. 1979. *The Audubon Society field guide to North American wildflowers, Western Region.* New York: Alfred A. Knopf.

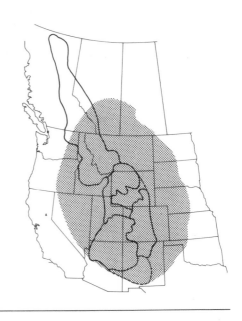

Section V

Western Drylands: Plains and Plateaus

Photo courtesy U.S.D.A. Forest Service

Claude A. Barr, age 91,
at his home near Smithwick, S.D.
Photo by Linda Rector Brown

21

Bounty of the Grasslands: The Legacy of Claude A. Barr

by Cynthia Reed, Joyce Phillips Hardy and Ronald R. Weedon

Just enough work has been done with rock garden cultivation of the beautiful bounty of the grasslands for us to know that these vast acreages harbor many fine plants which will reward us well when we understand their individual requirements. The late Claude A. Barr, who homesteaded the gumbo clay plains of western South Dakota in the early 1900s, introduced rock gardeners to these distinctive plants, so secluded among the grasses that they had largely escaped notice. In this description of a small selection of plants drawn from Barr's work, we believe you will find plants of unusual interest to add to your collection.

To begin to understand plains wildflowers as a group, one must consider the grasslands in general. These mostly treeless expanses offer harsh climate and soils, requiring special adaptations by the flowering plants. Wide variations in daily as well as annual temperatures have fostered an amazing level of adaptability in these plants, allowing us to grow them far outside their normal range of occurrence. However, the prevalence of strongly alkaline soils has produced not only a preference for the higher pH levels, but in some cases a nearly absolute intolerance of acidity. This harshness of soil and temperature is not muted by the moisture nature provides. General aridity is the rule for these grasslands, with the little available moisture usually not well distributed throughout the year. The plants must be able to withstand lengthy periods with no rainfall, immediately followed by steady drenching for several days. It is not just a matter of relatively low amounts of available precipitation that plains plants must endure; they must also be able to survive the high degree of unreliability of available moisture. Extremely drying winds are intermittent but common and require compensation by those sturdy survivors that endure and provide the flashes of colorful bloom Claude Barr called "Jewels of the Plains."

Cynthia Reed, president of the Great Plains Botanical Society, is pursuing an MS degree in biology at South Dakota State University. She specializes in Great Plains native ornamentals and is a research associate, Chadron State College Herbarium.

Joyce Phillips Hardy, research associate, Chadron State College Herbarium, is pursuing an MS in biology at Chadron State College, specializing in Great Plains native plant taxonomy.

Dr. Ronald R. Weedon, professor of biology at Chadron State College, serves as curator of the Herbarium and of the Claude A. Barr Archive. He is a taxonomist who collects extensively in the Great Plains and the Black Hills.

Selections from the Grasslands

The furry lavender "crocus" which figures affectionately in so many Western memories is *Pulsatilla (Anemone) patens*, commonly famous as the pasqueflower. It is a perennial on crowns just under the ground which send up their furry buds in early spring, often blooming between late snowfalls. The six pinkish to lavender petals and sepals are set off by a handsome golden center of many stamens to produce flowers ranging from 1–4 in. in diameter. Wide, but very finely divided leaves appear after flowering, and soon the large, silky plumed seed pods take center stage, especially in any slight breeze. Transplanting *P. patens* is not easy, and must involve a soil ball sufficient to leave the roots undisturbed. Fresh seeds are a surer source of success. Excellent drainage is vital, and the sandy soil should have a bit of richness near the surface. Plenty of sun is required, but mid-day shading is common in the native locations. *Dodecatheon pulchellum* and *Viola nuttallii* are among the usual associates of *Pulsatilla patens*.

A cushion-forming beauty of the habit so highly prized by alpinists, *Astragalus barrii* (Barr's milkvetch) is smothered in a rosy pink drift of flowers during May. The small, tripartite, bluish gray leaves form a dense mound, slowly reaching 8 in. in diameter, that is attractive through the entire year as it curves over any slope or soil ledge. The flowers are borne 3 to 5 per scape, on short stems that lift them to the surface of the leafy tuft. *Astragalus barrii* is rare in our grasslands, an endemic on its preferred rocky clay barren areas of eastern Wyoming, southeastern Montana and southwestern South Dakota. Propagation is by seed as the crown formed by the branching taproot may not be divided. In its natural setting, *A. barrii* is to be found with *Oenothera caespitosa*, *Phlox andicola*, and *Viola nuttallii*, but it should also tolerate other more xerophytic clay-lovers such as cacti, *Cryptantha celosioides*, *Oxytropis multiceps*, and various species of *Townsendia*. Barr's discovery of this gem a few miles south of his house figured strongly in his selection as recipient of the American Rock Garden Society's first Dr. Edgar T. Wherry Award in 1973.

In making rock garden selections from the grasslands one should not overlook the diminutive native grasses. *Bouteloua gracilis*, commonly known as blue grama, is present on clay soils in native prairies. It forms small mats by its short rhizomes, and from June to August sends up a distinctive "flag" inflorescence to a height of 6 in. A close relative, *B. hirsuta* (hairy grama), looks quite similar, but prefers more sandy or rocky soil. It flowers from July to October. *Bouteloua curtipendula* is called sideoats grama because its oatlike seeds are borne on one side of the 16 in. stem. It blooms from June to August. *Buchloe dactyloides*, commonly called buffalo grass, is another small, mat-forming perennial grass, which slowly spreads by stolons to form a dense colony. In the flowering state all of these grasses are attractive additions to a garden, yet even without the persistent inflorescence the growth habit and leaves are endearing. Propagation, from seed sown in early spring, or division in either the spring or fall, is easily accomplished. Blue grama and buffalo grass are suitable alternatives to Kentucky bluegrass and others for lawns in dry areas where available water is at a premium.

The frequent cacti of the grasslands are mostly to be found within two genera, *Coryphantha* and *Opuntia*. Our choice of two interesting species is based on their attractive reddish flowers, somewhat less common than the prevalent yellows. *Coryphantha vivipara* grows in the form of a globe which produces carmine pink flowers with many narrow pointed petals around a brilliant yellow center. Small offsets may arise to produce a clump up to 8 in. in diameter. The forms of *Opuntia polyacantha* which produce orange or pink flowers were favorites selected by Barr at his Prairie Gem Ranch in southwestern South Dakota. This opuntia is a member of the famed prickly pear group and propagates easily by division. As do most if not all cacti, these two species favor sandy, rocky locations, but they are frequently found in clay in our very dry habitats. Native associates include grasses of the high plains such as those mentioned above. With adequate drainage, cacti should do well as companions to most rock garden plants.

Cryptantha celosioides, the butte candle of the high plains, will provide a shining white light of bloom from May to July. During its first year this biennial forms a pleasing small rosette of narrow oblanceolate grayish leaves with stiff hairs which render it unpleasant to grazing animals. The second summer sees the production of a "candle" of 8–14 in., highlighted by delicate, tiny, white florets densely packed on the spike. Early in the blooming season the spikes are simple, but they later branch from the column in scorpoid fashion to form a candelabrum effect. *Cryptantha cana*, a perennial, was considered by Barr to be the choice of this genus, but difficult to grow, and "a challenge still to be met." The fact that these cryptanthas grow from a small crown on a deep taproot indicates to us that propagation will be best accomplished from the seeds.

A rare intensity of deep color is found in *Delphinium bicolor*, the larkspur of the northern Rocky Mountain areas. The several dark rich purple 1.2 in. flowers are set high on the main stem which is usually about 12 in. tall and appear early in June. The basal leaves, much divided in characteristic delphinium manner, follow the flowers into early dormancy. *Delphinium bicolor* does better on sandy soil with added humus in which to nestle its cluster of small tubers.

The shooting star of the plains, *Dodecatheon pulchellum* survives by a sensitive reaction to warmth and moisture, flowering early on speedy growth during an energetic spring, but later or not at all if warmth and moisture are too slow to arrive. *Dodecatheon pulchellum* is much more tolerant of drought than other shooting stars, thriving on less than 16 in. annual rainfall. The white roots may wither during drought, only to regain turgidity when moisture returns. This dodecatheon is perennial, producing simple leaves in a small basal rosette giving rise to scapes 6–12 in. tall topped with the familiar downward-pointing stamens from which the five rosy red, recurved petals fly. The shooting star responds well to a small addition of humus but still requires perfect drainage and freedom from lingering dampness. Propagation is to be undertaken during the autumn by crown division. One must mark the location, however, as the leaves die early. Barr selected and successfully propagated two outstanding color forms of this species, the one 'Prairie Ruby,' an intense velvety ruby red, the other 'White Comet,' a pure white with a thread of gold at the petal base.

Gaura coccinea is a common little flower of the grasslands whose main attractions are its delicate appearance and pleasant fragrance. The narrow leaves may attain a 2 in. length but are overpowered by the spikelike raceme up to 12 in. tall, closely covered with the delicate white flowers which age to pink and red. The long filaments of the stamens add to the decidedly airy effect. Such delicacy of appearance is belied by the sturdy strength of the rhizomes which may have you hoeing in your rock garden. It prefers sandier soils, so perhaps by using a heavier soil its tendency to spread may be curbed.

A showy bloomer in early spring, *Leucocrinum montanum*, known in the Plains as sand lily and elsewhere as mountain lily, is a premium candidate for culture in the rock garden for more interesting reasons than its considerable beauty alone. The mature perennial plants form multiple crowns about 2 in. underground from which several dozen flowers may arise, each with its long underground tube wherein the seeds will form. (Harvest of seeds requires a bit of excavation.) The narrow, straplike leaves surround the white flowers which open near the surface of the ground, spreading six petals around the golden anthers to a width of 1–2 in. Extended bloom season (early April to the end of May) may be accomplished in a colony by varied exposure. Thick, moisture-storing roots spread widely, but not deeply, from the crown. Transplanting is usually successful even with the loss of a great portion of roots, although a year's flowering may be sacrificed. This leucocrinum prefers clay, from firm gumbo to sandy clay loam or gravelly clay, but does poorly on sand.

Leucocrinum montanum. Photo by Vernon Tomppert

The gayfeathers of these sub-montane Western grasslands are especially adapted to drought with strong, moisture-storing roots. The taprooted *Liatris punctata* will bear its many purple-flowering spikes even in a very dry year. Its mostly basal leaves are rough and dotted, forming a tuft below the blooming stems, which are usually 10–12 in. tall. In areas of greater rainfall, this liatris may need extra lime and/or potash to maintain the normal erectness of its stems. During August when *L. punctata* shows its purple, the flowering stems may be cut and allowed to dry for an everlasting bouquet with color as fine as fresh. Liatris is easy to grow in dry, sunny areas, especially on sandy soils, from seed sown in autumn. It is well adapted as a companion to all these alkaline-oriented choices except those showing preference for heavy clays, such as *Oenothera caespitosa*.

The American Indians gave the showy golden gems of *Lithospermum incisum* their common name "puccoon." This is the Western puccoon, and may be the most delightful, giving us its five ruffled, glowing yellow petals on abundant 0.75 in. flowers in May. *Lithospermum incisum* shows definite preference for looser, sandy soils but can survive a bit of heavy clay. The small thin roots are easy to transplant during dormancy, with caution that the chosen site must be well-drained. Although these flowers are quite showy, the grayish leaves are narrow and small, not providing much impact during the rest of the year.

The infamous gumbo clays of the American West have given their coarse appellation to the large, delicate, much-loved flower we call "gumbo lily," *Oenothera caespitosa*. This improbable beauty produces flowers of 2–4 in. width composed of four heart-shaped white petals that open rapidly in late afternoon and usually fade to pink or rose-purple and wither the next day. Flowering from early May to August, sparse rosettes of irregularly margined, oblanceolate leaves are frequently found on the stickiest and slimiest patches of clay soils, but live longer where drainage is not impeded. Gardeners do well to use soils of at least one-third sand to cultivate this rewarding perennial. Barr indicated that although the thick taproots may branch to give rise to new crowns, rarely may a plant be successfully divided. The delightfully sweet fragrance seems to exist in total contrast to the heavy, clinging, pervasive clays called "gumbo." Any of the grasslands plants do well cultivated with *O. caespitosa* except those which prefer a moister habitat such as *Rosa arkansana*, *Dodecatheon pulchellum*, and *Ratibida columnifera*.

Among the many beautiful locoweeds of the grasslands, *Oxytropis multiceps*, one of the "crazy weeds," is dwarfed to a charmingly dense bun of short, silvery, silky, pinnate leaves, neatly attractive year-around. A taprooted perennial, *O. multiceps* flowers in late April and early May giving us up to four relatively large, well-rounded, purplish pink, pealike blossoms per short scape. During a favorable season the rosettes of up to 6 in. diameter will be almost covered with the flowers which give way to another attraction—the silky, red-purple pods, all held close to the surface of the mound of leaves keeping to our preferred tidy habit. This gemlike dwarf is normally found on stony open hilltops in the neighborhood of *Phlox andicola*, various species of *Townsendia* and *Viola nuttallii*.

The *Phlox* species are so common in Western grasslands that our discussion would be incomplete without inclusion of the favorite *Phlox alyssifolia*, which forms the typical low mat of hard small foliage. Its small 0.75 in. leaves form a solid mat which hides the soil, and in late April and May sends up the flowers whose scent and color elevate its standing in the garden. For a plant usually 1.5 in. in height, *P. alyssifolia* certainly provides large flowers. From 0.8–1.2 in. in width, they include white, pink or lavender blossoms. *Phlox alyssifolia*, like the other little phloxes of the West, requires open sun on limy soils, preferring a bit of loosening sand or gravel in the loam, yet tolerant of the heavier clays. A good colony retains its original central woody root, sending out rhizomes to form new plants which may be safely separated by their second or third year. Barr's extensive work with *Phlox* species led to the recognition of a variety of *P. andicola* and the discovery of a genetic variant not yet named but similar to *P. alyssifolia*.

A fragrant composite, *Ratibida columnifera* lights up in July and August with its brown disk flowers first appearing at the base of the central cone surrounded by the rich yellow rays which are often streaked with a deep red or, rarely, nearly completely reddened. The entire inflorescence is about 1.25 in. wide and 2–4 in. tall, and is carried 16–24 in. off the ground by a rather freely branching stem, from which the deeply pinnatifid leaves also arise. *Ratibida columnifera*, listed as a perennial, often performs as a biennial, at least on the heavier clay soils. Propagation is successful from seed sown in the autumn or, if stratified, in early spring. The taproot which supports this graceful friend tolerates a fair variety of soils except for the purer clays or sands.

Who can resist adding a rose? *Rosa arkansana* is a well-behaved and fragrant little jewel, generally achieving 12 in. in height, spreading gently from its deep rhizomes. The *R. arkansana* we know does not die back to the ground annually and flowers from both old and new growth. Claude Barr distributed a double form named for its discoverer from the Black Hills of South Dakota—J. W. Fargo. The "Fargo Rose" was labeled by the Canadian specialist F. L. Skinner as the best double wild

Ratibida columnifera. Photo by Bob Heapes   *Sphaeralcea coccinea.* Photo by Roberts

rose he had seen, with a flower, larger than the normal 2 in. single, of around 40 pink petals opening to display the golden center. The typical single *R. arkansana* blooms mainly in June, but "J. W. Fargo" peaks in early July. These sturdy little roses tolerate a variety of conditions, only avoiding the heaviest of our clays.

We include *Sphaeralcea coccinea* because it provides an arresting color contrast in the grasslands from early May to July. This plant is known variously as scarlet mallow, flame mallow, or "cowboy's delight." The small, grayish green, rough and hairy leaves only add to the apparent brilliance of the pink through brick red to orange flowers. The 4–8 in. stems bearing the clusters of five-petaled 0.8–1.2 in. flowers centered by the large, yellow pistil are the products of a strong, potentially invasive, root system. Forming vigorous colonies in disturbed soils such as roadsides, *S. coccinea* may exhibit better behavior in heavier soils.

Barr called *Townsendia hookeri* a treasure for the rock garden, stating that it is longer lived and more successful from seed than its more well-known cousin, *T. exscapa*. Showing smaller leaves and flowers, *T. hookeri* creates a finer textured 3 in. bun of close-set, narrow, evergreen leaves, and the wide white flowers come two weeks earlier in April. These diminutive tufts completely lose their quiet style when covered with the disproportionately large composite flowers of daisylike rays surrounding the yellow disk center. *Townsendia hookeri* is usually listed as white, but definite pink colonies have been reported. This taprooted perennial chooses loose, limy soils of excellent drainage and is to be found sometimes in rock fissures. These species of *Townsendia*, or Easter daisy, are often so rare in the Great Plains they are considered endangered by some. Grow plants from seeds.

Another of the outstanding finds made by our friend Claude Barr is an extremely doubled form of *Viola nuttallii,* which in its common single form is well-known for its brilliant yellow color and the wide variety of habitats in which it can be found. *Viola nuttallii* is a perennial whose stem has very short internodes so that the leaves form a small cluster at the soil surface. Blooming from April through July and producing good quantities of seed are considerable accomplishments for a plant which retreats to underground dormancy during the dry summer and autumn. This violet is so widely adapted, accepting such a range of conditions from dry prairies to stream valleys, that it probably is to be found in the native neighborhood of most all the plants we mention here.

Other interesting plants which are found in the grasslands of the High Plains include:

Antennaria spp., pussytoes: Low mats of grayish rosettes producing clusters of furry, pinkish inflorescences very early in spring.

Astragalus ceramicus, bird's-egg pea: A skeleton plant which bears insignificant flowers, but forms an inflated, papery, green seed pod with reddish streaks.

Artemisia frigida, fringed sage: A low, non-invasive tuft of velvet with several tall flower stems to be clipped for best winter display.

Artemisia longifolia: A shrub sometimes attaining 3.3 ft. in height, with a lovely silvery effect when seedpods are kept clipped.

Calochortus nuttallii, mariposa lily or sego lily: A pristine white, 3-petalled "tulip" marked on the interior with gleaming yellow and maroon; its stem reaches 10 in. above grassy leaves.

Castilleja sessiliflora: Paintbrushes bearing intriguing, colored bracts, difficult to relocate because of their parasitic requirements.

Chrysothamnus spp., rabbitbrushes: Large shrubs valuable for their golden autumn color.

Echinacea angustifolia, purple coneflower: A spectacular composite of pink rays drooping around a wide prickly cone of mahogany tinge.

Hymenoxys acaulis: "little yellow daisies" arising to 6 in. above a small rosette; free flowering and very early.

Some recommended associations of the plants we have discussed might be:

For a rocky, clay soil: *Astragalus barrii, Oenothera caespitosa, Bouteloua gracilis, Buchloe dactyloides, Oxytropis multiceps, Phlox andicola, P. alyssifolia, Liatris punctata, Leucocrinum montanum, Ratibida columnifera, Viola nuttallii, Cryptantha celosioides,* and the various species of cacti.

For sandy soil with added humus: *Delphinium bicolor, Pulsatilla patens, Dodecatheon pulchellum, Rosa arkansana, Gaura coccinea, Phlox alyssifolia,* and *Viola nuttallii.*

Research on the ornamental cultivation of Great Plains natives is still in its infancy, with the work provided by the late Claude A. Barr remaining the clearest source of experience to which one may refer. The recent formation of the Great Plains Botanical Society provides a forum for information exchange and stimulates continued progress by gardeners who cultivate Great Plains native plants. The Society has selected as its first major project the design, installation, and maintenance of a living botanical collection to be known as the Claude A. Barr Memorial Great Plains Garden. This research and display garden will be situated on the grounds of the Mammoth Site at Hot Springs, South Dakota, a location which already attracts visitors of scientific leanings and is close to Barr's original Prairie Gem Ranch. Barr has willed that his collections and papers be curated by Ronald R. Weedon, and they are now housed as the Claude A. Barr Memorial Archive at the Chadron State College Herbarium. For more information contact the authors at either of the offices listed at the beginning of this chapter.

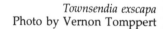
Townsendia exscapa
Photo by Vernon Tomppert

Acknowledgements

The authors acknowledge with appreciation funding provided by the Chadron State College High Plains Center for supporting the development of the Claude A. Barr Archive and the development of this paper. The High Plains Center is dedicated to conducting studies of the environmental, cultural, and historical resources of the High Plains region. We also thank Denise Kruger for assistance in preparing the manuscript and Jerry Ingram for assistance in photographic processing.

References

Barr, Claude A. 1953. "Germination of Great Plains species." *Bull. of the Amer. Rock Garden Soc.* 16(1): 9–11.

Dorman, Caroline. 1965. *Natives preferred.* Baton Rouge: Claitor's Book Store.

Taylor, Kathryn S., and Stephen F. Hamblin. 1983. *Handbook of wild flower cultivation.* New York: Macmillan Publishing Co., Inc.

22

Cacti of the Rockies

by Rod Haenni

Cacti are not generally thought to be able to withstand the rigors of an alpine or even a temperate winter but, indeed, many varieties of cacti are native to the Rocky Mountain region. They occur in habitats as diverse as pine forests at 10,000 ft. down to searing sand dunes below 4,000 ft. At least one species, *Opuntia fragilis,* ranges almost to the Arctic Circle in Canada.

Rocky Mountain cacti withstand winter temperatures from −20°F to −40°F and many of them frequent areas with more than 20 in. of rain per year. Cacti most often prefer well-drained limestone-dolomite slopes with a southerly or southwesterly exposure. Most of these plants prosper in alkaline soil conditions, but a few, such as *Pediocactus simpsonii,* will grow very well in the neutral to slightly acidic soil of decomposed granite.

Cacti from the Rocky Mountains are being successfully grown outside from Massachusetts to southern California, from Seattle to southern Florida, as well as in Canada, Europe, and Japan. They are more adaptable to climatic extremes than are many popularly grown rock and alpine plants, and they produce flowers which, although fleeting, rival the most spectacular the plant kingdom has to offer. Consequently, they deserve more respect from rock gardeners than they have received heretofore. Scholarly, and some not so scholarly, tomes on the Cactaceae abound, but hardy cacti in general, and Rocky Mountain cacti in particular, have been sadly neglected in the literature. This fact may have contributed to the lack of interest among rock gardeners in growing these deserving plants.

Taxonomic confusion is rampant, as many of the cacti are still rapidly evolving. The opuntias and the echinocerei are especially promiscuous and hybridize readily with other nearby species and varieties. This tendency is a nightmare for botanist and layman alike, often resulting in two or more names for the same plant. This confusion does not detract from the enjoyment to be derived from successfully growing and flowering these unusual plants and, in fact, allows room for many more "experts" than a more satisfactorily described family might permit.

Beginning with opuntias, I will progress from almost absolute chaos to some degree of order, ending with the sclerocacti. In between, expect a roller coaster ride of unfamiliar names, remote locations, and beautiful scenery.

Rod Haenni became interested in cacti while working as a geologist in the southwestern United States. When he became a rock gardener, he combined these interests by growing hardy cacti and other succulents alongside more traditional rock garden plants. He is known to readers of the *Journal of the Cactus and Succulent Society* for precise and witty accounts of his plants and travels. He now works as a landscaper in the Denver area and sells cacti and succulents by mail under the name Winter Country Cacti.

The Opuntias

The opuntias are commonly referred to as "prickly pears," a name which aptly describes the most common Rocky Mountain species of this genus, *Opuntia polyacantha*. This plant is extremely spiny and covers thousands of acres in Wyoming, Colorado, and New Mexico, scrambling up from the plains into the nearby mountains to approximately 8,000 ft. Spination varies tremendously in length, color, and in distribution on the "pad" or stem. Spines can be less than 0.25 in. to over 4 in. in length; spine color ranges from white to gray, to pink and to straw yellow; and spine distribution on the pads can be so thick as to obscure the pad's green epidermis or so sparse as to invest only the uppermost portion of the pads with a few scattered spines. Flower color is equally diverse, as *O. polyacantha* flowers range from a Claude Barr-discovered hybrid with cream-colored petals and red stamens, 'Crystal Tide,' to a deep pink form native to the eastern Colorado plains. Typically, *O. polyacantha* has a lemon to golden-colored flower. Bright orange flowers are not common but have been noted. *Opuntia polyacantha* forms clumps up to 2 ft. across and less than 8 in. high. This is not a plant for the small rock garden, but a clump 2 ft. across in full bloom, no matter what the flower color, is a sight many rock gardeners would welcome in their more spacious gardens. Like most opuntias, *O. polyacantha* is very easy to propagate from stem cuttings.

Two other opuntias are often found intermingled and hybridizing with *O. polyacantha*: *O. fragilis* and *O. phaeacantha*. In many places, these three species constitute a hybrid swarm with an almost infinite variety of spination, stem shape and size, and flower color.

The end member *Opuntia fragilis* is ideally a small, extremely spiny, prostrate plant, never over 4 in. high. Spines on *O. fragilis* are usually bone white but can vary to red or gray. *Opuntia fragilis* and its hybrids are not usually prolific flower producers but, when they do bloom, 2–3 in. flowers range in color from lemon yellow to light pink and can completely overpower the tiny stems. One *O. fragilis* form near Leadville, Colorado, grows at nearly 10,000 ft. and is completely spineless and almost free of glochids, those minute, barbed ancillary spines that cause so much discomfort to the unwary.

Opuntia phaeacantha, along with its varieties and hybrids, also exhibits a wide variety of spine density and colors as well as pad size and shape, and it displays an incredible diversity of flower

Opuntia macrorhiza
From report of the Whipple expedition

colors. My vote for the most beautiful *O. phaeacantha* goes to a hybrid growing near Gateway in western Colorado. Here, clumps of sparsely spined stems up to 3 ft. across present the fortunate observer with islands of deep tomato red blossoms surrounded by seas of *Artemisia, Ephedra, Eriogonum,* and numerous other xeric perennials.

Opuntia macrorhiza hybridizes readily with the *O. phaeacantha* varieties, but the end member can be readily distinguished by the glaucous, blue-green new growth, the sparse white-to-yellow spines on the upper third of the pads, and the thick, tuberous roots almost always present. Both *O. macrorhiza* and *O. phaeacantha* have juicy, persistent fruits which turn varying shades of red to purple when ripe. All of the other Rocky Mountain opuntias have dry fruits which do not persist into winter. Some of the *O. phaeacantha* fruits are large enough (2 or more in. in diameter) to make gathering and eating them worthwhile. They have a mild but refreshing flavor, similar to red plums.

Two other Rocky Mountain flat pad opuntias, separated by over 600 miles, deserve special note. The first, *O. arenaria,* is probably a depauperate form of *O. polyacantha,* stranded in the sand dunes of adjoining Texas and New Mexico during the last glacial epoch some 10,000 years ago. The plant adapted perfectly to its habitat of constantly moving sand by forming new stems directly from its rhizomelike root system, enabling parent plants buried by the sand to survive by sending up new pads several feet away in more favorable conditions. Despite the southerly location and the severe desert conditions, *O. arenaria* grows very nicely in temperate climates. Plants grown in Denver have thrived on around 20 in. of rainfall and survived subzero temperatures with no damage. The satiny saffron flowers arising from 1–2 in. high pads make this plant a choice addition to any rock garden with a hot, dry niche.

A northern cousin to *O. arenaria* is the recently described *O. heacockae,* named for the well-known Denver rock gardener and student of cacti, Mary Ann Heacock. This diminutive gem has bright pink flowers and grows above 8,000 ft. in the central Colorado Rockies. It, too, has developed a rhizomelike habit of producing new stems directly from areoles (dormant buds) on its roots. *Opuntia heacockae* probably developed this characteristic in response to the short growing season (less than 75 days) it experiences, as the plant grows in rocky, stable soil. The pads are usually almost naked, with few spines or glochids. *Opuntia heacockae* and *O. arenaria* are the only opuntias native to the United States exhibiting this rhizomelike growth habit. They represent a good example of convergent evolution, where both plants have arrived at the same growth mechanism to solve completely different problems of self-perpetuation.

Three "chollas" or cylindrical-stemmed opuntias of special interest occur in the Rocky Mountains. The first, *O. clavata,* is endemic to the Rio Grande Valley of New Mexico and is most abundant between Santa Fe and Albuquerque. This slow-growing mat-former can form masses 5 feet across of 2 in. high, club-shaped stems! Of course, *O. clavata* is slow growing, and mats this size could easily be fifty years old. Dense, daggerlike spines, white to gray in color, set this plant apart from all other cacti. The yellowish green flowers are not spectacular, but the plant is well worth growing for its interesting spination alone.

The "rat tail cholla," *O. whipplei,* is common in the southwest corner of Colorado and in the neighboring Four Corners states. The common name is appropriate, for certain low-growing dwarf forms of this plant do resemble rather large rats' tails. Larger forms grow to over 4 ft. tall and have a pleasing candelabrum effect. The white spine sheaths present on some forms glisten in the sun, giving the appearance of ice crystals. Unfortunately, the flowers are not particularly attractive as they are small and greenish yellow. However, the small "rat tail" forms grow in manageable clumps less than one foot high and would warrant a place in a large rock garden.

The giant of the Rocky mountain cacti is the "tree" cholla, *O. imbricata.* This monster can reach 7 or 8 ft. in height if protected from heavy snows. Commonly, plants will reach 4 ft. and then be broken by wet, heavy spring snows. Populations of *O. imbricata* are remarkably uniform, owing to their habit of reproducing mostly vegetatively instead of sexually. Stems detach readily, the barbed spines attaching themselves to animals and people, often ending up some distance away from the parent plant. A stem will root in just a few weeks during the growing season and will lie dormant for months in cold weather, waiting for the warm spring days that will allow it to root and form a plant genetically identical to its parent. *Opuntia imbricata* has beautiful magenta flowers and is the last of the Rocky Mountain cacti to bloom, usually throughout July. This cholla could be used for dramatic effect in any rock garden, perhaps taking the place of a dwarf conifer.

The opuntias, fascinating and variable as they are, represent only a portion of the cacti found in the Rocky Mountains. The genus *Echinocereus,* a group of cylindrical, single to multi-stemmed cacti, displays a bewildering variety of size, spination, and flower color. They hybridize with almost the same abandon characteristic of the opuntias. No rock garden including native plants is really complete without at least a representative of these outstanding, easy-to-grow plants.

Echniocereus viridiflorus
Photo by Vernon Tomppert

The Echinocerei

Only one member of this genus can be considered obscure to any degree: *Echinocereus viridiflorus*. The species epithet refers to the bright green flowers so typical of this plant. It prefers to grow among the grasses and is easily overlooked by anyone who, quite justifiably, would not expect to find cacti growing in a high altitude meadow.

Frequently, *E. viridiflorus* has a great deal of company from its relatives. One location in the San Luis Valley of Colorado includes *Coryphantha vivipara, Pediocactus simpsonii, Echinocereus triglochidiatus* var. *gonacanthus,* and *Opuntia polyacantha* and *O. macrorhiza.* This bounty of cacti occurs at an elevation above 8,000 ft. where winter temperatures can drop to −40°F.

Echinocereus viridiflorus is no exception to the general variability of cacti. Stem size varies from 1 in. high at maturity to almost 1 ft., depending on the altitude, soil conditions, and the genetic make-up of plants from a given location. Stems may be solitary or may coalesce into clumps of up to 15 stems, the whole perhaps 2 ft. in diameter. Spination is equally variable, with some plants having prominent white or red central spines, some with none. Often, plants with 0.5 in. long central spines grow next to plants completely lacking centrals. Plants without central spines have a neatly combed appearance given by their pectinate radial spines.

The *Echinocereus triglochidiatus* complex consists of six or seven varieties, four of which are abundant in the Rockies, from southern New Mexico to the Wyoming border. These are the "claret cups," the "king's crown" cacti. No one who has seen a mound of these plants in full bloom will ever forget the deep red flowers and prominent straw or gray spines the common names describe. Mounds of over 500 individual stems have been observed in many localities and, as one probably apocryphal account notes, can result in a mound "as big as a Volkswagen that in full bloom can be seen one mile away." Variability in spination (not considered by *any* taxonomists in the case of the obscure *E. viridiflorus*) is the primary means of differentiating amongst the *E. triglochidiatus* varieties. *Echinocereus triglochidiatus* var. *gonacanthus* has a few thick, gray spines; var. *melanacanthus* has many straw-colored spines, and *E. t.* var. *neomexicanus* is densely covered with gray to straw-colored spines that hide the green stem. Another common name for the echinocerei in general is hedgehog cactus, and none of the taxa in the genus typify this description more than *E. t.* var. *neomexicanus.* One other variety is *E. t.* var. *triglochidiatus.* This plant forms clumps of up to 5 stems, each stem growing to 1.5 ft. in height. The spines generally number 3 to 5 and are thick and triangular in cross section. The *E.*

Echinocereus triglochidiatus. Denver Botanic Gardens collection

triglochidiatus complex is genetically fluid. Intergradations are common among all the varieties, assuring that botanists will never quite get this species sorted out.

One very special form of *E. triglochidiatus* var. *melanacanthus,* forma *inermis,* illustrates the near impossibility of affixing a chiseled-in-stone label to any of these plants. In a small area on the Colorado-Utah border, plants with all degrees of spination grow contentedly together, unaware of the consternation they have inflicted on generations of field botanists. The choicest plants have no spines at all; when in flower, the red flowers appear to be sculpted onto symmetrical jade columns, each stem's ribs separately defined but abstract as a whole. No other cactus in the Rocky Mountain region can compare to this treasure for its perfection of form and flower. Associated with it in its pinyon-juniper habitat are *Sclerocactus parviflorus* var. *intermedius, Coryphantha vivipara* var. *arizonica, Opuntia fragilis,* and *O. phaeacantha.*

Two purple-flowered echinocerei are also found in the Rocky Mountains. The first, *Echinocereus fendleri,* is usually a solitary stem, 6–8 in. high. The attractive flower often does not open all of the way but is 2–3 in. across nonetheless. Upward-pointing central spines distinguish *E. fendleri* from *E. triglochidiatus* var. *gonacanthus* when not in flower. Both plants can be found growing together near Penrose, Colorado, and in other localities farther south, and at least one hybrid between the two is known. *Echinocereus fendleri* is common in much of New Mexico.

The lace cactus, *E. reichenbachii* var. *perbellus,* barely makes a Rocky Mountain appearance, growing along the drainage of the Arkansas River in southern Colorado. The white, pectinate spination gives this uncommon plant its common name. It is attractive in or out of bloom and is very easy to grow from seed, as are most of the Rocky Mountain native cacti.

Rock gardeners unfamiliar with native cacti might be surprised to learn that one species grows *only* in mountainous areas, between 6,000 and 10,000 ft. In fact, these plants qualify as the highest-growing cacti north of Mexico.

The Pediocacti

Despite its name, *Pediocactus simpsonii* and *P. simpsonii* var. *minor* do not grow on the plains. The mountain ball or mountain pincushion cactus is more aptly described by its common names, for it resembles nothing more than a fat pincushion. The generally pink flowers surround the growing center of the plant, blooming earlier than any other Rocky Mountain cacti. Blooming times range from early April to early June, depending on altitude. Again, size, spination, and flower color are variable. Plants up to almost 1 ft. tall are not uncommon, but neither are miniatures not much bigger than a thumb. In some localities, *P. simpsonii* forms mounds of 10 or more stems and grows with *Artemisia tridentata*. Individual colonies can contain plants with pure white to dark brown-red spines. Flower colors range from white with the barest flush of pink to magenta and even yellow. The type variety, *P. s.* var. *simpsonii,* can generally be distinguished from *P. s.* var. *minor* by the latter having more open spination and forming smaller stems than *P. s.* var. *simpsonii*. The two do grow together and intermediate forms are common in some areas. These plants range from the higher altitudes of New Mexico up into the Wyoming Rockies. They are the delight of hikers and amateur naturalists not expecting to find high altitude cacti.

The Coryphanthas

Two species occur throughout the Rockies and are quite dissimilar. *Coryphantha vivipara* grows from New Mexico well into Canada and superficially resembles *Pediocactus simpsonii*. However, *Coryphantha vivipara* has prominent grooved tubercles never found in the pediocacti. The central and radial spines of *C. vivipara* are also much longer than those of *Pediocactus simpsonii*. *Coryphantha* means "top blooming" and the pink, frilly, star-shaped flowers are produced at the very apex of the plants as opposed to the ring of flowers surrounding the apex that *Pediocactus simpsonii* produces.

The three *Coryphantha vivipara* varieties occurring in the Rockies are *C. v.* var. *vivipara, C. v.* var. *neomexicanus,* and *C. v.* var. *arizonica*. Intergradations between any two of the varieties commonly occur in parts of New Mexico and Colorado, but the flower color is a relatively constant bright pink in all of the varieties. Spination and stem size are, of course, quite variable.

The other native species is a very obscure little plant known as *C. (Neobesseya) missouriensis*. It is frequently associated with that other recluse, *Echinocereus viridiflorus,* in scattered localities along the Front Range. The appressed, "friendly" white spination, the yellow to pink flowers with brown mid-stripes, and the orange to red persistent fruits all serve to readily distinguish this plant from any of the *C. vivipara* varieties. In addition, *C. missouriensis* has a thick turniplike root system as opposed to the stringy rambling root system of *C. vivipara*. Forms and questionable varieties of *C. missouriensis* range from Texas to Montana. The red fruits, peeking through the melting March, April, and May snows, make this plant a fine addition to any rock garden.

One final group of predominantly hooked spine cacti occurs on the western fringe of the Rockies, with its distribution centered on the Four Corners area of Arizona, New Mexico, Colorado, and Utah. These "braided arrows," the sclerocacti, are presently being studied by several different professional botanists; new species and varieties are continually being described.

The Sclerocacti

Here is a group of plants that will challenge the most conscientious rock gardener. Difficult from seed and frequenting habitats often resembling moonscapes, *Sclerocactus parviflorus* and *S. glaucus* have unusually rigid cultural requirements, including soils with little or no organic material in them. The central spines of *S. parviflorus* are shaped like fishhooks, varying in length from less than 0.25 in. to more than 2 in. Plants are commonly solitary and range in height from 2–18 in. Flower colors cover a wide range, from chartreuse to cerise, yellow, and even white. This plant will grow where no other cacti can exist, in landscapes so barren, dry, and cold that the possible colonization of Mars comes to mind. Of course, less severe habitats will support *S. parviflorus* also, but its amazing adaptations to some of the extreme conditions it endures constantly surprise those who seek it out.

Sclerocactus glaucus commonly lacks the hooked central spine(s) present in *S. parviflorus* and has few radial spines, allowing the steely gray-green, ribbed body to show through. This is a rare plant, limited to just a few colonies in western Colorado. In habitat, these pink-flowered sentinels are found growing beneath *Artemisia tridentata* or on barren, open ground.

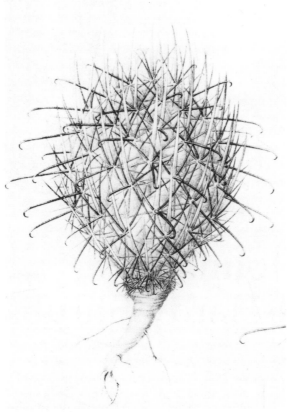

Sclerocactus whipplei
From report of the Whipple expedition

Conclusion

Rocky Mountain cacti are, as has been discussed, variable; they are as variable as the mountains and steppes they inhabit. Certainly the cacti are appropriate denizens of a region where soil and rock type, altitude and climate can change so drastically in such short lateral distances. My wonder never lessens when hunting these plants in the wild. Every colony is different, every previously unvisited locality a potential source of some yet unknown spined diadem. Cacti, and Rocky Mountain cacti in particular, are essential members of any dryland rock garden and welcome additions to moister, more traditional alpine gardens. No rock gardener will be disappointed should the decision be made to introduce a few choice cacti in the dry microclimates of a rock garden anywhere in the world.

References

Benson, Lyman. 1982. *The cacti of the United States and Canada.* Palo Alto, Calif.: Stanford University Press.

Boissevain, Charles H., and Carol Davidson. 1940. *Colorado Cacti.* Pasadena: Abbey Garden Press.

Earle, W. Hubert. 1980. *Cacti of the Southwest.* Phoenix, Ariz: self-published.

Taylor, Allan R., and Panayoti Callas (Kelaidis). 1979. "Cacti: America's foremost rock plants, part I." *Bull. of the Am. Rock Garden Soc.* 37:157–64.

_____ . 1980. "Cacti: America's foremost rock garden plants, part II." *Bull. of the Am. Rock Garden Soc.* 38:1–10.

_____ . 1980. "Cacti: America's foremost rock garden plants, part III." *Bull. of the Am. Rock Garden Soc.* 38: 59–66.

Weniger, Del. 1984. *Cacti of Texas and neighboring states.* Austin: University of Texas Press.

23

Rocky Mountain Drought-Hardy Shrubs

by Allan R. Taylor

In and among the Rocky Mountain foothills—3,500 to 6,000 ft. above sea level, depending on latitude—a large number of cold-hardy, drought-tolerant shrubs of possible interest to rock gardeners are found in or near the various ranges that comprise the Rocky Mountain chain.

In the Upper Sonoran Zone, again depending on latitude, winter lows can descend to −20°F or lower, while summer highs can reach above 100°F. This vast area—roughly from the Canadian to the Mexican borders, and from the Black Hills and the Little Rocky Mountains on the east to the Wasatch Mountains and the Colorado Plateau on the west—is characterized at lower altitudes and on warm south-facing slopes by more or less perpetual drought; rainfall varies throughout the area from 5 to about 15 in. per year. The moisture comes both as summer rain and as winter snow; the climate is definitely continental.

Most of the flora of this region, though now rather well-known and described (e.g., Weber (1976), Cronquist et al. (1972, 1977, 1984), Kearney and Peebles) is nevertheless almost entirely untested as ornamentals and garden cultivars. This is the result both of the recency of settlement and of the natural conservatism of gardeners, who, with but a few noteworthy exceptions, stick to tried and true plants already grown for generations elsewhere. This is regrettable, both because a host of desirable natives is ignored, and because many exotics tend to do rather poorly under our conditions in the Rocky Mountain region.

Descriptions of a few of these worthy natives will follow. They are primarily plants of the drier parts of the Rocky Mountains that I know to be of interest as rock garden subjects or that I suspect have promise. I will concentrate on woody and shrubby plants that are 3 ft. or less in height in their native habitat. Gardeners who may want to grow these plants should keep in mind that most of them are largely untried so it is at present impossible to state how they may respond to cultivation, even in this region. Plants that are charming dwarfs in their native habitat can become ungainly giants in the unnaturally lush conditions of a garden. The only safeguard against this undesirable result is to attempt to replicate the conditions under which the plant grows in nature.

Allan R. Taylor, Ph.D, is a Colorado native, born and raised in the rimrock country of western Colorado. His special interest in the species of plants of arid lands (particularly the Southwestern deserts) takes him all over western North America in search of superior forms of native plants. At his home in Boulder he maintains a large garden featuring Western cacti and drought-tolerant herbaceous plants and shrubs. Taylor is a professor of linguistics at the University of Colorado where his area of research is American Indian languages. He publishes frequently in his professional field, and he is now writing a book on dryland gardening in the western uplands.

Needle and Broadleafed Evergreens

Members of the Pinaceae are among the most important plants in a modern rock garden; our area, as broadly defined above, can contribute at least two plants that are superior for Rocky Mountain gardens because they are native here. *Juniperus communis* is found throughout the area in a number of forms. This taxon is normally scarcely in excess of 3 ft. in height, with bright green, sharp, scalelike needles and glistening blue berries on the female plant. The plant is less esteemed than it should be, since it is so often straggly, and usually has a dull brown winter color. Superior forms, however, are there for the finding: I know of several areas in Montana at the interface between mountains and plains where *J. communis* forms low, symmetrical mounds rather than an undesirable ragged clump.

Juniperus horizontalis also occurs at low altitudes in the northern' Rockies, especially on the eastern face of the mountains, continuing into the northern plains. These plants are a local race of a very widespread taxon, but our forms are far more drought-tolerant than those from Eastern (e.g., Newfoundland, New England) or Midwestern (e.g., Michigan) sources. Growth form and color can vary greatly: in the field one finds everything from steel blue to dark green in summer, and from purple to brown in winter; from ground-huggers to low, billowy shrubs 1–2 ft. in height.

Much of the fascinating variability I have observed in junipers in the Montana foothills is, I believe, the result of much introgression between these three sympatric juniper species: *J. scopulorum*, *J. communis*, and *J. horizontalis*. I have seen almost all of the characteristics of any of these present in a plant which is otherwise more like one of the others. The greatest promise for the rock garden is in plants that tend toward either *J. communis* or *J. horizontalis*. Selection and introduction from among these probable hybrid swarms seem very promising.

Before leaving the Pinaceae I would like to also suggest that dwarf forms of the pinyon pine (*Pinus cembroides, P. edulis* var. *c.*) in all of its varieties should be sought. Not to be overlooked, also, are witches broom derivates of all of the native conifers. These, too, would be handsome additions to Western rock gardens.

Author's garden
Photo by Deane Hall

The Ericaceae are traditionally a source of many rock garden cultivars, and we are fortunate in having members of the genus *Arctostaphylos,* which has its center west of the Sierra Nevada, native to the Rocky Mountains. *Arctostaphylos uva-ursi* is too well-known to require comment, though Rocky Mountain gardeners should always be on the lookout for superior or unusual local forms of this beloved plant. A close relative of the latter, and in some respects a look-alike, is *A. nevadensis,* which occurs in chaparral areas in the Colorado plateau. An excellent form of this plant was selected by T. Paul Maslin years ago on the Uncompahgre Plateau of southwestern Colorado. This form has recently been introduced under the clonal name 'Chipeta.' It forms a billowy mat about 4 in. high and in the spring covers itself with bright pink flowers. Many other worthy selections could be made from *A. nevadensis* emphasizing other characteristics such as fruit size and color.

Also worthy of selection and introduction is another manzanita, *Arctostaphylos patula,* which is at home on the Colorado Plateau along with *A. nevadensis.* Dwarf forms of this taxon under 3 ft. tall occur in the colder parts of the Plateau (e.g., the Uncompahgre Plateau, the Paunsaugunt Plateau). All individuals of this taxon have attractive, mahogany-colored stems and bright pink flowers, but great variability in leaf size and shape occur, as well as in time of flowering. A selection from this taxon was also made several years ago from the Uncompahgre population by the late Dr. T. Paul Maslin of Boulder and Panayoti Kelaidis; it has been informally designated 'Big Red.' The plant grows about 3 ft. tall and has large, quite red flowers.

Growing among the manzanitas on the Colorado Plateau, as well as in many other places west of the Continental Divide, is an evergreen Tertiary relict, *Pachistima (Paxistima) myrsinites.* This low, evergreen shrub, which belongs to the Celastraceae, is a prime subject for the native rock garden. Although the flowers are inconspicuous, as is usual in members of the staff tree family, the shrub itself is very tidy and ornamental. It grows in either shade or sun.

Three evergreen members of the rose family are among the best for arid plantings. These include *Cercocarpus intricatus,* native throughout the Colorado Plateau, and *Coleogyne ramosissima,* which is found from the western foothills of the Rockies all the way to the Pacific Coast. In both cases the shrubs are twiggy and have reduced, dark green but very lustrous leaves. The flowers are of little interest in both, but *Cercocarpus intricatus* has the attractive, tailed fruits typical of the cercocarpus and their close relatives. Since both of these handsome shrubs can grow head-high, selection for especially low-growing forms is indicated. *Cercocarpus intricatus* can also be heavily sheared, which replicates in the garden the clipped appearance of the plant in nature, where it is heavily browsed by deer and livestock. Another rosaceous plant normally occurring at low, dry elevations, *Purshia tridentata* also reaches very high elevations where the environment is right. A population of this plant is found near Dillon, Colorado, (above 9,000 ft.) which is barely 1 ft. tall. It is a superb shrublet for rock·garden planting.

Another broadleafed evergreen of possible interest to some is *Berberis (Mahonia) repens.* The brilliant yellow flowers of this plant are very showy, as is the lustrous green, hollylike foliage, which turns to red or purple in hot winter sun. Under very favorable conditions the plant can grow as high as 18 in., but it is normally 6 in. or less in height. *Berberis repens* has one characteristic, however, which can vitiate all of its many attractive features: it is extremely invasive. If this trait can be curbed or otherwise managed, it is a lovely addition to the native rock garden.

Shrubs with Gray, White, or Silver Foliage

A characteristic that unites many drought-tolerant plants is gray, white, or silver foliage. Usually this is because of the presence of some structure on the leaves and stems such as minute hairs or farina, presumably to impede water loss. Plants with these traits often have a specific epithet such as *lanata* (wooly), *canescens* (hoary), or *pulverulenta* (dusty). Needless to say, gray, white, and silver-foliaged plants are highly esteemed in the rock garden, where contrasting color and texture of foliage is prized.

A number of such shrubs belonging to many genera are found in the drier parts of the Rockies; some of these, e.g., *Artemisia frigida,* are already esteemed garden cultivars; others are just beginning to be discovered.

Certainly, the quintessential gray plant of the American West is sagebrush, the genus *Artemisia.* Several native woody species of *Artemisia* are apt rock garden subjects.

The most typical Western "sage" is probably *Artemisia tridentata,* but most forms of this taxon are really too tall for all except very large gardens. There are, however, several charming dwarf forms of this species—the varieties *A. t. nova, arbuscula, rothrockii* (these are classed as separate species by some taxonomists)—which are fine shrublets for a dry rock garden. Also of interest are *A. pedatifida, A.*

Author's garden
Photo by Deane Hall

porteri, and *A. bigelovii. Artemisia filifolia,* a sagebrush native to the Colorado Plateau, has attractive, threadlike leaves, but its open, rather rangy growth habit makes it less desirable than the forms cited above. Looking rather different from the other sages, and definitely worthy of cultivation, is *A. spinescens.* This plant is low and has yellow-green flowers that are rather large for a sagebrush. These flowers come in the early spring, rather than the fall, which is the usual flowering time for sages. The specific epithet comes from the fact that the flower stems dry into 1 in. long woody spines after the flowers drop.

At least two species of the rabbitbrush complex, *Chrysothamnus nauseosus* and *C. viscidiflorus,* are of interest for the dry rock garden where sufficiently diminutive forms can be found. I am growing a very handsome form of *C. nauseosus* which is only a foot high. This plant was introduced a number of years ago by Harry Swift of Golden, Colorado.

The genus *Senecio* is one of the largest and most widespread of all genera. Many members of the genus are attractive plants, and it would be unusual indeed if the Rocky Mountain region had no interesting representatives. In fact there are several, although most occur at higher altitudes than we are concerned with here. One that is definitely of interest is *Senecio douglasii.* This plant grows about 2 ft. tall and has the predictable beautiful yellow flowers in clusters at the ends of the stems.

Also producing handsome yellow "daisies" are *Encelia farinosa* and *Sphaeromeria (Tanecetum) capitata. Encelia farinosa* grows to between 2–3 ft. in height, and has glistening white foliage. It is really most characteristic of the Lower Sonoran Zone in areas of winter rainfall (e.g., the Mojave Desert, but also inside the gorge of the Grand Canyon), and it is probably too tender for most gardens in the Upper Sonoran or higher zones. However, an unusually hardy population may yet be found (possibly somewhere on the Colorado Plateau) that will permit wider cultivation of the plant than presently is possible. *Sphaeromeria capitata,* by contrast, is very frost-hardy. It is a subshrub (only 2 in. in height) that forms a tight, wide mound of brilliant silver. It produces myriad yellow flowers, shaped like little balls, held aloft on slender, 4 in. stems.

Another composite of shrub size is *Tetrademia canescens.* This plant grows as a low, rounded, shrub 1–2 ft. in height. It blooms freely from June to September with yellow, star-shaped flowers in clusters at the ends of the branches. A related species, *T. glabrata,* should also be tried.

The Chenopodiaceae are another family represented in the Rocky Mountain region by many dryland plants. Several of these possess qualities making them of interest to rock gardeners.

The shadscale complex, members of the large genus *Atriplex,* are abundant in areas of low rainfall, particularly where the soil is alkaline. Most of these possess small, silvery gray, succulentlike leaves. Probably the most interesting of these to rock gardeners are *Atriplex confertifolia* and *A. corrugata. Atriplex confertifolia* is a spiny shrub that grows up to 3 ft. It is a handsome, open shrub. *Atriplex corrugata* is a very low subshrub, just 3 in. tall. Both of these species of *Atriplex* are characteristic of cold steppe landscapes such as those found in the Colorado Plateau and high mountain basins elsewhere in the Rockies.

Other silver-gray chenopods are *Ceratoides lanata* and *Grayia brandegei. Ceratoides lanata* grows in sandy, alkaline soil; it can reach 3 ft. The shrub has many upright branches with densely hairy, threadlike leaves. The fluffy fruits are often used in dry arrangements. *Grayia brandegei* is also an erect shrub; it is typically about 2 ft. tall. The leaves of *G. brandegei* are long, narrow, and somewhat fleshy. The fruits are heavily winged, each seed having a wide, pinkish, papery keel completely surrounding it. The plant is especially attractive in fruit.

Among the most elegant wildflowers of the Pacific Coast, particularly California, are the wild buckwheats, which belong to the genus *Eriogonum* of the Polygonaceae. All, whether herbaceous or shrubby, tend to have tomentose, whitish foliage and straw-toned flowers.

A number of species of eriogonums reach the Rockies, most through the Great Basin. Particularly attractive for rock garden cultivation in our area are four species: *Eriogonum thymoides, E. sphaerocephalum, E. microthecum,* and *E. corymbosum. Eriogonum thymoides* and *E. sphaerocephalum* occur in the sagebrush zone of the western slopes of the northern Rockies, e.g., the Snake River Plains. *Eriogonum thymoides* is the taller of the two, growing to around a foot high. Its flowers are yellow, orange, or red. *Eriogonum sphaerocephalum* is a subshrub only 4–8 in. in height, with yellow flowers. *Eriogonum microthecum* is a bushy plant about a foot tall with narrow leaves which have inrolled margins. The flowers are yellow, white, or pinkish. *Eriogonum corymbosum* is native to the Colorado Plateau; it becomes, in late summer, a stunning mound of white or yellow which is very reminiscent of a gypsophila.

Probably the handsomest silver-foliaged shrub of all is *Shepherdia rotundifolia.* A member of the oleaster family, it is native to the Colorado Plateau. This plant is actually somewhat taller than the limits I have placed on myself here, but it is of such stunning beauty that people who are in a position to do so should begin selection of superior cultivars, some possibly dwarf. Like other shepherdias, *S. rotundifolia* is dioecious; the small yellow flowers are fragrant but inconspicuous in both sexes. The plant's real beauty is in its oval, evergreen (better: eversilver) leaves, whose appearance resembles nothing more than aluminum foil. It is a choice plant, able to stand harsh conditions, and certainly one destined to become an important element in western landscaping.

Several other gray- or silver-foliaged shrubs belonging to other families could be mentioned, e.g., certain mints (*Poliomintha incana, Salazaria mexicana*) and mallow species belonging to the genus *Sphaeralcea* (e.g., *S. coccinea*). Readers can use Western floras for additional information about these, and indeed to discover additional likely taxa of gardening interest.

Eriogonum corymbosum
Photo by Allan Taylor

Shrubs with Green Foliage

A number of members of the rose family are low shrubs of great interest for rock gardens. One, *Potentilla fruticosa (Pentaphylloides floribunda)* is already used extensively for this purpose. Concerning this taxon I should note, however, that no Rocky Mountain native forms are in general cultivation. Gardeners in the Rocky Mountain region should therefore watch for local forms that are possibly superior to those already available. Also very well-known are *Prunus besseyi* and *Amelanchier alnifolia*. The latter is usually a tall shrub or a small tree, but dwarf forms are known to occur and are indeed already available from commercial sources. I am also testing what I believe to be a dwarf form from the Little Rocky Mountains in Montana. My form is low, 18 in. tall, very floriferous, and both drought-tolerant and extremely cold-hardy. Most forms of *Prunus besseyi* grown are medium-sized shrubs. Not widely known is that fact that foothill and mountain forms of the shrub are very dwarf; several populations occur along the Front Range in Colorado that are less than 6 in. tall.

A prime candidate for cultivation in this category should be shrubby forms of species of the wild rose itself, e.g. *Rosa arkansana*. These species are low-growing in dry areas, and display a great variety in flower color and form. Much selection on the native roses has been done in the Canadian Prairie Provinces (the wild rose is the provincial flower of Alberta), and improvement on the Canadian experiments would probably be difficult. Nevertheless, a sharp eye is in order, since the Canadian forms are selected for a slightly cooler summer climate than prevails farther south. A successful example of the latter is *R. arkansana* 'J. W. Fargo,' an introduction made by Claude Barr many years ago. One caution: all wild roses sucker freely, and they are difficult to eliminate if suckering is undesirable or intolerable.

Several other rosaceous genera contain shrubs that make exceedingly graceful ornamentals. Sufficiently well-known to require no comment is *Petrophytum caespitosum*. Not as well known, however, is *Kelseya uniflora*, a plant very much like *Petrophytum caespitosum*. *Physocarpus monogynus* and *Holodiscus dumosus* are two additional shrubs worthy of cultivation. Both grow at higher elevations and favor cooler, moister locations than most of the plants discussed here. *Holodiscus dumosus* is the taller of the two, so selection for low-growing forms is in order.

Another plant family which has many drought-tolerant members in western North America is the Rhamnaceae. The Rocky Mountain region offers rock gardeners five handsome members of this family: *Ceanothus greggii, C. velutinus, C. fendleri, C. martinii,* and *C. herbaceus.* In *C. greggii*, which does not occur north of the Colorado Plateau, the leaves are tiny, round, and very shiny. The handsome flowers are typically white, but bluish and pinkish forms occur as well. Selection on this taxon should definitely be done, primarily for size and cold hardiness, since they are typically less hardy than most Rocky Mountain native shrubs. *Ceanothus velutinus* is of interest mainly for its very large, shiny,

Ceanothus velutinus. Photo by Jim Borland

evergreen leaves, but its sprawling habit can also be useful. *Ceanothus fendleri* is a very spiny plant with small, oblong, deciduous leaves and lovely white, foamy flowers. *Ceanothus martinii* occurs west of the Continental Divide. It is very much like *C. fendleri*, but it is a little taller and lacks the spines. *Ceanothus herbaceus* is really a survivor in the eastern Rockies of plant populations presently centered farther east. It is frequently found in the foothills near Boulder, Colorado, where it hybridizes with its relative, *C. fendleri*. All of the last mentioned species have white flowers.

The oleaster family has several representatives in the Rocky Mountain area; one, *Shepherdia rotundifolia,* has already been mentioned. Another of definite rock garden interest is *S. canadensis*. This dioecious plant occurs from foothills to the subalpine throughout the region. Its leaves are a rich dark green, covered with peltate scales, giving the foliage a unique sheen. The fruits, which range in color from amber to deep red, also have a plated appearance. Superior forms of this shrub are among the most handsome of our native plants.

Belonging to the closely related olive family is *Menodora scabra*. This twiggy subshrub, which reaches 1 ft. in height, occurs in the southern Rockies. From May to August it displays bright yellow flowers exactly like those of a flax.

Saxifrages are ordinarily thought of as alpine plants, but three shrubs belonging to this family are native to lower, drier areas in the Rockies. Probably the best known of these is *Philadelphus microphyllus*. Unlike the traditionally cultivated mockoranges, this shrub is exceedingly shapely. It forms a low mound; because of its tiny leaves and its showy, fragrant white flowers, it is a first class rock garden subject.

Also rather well-known is *Ribes aureum*. Some forms of this attractive currant are small enough to be of use in the rock garden. Its tubular, spicy flowers in early spring make this native plant a prized garden ornamental. Possibly also of interest are other native currants such as *R. inebrians, R. cereum,* and *R. velutinum*.

The last saxifrage which I will mention is *Fendlerella utahensis*. This plant is much like a mockorange, and occurs in the southern area of our region, as the specific epithet implies.

The composite family has a number of shrubby species which belong to the category of green-foliaged plants. One of the choicest is *Gutierrezia sarothrae*. This plant forms a low mound 8–24 in. high. It occurs throughout the Rocky Mountains, and its attractive yellow flowers appear in the late summer. It is similar to *G. microcephala* (*G. s.* var. *microcephala*)

A number of native composites in the genus *Haplopappus* are also worthy of planting, e.g., *H. laricifolius* and *H. (Stenotopsis) linearifolius*. Readers of floras should be warned that this genus is a catch-all, and some authors may place elsewhere plants which other authors place here.

The Leguminosae are a family much represented in warm, arid climates, and many herbaceous legumes, e.g., astragalus and lupines, are choice rock gardens subjects already. Unfortunately, there are only a few shrubby legumes in the Rockies which seem likely to be good additions to the rock garden plant palette. Probably the best candidates are from the genus *Dalea: D. fremontii, D. formosa,* and *D. wislizenii*. *Dalea formosa* and *D. fremontii* are both quite handsome; the former has brilliant blue flowers, while the latter has blossoms that vary from indigo to rose-purple. *Dalea wislizenii* is of such southern occurrence (near the Mexican border) as to make it of questionable cold-hardiness farther north. Another dalea which occurs in the canyon country of west Texas is *D. frutescens*; it, too, has potential as a rock garden plant, but it is questionable whether it should be regarded as a Rocky Mountain plant.

Also deserving mention here are two species of *Amorpha. Amorpha fruticosa* is a tall shrub with dark blue-purple flowers. *Amorpha nana* is a very attractive low shrub which is very rare—it occurs in only two sites on the eastern face of the Rockies in Colorado.

Well-known herbaceous perennial plants in the foothill areas of the Rockies are the various native species of *Oenothera*. They are much appreciated for their large, showy flowers, some blooming by day, others by night. Several of these attain subshrub size. *Oenothera greggii* and *O. lavandulifolia* form wide mounds about 10 in. high. The flowers on both are large and clear yellow. Both occur widely on both sides of the Continental Divide. In the eastern foothills of the Rockies, and into the western Great Plains, is found *O. (Calylophus) serrulata*. This delicate, twiggy subshrub, reaching a height of 6–10 in. is probably my favorite of this choice group of plants. It produces an abundance of small, crinkly yellow flowers, 1 in. wide or less, which are miniatures of the flowers of its relatives. There is apparently considerable local variation in this plant: the Colorado form I know from the Boulder area has much smaller flowers than those described by Claude Barr.

There remains to be mentioned a scattering of shrubs belonging to several different families. To the Celastraceae belongs *Glossopetalon spinescens*, a spiny, olive green, many-stemmed dwarf shrub. *Frankenia jamesii* (Frankeniaceae) is a handsome dwarf shrub partial to alkaline or saline soils. Its bundles of dark green, awllike leaves (the edges roll under) make the plant resemble a heather somewhat. The 5-petaled flowers are present at the ends of the upright branches from May to October. This is certainly one of the more interesting shrubs of the southern Rockies. To the Caprifoliaceae, in the genus *Symphoricarpos,* belong the many species of snowberries. A number of these occur in the Rocky Mountains. Foothills forms are such species as *S. occidentalis, S. albus, S. longiflorus, S. oreophilus,* and *S. rotundifolius.*

To the Anacardiaceae belongs a sumac which is widespread in chaparral areas in the foothills, *Rhus trilobata.* This plant usually occurs in low forms around 2 ft. tall; its trilobed foliage is attractive during the summer, while during the late summer and fall it has brilliant red fruits.

For last mention I have saved a very distinct—and distinctive—plant which is a favorite of mine. This is an unidentified *Yucca* species which occurs from the foothills of the San Juan Mountains in Colorado west across south-central Utah to at least the eastern edge of the Aquarius Plateau. This yucca is probably a hybrid, since it never sets fertile seed, though it flowers normally. At maturity the plant is only 5 in. high. The plant forms colonies based on thick, subsurface runners. This seems to be its only method of reproduction. This is certainly one of the most beautiful members of a very large genus, and it is a rock garden plant of absolutely first quality.

Yucca harrimaniae
Photo by Allan Taylor

Conclusion

I have attempted to call the reader's attention to Rocky Mountain native shrubs that are, or could be, attractive additions to rock gardens in the Intermountain West. I feel that I have managed to mention the best; a dedicated explorer, however, could doubtless discover many others by careful research in the field and in the manuals. I urge such people to do so, for, as did Jefferson, I feel that one of the major accomplishments of any life is the discovery of another choice plant for our gardens.

References

Kearney, T. H., and R. H. Peebles. 1960. *Arizona Flora.* 2nd ed. Berkeley: University of California Press.

Patraw, Pauline M. and Jeanne R. Janish. 1976. *Shrubs and Trees of the Southwest Uplands.* Globe, Arizona: Southwest Parks and Monuments Association.

PART THREE
Rocky Mountain Plants in Cultivation

Section I

At Denver Botanic Gardens

Photo by Deane Hall

24

Rocky Mountain Landscaping Alternatives

by Gayle Ann Weinstein

Our discussions of Rocky Mountain climate, geography and flora are, in essence, descriptions of the natural world as it is before alterations are made by man. In the urban environment and in the world of landscaped gardens, things are somewhat different; we have the ability to make choices and to create beauty by design. But to do so successfully, we must understand and cooperate with the natural forces that govern both the natural and the created landscape.

In gardens and natural landscapes each region has unique styles. The trademarks of the Plains and the Intermountain Areas are bright sunshine, warm days, cool nights, and little precipitation. The scene here is of flat land to rolling hills with vistas clear to the horizon.

It is a characteristic visual image we have that sets our region apart from others and renders it a style all its own. It is appropriate that each region's landscaping and gardening style should be prescribed by its climate and topography. A type of beauty from one region—the ideal of lush greenery typical of the U.S. colonial eastern seaboard—has been imposed on other regions. Landscapes in the Rocky Mountain states are treated the same as those in New England, using broad expanses of lawn, foundation shrubbery and trees.

We have the opportunity and the ability to create a distinct beauty for distinctive regions. Yet, we have inherited and accepted without question high water-demand, heavily irrigated landscapes.

The problem now is not only that we lack a geographical identity; we are also making exorbitant demands on our water resources. We are attempting a life style independent of our climate. The pressure of today's larger population increases demand and depletes available resources. This is a serious concern. Water is becoming a very precious commodity.

In our arid to semiarid country, we are engulfed with landscape designs using plants from mesophytic habitats. No wonder there are so many stressed landscapes and frustrated gardeners.

To promote alternatives, we must keep these facts in mind:

1. Elements such as temperature, precipitation, soil type, solar radiation and air movement

Gayle Ann Weinstein is a Denver Botanic Gardens (DBG) Botanist-Horticulturist, responsible for development, plant selection and the outside gardening staff. She holds an MA in special education and an MS in landscape horticulture. She contributes regularly to DBG publications and professional journals. Special interests include the introduction and use of native plants in urban landscapes, and the promotion of greater environmental consciousness in horticultural design and water use.

cannot be ignored. When plants are pushed beyond their comfort zones, metabolic efficiency lessens; stress and possibilities for disease or insect attack increase. A plant's ability to adapt to these conditions depends on its innate cultural requirements and genetic makeup.

2. Success in growing plants depends not so much on which of the various techniques of seed-sowing, planting, pruning, or watering is used but on the kinds of plants chosen, the growing medium, and timing.

3. Plants for landscapes are usually chosen and used intuitively, not scientifically. There is a real need to gather more technical data specific to this region.

Rocky Mountain Horticultural Challenges

The major elements that influence plant growth in the Rocky Mountain region are abundant sunny days, low precipitation, low humidity, dry winds, and large differences between day and night temperatures.

Abundant sunny days are often a blessing on human activities. But day after day of absorption of the sun's heat by a plant's foliage robs the plant of its necessary moisture. Because of low precipitation, there is insufficient water to replace what the plant loses in transpiration. Less water also means less plant growth. With less plant growth, the amount of vegetable matter returned to the soil when the plants die and decay is smaller. Soils, therefore, have less organic matter which, in turn, reduces the microorganism population. With little precipitation, soils are not thoroughly leached and there may be an accumulation of soluble salts.

Low humidity also decreases the moisture in the plant's tissues. The less vapor that surrounds the plant's surfaces, the more moisture will diffuse out from within the plant. Any air movement quickly removes the moisture around the plant's tissues. Thus, winds also cause dehydration.

Temperature differences between day and night affect plant growth. During the growing season, cool nights tend to slow the growth of plants, reducing their overall size and prolonging the time it takes for them to reach maturity. Warm sunny days during the winter months raise the internal temperatures of plant tissues. As evening approaches, temperatures plunge and tissues that were warmed during the day are often damaged.

New dryland Xeriscape Garden
at Denver Botanic Gardens.
Photo by Deane Hall

Rocky Mountain Natives Versus Traditional Plant Material

The most obvious critical element that affects plant growth in the Rocky Mountain region is water. Low precipitation, winds, low relative humidity, and bright sun all deprive plant tissues of water. Plants indigenous to the Rocky Mountains have adapted survival capabilities for these conditions. The overall impression of the vegetation of the Rocky Mountain States is one of a pale green, rigid, small-leaf foliage that is often gray to bluish in color. Looking closely at the plants, it can be seen that the foliage is coated by either hairs, wax, or scales. All are adaptations the plants have made to conserve moisture. Some other adaptations, such as extensive root systems, storage organs, and root hairs that are below the ground are not as obvious.

Given the diversity of habitats in the Rocky Mountain states, a great native flora is available, and we have yet to take advantage of it. While it is true that some plants from our region—such as Colorado spruce, potentilla, and red osier dogwood—are already used regularly in the landscape, they are few in comparison to those available.

Plant for plant, there is a Rocky Mountain substitute that will serve the same function in the garden and withstand conditions with much greater ease than those plants traditionally used. For example, *Ribes aureum* (golden currant) can be substituted for *Forsythia* × *intermedia* (forsythia) to produce early yellow flowers. *Arctostaphylos patula* (green manzanita) may be substituted for *Euonymus kiautschovica* 'Manhattan' (spreading euonymus) as a broad leaf evergreen. *Cowania mexicana* (cliffrose) may be substituted for *Spiraea* × *vanhouttei* (Vanhoutte's spirea) to produce a massive show of flowers.

Rocky Mountain Landscape Design

Both landscaping and gardening are regarded as luxuries. The success of a landscape installation today must first be measured by its viability in spite of restrictions imposed when water conservation measures must be instituted. Landscapes designed for humid climates use twice as much water when placed in arid regions. Under conservation restrictions these will be the first to show signs of stress. The resulting loss to the gardener will be great emotionally as well as financially.

Few landscapes have been conceived to include plants with low water requirements. The idea of using native plants, with its accompanying concern for water conservation, is just beginning to find its way into the general consciousness.

To change styles, however, keen perceptions of the needs of the area and the individuals involved, as well as of environmental factors, are required. Moreover, the mere presence of plants does not make an attractive landscape. To create a regional design style that enhances the geographical environment is the challenge before us.

What, then, are our alternatives?

1. We can continue to grow the same plants in the same landscape styles.

2. We can continue to design in familiar idioms, changing only by substituting low-water-demand plant materials.

We must note, however, that neither of these possibilities creates regional identification.

Or:

3. We can abandon traditional styles and move toward more naturalistic designs—naturalistic for our own region, that is—a style that looks to its surroundings and tries to fit the landscape to the environment rather than forcing the environment to fit the landscape.

This last possibility is most challenging. It offers the use of a variety of new plant materials. It gives the desirable sense of regional identity—but it sometimes presents problems for which we have yet to find the answers. This is the style of design we are calling "naturalistic." Where does it best fit in? Ideally, perhaps, in new suburbs yet to be developed, either at the base of the foothills or on the high plains in open country. Unfortunately, some developers and some neighborhood associations restrict the use of this type of design, still insisting on irrigated lawns to set the landscaping stage.

The natural-to-the-region garden style requires that we look at our surroundings and fit the site plan to those surroundings. If the site is in the prairies, then the overall feel should be of short to midgrass prairie with forbs and shrubs interspersed in an appropriate manner. If it is in the hills, the appropriate setting may mean more shrubs and trees with a cover of grasses and forbs. The style may mean that plants are no longer arranged in terms of texture, balance, or size. The landscape becomes a part of its surroundings. It is one part of the whole. It is as if nature is being recreated.

This is a difficult way to landscape initially because it requires knowledge of the area and insight into the plant material. Across-the-board designs once used in Ohio or New York cannot be used in Colorado. It means an intense observation of the area and an understanding of the needs of the persons who will be using it. There are few examples to follow and many questions exist. It is also difficult to educate individuals to the desirability of natural landscapes, especially those who have not been exposed to the land before it was developed and irrigated.

Plant Testing at Denver Botanic Gardens

Many of the plant materials at Denver Botanic Gardens are on trial, whether they are confined to a test area or not. Shrubs and trees have been given various exposures with restrictive irrigation. A variety of grasses and ground covers with low water demands have been planted in trial and demonstration areas. A wildflower testing program seeks information on initial establishment as well as ongoing growth. An area has been set aside for the establishment of a High Plains Garden representative of the short to midgrass prairie of the Rocky Mountains. An area has been established for a Xeriscape Garden representing the dryland areas: desert, desert grassland, open woodlands, scrubland. Trials of annuals, ornamental grasses, and herbaceous perennials for use in ornamental displays with low water requirements are ongoing.

With these trials DBG hopes to contribute answers to some of the current questions involving plant material, water requirements, and cultural methods.

Those of us who are a part of this trend—moving from a mesophytic to a xerophytic landscape—find it an exciting endeavor. We are searching for new plant materials, techniques, and styles that, if we are successful, could affect the landscapes and gardening styles of several generations to come.

New dryland Xeriscape Garden at Denver Botanic Gardens. Photo by Deane Hall

References

Kelly, George. 1967. *Rocky Mountain horticulture.* Boulder: Pruett Publishing Co.
Taylor, Ronald J., and R. Valum. 1974. *Sagebrush country.* Beaverton, Oregon: Touchstone Press.

25

A Rock Garden for the Rockies

by Panayoti Kelaidis

Just as a moraine marks the culmination of a glacier, a large institutional rock garden is the result of lengthy processes. Its creation sometimes seems to come about with glacial speed as well. Yet many visitors pass swiftly through Denver Botanic Gardens Rock Alpine Garden, glancing quickly at the giant boulders and the tiny alpines they harbor, never suspecting the depth of the local gardening tradition necessary to produce it.

Although large public rock gardens are commonplace in Europe, relatively few botanic gardens in the United States have attempted to construct large-scale rockwork. For whatever reason—the looming presence of the Rockies, the influence of Sacco DeBoer and his illustrious colleague M. Walter Pesman—monumental rockwork has been incorporated into many features at Denver Botanic Gardens since its inception.

The first major garden undertaken on the grounds of the York Street gardens was an extensive rock garden: The Gates Garden. Still in existence, it was built by funds donated by the Gates Foundation (of Denver's Gates Rubber Company), and planted and maintained by gardeners who worked for the Gates family. This garden features a large pool bounded on the west by some 100 feet of granite rockwork, amounting to well over 100 tons and culminating in a waterfall, the whole planted with native conifers and shrubs. Obviously, this wasn't intended to be an "alpinarium" for high altitude cushion plants, but it helped prepare the way for more extensive rockwork 20 years later.

In the intervening years, the grounds at Denver Botanic Gardens were planted with a greater and greater variety of plants and gardens. A master plan for the various gardens was orchestrated under the baton of Warren Eckbo, one of the founders of the now nation-wide landscape architecture firm of EDAW. Since the Gates Garden was already in existence, there seemed to be little call for a naturalistic garden, including rocks and regional wildflowers, for many years. Meanwhile, the early generation of horticulturists most responsible for promoting this type of garden at DBG was passing away.

Beginnings

It is difficult to determine at this point what convinced the planning board in the mid-seventies that another rock garden was needed at DBG. There were many advocates: well-known Denver

Curator of Denver Botanic Gardens Rock Alpine Garden since its creation in the spring of 1980, **Panayoti Kelaidis** is responsible for the design and maintenance of its plantings and has written extensively on the garden in many specialist publications. Currently president of the American Penstemon Society, Kelaidis has lectured in twelve states, Canada and Britain. He enjoys studying plants in their native haunts and collecting seed both in the garden and in the wild. His garden favorites are phlox, penstemons and irises.

nurseryman George W. Kelly, who has written eloquently on rock gardens for the Brooklyn Botanic Garden's handbook on the subject; Bernice Petersen, long-time editor of the DBG's *Green Thumb* magazine, who not only constructed and planted an ambitious rock garden at her home, but also wrote extensively about rock gardens in that publication. Both William W. Gambill, director of the Gardens in this crucial phase, and Beatrice Willard, co-author of *Land Above the Trees,* were local botanists who advocated the development of a naturalistic garden where wild plant material could be grown.

The late T. Paul Maslin of Boulder was also a decisive influence. Not only was Maslin active in the affairs of both Denver Botanic Gardens and the American Rock Garden Society, he was well-known and loved by horticulturists throughout the region, and his eminently creative garden captivated their imaginations. Here was a garden where plants and rocks combined to form an artistic unity, yet it also harbored an extensive collection of fascinating plants that were simply not encountered elsewhere in the region. Maslin was an active and effective advocate of a rock garden at Denver Botanic Gardens.

Whatever the influences, the crucial spark came from Herb Schaal, principal of the Rocky Mountain regional office of EDAW. Schaal was fascinated by the concept of nature used to enhance a city landscape. He was to spend hundreds of hours researching the tradition of rock gardening, studying rocks in nature and in gardens, before producing the final design for the Rock Alpine Garden. This process has been well documented in articles published in The *Green Thumb* and the *Bulletin of the American Rock Garden Society.*

Funds for the design and construction of the Rock Alpine Garden were raised as part of "To Fulfill a Promise," the largest capital fund drive initiated by the Gardens during the decade.

Most of the construction of the Rock Alpine Garden took place in 1979, with final touches completed the following year. Planting began in June of 1980. Many of the plants were grown at DBG; many more were purchased from specialty nurseries over the next few years. The planting scheme consisted of a general design executed by Herb Schaal with my collaboration, along with an extensive plant list of some 1,000 species of plants that had been drafted the previous winter.

Rock Alpine Garden and alpine house, DBG.
Photo by Deane Hall

Fulfillment

It is both instructive and amusing to compare the list of plants first suggested for the Rock Alpine Garden with the inventory that has gradually evolved *in situ*. The initial planting guide reads like the index of a popular rock gardening book, and indeed, most of the plants included there were gleaned from the current literature as well as the catalogs of leading nurseries. As a result, the first year's plantings consisted of all the usual sorts of alpines from primroses and saxifrages to gentians and dianthus. These were often grown from seed derived from the seed exchanges of various rock garden societies. Sometimes they were grown from plants purchased from outstanding rare plant nurseries in various parts of the United States and Canada. By the end of the first year, 1,400 taxa of rock plants had been planted in the Rock Alpine Garden. Most of these were state-of-the-art plants, those basic alpines most often grown and sold in the United States.

After the first planting season was completed, an inventory of plants was made, and a plant list published. The first thing that strikes one in retrospect is how quickly extensive collections of plants were put together. The following chart shows the status of some genera of plants in the garden after the first growing season, as compared with the same inventory at present.

Table 25.1 Number of Species within Genera of Plants in the Rock Alpine Garden, 1980 and 1985

Genus	1980	1985
Sempervivum	81	62
Saxifraga	43	91
Iris	38	273
Gentiana	34	31
Dianthus	34	60
Campanula	25	70
Draba	23	21
Silene	23	16
Penstemon	22	78
Phlox	14	45
Achillea	5	17
Artemisia	4	15
Cytisus	4	14
Dracocephalum	3	21
Eriogonum	2	21
Nepeta	1	8
Scutellaria	2	18

Why are there so many dramatic shifts in numbers over this five-year period? The answer is simple: The Rock Alpine Garden underwent a sort of Darwinian survival of the fittest. Plants best suited to our climate flourished, while plants not suited simply perished. The garden served as a sort of laboratory where many kinds of plants were tested in the region for the first time. Those plants that thrived were encouraged, while those that died were not replaced.

Obviously, plants requiring shade or cool conditions were the first casualties. Only those primulas that could withstand considerable sun would make it in this very sunny rock garden. Even saxifrages and gentians, groups known for their need for sun in maritime climates, seem to benefit from some protection here: the cool side of a rock and richer soils than they need in the mountains. Each passing year winnows out more and more of those plants that will not take full exposure in this very sunny continental climate.

Meanwhile, whole groups of plants not widely grown before in American rock gardens are assuming an entirely new role here; the many species of Lamiaceae, for example, which are especially abundant in central Asia and the Mediterranean, thrive in our sunny climate. The genus *Origanum* is usually thought of as an oddity for the alpine house. Here, *O. amanum* is a spectacular fountain of long-tubed blossoms all summer long, and many other oreganos are equally ornamental. Other genera of mints that have become important in this garden include *Dracocephalum*, *Scutellaria*, *Marrubium* and *Ballota* as well as the more conventional thymes and lavenders. Why is this so? Because these are plants adapted to virtually the same climatic regime in Eurasia.

Other Eurasian groups that have assumed great importance in this garden include *Acantholimon*, *Dianthus* and *Veronica*, which are not often featured in public gardens in America. Many of the species in these genera are especially good garden plants in Colorado.

Aside from plants from homologous climates in Eurasia, it is hardly surprising that native plants have proven to be especially successful in this garden; after all, these are the plants that have chosen to grow here in the first place. *Penstemon, Eriogonum* and a wealth of composites have flourished in the Rock Alpine Garden. Even the dryland species in these groups will tolerate the supplemental irrigation provided here because of the quick-draining soils and open exposure.

Thus the Rock Alpine Garden has evolved from a showplace for "generic" alpines to a laboratory for the study and display of continental alpines, those plants emanating from the hundreds of mountain ranges that occur in the sunny, dry continental landmasses of America, Eurasia and even the Southern Hemisphere. No other public garden has attempted to highlight the rich flora of steppe regions throughout the world. And no other garden has sought to feature the native rock plants of the Rocky Mountain region. These are the complementary goals of our Rock Alpine Garden.

Rock Alpine Garden, DGB. Photo by Deane Hall

A Selection of Fifty Rocky Mountain Rock Plants

Androsace chamaejasme var. *carinata.* The Rockies are not nearly as rich in androsaces as other mountain ranges; this form of this widespread species is easily grown from seed and appears to be garden-worthy. It is quite woolly and the flowers are large for the species (more than 0.25 in. across) and practically stemless. In nature, it appears to be restricted to the Front Range of Colorado.

Anemone narcissiflora var. *zephyra* is restricted to the Southern Rockies, particularly abundant on the eastern slope of Trail Ridge Road in Rocky Mountain National Park and the mountains ringing South Park in Colorado. The flowers of this form are large for the species, carried in thick clusters on relatively short stems rarely exceeding a foot in height. Because seed must be sown fresh to germinate, it is rarely seen in cultivation.

Aquilegia jonesii. Rock gardeners are always struggling with this most dramatic alpine columbine. In Denver, it has bloomed and grown quite well for three successive years in a hot, limestone scree alongside various Mediterranean and Western desert plants such as a hedgehog cactus (*Echinocereus reichenbachii*), *Acantholimon acerosum*, *Origanum scabrum* and Oncocyclus iris. In order to bloom, it apparently requires heat, perfect drainage and a very limy soil.

Aquilegia saximontana. This endemic of the Front Range of the Colorado Rocky Mountains occurs only on rockslides and screes at or near timberline. For a plant of such restricted occurrence in nature (it has even been proposed for endangered status on the Federal endangered species list), it is extremely adaptable in the garden, thriving under ordinary scree conditions in sun or part shade. The flowers are distinctively shaped—with large sepals and tiny hooked spurs—and bloom over a three-month period in the garden.

Arenaria hookeri. One of the two most pulvinate sandworts in the Rocky Mountain region is not an alpine plant at all. Hooker's sandwort is universal throughout the eastern portions of the Great Basin, and especially in the dry plains of Wyoming and Montana south through the high plains of Colorado. It is tremendously variable in rosette form and size: its rosettes can range from lax, inch-wide green starfish to less than an eighth of an inch across. The flower stalks are usually several inches long, forming a dome of good white flowers in late spring. When the seed ripens, the entire stem breaks off at the cushion revealing the dome of tight, green growth. Give heat, drainage and lime.

Arenaria (Minuartia) obtusiloba is the universal cushion sandwort throughout the alpine zones of the Rocky Mountains. Unlike the eritrichiums and *Silene acaulis* with which it so often grows, this tiny mat plant adapts readily to cultivation and blooms well in gardens as well.

Artemisia is ubiquitous at all elevations throughout the West. Indeed, the sagebrushes are probably the most common plants in this region, growing from the lowest deserts to the highest mountain tops. Even the smaller forms of common sagebrush, *Artemisia tridentata*, grow several feet high. There are several closely related species, however, that are much shorter. Black sage, *A. nova*, grows at high elevations and makes a perfect 8–12 in. replica of the common species. *Artemisia arbuscula* is similar in habit. *Artemisia pedatifida*, which grows throughout Wyoming, is actually a prostrate sagebrush rarely more than a few inches tall.

Artemisia frigida is undoubtedly the most common herbaceous sagebrush in the West, forming mounds up to a foot in height when not in bloom. Few people realize that this same species grows in alpine areas in the drier Western ranges, and that these alpine forms are not only much tinier, but seem to be longer-lived under garden conditions. One other tiny sagebrush demands consideration: *Artemisia tripartita* var. *rupicola* from the dryland stretches of Wyoming is perhaps the tiniest of native sages. In the wild it rarely grows more than a few inches in height or breadth, and grows only slightly larger in cultivation. Its quite attractive miniature yellow powderpuff flowers are produced all summer. This is the best artemisia for troughs.

Aquilegia elegantula. Photo by Sandy Snyder

Arenaria hookeri. Photo by Jim Borland

The genus *Astragalus* is perhaps the special glory of the Rockies. The West abounds with dramatic and showy milkvetches, but many of the tiniest and most colorful cushion forms are restricted to the Rocky Mountain region. Surely the smallest and most widespread of these is *Astragalus kentrophyta* ssp. *implexus.* This is a rather variable little milkvetch that occurs both on cold desert as well as on the tundra. In Colorado it is found on the mountain parks where the growth is so compact and tight that it resembles a rather bluer-leaved raoulia. In bloom, the flowers vary from bluish to pink-purples. In a good year, these justify Dwight Ripley's description as "amethyst scatter-rugs." In Wyoming and Montana the same plant is much more common above timberline, where it grows a bit lusher, but has flowers almost twice the size. Very difficult to grow, it is best established from the tiny seed capsules that are painful to retrieve among the prickly leaves.

Astragalus sericoleucus is one of the most widespread representatives of the Orophaca section of *Astragalus.* These are unquestionably the most colorful and glamorous plants of the genus in America. These typically form tight mounds or mats only an inch or two in height made of myriad short stems that are tightly clothed with three-parted, white haired leaves. The flowers vary from bright reddish pink in some forms to bluish lavender in others. Most species of this section are prodigal bloomers. Like most other members of this genus, these are taprooted dryland plants that resent disturbance. They do produce quantities of seed, and can be grown rather easily when provided with a fast draining soil. *Astragalus sericoleucus* is an especially tiny-leaved mat former with vivid magenta flowers. *Astragalus tridactylicus* has larger leaves and flowers common over much the same range. *Astragalus aretioides* is an especially compact mound former with spectacular purple-red flowers. *Astragalus barrii*, named for Claude Barr, is reputed to be the easiest to grow, as well as the largest flowered of the section, but we have yet to attempt it.

Astragalus spatulatus deserves separate mention. This is perhaps the most widespread cushion astragalus in the Western deserts. It occurs in immense colonies throughout the eastern Great Basin and is universal throughout the scablands of Wyoming. For a few weeks in June, *A. spatulatus* forms a tremendous spectacle wherever it grows, for the tight white vegetable sheep are covered with vivid pink to purple blossoms. It is easily distinguished from its relatives since its leaves are not divided but consist of simple, lanceolate leaflets that are crowded into a tight cushion. The size and length of leaf is variable, however, sometimes reaching an inch, although the best forms are less than a quarter of an inch in length. This one is much easier to grow than most other members of the genus, even propagating from cuttings.

Atriplex corrugata occupies literally hundreds of acres in the Intermountain Area. This is a wonderful cushion plant, although the flowers are not at all showy. Under ordinary garden conditions, however, the tight mounds quickly etiolate and rot at the first prolonged wet spell. This is a desert plant that needs the driest, most austere conditions to grow. Provided it has a perfectly drained hot spot with no competition, it can form fleecy white mounds from cuttings or seed.

Besseya alpina produces wooly candles of purple bloom in the earliest spring in the high mountains of Colorado. These are followed by small clusters of round, scalloped leaves. In nature, this is largely restricted to rocky cliffs at higher elevations. Surprisingly, it has proven to be long-lived and easy with scree conditions in the garden.

Campanula parryi is much rarer than the common harebell. The flowers are much larger, however, and their shallow, upright salvers are usually produced on shorter stems. This is not a difficult plant to grow either from cuttings or from seed, and it will quickly spread to fill an entire bed. It tends to bloom in a desultory way unless it is fertilized.

Chrysothamnus viscidiflorus, both this and the better known *C. nauseosus* produce tiny, high mountain forms that literally smother the low, silver mounds with yellow brushes of bloom. *Chrysothamnus viscidiflorus* often produces individuals with foliage twisted in spirals that are especially decorative. All are best grown from seed.

Cryptantha has yet to be discovered. These bristly relatives of the forget-me-nots are numerous and abundant throughout the drier portions of the West. Some, like *Cryptantha jamesii* or *C. grahamii,* have tight rosettes crowned with creamy white flowers that resemble nothing so much as a superior androsace. All seem to be taprooted, and should always be grown from seed.

Draba oligosperma is perhaps one of the most widespread species of Western drabas: it is extremely common throughout most of the Wyoming Rockies and locally abundant both north and south of there. Its tiny, silver rosettes form mats which can sometimes spread to a foot across. These are smothered in the spring with tiny yellow flowers. It is easily propagated by division,

Cryptantha jamesii
Photo by Bob Heapes

cuttings or seed. In Colorado this can be found with *Draba aurea*, which is much showier in cultivation than in the wild. It forms a tuft of extremely hairy rosettes 2 in. wide that are a delightful addition to a trough or small rock garden. The flowers are typical, bright yellow crucifers.

Erigeron pinnatisectus is just one of legions of fleabanes that seem to grow in virtually any habitat throughout the West. There are many tiny, cushion-forming species with vivid pink, blue or white flowers and even some showy yellow-flowered daisies. Some of these will undoubtedly prove to be indispensible rock plants in the future. *Erigeron pinnatisectus* deserves special mention not only because it is largely restricted to tundra in the Southern Rockies, but because the bright daisies, produced on short stems, are invariably a vivid blue or even deep violet in color. The leaves are usually deep green—with six or more divisions—which distinguish it from the commoner *E. compositus* that usually has only three to five segments on its grayer foliage. The latter can be weedy in a garden, but *E. pinnatisectus* is well-behaved and elegant.

Delphinium alpestre is a rare endemic of the Southern Rockies that has yet to be tamed. It forms mats of deep green foliage only a few inches tall, with dark blue flowers towering to 6 or 7 in. Similar but much commoner are the legions of tuberous dryland delphiniums that color much of the West with dazzling blue sheets of color in late May or early June. These demand the same sorts of conditions as *Lewisia rediviva,* and disappear just as promptly and completely after they set seed. They have persisted for five years in the Rock Alpine Garden, improving every year. *Delphinium nelsonii* and *D. menziesii* are typical of these.

Eriogonum acaule is the tiniest and most condensed of all eriogonums. It is found widely scattered throughout Wyoming, extending beyond the state only a short distance into northwestern Colorado. It has deep green or gray-green cushions that are studded with yellow to orange clusters of flowers in mid June. This is a cold desert plant that needs all the care of a dionysia (and the heat needed for cactus) to adapt to cultivation.

Eriogonum caespitosum is only slightly larger than the previous species and it is almost as difficult to grow in gardens. It is a sin to collect the ancient cushions of this plant that occur throughout the entire Intermountain Region, especially since collected plants never reestablish properly. Grown from seed or cutting it matures very slowly. A five-year-old seedling in the

Rock Alpine Garden is the size of a fifty-cent piece. An ancient specimen of this, covered with yellow, orange or reddish clusters of papery flowers over powdery white foliage, is a sight to remember.

Eriogonum flavum in its typical form is a fine small plant that thrives in dry scree conditions even in moist climates. This has a high mountain form, subspecies *E.f. xanthum,* which forms broad mats of silvery foliage on sunny alpine screes in parts of the Colorado Rockies. It has proven to be one of the easiest of the genus to grow in cultivation, forming a large mat in only a few years. The flowers are practically stemless, opening bright yellow and fading to a burnt orange-red. There are literally dozens of other garden-worthy eriogonums. This is surely one of the most aristocratic genera of Rocky Mountain plants.

Eriogonum ovalifolium occurs in a profusion of forms from hot desert to alpine tundra throughout the Rocky Mountain Region. Fortunately, this is not only one of the loveliest of the genus, but also one of the easiest to grow. Seed is produced in abundance, and plants quickly attain a respectable size in the garden. This is a superb silver-foliaged plant in all forms, but it is worth searching out the brighter pink or yellow flowered forms which are outnumbered by dirty whites and dingy grays in the wild. There is at least one mountain in the Northwest where the flowers open a deep rose. It only asks for sun and drainage.

Haplopappus acaulis occurs in great numbers from the crest of the Sierra to the foothills of the Rocky Mountains in the east. Most forms of this are fine rock garden mat plants that will thrive in warm scree conditions, producing a mass of yellow daisies in early summer. In certain portions of the Great Basin, tiny ecotypes of this occur with leaves only a quarter or half inch in length rather than the 2 in. more commonly encountered. These are as easy to grow as the type and constitute delightful trough plants.

Heuchera is universal from plains to mountaintops throughout the Rockies. All are decorative in evergreen rosette, although only *H. hallii* from the Pikes Peak region and *H. rubescens* from the Intermountain Region are really pure white in color. The common, tiny *H. bracteata,* with bronzy, green flowers, may appeal to sophisticated tastes.

Hymenoxys acaulis is one of the most abundant plants of the West. Practically any dry meadow from the Great Basin to the Great Plains up to the highest tundra throughout the Rockies seems to boast some form of this endlessly variable species. In the garden, most have lovely silvery foliage that is decorative at all times of the year. The flowers are showy, and some

Eriogonum ovalifolium. Photo by Panayoti Kelaidis

forms are everblooming. It is long-lived and easy to grow. With so many good qualities, it's surprising that it is so rarely seen in cultivation.

Lesquerella alpina is perhaps the most widespread of this immense genus of Western plants. It forms miniscule clumps of silver rosettes studded in the early spring with yellow cruciform flowers which in turn are succeeded with tiny balloonlike seedpods. This is a superb trough plant. Many are the bladderpods in the West, and virtually all of them have interest in leaf, in rosette, in flower and in seed. Many are small enough for the smallest trough, and others are of the proper stature for the scree. All need superlative drainage and most like hot, dry conditions.

Machaeranthera coloradoensis and *M. pattersonii* are two little-known endemics of the Southern Rocky Mountains. The first was known to Dwight Ripley as *Aster coloradoensis* and considered by him to be the finest American aster. It is found sparingly in the Mosquito Range of central Colorado and on the neighboring parklands where it forms tiny mats of toothed, silvery foliage with comparatively huge flowers of bright pink produced on short stems for most of the summer season. Patterson's aster is a larger plant, with toothed, deep green leaves forming lush rosettes several inches across. These produce short stems with positively huge heads of blossom, occasionally 3 in. across. The ray flowers are shimmering violet and the disk flowers are a pure, contrasting yellow. This is a rare endemic of the Front Range in Colorado, usually found right at tree line.

Melampodium cinereum, sometimes called the blackfoot daisy, shares the same overall range as *Zinnia grandiflora* in the plains bordering the Southern Rockies. It too is an everblooming perennial forming symmetrical mounds of pure white, 5-rayed flowers that create a vivid mass of color from late May to frost.

Mertensia alpina is the tiniest and perhaps the most distinctive Western chiming bells. I know it only from Pikes Peak, although similar plants have been found on the Beartooth Plateau. Unlike most chiming bells, the flowers are born upright on very short stems. The corollas are flat rather than bell-shaped, and the flowers are quite fragrant. There are numerous attractive dwarf *Mertensia* species throughout the mountains and deserts of the West. All are easy to grow in scree conditions in gardens from seed.

Oenothera lavandulifolia and its close relatives, *O. greggii* and *O. (Calylophus) serrulata* are widespread throughout the drier portions of the West. Unlike the better known evening

Lesquerella alpina. Photo by Jim Borland

primroses, these are all day-flowering plants. They are also subshrubby in habit, bearing their comparatively huge flowers over tiny mounds of twiggy stems with tiny leaves. Like most *Oenothera* species, they are easily grown from cutting or seed, but need good drainage and a hot position to grow in cultivation.

Oxytropis lambertii is the famous showy locoweed that stains plains and mountain meadows magenta with its vivid flowers in June and July. At Denver Botanic Gardens we find that this is easily grown from seed (which requires scarification), and that it thrives in a variety of soils and exposures. Other locoweeds are almost as showy, and often as easy to grow. *Oxytropis sericea* is larger, and white with even more silvery foliage. *Oxytropis multiceps* is a cushion-forming species that needs fast drainage and a warm position to persist in cultivation.

Paronychia pulvinata from the tundra of the Southern Rockies forms a rock hard dome in the wild. A few botanists have lumped this highly distinctive plant with the abundant lowland nailwort, *P. sessiliflora*. This latter plant is very easy to grow in cultivation, as is the similar *P. jamesii*, although neither is very showy. These are universal plants of parkland and desert throughout the Rocky Mountains.

Pellaea occidentalis is a magnificent rockfern that abounds on limestone in the Northern Rockies. The closely related *P. suksdorfiana* from farther south is also a difficult plant, and neither should be attempted except from spores. We find that it is possible to grow them in pots, but impossible in the open garden. *Pellaea atropurpurea* is occasionally encountered in the Southern Rockies, and is much easier to grow in the rock garden. There are many other fine rock ferns throughout the West, few of which seem to persist in open soil. Plants in the wild are probably decades—if not centuries—old, and it is irresponsible to collect these. All ferns can be grown from spores.

Penstemon contains a treasure chest of plants suited to sunny rock gardens, troughs and the wildflower patch. The Rockies include many of the tiniest and largest flowered members of the genus. *Penstemon acaulis* and *P. yampaensis* are unquestionably the smallest plants of the genus, forming tiny mats of needle-thin foliage with stemless blue flowers in early spring. They come from desert areas and need perfect drainage to survive in cultivation. The bewildering complex of "heather" penstemons (usually assigned either to the section Ericopsis or else subsection Caespitosi) are fine plants in drier climates. *Penstemon caespitosus* and *P. crandallii* are the best known species in this section, although *P. teucrioides* and *P. tusharensis* are proving to be more adaptable to the Rock Alpine Garden. All penstemons in this section are eminently desirable. The closely related *P. linarioides* is larger, but excellent as well. *Penstemon laricifolius* in both the larger pink and tiny white varieties is a fine trough plant, or specialty plant for tiny rock gardens. *Penstemon eriantherus* occurs throughout the dry portions of the Northern and Southern Rockies. It is a very showy dwarf plant demanding dry conditions. *Penstemon humilis* is equally abundant throughout the Intermountain Region, most forms of which are quite small-leaved and low, with vivid blue flowers. *Penstemon aridus* is like a microscopic version of this last species, while *P. virens* is similar to *P. humilis,* only still larger. *Penstemon fruticosus* and *P. montanus* are two representatives of the primarily Northwestern section of *Dasanthera*. Both are dwarf and superb in bloom, although the latter is a challenge to grow. New species of penstemon from the Rocky Mountain region are still being described, and the last word will not be said about them for some time.

Phlox abound at all levels in the Rocky Mountains from the hottest deserts to the highest tundra. There are so many species, which in turn so often hybridize, that some people are intimidated by this richest of native genera. With care and attention, the famous cushion phlox of the West can indeed be grown. Of these, the tightest cushions are formed by the rare *P. tumulosa* from east central Nevada. Almost as condensed—and magnificent in their own right—are *P. condensata* (an alpine of the Southern Rockies and Great Basin), *P. muscoides* (which has tiny flowers and is widely rhizomatous, with tiny, deep green rosettes), *P. bryoides* with silvery white imbricate leaves and pure white flowers.

Phlox pulvinata is often blue-flowered, and largely alpine in the Southern Rockies. *Phlox caespitosa* is also alpine, with longer, narrower leaves and variable flower color. *Phlox hoodii*, however, is surely the most widespread and variable of all—occurring throughout the range of *Artemisia tridentata* and often carpeting the ground under the common sagebrush. This, and all other Western cushion phloxes, are intensely fragrant—and worth the effort to grow for this quality alone. All appear to need scree conditions in the garden.

Physaria alpina is the most aristocratic of this fine race of crucifers not only because it is a high alpine endemic of the Mosquito Range of Colorado, but also because of the size and splendor of the orange-yellow blossoms that surround the silvery, starfish rosette. All twinpods are easily cultivated in warm, fast-draining scree, and often self-sow. This is quite a large genus, with new species constantly being described from the vast desert stretches of Wyoming. They are also fine plants for trough gardens.

Primula angustifolia occurs in great numbers throughout the tundra of Colorado. It never seems to establish properly in a garden from collected plants, but seedlings appear to be quite adaptable. In the garden, however, this primrose goes dormant during the long summer season, so mark its place well. It has persisted three years in the Rock Alpine Garden.

Four variable and lovely dwarf willows occur throughout the Rocky Mountain region. *Salix nivalis* is closely allied to the arctic *S. reticulata,* and likewise has deep green reticulated leaves. This and the pointier-leaved *S. arctica* are the commonest species throughout the Rockies. *Salix rotundifolia* is more common in the north part of the range, and has tiny, round-leaved foliage. *Salix cascadensis* is scattered in occurrence throughout its range, with narrow, gray leaves. All willows are best struck from cuttings made in late winter.

Saxifraga serpyllifolia, also known as *S. chrysantha,* is a high alpine that is quite common at the highest elevations of the Colorado Rockies. It forms extensive colonies with tiny, concise, apple green rosettes less than an inch across. In the mountains this comes into bloom in July and August, with comparatively huge yellow bells of bloom that can color the tundra gold. It is extremely difficult to grow at lower elevations. There are quite a number of other interesting saxifrages in the Rockies, including *S. oppositifolia* in some fine and easily grown forms.

Telesonix jamesii is found in abundance throughout the Northern Rockies where the petals are rarely more than a quarter of an inch in length. On Pikes Peak and a few other mountains in central Colorado the petals are three or four times as large, and the plant suddenly attains star status. It was known for many years as *Boykinia jamesii.*

Townsendia is a large and confusing genus in the Rocky Mountains. A few species, such as the large, summer-blooming *T. eximia* or *T. grandiflora* are easily recognized and keyed out. In the eastern Intermountain Region, a variety of species occur which are harder to distinguish. These include quite a number of mat-forming, everblooming composites that will be fine additions to troughs and rock gardens of the future.

Zinnia grandiflora occurs on the flanks of Pikes Peak up to 6,000 ft. in elevation—surely it must qualify as a Rocky Mountain plant. In dry climates on warm exposures this is a long-lived mat-forming plant that blooms for over four months in the garden. In wetter climates it must be grown in sand or scree conditions in order to survive the winter.

References

Callas, P. P. (Kelaidis). 1980. "First Summer: Planting the Rock Alpine Garden." *The Green Thumb.* 37(4): 113–120.

Callas, P. P. (Kelaidis). 1981. "The Rock Alpine Garden in historical perspective." *The Green Thumb.* 38(2): 57–62.

Pierce, A. 1981. "Plants for Denver's new rock garden." *Bulletin of the American Rock Garden Society.* 39(1): 21–23.

Schaal, H. R. 1979. "Alpine Rock Garden under construction." *The Green Thumb.* 36(1): 13–15.

Schaal, H. R. 1981. "Denver Botanic Garden's Alpine and Rock Garden." *Bulletin of the American Rock Garden Society.* 39(1): 20–23.

26

Seed Propagation of Rocky Mountain Alpines

by James Borland

Of the 55,000 plants annually requested of the propagator at Denver Botanic Gardens, 25 percent are destined for the Rock Alpine Garden. Ninety-five percent of these 10,000–12,000 requested plants are received as seed acquired from worldwide botanic gardens, personal gardens and from private and commercial seed collectors. Although the sources are global, they rarely represent plant life zones other than those present in the Rocky Mountain region. As expected, then, seed survival and germination characteristics of our desert-to-alpine species are essentially similar to those of species from other continents.

Although a great amount of research has been done on the physiology and characteristics of seed germination, very little is known about the seed of typical rock garden plants. We are fortunate that the economic realities of seed research include the weeds of agronomic crops as well as species for revegetating human- or cattle-disturbed lands. Many of these species are either already considered to be rock garden plants or are so closely related that information regarding their germination can be directly or indirectly applied to their smaller or flashier cousins. Unfortunately, this information applies to only a small fraction of the total number of species received at Denver Botanic Gardens. The rest fall into a category whose germination requirements are entirely unknown.

Extraneous human elements involved with the seed often affect its ultimate germinability. The seed may have been harvested before it was sufficiently ripened, or it may have been subjected to unfavorable high temperatures or high humidity, both of which can quickly sap its vitality. Conversely, seeds of the Salicaceae, Fagaceae, and Aceraceae are short-lived and should be planted immediately before they desiccate and die; *Salix* seeds remain viable only a few days. Experience indicates that members of the Ranunculaceae, Fumariaceae and Asteraceae families might be added to this list as well.

Assuming that the packet received contains seed and not chaff and that the seed has not suffered any of the aforementioned mishaps and is still viable, consideration is then given to the type of potential dormancy involved with that seed and the means to overcome it.

A native of western Pennsylvania, **James Borland** moved west to study horticulture at Colorado State University. He quickly fell under the spell of the Western landscape, particularly dryland native plants, which he has studied extensively throughout the West. His favorites include the many permutations of *Atriplex, Eriogonum, Penstemon* and the numerous varieties of native Asteraceae. After graduation, he worked several years at Weddle Native Plant Nursery in western Colorado, growing a broad spectrum of Western wildflowers, trees and shrubs. He moved to Denver in the fall of 1982 to become chief propagator at Denver Botanic Gardens. At DBG, he grows an impressive range of native and exotic plants; this experience forms the basis of this paper.

SEED GERMINATION PRETREATMENTS

Impermeable Seed Coats

Seeds must imbibe or absorb water before germination processes can commence. Certain seeds are immediately prevented from doing so by hard, dense or hydrophobic layers or by a netted arrangement of cell layers that rely on the surface tension of water to prevent absorption. Through the natural action of weathering, soil microorganisms, and occasionally higher forms of animal life, these coats are abraded sufficiently to allow water penetration. Several methods are used to artificially mimic and hasten these natural processes which may otherwise take years to accomplish.

Mechanical Scarification: Seed coat abrasion is accomplished through the action of sandpaper, file or knife. Particular care must be taken to avoid injury to the embryo, especially around the seed's point of former attachment to the fruiting body. Seeds treated in this fashion should be sown immediately, since internal moisture can now be lost and may be reduced to a deficient and lethal quantity.

Acid Scarification: This method should be used *only* by those knowledgeable of the dangers involved with handling acid and the absolute necessity for following the proper safety precautions. Seeds with especially recalcitrant, water-impermeable seed coats are soaked in concentrated sulfuric acid for periods ranging from only a few seconds to several hours. It is advisable to occasionally stir the mixture gently with a glass rod to ensure proper contact with the acid. Immediately upon removal from the acid bath the seeds must be washed in several changes of fresh water and sown immediately. Since different seed lots or accessions of the same species may require different acid soaking periods, the progress of the acid soak should be checked periodically by withdrawing a few seeds and checking the thickness of the seed coat. When the seed coat has become paper-thin, the treatment must be terminated. Penetration by the acid to the interior embryonic tissues will quickly kill the embryo.

Hot Water Soaks: This scarification treatment involves either soaking seeds in 4 to 5 times their volume of hot water 77° to 100°C or pouring boiling water over the seeds and allowing the water to cool naturally for 12 to 24 hours. Prompt sowing following this treatment is advised.

Warm Moist Scarification: This treatment most closely resembles natural conditions where seeds are sown in a non-sterile, moist, warm medium and left for several weeks to several months. This can be achieved easily through summer or early fall outdoor sowings where microorganism activity will eventually penetrate the seed coat.

Seed Coat Chemical Inhibitors

Fruits, seed coats and associated seed parts (e.g., tails, wings, etc.) of some seeds may contain germination-inhibiting chemicals, some of which may be removed by running water or by removal of the offending part. Inhibitors have been found or are suspected in seeds of Chenopodiaceae, Portulacaceae, Brassicaceae, Linaceae, Violaceae, Ranunculaceae, Lamiaceae, Rosaceae, Vitaceae and Polygonaceae.

Internal Seed Dormancy

This very general term includes many not fully understood physiological and morphological conditions within the seed that can delay germination (e.g., rudimentary or undeveloped embryos, thermodormancy, photodormancy, embryo dormancy). Most of these sometimes complex and interacting conditions can be overcome by subjecting the seed to periods of specific environmental conditions.

Dry Afterripening: Seeds of several species require only a period of exposure to warm temperatures after harvest to allow interior conditions to become receptive to subsequent favorable germination conditions.

Stratification: With this treatment seeds are subjected to moist conditions at low temperatures (2°–5°C) for a prescribed period for that species or seed lot. Seeds can be mixed with moistened sand or peatmoss and enclosed within a plastic or glass container which then can be stored in the refrigerator. The container should be checked periodically for media moisture content and for early germination. The seed should be sown immediately upon signs of germination or after the stratification treatment. Drying of the seed at this point may force the seed back into an even more complex dormancy at best or prove fatal at worst. Stratification conditions are *not* satisfied by subjecting seed to low temperatures only. It must be moist and fully imbibed as well.

Other Treatments

Chemical: Certain seeds can be stimulated to germinate by soaking them in single or combination low concentrations of chemicals for prescribed periods. Chemicals commonly used include: gibberellins (200–1,000 ppm for 1–24 hours), kinetin (100 ppm for 1–10 minutes), ethylene, thiourea (0.5–3.0% for 24 hours), sodium hypochlorite (1% solution) and potassium nitrate (0.1–0.3%). Some of these chemicals are expensive and dangerous and require thorough knowledge of the safety precautions involved with their handling.

Freezing: Probably the only benefit to be derived from this treatment is the possible cracking of the seed coat during the actual freezing cycle which for most seeds placed in the home freezer unit takes place in less than an hour. Since most physiological activity essentially stops at below freezing temperatures, the potential benefit of cracking the seed coat with this process can be derived more expeditiously through other scarification procedures.

Temperature: It has been found that most seeds germinate better with a daily alteration of temperatures not unlike that found in nature. Two common combinations are 15° and 30°C or 20° and 30°C, with seed subjected to the lower temperature for 16 hours and then to the higher temperature for 8 hours.

Light: Although a few species (e.g., the genera *Phacelia, Nigella, Allium, Phlox*) are inhibited from germination by the presence of light, most are either not affected or are promoted. Light can be provided with cool-white fluorescent lamps so that they provide an intensity of 75–125 foot-candles (800–1345 lux) for at least 8 hours daily.

These treatments and conditions include only a few of the known means of overcoming the most common seed dormancies. Additional, more complex dormancies, including combination or double dormancies, make it practically impossible to determine what pretreatment is necessary to enhance or promote germination.

It is no wonder that with so many unknowns and complexities involved with the seed of these little-studied species that rock gardeners everywhere resort to the one time-honored method available to everyone—Mother Nature. Even at Denver Botanic Gardens a significant number of species are sown in small pots and placed outdoors in a protected cold frame, kept moist and allowed to germinate naturally.

Seed germination is only one of a number of indispensable subjects regarding the culture of rock garden plants. Equally important are soils, light, disease, pests, nutrition and temperature. The reader is advised to research these subjects in one of the greenhouse texts listed at the end of this article.

References

Hanan Joe J., Winfred D. Holley, and Kenneth L. Goldsberry. 1978. *Greenhouse management.* New York: Springer-Verlag.

Hartman, Hudson T., and Dale E. Kester. 1983. *Propagation: principles and practices.* Englewood Cliffs, N. J.: Prentice-Hall, Inc.

Mastalerz, John W. 1977. *The greenhouse environment.* New York: John Wiley and Sons.

Redente, E. F., P. R. Ogle, and N. E. Hargis. 1982. *Growing Colorado plants from seed: a state of the art.* Vol. 3, *Forbs.* FWS/OBS-82/30. Washington: United States Dept. of the Interior, Fish and Wildlife Service.

United States Department of Agriculture. 1974. *Seeds of woody plants in the United States.* USDA Handbook no. 450. Washington: USDA, Forest Service.

———. 1978. *Collecting, processing and germinating seeds of Western wildland plants.* Science and Education Administration, Agricultural Reviews and Manuals no. ARM-W-3/July 1978. Berkeley: USDA, Office of the Regional Administrator.

Vories, Kimery C. 1980. *Growing Colorado plants from seed: a state of the art.* Vol.1, *Shrubs.* Ogden, Utah: Intermountain Forest and Range Experiment Station.

SEED GERMINATION PRETREATMENTS

Species	Pretreatment	Species	Pretreatment
Abies concolor	stratify 1–2 mo.	*Arctostaphylos nevadensis*	acid scarify 1–7 hr. then stratify 2–4 mo.
A. grandis	stratify 3–4 wk.	*A. patula*	acid scarify 4 hr. then stratify 6 mo.
A. lasiocarpa v. *lasiocarpa*	none	*A. uva-ursi*	acid scarify 1–7 hr. then stratify 2–4 mo.
A. lasiocarpa v. *arizonica*	none	*Arenaria fendleri*	none
Acer glabrum	subject to warm (20°–30°C) moist conditions for 6 mo. then stratify 6 mo.	*A. (Minuartia) obtusiloba*	none
		Arnica fulgens	none
A. grandidentatum	stratify 1–2 mo.	*Artemisia arbuscula* (*A. tridentata* ssp. *a.*)	none or stratify 10 days
Achillea lanulosa	none	*A. cana*	none
Actaea rubra	stratify at 22°C day and 17°C night for 3 wk. then stratify at 2°C for 3 mo.	*Artemisia filifolia*	none
		A. frigida	none
		A. ludoviciana	fresh seed may need stratification
Agoseris glauca	none	*A. nova* (*A. tridentata* ssp. *n.*)	none
Allium brevistylum	none or stratify 4 mo., scarify or none, use fresh seed only	*A. pedatifida*	none
		A. porteri	none
A. cernuum	none or stratify 4 mo., scarify or none, use fresh seed only	*A. scopulorum*	none
		A. (Picrothamnus) spinescens	none
A. geyeri	none or stratify 4 mo., scarify or none, use fresh seed only	*A. tridentata*	none
		Asclepias tuberosa	seed younger than 2 yrs. old may show dormancy
Alnus tenuifolia	none	*Astragalus aretioides*	sandpaper scarify
Amelanchier alnifolia	stratify 4–6 mo.	*A. barrii*	sandpaper scarify
A. utahensis	stratify 1.5–6 mo.	*A. bisulcatus*	sandpaper scarify
Amorpha canescens	hot water soak or sandpaper scarify	*A. canadensis*	sandpaper scarify
		A. crassicarpus	sandpaper scarify
A. fruticosa	hot water soak or sandpaper scarify	*A. drummondii*	sandpaper scarify
		A. hyalinus	sandpaper scarify
A. nana	hot water soak or sandpaper scarify	*A. kentrophyta*	sandpaper scarify
		A. sericoleucus	sandpaper scarify
Androsace chamaejasme ssp. *carinata*	none	*A. spatulatus*	sandpaper scarify
		A. tridactylicus	sandpaper scarify
Anemone multifida	1–2 mo. stratification may be helpful, use fresh seed only	*Atriplex canescens*	after-ripen for several mo. or stratify 3 mo.
		A. confertifolia	after-ripen 3–6 mo.
A. narcissiflora spp. *zephyra*	1–2 mo. stratification may be helpful, use fresh seed only	*A. cuneata* (*A. nuttallii* ssp. *c.*)	stratify 1–2 mo.
		A. gardneri (*A. nuttallii* ssp. *g.*)	stratify 1–2 mo.
A. (Pulsatilla) patens	stratify 2 mo.	*A. obovata*	after-ripen 3.5 mo.
Antennaria alpina	none	*Baccharis emoryi*	none
A. parvifolia	none	*B. glutinosa*	none
A. rosea	none	*Balsamorhiza sagittata*	stratify 3 mo.
A. umbrinella	none	*Berberis haematocarpa*	none
Aquilegia caerulea	3 wk. stratification helpful	*Brickellia californica*	none
		Brodiaea douglasii	none
A. chrysantha	3 wk. stratification helpful	*Calochortus nuttallii*	stratify 1–3 mo.
A. elegantula	3 wk. stratification helpful	*C. gunnisonii*	stratify 1–3 mo.
A. jonesii	3 wk. stratification helpful	*Campanula rotundifolia*	stratify 1–2 mo.
A. saximontana	3 wk. stratification helpful		

Species	Pretreatment
Cassiope tetragona	none
Castilleja chromosa	stratify 3 mo.
C. foliosa	stratify 3 mo.
C. integra	none
C. linariifolia	none or stratify 1–2 mo.
Ceanothus fendleri	hot water soak then stratify 1–3 mo.
C. velutinus	stratify 1–3 mo.
Celtis reticulata	stratify 2–4 mo.
Cerastium beeringianum	after-ripen 4–12 mo.
Ceratoides (Eurotia) lanata	after-ripen 2–3 mo.
Cercis occidentalis	acid scarify 25–60 min. then stratify 3 mo.
Cercocarpus intricatus	acid scarify 20 min. then stratify 1–3 mo.
C. ledifolius	acid scarify 20 min. then stratify 1–3 mo.
C. montanus	acid scarify 20 min. then stratify 1–3 mo.
Chilopsis linearis	none
Chrysopsis (Heterotheca) villosa	none
Chrysothamnus nauseosus	none, use fresh seed only
C. viscidiflorus	none, use fresh seed only
Clematis hirsutissima	stratify 4 mo.
C. ligusticifolia	stratify 2–6 mo.
Coleogyne ramosissima	stratify 8 days
Coreopsis lanceolata	none
Cornus canadensis	acid scarify 1–3 hr. then stratify 4–5 mo.
Cornus nuttallii	stratify 3 mo.
C. sericea (stolonifera)	stratify 1–3 mo.
Corydalis aurea	erratic germination, use fresh seed only
Coryphantha spp.	none or sandpaper scarify
Cowania mexicana	stratify 1 mo.
Crataegus douglasii	acid scarify 0.5–3 hr. then stratify 3–4 mo.
Cupressus arizonica	stratify 1 mo.

Species	Pretreatment
Delphinium nelsonii	stratify 2–3 mo., use fresh seed only
Dicentra uniflora	stratification probably needed, use fresh seed
Draba aurea	none
D. crassa	none
D. crassifolia	none
D. oligosperma	none
D. paysonii	none
D. streptocarpa	none
Echinacea angustifolia	none or stratify 1–3 mo. for fresh seed
Echinocereus triglochidiatus	none or sandpaper scarify
Eleagnus commutata	stratify 2–3 mo.
Ephedra torreyana	stratify 1–2 mo.
E. viridis	stratify 1–2 mo.
Epilobium (Chamerion) angustifolium	none
Erigeron compositus	none
E. simplex	none
E. pinnatisectus	none
Eriogonum fasciculatum	none
E. flavum v. flavum	stratify 1–2 mo.
E. flavum v. xanthum	stratify 1–2 mo.
E. umbellatum	stratify 3 mo.
Erysimum nivale	none
Erythronium grandiflorum	stratify 3–5 mo.
Eustoma grandiflorum (Lisianthus russellianus)	none, slow growing
Fallugia paradoxa	none
Forestiera neomexicana	stratify 1 mo.
Gaillardia aristata	none
G. pinnatifida	none
Galium boreale	none
Garrya wrightii	none or stratify 1–4 mo.
Gaultheria (Chiogenes) hispidula	stratify 3–5 mo.
Gentiana (Pneumonanthe) affinis	none

Cercocarpus intricatus
Photo by Jim Borland

Species	Pretreatment
G. (Pneumonanthe) andrewsii	stratify 1 mo.
Geranium caespitosum	sandpaper scarify
G. viscosissimum	sandpaper scarify
Geum (Acomastylis) rossii	none, germination improved with 6–12 mo. dry storage
G. (Erythrocoma) triflorum	1 mo. stratification improves germination
G. turbinatum (G. rossii ssp. t.)	none, seed sensitive to drying
Grayia brandegei	stratify 2–3 mo.
G. spinosa	stratify 2–3 mo.
Guttierezia sarothrae	none
Haplopappus glutinosus	none
H. spinulosus	1 mo. stratification may improve germination
Hedeoma drummondii	none
Hedysarum boreale	sandpaper scarify
Heliomeris (Gymnolomia, Viguiera) multiflora	none
Heuchera hallii	none
H. parvifolia	none
H. rubescens	none
Holodiscus discolor	after-ripen 6 mo. or stratify 18 wk.
H. dumosus	stratify 4 mo.
Hymenoxys acaulis	none
H. grandiflora	none

Species	Pretreatment
Hypericum formosum	none
Hypoxis hirsuta	stratify 3 mo.
Iris missouriensis	sandpaper or acid scarify then stratify 1–2 mo.
Juncus spp.	store fresh seed in water in the refrigerator then sow in the spring
Juniperus communis	store warm (20°–25°C) and moist for 2–3 mo. then stratify 4 mo.
J. deppeana	none or stratify 1–4 mo.
J. horizontalis	store warm (20°C) and moist for 2 mo. then stratify 3 mo.
J. monosperma	none or stratify 1–4 mo.
J. occidentalis	subject to warm (20°–30°C) moist conditions for 1.5–3 mo. then stratify 1–4 mo.
J. osteoperma	subject to warm (20°–30°C) moist conditions for 1.5–3 mo. then stratify 1–4 mo.
J. scopulorum	subject to warm (20°–30°C) moist conditions for 1.5–3 mo. then stratify 1–4 mo.
Kalmia microphylla	none, surface sow
Larix laricina	none or stratify 1–2 mo.
L. lyallii	none or stratify 1–2 mo.

Juniperus osteosperma. Photo by Loraine Yeatts

Species	Pretreatment
L. occidentalis	none or stratify 1–2 mo.
Larrea tridentata	sandpaper scarify
Lathyrus spp.	hot water soak or sandpaper scarify
Ledum palustre	none, surface sow
Lesquerella alpina	none
L. fendleri	stratify 1–2 mo.
Lewisia pygmaea	stratify 2–4 mo.
Liatris ligulistylis	none
L. punctata	stratify 1–2 mo.
L. squarrosa	stratify 2 mo.
Lilium philadelphicum	store 3 mo. warm (20°C) and moist then stratify 6 wk.
Linanthastrum nuttallii	1 mo. stratification may improve germination
Linnaea borealis	none
Linum flavum	none
L. lewisii	none
L. rigidum	stratify 1 mo.
Lithospermum ruderale	none
Lobelia cardinalis	none or stratify 1–3 mo.
Lomatium dissectum v. *multifidum*	stratify 11 mo.
Lupinus spp.	hot water soak or sandpaper scarify
Lychnis apetala (*Silene uralensis*)	none
L. (*Silene*) *kingii*	none
Lycium andersonii	none
Lygodesmia juncea	stratify 1–2 mo.
Mahonia (*Berberis*) *repens*	stratify 1 mo. then 2 mo. moist and 20°C then stratify 6–7 mo.
Menodora scabra	none
Mentzelia decapetala	stratify 1 mo.
Mertensia alpina	stratify 1–3 mo.
M. fusiformis	stratify 1–3 mo.
M. lanceolata	stratify 1–3 mo.
M. longiflora	stratify 1–3 mo.
M. viridis	stratify 1–3 mo.
Mimulus glabratus v. *fremontii*	none
M. guttatus	none
M. lewisii	none
M. primuloides	none
Mirabilis multiflora	none
Monardella odoratissima	none for fresh seed, stratify stored seed 3 mo.
Oenothera caespitosa	none
O. (*Calylophus*) *lavandulifolia*	none
Opuntia spp.	none or sandpaper scarify
Oxyria digyna	none
Oxytropis ssp.	none or sandpaper scarify

Species	Pretreatment
Paeonia brownii	stratify 2.5 mo.
Papaver nudicaule	germinate at 12°C
Parthenocissus inserta	stratify 2 mo.
Pediocactus simpsonii	none or sandpaper scarify
Penstemon albifluvis	stratify 1–2 mo.
P. alpinus	stratify 1–3 mo.
P. angustifolius	stratify 1–2 mo.
P. barbatus	none or stratify 1–3 mo.
P. bridgesii (*P. rostriflorus*)	stratify 1–3 mo.
P. carnosus	stratify 2 mo.
P. cobaea	stratify 2 mo.
P. confertus	stratify 2 mo.
P. digitalis	stratify 1–2 mo.
P. dissectus	stratify 1–2 mo.
P. eatonii	stratify 2 mo.
P. eriantherus	stratify at least 4 mo.
P. euglaucus	stratify 2 mo.
P. fruticosus v. *serratus*	stratify 3 mo.
P. gairdneri v. *gairdneri*	stratify 3 mo.
P. glaber	stratify 3 yr. old seed 4 mo.
P. grandiflorus (*P. bradburii*)	none
P. heterophyllus	stratify 2 mo.
P. heterophyllus v. *purdyi*	stratify 2 mo.
P. laricifolius	stratify 2 mo.
P. mensarum	stratify 2 mo.
P. moffattii	stratify 3 mo.
P. montanus v. *montanus*	stratify 2 mo.
P. neomexicanus	stratify 3 mo.
P. newberryi	stratify 3 mo.
P. nitidus	stratify 3 mo.
P. palmeri	stratify 1–3 mo.
P. parvulus	stratify 3 mo.
P. peckii	stratify 2 mo.
P. pennellianus	stratify 3 mo.
P. richardsonii	stratify 1 mo.
P. rydbergii	stratify 2 mo.
P. serrulatus	stratify 2 mo.
P. speciosus	stratify 3 mo.
P. virgatus ssp. *asa-grayi* (*unilateralis*)	stratify 1–3 mo.
P. utahensis	stratify 2 mo.
P. virens	stratify 2 mo.
P. whippleanus	stratify 3 mo.
P. wilcoxii	stratify 2 mo.
Peraphyllum ramosissimum	stratify 1.5 mo.
Petalostemon (*Dalea*) *candidum*	none
P. (*Dalea*) *purpureum*	none

PLATE 21

Penstemon teucrioides
Photo by Bob Heapes

Townsendia grandiflora
Photo: Grand Ridge

Geranium fremontii
Photo by Ted Kipping

Garden of the Gods
Photo by Patricia Moore

PLATE 22

Notholaena fendleri
Photo by Ray Radebaugh

Montane stream
Photo by Ray Radebaugh

Oenothera caespitosa
Photo by Sharon Sutton

Betty Lowry's garden
Photo by Ned Lowry

Species	Pretreatment
Phacelia heterophylla	none
P. sericea	none
Philadelphus lewisii	stratify 2 mo.
Phlox hoodii	none
P. pulvinata	none or stratify 2 mo.
Physocarpus malvaceus	much unfilled seed
P. opulifolius	none
Pinus albicaulis	stratify 3–4 mo.
P. aristata	none for fresh seed, stratify stored seed 0–1 mo.
P. contorta	none for fresh seed, stratify stored seed 1–2 mo.
P. edulis	none for fresh seed, stratify stored seed 2 mo.
P. flexilis	stratify 1–2 mo.
P. monophylla	stratify 1–3 mo.
P. monticola	stratify 1–4 mo.
P. ponderosa	none for fresh seed, stratify stored seed 1–3 mo.
Physaria australis	none
P. didymocarpa	none
Picea engelmannii	none
P. glauca	none
P. pungens	none
Polemonium confertum	none
P. foliosissimum	none
P. viscosum	none
Populus spp.	none, sow only fresh seed
Potentilla anserina	stratify 2 mo.
P. arguta	stratify 1 mo.
P. diversifolia	none
P. fruticosa (Pentaphylloides floribunda)	none or stratify 1–3 mo.
P. glandulosa	none or stratify 1 mo. or scarify
P. gracilis	none
Primula angustifolia	none
Prunus americana	stratify 3–5 mo.
P. besseyi	stratify 4 mo.
P. emarginata	stratify 3–4 mo.
P. pensylvanica	subject to warm (20°–30°C) and moist conditions for 2 mo. then stratify 3 mo.
P. virginiana	stratify 4–5.5 mo.
Pseudotsuga menziesii v. *glauca*	none or stratify 1 mo.
Psilostrophe bakeri	1 mo. stratification improves germination
Ptelea trifoliata	stratify 3–4 mo.
Pulsatilla (Anemone) patens ssp. *multifida*	none

Species	Pretreatment
Purshia glandulosa	stratify 2–3 mo.
P. tridentata	stratify 1–3 mo.
Quercus gambelii	sow seed immediately upon harvest
Q. macrocarpa	stratify 1–2 mo. sow seed immediately upon harvest
Q. turbinella	sow seed immediately upon harvest
Q. undulata (Q. × pauciloba [gambelii × turbinella])	sow seed immediately upon harvest
Ranunculus spp.	seed viability lost quickly, sow only fresh seed, wash in running water several hours to rid of water soluble germ. inhibitors
Ratibida columnifera	none or scarify
Rhamnus alnifolia	none for fresh seed, stratify stored seed 2 mo.
R. purshiana	stratify 3 mo.
Rhododendron albiflorum	none, needs light to germinate
Rhus glabra	acid scarify 1–3 hr.
R. trilobata	acid scarify 1 hr. then stratify 2 mo.
Ribes americanum	stratify 3–4 mo.
R. aureum	stratify 2 mo.
R. cereum	stratify 4–5 mo.
R. hudsonianum	none
R. inerme	stratify 4–7 mo.
R. irriguum	stratify 3 mo.
R. lacustre	stratify 4–7 mo.
R. montigenum	stratify 4 mo.
R. odoratum	stratify 3–4 mo.
R. viscosissimum	stratify 4–5 mo.
Robinia neomexicana	hot water soak
Rosa acicularis	subject seed to warm (25°C) temperatures for 115 days then strat. 3 mo.
R. gymnocarpa	stratify 3 mo.
R. nutkana	stratify 5 mo.
Rubus occidentalis	subject seed to warm (20°–30°C) moist conditions for 3 mo. then stratify 3 mo.
R. spectabilis	subject seed to warm (20°–30°C) moist conditions for 3 mo. then stratify 3 mo.
Rudbeckia laciniata	stratify 1 mo.
Rumex venosus	none
Salix amygdaloides	none, seed is viable only 10–30 days after harvest
S. bebbiana	none, seed is viable only 10–30 days after harvest

Species	Pretreatment	Species	Pretreatment
S. discolor	none, seed is viable only 10–30 days after harvest	*S. occidentalis*	acid scarify 60–75 min. then subject seed to warm (20°–30°C) moist conditions for 1–4 mo. then stratify 4–6 mo.
S. exigua	none, seed is viable only 10–30 days after harvest		
S. interior (S. exigua)	none, seed is viable only 10–30 days after harvest	*S. orbiculatus*	acid scarify 30 min. then subject seed to warm (30°C) moist conditions for 4 mo. then stratify 6 mo.
S. lasiandra	none, seed is viable only 10–30 days after harvest		
S. petiolaris	none, seed is viable only 10–30 days after harvest		
S. rigida	none, seed is viable only 10–30 days after harvest	*Taxus brevifolia*	subject seed to warm (20°–30°C) moist conditions then stratify 9 mo.
S. scouleriana	none, seed is viable only 10–30 days after harvest	*Telesonix (Boykinia) jamesii*	none
Sambucus caerulea	stratify 3–4 mo.	*Thalictrum fendleri*	wash in running water 4 hr.
S. canadensis	subject seed to warm (20°–30°C) moist conditions then stratify 3–5 mo.	*Thermopsis rhombifolia*	sandpaper scarify
		Thlaspi alpestre (T. montanum)	none
S. glauca (S. caerulea ssp. g.)	stratify 3–4 mo.	*Thuja plicata*	none or stratify 1–2 mo.
S. pubens (S. racemosa v. p.)	subject seed to warm (20°–30°C) moist conditions for 1–2 mo. then stratify 3–5 mo.	*Townsendia exscapa*	none
		T. eximia	none
		T. incana	none
		T. grandiflora	none
Sarcobatus vermiculatus	none	*T. sericea (T. exscapa)*	stratify 1–2 mo.
Saxifraga rhomboidea	up to 1.5 yr after-ripening increases germination	*Tradescantia* spp.	use fresh seed only, probably no pretreatment necessary
Sedum lanceolatum (S. stenopetalum)	none	*Trifolium dasyphyllum*	none or sandpaper scarify
Senecio canus	none	*T. nanum*	none or sandpaper scarify
S. integerrimus	stratify 4 mo.		
S. mutabilis (S. neomexicanus var. m.)	none	*T. parryi*	none or sandpaper scarify
S. serra	stratify 4 mo.	*Trillium ovatum*	scarify
Shepherdia argentea	stratify 2–3 mo.	*Tsuga heterophylla*	stratify 1–3 mo.
S. canadensis	acid scarify 20–30 min then stratify 2 mo.	*T. mertensiana*	stratify 3 mo.
		Vaccinium caespitosum	none, very erratic germination
S. rotundifolia	none	*Vernonia fasciculata*	stratify 1 mo.
Sibbaldia procumbens	none	*Viburnum lentago*	subject seed to warm (20°–30°C) moist conditions for 5–9 mo. then stratify 2–4 mo.
Silene acaulis	none		
S. laciniata	none		
Smilacina racemosa	stratify 3–4 mo.		
Solidago mollis	none or stratify 1 mo.	*Viola nuttallii*	stratify 1–2 mo.
S. rigida	none	*Wyethia amplexicaulis*	stratify 1 mo.
Sorbus scopulina	stratify 2 mo.	*Xerophyllum tenax*	none
S. sitchensis	stratify 3–5 mo.	*Yucca angustissima*	none
Sphaeralcea coccinea	scarify	*Y. baccata*	none
S. parvifolia	none	*Y. elata*	none
Spiraea betulifolia	none	*Y. glauca*	none
Stanleya pinnata	none	*Y. harrimaniae*	none
Symphoricarpos albus	acid scarify 60–75 min. then subject seed to warm (20°–30°C) moist conditions for 1–4 mo. then stratify 4–6 mo.	*Zauschneria garrettiae (Epilobium canum ssp. g.)*	none or lightly sandpaper scarify
		Zinnia grandiflora	none

Section II

In the Garden: Adapting to Microclimates

Photo by Lee Raden

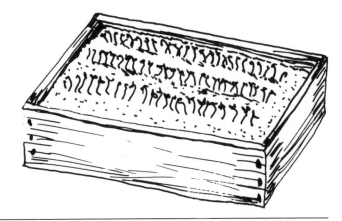

27

Commercial Production of Rocky Mountain Alpines

by Ronald D. Arpin

When I think about the Rocky Mountains, I think of how many species exist there—many more than I know now or may ever know. It fills me with excitement to imagine the vast amount of plant material not currently used in the nursery industry in this region, awaiting discovery—plant material that is only beginning to be studied for its landscape value.

Think for a moment about the process of introducing a plant to the industry. First, someone finds and identifies a plant that strikes his fancy. If he wants people to grow it, they will need seeds or cuttings. The plants he starts must then be planted out and observed to determine value and character. Usually at the same time, additional seeds or cuttings are being collected to increase the number of individuals in preparation for the anticipated release of the new plant. We are talking about years of work for one new introduction, even if the plant is easily propagated.

Continuing the process, perhaps this potential new introduction strikes the fancy of plant breeders. Now we have the potential for the development of new cultivars. The number of selections made depends on the breeder and the variability of the plant species being tested. Meanwhile, more plants are being planted in gardens where people can learn about them, enabling them to educate others.

But now the exciting part—have you realized how many people this new introduction has touched? We are only talking about one plant. Multiply this by hundreds or maybe even thousands of plant species, and you begin to see how essential enthusiasm is to this whole process. A new frontier exists here; this is only the beginning.

To be realistic, however, the scenario I have just drawn for a newly introduced plant seldom materializes. It happens on rare occasions, but many more new introductions fail, the plants destined for ultimate rediscovery. The successful introduction of a new plant requires not only a good plant, but hard work, good luck and the sustained enthusiasm of many people.

I don't mean to say the Rocky Mountain region has a monopoly on new plant material; it doesn't. Plant enthusiasts all over the world look in their own backyards for noteworthy plants which have been ignored. We also continue to look and trade with people in other countries, and this is as it should be.

Ronald D. Arpin began his nursery career working at Twin Valley Garden Center in Salina, Kansas, during his sophomore year in high school. He worked there until graduating from Kansas State University with a BS from the College of Agriculture, including a minor in Horticultural Business. He is now chief propagator for Little Valley Wholesale Nursery in Brighton, Colorado, where he grows a broad range of perennials, shrubs and trees in addition to native plants, which are his favorites.

We don't yet grow a large selection of alpines at Little Valley Wholesale Nursery, but the list does lengthen each year. So far the species we do grow are from seed only. We grow and offer for sale a full line of plant material, from large caliper trees to 2.25 in. perennials. Our perennial line includes familiar garden perennials, ground covers, and wildflowers, including the alpines.

Let us follow this process from seed to the finished plant. Along the way I will describe procedures I have found helpful, point out certain problems, and offer some solutions.

The first step in production is always the seed itself. Since seed for most alpines is difficult to find, especially in quantity, collecting our own is often a necessity. The seed may come from Denver Botanic Gardens, or from others who want to see the plant produced. No matter where the plant originates, to mass produce it we will need a good quantity of seed. We begin with the small amount of original seed we have acquired; the plants from these seeds are planted around the nursery to increase next year's seed supply.

If we are collecting the seed in the wild, we need to know the plant well enough to determine when the seed is mature. It also helps to know how the seeds are dispersed. If they are catapulted, we must be sure to collect them prior to dispersal. In general, the pods should be brown, turning brown, or beginning to open. Observation and experience are the best teachers for learning when to collect seed.

Gathering seed in the wild. Photo by Martin Jones

The collecting itself is done by hand. In the field, the seed is placed in zip-lock storage bags, a good choice because they are readily available and can be sealed to prevent spillage. Once we have collected the seed and returned from the field, it is important to empty the contents of each bag into a bucket or box to promote air circulation and prevent mold growth. We then let the seed dry 7–14 days. Not only does this allow the seed to finish maturing, but the extra plant material collected also dries and crumbles very easily when we clean the seed.

One of the first things we must do during this process is identify the seed. This may sound ridiculous, but there are times when it is difficult to differentiate seeds from plant debris. Once the seed are recognized, a screen is selected such that all of the seeds fall through, leaving behind any chaff that is larger than the mesh. The next screen selected is small enough to catch the majority of the seed. Of course, the plant residue that is the same size as the seeds remains also.

Thankfully, in nearly all circumstances the seed is heavier than the chaff. We then make use of an empty half-pound coffee can and a small "squirrel cage" fan removed from a salon hair dryer. By directing the stream of air from the fan into the coffee can, the chaff is blown away, leaving the clean seed. The amount of air is controlled by how close the fan is held: too much air will blow the seed out along with the chaff. This works surprisingly well, although it is time-consuming.

Separating seed from chaff
with hair dryer.
Photo by Deane Hall

Now that we have a quantity of seed, we are ready to start production. Germinating most seeds is merely a matter of sowing them and then transplanting the seedlings when they reach a suitable size. If we have no prior information or previous experience germinating a particular species, our first step is simply to sow a small quantity of seed and wait. If we get good germination we are in business; if germination is poor or nonexistent we begin experimenting.

First we try putting the seed through a 30-day cold treatment. Of the various perennial seeds that we cold-treat, all germinate well after 30 days, so we have never used a longer period of time.

A substitute procedure we used for the first time this spring involved treating the seeds at 0–15°F for 5 days. We were pushed for time, had nothing to lose and a great deal to gain. The results were very good; see Table 27.1.

In both cold treatments we place the desired amount of seed in a zip-lock plastic bag. If the seeds have a diameter of .062 in. or larger we mix a medium with the seed to keep it moist; if they are smaller, we do not. We save ourselves a little time by not mixing medium with the seed, and it is also easier to control seedling density when we sow later.

Small seed exhibits water-holding characteristics similar to soil. Water is actually held in the minute spaces between the seeds. The spaces between larger seeds are too large, and water cannot be held, which is why a medium must be used. Typically, we add a volume of the medium equal to the volume of seed.

After the seed and medium are in the bag, we add water. We take a great deal of care to use just enough water to moisten the seed. Free water moving from side to side across the bottom when the bag is tilted indicates that we have added too much. This excess must be poured off or the seeds will rot.

When we treat the seed for 30 days, we check it after a week for adequate moisture. The medium should be moist, not dry or soggy. The seed without a medium should have a film of water inside the bag, but no free water.

After the cold treatment, we dry the seed for a short period of time. One to two hours are needed for the naked treatment, 2–4 hours for the treatment with medium. We dry the treatments on a smooth, non-fibrous surface such as a table top or a piece of notebook paper. I made the mistake of using a paper towel once. The drying seeds attached themselves to the towel fiber, and I ended up sowing paper towel as well as seeds.

It is necessary to dry the seed because moist seeds cling together, making it difficult to sow them uniformly. Be careful not to let them dry too long because viability will decrease rapidly. The seeds are sown when they no longer cling together.

We fill 11 in. x 21 in. seed flats with MetroMix 200, a commercially-produced medium containing milled sphagnum moss, fine grade perlite, and small amounts of fertilizer. The flat is filled by hand and the excess medium leveled off with a piece of lath. This leaves us with a flat, smooth surface on which to sow the seed. The seeds are sown by taking a pinch between the thumb and index finger and rubbing them together—much the same as you take a pinch of an herb to season food. At the same time we make a pattern of overlapping ovals traveling from side to side until we cover the length of the flat. Then, if necessary, additional medium is spread over the top of the seeds. Care must be taken to apply the medium evenly and to the proper thickness. The seeds are covered to a depth approximately equal to twice their diameter. For very fine seeds, no additional medium is needed on top. The seeds are fine enough to settle in between the particles of the medium. Placing additional medium over the seeds retards germination.

After sowing, the seed flats are placed on benches and watered thoroughly with a mist nozzle. We apply water until the medium is moist to the bottom of the seed flat. Care must be taken to keep the nozzle at least 1 ft. away from the surface, or fine-seeded species can be washed into adjacent flats.

Once we start watering, the medium is never allowed to dry out, lest germination be adversely affected. The moisture is checked twice daily, 7 days a week, until time to transplant.

Before I tell you when and how we transplant our seedlings, I want to say a little bit about seedling density. We sow our seeds to harvest 200 to 600 seedlings per flat. The smaller the seeds, the smaller the seedling and the higher the seedling density. With larger seeds the seedling density must be lower. We want to maximize the number of seedlings per seed flat, without affecting the quality. We know seedling density is too high when the seedlings are stretched, brittle, and difficult to separate for transplanting. Damping-off is also a common occurrence when seedling densities are too high. When these problems occur, we make adjustments in later sowings.

The rule we use when we have no previous experience is to transplant when the first set of true leaves has emerged. If we notice, a few weeks after transplanting, that losses are high on a particular species, everything from seedling density to transplanting is considered for possible cause. We have found damage to the root system during transplanting to be the most common cause of our problems. Solutions to this include decreasing the seedling density, transplanting more seedlings per pot, or a combination of lowering seedling density and waiting longer before transplanting.

The transplanting itself is done by hand, a method that has been used for years in the horticulture industry. The seedlings are pricked from the seed flat one to several at a time and are dibbled into the pot. The pots themselves are 2.25 in. x 2.25 in. x 3 in., with 25 pots per flat. Our potting medium is a commercially-prepared mix called Sunshine No. 1. It is a soilless mix, again containing peat, perlite, and fertilizer, but with coarser particle sizes. We amend the mix by adding 33 percent more No. 8 perlite to reduce the amount of water retained by the mix. We believe the original mix holds too much water, thereby contributing some problems.

After transplanting, the flats are placed on the floor in beds 15 flats wide and 120 flats long. They are hand-watered thoroughly and immediately. Then, until the flats are shipped out, watering is handled with an overhead water system supplemented by daily spot watering. Our seedlings are well on their way to becoming healthy and beautiful garden plants.

Zinnia grandiflora
Photo by Bob Heapes

References

Forest Service, USDA. 1974. *Seeds of woody plants in the United States,* USDA Handbook No. 450. Washington: USDA, Forest Service.

Hartman, Hudson T., and Dale E. Kester. 1975. *Plant propagation principles and practices.* 4th ed. Englewood Cliffs, N. J.: Prentice Hall.

Table 27.1. Native Species Grown

Species	No Treatment	30 day Cold Treatment Naked	30 day Cold Treatment With Medium
Achillea millefolium	X		
Anemone (Pulsatilla) patens	X		
Antennaria spp.	X		
Aquilegia caerulea*		X	
A. saximontana*		X	
Artemisia frigida	X		
A. ludoviciana	X		
Asclepias tuberosa	X		
Calochortus nuttallii			X
Campanula rotundifolia	X		
Castilleja integra	X		
Corydalis aurea	X		
Epilobium angustifolium	X		
Erigeron caespitosus	X		
E. compositus	X		
E. speciosus	X		
Gaillardia aristata	X		
Iris missouriensis**			X
Lewisia pygmaea	X		
Liatris punctata	X		
Lupinus argenteus	X		
Mentzelia nuda	X		
Oxytropis lambertii	X		
Penstemon barbatus		X	
P. brandegei		X	
P. bridgesii (rostriflorus)		X	
P. cobaea		X	
P. eatonii		X	
P. glaber		X	
P. jamesii		X	
P. strictus*		X	
P. virens		X	
P. whippleanus		X	
Physaria australis	X		
Psilostrophe bakeri	X		
Ratibida columnaris	X		
Silene acaulis	X		
Telesonix (Boykinia) jamesii	X		
Thermopsis divaricarpa			X
Townsendia exscapa	X		
T. eximia	X		
Tradescantia occidentalis			X
Zinnia grandiflora	X		

No Treatment: No cold treatment of seeds necessary
Naked Treatment: No medium used with seeds during cold treatment
Medium Treatment: Medium used with seeds during cold treatment

*   Seed was frozen for 3–5 days at 0–15°F.
** Seed was treated with cold temperatures for 365 days.

All cold treatments were performed at 36–38°F.

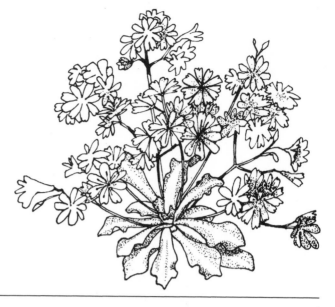

28

In a Rare Plant Nursery

by Jerry Cobb-Colley and Baldassare Mineo

The long, hot, dry summers of the Rogue Valley in southern Oregon are a far cry from the high, cool, moist alpine meadows and peaks of the Rocky Mountains. It may be surprising to some that there are those who dare to try to propagate, grow, and eventually market many of the desirable plants from the Rockies in such a hostile environment.

However, the process of overcoming the many obstacles that plague such a venture as Siskiyou Rare Plant Nursery actually opens many doors to understanding the curious needs and habits of these plants that inhabit the higher altitudes. Perhaps the greatest asset a plant propagator can possess is a finely developed power of observation; studying the plants in their natural habitat is all-important. The key to success in this field is the ability to see and become totally absorbed in this specialized environment—becoming familiar with the soil, analyzing the protective features of the terrain, delving into the seasonal fluctuations of temperature, knowing the approximate beginning time of spring rains and the likely duration of moisture throughout the growing season. On and on we observe because ultimately we must transfer and translate these conditions to our nursery propagation houses and growing grounds.

Siskiyou is located in the center of a valley 1,300 ft. in elevation, surrounded by the Siskiyou and Cascade Mountains, 60 miles, as the crow files, from the Pacific Ocean. Our summer days are hot and dry with temperatures ranging from 85–114°F. The nights are cool, with the coolness continuing well into midmorning. Each day from 10 to 4 o'clock, the winds come from the northwest at 10–20 mph. These conditions can be seriously debilitating to plants if effective precautionary measures are not taken. We have 20,000 sq. ft. of medium-to-heavy shade areas, and all of our pots are plunged into a 6 in. deep layer of sand. This enables the plants to have continuous moisture for the roots; the surface of the soil in the pot can become extremely dry without apparent damage to the plant. We try to eliminate excessive drying of the soil in the pots by top dressing with chips of granite 0.25 in. or smaller.

Let us now examine in detail how observation has helped us grow the many difficult and choice plants from the Rocky Mountains and the Great Basin area.

Well in the forefront of those botanical wonders deemed difficult is *Aquilegia jonesii* from the Bighorn Mountains of Wyoming. To see *A. jonesii* growing and flourishing in the wild—we were for-

---

Jerry Cobb-Colley and **Baldassare Mineo** own and operate Siskiyou Rare Plant Nursery in Medford, Oregon. Siskiyou offers a constantly changing palette of native and exotic alpines and is perhaps universally regarded among rock gardeners as the finest rare plant nursery in America. Both men have been in the nursery business for many years. They first collaborated in the operation of a perennial nursery in San Luis Obispo, California. In 1977, while passing through Medford, they met Lawrence Crocker and Boyd Kline, Siskiyou's first proprietors, with whom they developed an instant rapport that continues to this day.

tunate enough to observe it blooming profusely—is unforgettable. The broad treeless slopes near the summit of Mount Duncum are strewn with tiny bits of limestone, indicating that *A. jonesii* is indeed a lime-loving, lime-needing plant. Snow falls as early as mid-September, covering the aquilegia until late in the spring. By the latter part of June the light, puffy soil seems devoid of moisture, while brisk ground currents of wind knock the plants back and forth relentlessly. We sow the seed of *A. jonesii* in December, planting them in 4 in. square pots with 1 in. of drainage material. The soil is our standard mix, used for all seed except that from ericaceous plants. For *A. jonesii*, one heaping tablespoon of lime is mixed into each 4 in. pot. The standard mix consists of 6 parts of sharp sand, 2 parts peat, 2 parts perlite, 1 part granite chips and 1 part fine red cinder grit, sifted. The seeds are covered 0.25 in. deep with clean No. 2 granite, known as turkey grit. After sowing, the pots are soaked in a pan of water and, when saturated, are lined out in the open to freeze and thaw until the seeds sprout in early spring. If frost persists after sprouting, they are placed under cover to prevent heaving. The seeds are sown sparingly to prevent crowding since they will remain in the pot until the spring of the second year.

If you have ever seen *Cypripedium montanum* in its natural habitat, you noticed how it loves the bright morning sun from the east, but is protected from hot midday and western sun by canopies of spruce, madrone (*Arbutus menziesii*) and pine. It is well anchored in its soil—usually a light, very rocky, loamy earth, which provides a cool run for the roots. *Cypripedium montanum* has a reputation of surviving only a year or so in the garden. We have grown it for 5 years with each year bringing an increase in clump size and an ever increasing vigor. During winters in the wild it is protected from wetness by snow cover or by the thick mats of overhead branches or conifers. To imitate these conditions without unnecessary bother, we dig a pit 12 in. deep and wide enough to accommodate the plants without undue crowding, just as they are observed in the mountains. The pit is filled with 6 in. of rich compost and covered with 6 in. of coarse sand into which the orchids are planted, allowing their roots to penetrate the compost as needed. The purpose of the sand is to keep the crowns of the plants moist, but not soggy, which is sure death. After the third year the plants can be divided and planted in other locations in this same compost-sand situation. They are given 55 percent shade and watered abundantly, but never fertilized.

The attempt to obtain *Gentiana (Pneumonanthe) calycosa* from seed produced continuing consternation for us for several years. It just would not sprout beyond a few seedlings per pot, although we knew the seed was fresh. It became apparent that this gentian grows in a very heavy, peaty soil, with hardly any rubble or shrubs providing compost to cover the seed. Consequently we began sowing the seed without any cover, and a remarkable amount of sprouting occurred. This gentian does not transplant from the wild with continuing vigor. Usually it simply languishes without recovery. Boyd Kline, one of Siskiyou's previous owners, suggested we plant them in sand to allow the broken roots to mend and recover. Three years after our specimens were dug they

J. Cobb-Colley
tending seed tables.
Photo: Siskiyou

displayed remarkable sets of roots, and when transplanted to peat beds continued their healthy growth. *Gentiana algida* requires the same treatment, but it must remain dry during the winter months. A cover should be placed over the plants even if they are grown in sand.

Lewisia rediviva, which for so many never revives beyond the second year, undergoes perhaps the most austere, desiccating conditions during dormancy of any plant including *Astragalus coccineus.* In mid-to-late summer, when we find its frizzled remains in the rocky, hot flats it calls home, it is indeed hard to believe that it will ever be restored to growth. Plants grown from seed are planted in coarse sand and given a northern exposure. By the following spring their roots are fully established. They can be planted in a loamy, rocky soil, given full exposure to the sun, and watered until flowering time. After this they should be left on their own, allowing the early fall rains to bring them to life once again.

Many Rocky Mountain penstemons such a *Penstemon hallii, P. montanus, P. teucrioides,* and *P. caespitosus* all come well from seed. These are the more diminutive species of the genus, and they do not seem to suffer from overwatering in late summer like the coarser, taller-growing penstemons. We grow all penstemons in our standard scree mix which is the same as our seed mix plus a time-released fertilizer with a 14-14-14 formula. The penstemons are isolated from the other beds that are watered automatically. Only the sand in which the pots are plunged receives water, and this only after the flowers have faded and all signs of growth have ceased. We propagate all penstemons under mist from June to October.

The sagebrush violets such as *Viola beckwithii* are found in various types of soil and habitats throughout the Great Basin area. Some grow in heavy, wet, mucklike soil, and flower in early April. Since the soil dries to cementlike hardness by June, they remain dormant beneath the surface with only occasional spent, shriveled seed pods marking their sites. Sagebrush violets are also found in light, rocky soils which dry to a talcum powder consistency by early summer. These observations tell us that in order to keep these violets alive, we must keep them free of any lingering moisture for 6 months of the year. Again the sand pits are utilized and work very well. In this situation the roots never shrivel but remain plump, adapting to the minute moisture content that lingers in the sand. In our climate it is not necessary to cover the sand when the rains begin in October. *Leucocrinum montanum,* the sand lily, which has a large, fleshy root system, insists on complete dryness from dormancy in late spring until growth begins in late winter. Fiberglass panels are placed over beds of sand in late summer.

Many of the lovely Rocky Mountain plants grow well from both seed and vegetative propagation for us. Among those that adjust readily are *Aquilegia saximontana, Boykinia (Telesonix) jamesii, Heuchera hallii, Agave utahensis,* numerous townsendias and, surprisingly, *Mertensia alpina.* This difficult mertensia demands protection from the wetness of early fall rains and must remain very dry throughout the dormant season. It is also important to grow it in a cool position in the garden, providing bright light but no heat. We have found that a north wall exposure is very satisfactory. We grow *Mertensia alpina* in a scree mix with a small amount of bog peat mixed in to reduce bacterial growth.

Zinnia grandiflora, the small caespitose subshrub of Colorado and Kansas, is perhaps not generally classified as a Rocky Mountain classic. However, to eliminate it from this list would be a disservice to those who seek unusual, garden-worthy plants of that area. Despite our mild winter in southern Oregon, the combination of detrimental effects produced by a wet root zone and near-freezing temperatures is fatal to many of our alpine and prairie plants. For several years we seemed to be in a vicious cycle of obtaining seed, sprouting them, transplanting and successfully growing them through the summer, and then invariably, as the frenzy of battening down the hatches for winter moved at full speed in the nursery, *Zinnia grandiflora* somehow always seemed to be left out in the cold, only be discovered in early spring as a casualty. This zinnia is not, for all practical purposes, an ideal pot plant since it does ramble, throwing up occasional shoots perhaps a foot or more away from the original plant. This is not to say that *Z. grandiflora* is not a hardy plant, but in order to come safely through the winter for us, it must either be planted out or kept under cover to insure that the roots and crowns are kept on the dry side in a container or given very free drainage in the ground. Its flowering in mid-June is a delight, and it has definitely gained a place of importance in the Siskiyou display garden where it grows happily in sand and peat.

The fabulous *Claytonia megarhiza,* which we first saw on Mount Evans, produced a spectacular moment for those of us who stood in awe of its perfection. Not until Boyd Kline casually mentioned that he had seen a double flowered form in the vicinity did we come back to earth. Of course, after scouring the peak trying to ignore *Eritrichium elongatum (E. nanum),* we gave up the search and returned to study our magnificent *Claytonia megarhiza.* Though we have never seen this plant in any nursery catalog, it seems only logical that someday this lovely spectacle of a perfect rosette of white,

Baldassare Mineo with stock plant *Aquilegia jonesii*. Photo: Siskiyou

as well as the deep rose-pink variety *C. megarhiza* var. *nivalis* of the Wenatchee's in Washington, may possibly be listed in our own catalog. Cuttings of the rosettes were taken, inserted under mist back in Medford and rooted in a surprisingly short time. One of the first indications of difficulties with this plant was that our cuttings, well-rooted and thriving, increased remarkably in size but flowered only very sparingly. All clues indicate that the rosettes must age several years before flowering—perhaps 4–6 years before the plant achieves the size and root growth it needs to settle down. We think it is also imperative that, although *Claytonia megarhiza* grows in the open while *C. megarhiza* var. *nivalis* prefers a nook on the protected north side of rocks, both should be given winter cover and grown in deep pots in an unheated greenhouse. It is a joy to see their steady increase, indicating the good probability of listing them for sale in the not-too-distant future.

Now, back to *Eritrichium elongatum* (*E. nanum*), the weed of the high country. There are rumors of growers in Europe who are successfully growing and flowering the European *E. nanum* and *E. nanum* ssp. *jankae*. As an unsolicited opinion, we venture to say that by using cuttings one is attempting the shortest route to failure, while by using collected plants one can also expect a miserable record of success. Seed seems by far the most encouraging method of beginning this almost religious undertaking. A further bit of speculation gives merit to the idea of sowing the seed in a permanent alpine house container and avoiding the great risk of transplant loss. It would also seem valuable to keep the root system as cool as possible. Who knows? Even a refrigerated plunge table could become the ticket to success with this high alpine. Such a fine, shallow root system would have to benefit from the constant cool temperatures to which it is no doubt accustomed. We have a pot of 4-year-old seedlings of *E. howardii*, healthy, not a brown spot on the clump, but also no flowers. One 3-year-old *E. elongatum* collected in the Bighorns has neither advanced nor receded in its 6 in. pot. There always seems to be the hint of a flower bud developing each spring. It is amazing what the imagination can do for us.

Finally, we must include the magnificent salix of the high country. These minute willows can be difficult to propagate. Take, for instance, *Salix dodgeana* (*S. rotundifolia*) from the Bighorns, where the snow cover lasts until late June. Cuttings taken at that time simply do not have time to root and grow, storing enough vitality to break bud growth in the spring. It seems logical to take small, rooted clumps and plant them out in a bog peat bed. After a season's growth, cuttings can be taken much earlier in the spring, inserted in a mixture of sphagnum peat and perlite, and rooted under mist. As soon as roots of 1–2 in. have formed, the salix are potted in our regular mix with additional bog peat added, then placed back under mist and hardened off. This produces a well-rooted plant in one season. In a dry, breezy climate such as ours, red spider mites are the chief nuisance of the growing season. Salix must have abundant moisture but good drainage, and they respond dramatically to heavy feeding.

Conclusion

While laying the groundwork for this report, we searched the catalog to see how many Rocky Mountain and Great Basin plants were offered. To our astonishment, from an overall list of nearly 1,000 plants fewer than 20 came from these great plant areas. Why? Certainly not because there are so few desirable plants, nor are they desirable but ungrowable. Nor could one call this area virgin territory for plants. However, these famous favorites such as *Boykinia jamesii, Eritrichium elongatum,* and *Polemonium viscosum* seem to have stolen the limelight over the years. For these who now dare to investigate other possibilities, the fields are ripe for harvest.

Perhaps more than any other area on our continent, the Rockies await the eager plantsman with scores of good, growable plants. Undeniably, many of those most wanted have proved difficult to tame, but isn't that what it's all about? The Rockies are teeming with promising plants for the alpine enthusiast. We as propagators and growers have been introduced to only a small part of this vast area and its treasures.

29

Rocky Mountain Alpines in Troughs

by Waid R. Vanderpoel

My love affair with troughs began at the 1976 First Interim International Rock Garden Conference in Vancouver. Our rock gardening friends from British Columbia had arranged plants in groupings representing various North American mountain ranges, a concept I immediately found appealing. By using a regional grouping technique, substantial and pleasing variations in form, color, and foliage texture are effortlessly achieved, and the viewer is also provided with a quickly comprehended demonstration of the differences between plants from widely separated mountain areas.

Since the construction, planting, and maintenance of troughs involves extra effort, a gardener considering troughs for the first time can logically ask "Why?" I sometimes debate this ultimate question myself when we are stuffing the 79th plastic bag of oak leaves for a winter wind shield. Let's face that question, "Why troughs?"

One very personal reason: I am 6 ft. 4 in. tall—a long way up from the tiny alpine treasures we cultivate and love. When spring finally warms my garden, it is a genuine pleasure to be a few feet closer to the exquisite, but tiny, blossoms of an androsace or a *Lewisia pygmaea*.

I also find the opportunity to create a wee slice of mountain scenery an irresistible challenge. Many troughs I've seen are simply containers planted across a level surface. It need not be so! We have a number of troughs whose outer dimensions are 3 ft. x 2 ft.; with 2 in. thick walls, the inner dimensions total 704 sq. in.—less than 5 sq. ft. Yet in that limited space enough vertical rise can be achieved to allow placement of plants on at least three distinctly different height levels. With perhaps 45–60 plants, one trough can provide amazing variation in bloom color and foliage. The total effect brings a "mountain miniature" to the flatlands of Illinois. When photographed with a close-up lens, the rocks in our troughs appear to loom up behind the plants like a massive rock outcropping or a steep scree in nature.

One final reason for regarding troughs with affection is the ease with which an occasional weed can be swiftly extracted. Few weeds spring up in troughs, but when one does it is a small pleasure to dispatch it with neither a stoop nor a bend.

A rock gardener for 24 years, **Waid Vanderpoel** and his family have developed a series of different kinds of gardens: a garden for native woodland plants, a large rock garden, a high plains garden and his son Tom Vanderpoel's special project—a restored prairie. They have collected seed all over the West and in Europe. He is active in the Illinois chapter of the Nature Conservancy and; of course, has a special interest in troughs.

I hope many gardeners will be tempted to experiment with developing their own custom-designed troughs. Before we consider some of the factors to be thought out in adapting troughs and plants to the prevailing conditions encountered by individual gardeners, I will describe our northern Illinois location, climate and growing conditions. Our garden is about 35 miles northwest of Chicago at an altitude of just under 900 ft. We live in an area of 5-acre suburban lots—thus we have wind in abundance. Most of our troughs receive considerable sun, perhaps 60 to 75 percent of the day. Our garden is in the coldest part of Zone V and, since we have shivered through record-setting lows of −25°F in 1984 and −27°F in 1985, perhaps we will be reclassified as Zone IV. We receive an average of just under 40 in. of precipitation per year, with snowfall of anywhere from 30 in. up to 80 or 90 in. Our spring blooming season begins about April 1st and summer heat is upon us by late June. To state it mildly, our weather is changeable—especially in spring. We usually have adequate rainfall, but it is erratic and undependable and it seldom comes in measured, gentle applications. Our summer days are often humid with temperatures in the 80s and, frequently, the thermometer reads in the 90s. Autumn arrives by mid-September and winter descends across our land by late November.

Quite obviously, gardening in a climate of quick, often violent, weather changes and temperature extremes demands both tolerance and adaptability on the part of the plants we grow. It never ceases to amaze me just how many alpine and mountain basin plants, with just a bit of help, will adapt to our enormously different and often harsh conditions so far from the conditions of their natural homes.

Just as in our gardens, we attempt to create microclimates for our troughs. This can be accomplished by the placement of the troughs in relation to buildings and trees. Sun exposure can be maximized by utilizing a vertical slope toward the sun, and reduced by placing plants on the shady side of rocks. On certain troughs, particularly those featuring European plants, we place summer screens above the troughs. The screening is mounted on a wood frame attached to 2 in. x 2 in. wood posts which rest on each corner of the trough. However, we have found that many groupings of Rocky Mountain plants do not appear to require this reduction of heat and sun. The screens do nothing to enhance the appearance of the trough, so we utilize them only during the hottest summer periods.

Author's rectangular trough. Photo by Gwen Kelaidis

By using the technique of placing rocks and soil in the trough so as to achieve as much vertical effect as possible, the gardener can accomplish a variety of objectives:

(1)   the potential for varying microclimates is enhanced;
(2)   superb, quick drainage is achieved;
(3)   most plants are given a background of rock which provides an attractive setting and also delineates the space allotted to that plant;
(4)   plants are better separated and can be viewed and studied in their entirety when displayed on varying vertical levels;
(5)   the "composition" of a trough is more varied, hence more interesting, when several altitude levels are achieved; and, finally,
(6)   vertical variation helps create that magical illusion that the gardener has somehow transported a tiny slice of, say, the Bighorns to his or her faraway garden.

PLATE 23

Garden designed by Herb Schaal
Photo by Herb Schaal

Lee Raden's "Alpineflora"
Photo by Lee Raden

Rock Alpine Garden at Denver Botanic Gardens
Photo by Deane Hall

PLATE 26

Townsendia jonesii
Photo by Elizabeth Neese

Penstemon barbatus
Photo by Bob Heapes

Talinum breviflorum
Photo by Elizabeth Neese

Eriogonum brevicaule
Photo by Elizabeth Neese

Eriogonum shockleyi
Photo by Ned Lowry

One of the advantages of trough gardening is that the gardener can develop widely differing soil mixes specially tailored for various plant groupings. These soil mixes, be they of an acid pH, neutral, or alkaline, and whether high or low in humus content, can be fairly well maintained—if kept free of earthworms, whose fervent desire seems to be to change any and all specially prepared soil pockets to the characteristics of the surrounding soil.

As I wrote this, however, I decided to measure pH with my new mechanical tester. My two Bighorns troughs, featuring limestone rock and top chips, measured 6.96 and 6.91. My Colorado trough, using Royal Gorge granite and chips, measured 7.0, as did my Idaho trough using a hard brown and white Western rock. The one trough in which I'd tried to concoct an acid soil measured 6.93. While I am not prepared to argue the merits or accuracy of my pH tester, it might well be that my troughs all have a neutral pH—admittedly by happenstance, not design.

I will confess to using a general purpose soil mix for all but one of my Rocky Mountain troughs (3 parts gravel and grit, 3 parts coarse sand, and 2 parts leaf mold or peat moss). I suspect that specialized soil mixes would produce superior results for certain plants. I will leave these potentially rewarding experiments to others while conceding that my successes may reflect only the inherent ability of mountain plants to adapt to a diversity of conditions, while my failures may highlight my inability to locate or absorb available know-how.

In addition to creating microclimates by trough, by rock and plant placement, and by providing a gritty soil, we also top-dress our troughs with stone chips. In warmer climes, I recommend using a light colored stone, such as limestone, to better reflect sunlight and heat. However, we match the top chips with the rock and thus have reddish, mica-laced chips on our Colorado trough. The top stones keep the soil cooler, help retain moisture in the soil, and prevent direct contact between plant crowns and soil (which can be very wet during some rainy periods).

Troughs do dry out, smaller ones far more quickly than our two monsters (one 4.5 ft. long; one over 5 ft. long and almost 4 ft. wide). The amount and frequency of watering depends on temperature, sunlight and wind velocity. Most Rocky Mountain plants are quite drought-resistant. The plants that need extra moisture may be grouped together in one area of a large trough or be given their own trough. Watering may be unnecessary for extended periods if there is sufficient rainfall. During a warm, dry, breezy period, a 3 ft. x 2 ft. trough will usually require water every 4 or 5 days. Beyond this general guidance, I can only state that watering is an art form, not an exact science. As in so many other activities in life, experience and observation are the best teachers.

We have found that plants in a new trough may initially grow vigorously, reflecting the new leaf humus in the soil. After a year or so, the growth spurt is over. We then give our troughs two or three applications each spring of a general purpose liquid fertilizer (I use one with a 15-18-15 formula). Occasionally, we add bone meal to some troughs and have been experimenting with liquid fertilizer combinations in which we have reduced the nitrogen content by adding soluble phosphorus and potash to a half-strength solution of the standard liquid fertilizer. We have not arrived at hard and fast conclusions on feeding other than a general belief that the feeding is easily accomplished, is probably beneficial, and, importantly, has produced no ill side effects.

In our climate we also give our troughs some winter protection. The smaller, portable ones are simply placed on the ground and surrounded by oak leaves up to the top of the sides of the troughs. The larger ones are not really portable. We initially took them down for the winter, but since even a 3 ft. x 2 ft. landscaped trough can weigh 350 pounds, this was difficult. When we built our two largest troughs (one weighs about 800 pounds), moving became out of the question, and so they stand upon their 18 concrete blocks which, in turn, sit on a below-grade concrete base. The troughs now face winter on their normal mountings but surrounded by bags of oak leaves. The surfaces of the troughs are never covered except by snow. Since snow cover is unpredictable, the troughs are exposed to winter rain, snow, sun, wind and freeze/thaw action. The bags, and loose leaves stuffed into any open spaces, block quick-freezing winds from the sides of the trough thus protecting roots. Since adopting this technique, our winter losses have been minimal. Casualties were numerous, however, beforehand. The plants' high survival rate is testimony to their rugged mountain heritage.

While every gardener will accept a dissertation on construction, growing conditions, problems, etc., eyes light up when the discussion turns to specific plants. We grow Rocky Mountain plants in seven troughs: Colorado (our largest), Bighorns (two troughs), Idaho, Canadian Rockies (Banff, Jasper, and Yoho), Great Plains/Intermountain Valleys, and a "mixed western" trough. Several plants, *Penstemon aridus,* for example, grow in more than one trough. Remember, too, that by accident or design, our soil mix differs little from trough to trough. Now, to the Rocky Mountain plants which dwell in these troughs.

CODES:
(+)   grows better in troughs than in the garden
(++) grows unusually well in troughs compared to the garden
(−)   grows less well in troughs than in the garden
(0)   tiny plant that is much better observed, hence more enjoyed, in a trough than in the garden
(?)   has grown for a year or more, but has not bloomed or does not persist in troughs (or in the garden)
No indication means the plant does well in troughs and in the garden.

Androsace: excellent trough plants.
    A. chamaejasme: (++, 0) so much better enjoyed in a trough.
    A. septentrionalis: (0) annual; once established, the species will continue indefinitely from plentifully set seed.
Antennaria: a dwarf species or form; makes a tight, gray mat. Accept only neat, slow-growing forms.
Aquilegia: small *Aquilegia* species, or hybrids, make fine trough plants if compact and if they remain of size appropriate for the trough.
    A. jonesii: (+) I dream they will someday bloom.
    A. sp. (hyb.?): We have 2 forms of uncertain western parentage; however, one rewards us with dark blue flowers, the other with white, blue-tinged flowers and produces like offspring. Our little aquilegias must certainly be descended from *A. saximontana* which, along with dwarf forms of *A. scopulorum,* would make excellent trough plants.
Arenaria: a genus that produces tufts, buns, and flat mats. A number are good, easily-grown trough plants. We grow:
    A. hookeri: a high plains dweller attractive for its green foliage tufts.
    A. (Minuartia) obtusiloba: makes a low, flat mat. Little dodecatheons or *Lewisia pygmaea* attain a special charm reaching skyward through the arenaria mat for their brief spring moments in the sun.
    A. (Minuartia) rubella: (0).
    A. species: (0) we have two small arenarias from the Bighorns with tight, humped buns which thrive in troughs. Visitors often find them irresistibly pettable.
Aster: small, tidy asters provide color and variety to a trough. We have two species, grown from collected seed, one a mat-former with attractive oblanceolate foliage and rich blue flowers on short, uniform stems.
Astragalus: many species have potential for troughs. At this time we have only:
    A. alpinus: vigorous.
Besseya alpina: (?) has bloomed but does not thrive.
Boykinia (Telesonix) *jamesii:* (+, ?—won't bloom).
Claytonia megarhiza: not easy; one specimen lived 3.5 years and bloomed twice. Probably needs some extra shade and a deep root run.
Dodecatheon: better display of petite flowers from the higher elevation of a trough. Experiment with various small dodecatheons in troughs. We now grow:
    D. pulchellum: (+, 0).
    D. hendersonii (dwarf form): (+, 0) these are more easily remembered when dormant if in a trough.
Douglasia montana: (?) haven't yet mastered its requirements.
Draba: nearly any compact Western draba appears at home in a trough. Some we grow include:
    D. densifolia: (0).
    D. incerta.
    D. oligosperma.
    D. sp. (from Stanley, Idaho): (0) a tiny cushion of .125 in. rosettes.
    D. sp. (Wallowas): a gray, hairy species of small rosettes.
Dryas: (−) usually too large for troughs. However, *D. octopetala* cv. 'Minor' will remain trough-sized for years.
Erigeron: a genus which produces a host of trough-sized species which live and bloom happily in a trough. A gardener's objective in choosing erigerons should be to obtain species and forms which are compact, neat, varied as to both foliage and flower, attractive in bloom, and which will remain at a size appropriate for troughs. With careful selection a gardener can obtain a wide range of foliage types as well as blossom colors. The form may be even

more important than the species when selecting erigerons for troughs. Our trough erigerons include:

E. allocotus: ideal for a dry, sunny spot.

E. aureus: (0;?) not easy for us, but glorious in bloom. It is reputed to favor acid soil. Attractive foliage, too.

E. compositus: produces forms galore. The best ones we have are a lacy green-foliaged type with dainty white flowers from somewhere in Colorado and a low pink-blue flowered one from the Wallowas.

E. leiomerus.

E. ochroleucus: (0) erratic; some specimens delight for years; others perish rather quickly.

E. pinnatisectus: long-lived; obtain a form with rich blue flowers; trouble-free.

E. simplex: showy flowers; not dependably long-lived, although some specimens live for years.

E. sp. (Idaho): a late-blooming species with fine blue flowers over green, oblanceolate leaves.

Eriogonum: these have not yet grown well in our troughs. We intend to experiment with different plants and species beyond the three we are attempting now:

E. caespitosum: (new: no rating) doing better in a pot.

E. flavum: (−).

E. ovalifolium: (−).

Erysimum: provide fine bloom color and are of a suitable scale for troughs.

E. amoenum: pink flowers, too new to rate (*E. wheeleri,* according to Harrington, *E. nivale* f. *amoenum,* according to Weber).

E. nivale (yellow form): (?) bloomed gloriously, perished ingloriously. However, it was thoughtful enough to seed a bit before departing.

Heuchera: grow contentedly in a trough just as they do everywhere else in the garden. Again, the trough proprietor is best served by small, neat forms or the most diminutive of species. We grow:

H. rubescens: (+, 0) with genuinely graceful little stems and flowers. Its proximity in a trough leads to added appreciation of the fine foliage.

H. sp. (Colorado): will grace any rock crevice even though the flowers are insignificant.

Hymenoxys: can be excellent trough plants.

H. acaulis: best forms are small and silvery-foliaged with sizable, full-rayed flowers on short stems. Alas, the better the form, the less chance seed will germinate or the plant will thrive. Definitely worth growing.

H. grandiflora: both monocarpic and an erratic bloomer. Like an undisciplined performer, it often "can't get its act together." Season of bloom is unpredictable; flowers do not always form well. On those rather infrequent occasions when it does "get its act together," it is a show-stopper.

Author's large trough.
Photo by Gwen Kelaidis

Shale trough
Photo by Deane Hall

Lesquerella/Physaria: grow well in troughs as do many other crucifers. We grow several species, mainly for their neatly displayed gray foliage, all of which are often overwhelmed in the garden but provide quiet pleasure in a trough:

L. alpina: (0).

L. occidentalis: (0).

P. dornii: (0).

Lewisia: appear well-suited for troughs. We host:

L. columbiana: (+, 0).

L. pygmaea: (++, 0) shows nicely in a trough. Very important to obtain a richly colored form.

L. rediviva: easier to remember where it is after die-down, in a trough.

Linum: usually too tall for a trough. We grow an exception:

L. lewisii (dwarf form, Bighorns): a 3–4 in. gem which graces many a spring morning with its 0.75 in. sky blue flowers. In the fall it gives a delightful encore. A winner!

Mertensia: dwarf forms and species offer potential. To date we have grown only:

M. viridis: it has persisted for three years while blooming twice.

Myosotis alpestris: came to us years ago in a tiny clump of Western grass from the Bighorns. Each year blue forget-me-nots poke up through the grass (0).

Penstemon: These are special favorites. Many fare well in troughs. With a vast array of species, forms, and sizes from which to choose, a number appear most suitable for trough use. Some we grow are:

P. aridus: (0) ideally scaled for a trough.

P. caryi: somewhat tall but sparsely foliaged so it never appears to crowd its neighbors; flowers are large and most attractive.

P. eriantherus: (0) loves a warm spot and rewards with fascinating, exotic flowers.

P. laricifolius: (0) is for those of us who cherish insignificant little plants.

P. procerus: only use compact forms.

P. davidsonii, P. davidsonii var. *menziesii:* neither has performed as well as those in our garden. This by no means exhausts the list of appropriate penstemons. Next year we hope to add *P. hallii* to our Colorado trough. However, most of the creepers (e.g., *P. caespitosus*), though flat, spread too wide for a trough.

Petrophytum caespitosum: grows slowly, persists (usually) but doesn't bloom for us. We remain hopeful.

Phlox: the small, low, Western species represent an unmet challenge to us. We have tried:

P. caespitosa: (?, alas).

P. diffusa: does not grow well nor does it bloom beyond an occasional blossom. Perhaps a tailored soil mix would be the answer. I encourage rock gardeners to try various species under a variety of soils and conditions.

Physaria: see *Lesquerella*

Polemonium: often proves rather short-lived in our garden. However, some plants live for years. We have:

P. brandegei: (not at all happy, thus ?).

P. delicatum: we have a delightful, neat form from Stanley, Idaho.

P. viscosum: has proven difficult for us (?).

Potentilla: a genus which provides some neat, properly scaled species which grow well in troughs. We have an attractive, not overpowering species from the Bighorns and an even more compact, tight-foliaged species from the Canadian Rockies which provides fine maroon fall color. *P. villosa,* which we grow only in the garden, would be a satisfactory, easy trough plant.

Primula: from the Rockies. The American species challenge the gardener—in troughs and in the garden. We attempt:

P. angustifolia: (?) our accomplishment to date is merely that they have survived for 2.5 years.

P. ellisiae: after 7 years one bloomed in 1985—a modest victory of the type which gives new inspiration to rock gardeners. It was beautiful!

P. rusbyi: clings to life, but does not bloom (?).

Saxifraga: provide potential for further experimentation. It is not easy to obtain either plants or seed of many American saxifrages. We grow:

S. bronchialis: (+, 0) in two forms. One from Colorado is a fine trough plant with dainty white flowers on short stems. Underrated and highly recommended. We would like to be able to grow *S. serpyllifolia,* and *S. oppositifolia* in our troughs.

Sedum: if small and non-invasive, can find a home in a trough. Our quest must be for species which conform to our criteria and to their allotted space. One which measures up is the common

S. lanceolatum (0) (formerly *S. stenopetalum*): both attractive and easily grown.

Senecio: even more than other genera, these should be selected for form and diminutive size. The gray foliage can be pleasing.

Silene acaulis: (++) a plant placed all over the Northern Hemisphere on tundra and mountains just so rock gardeners cannot miss it and will thus use it in just about any regional trough they may design. Its bright green cushions attain near perfection in several of our troughs. We even have a Canadian form which dependably produces good-sized, dark pink flowers.

Solidago: contains some dwarf species suitable for troughs. We grow:

S. multiradiata var. *scopulorum*—an amicable species with modest, pleasing flowers and foliage.

Talinum okanoganense: (0) appears to perform well when finally established. In the garden it will be overrun, overlooked, or both.

Townsendia: includes several species suitable for troughs. In fact, the size of most smaller townsendias is just right for troughs. We use:

T. exscapa.

T. hookeri: attractive, even if often short-lived.

T. sp. (0) (Double Springs Pass, Idaho): a dwarf species with tight, dark green foliage and dark, purple buds, with small blue flowers. Has been long-lived with very neat attractive foliage.

In addition to forbs, we allow an occasional clump of short western grass and a sedge or two to add a vertical accent to the troughs. We remain constantly on the lookout for new Rocky Mountain plants and superior forms of existing plants. Some scheduled for near-term introduction to our troughs include *Erigeron bloomeri, E. chrysopidus,* and *E. elegantulus,* a number of eriogonums, *Erithrichium howardii,* several *Astragalus* and *Oxytropis* species, and one or two additional townsendias. Some day we hope to learn the secret of providing a happy home for *Phacelia sericea* which now will grow and bloom but does not persist. *Phlox* and *Saxifraga* remain a long-range challenge. Dwarf rock ferns could be worked into the trough mosaic.

In summary, the alpine gardener has a marvelous selection of Rocky Mountain plants with which to grace troughs. There are flat mats, tight buns, and complementary vertical accent plants. Some are easily grown, others may be outside the knowledge of even the most skilled grower. In all, the possibilities for both experimentation and the construction of fascinating alpine compositions appear limited only by our own energy and imagination.

References

Elliot, Joe. 1974. *Alpines in sinks and troughs.* Woking, Eng.: Alpine Garden Society.

Brooklyn Botanic Gardens. 1952. *Handbook on Rock Gardens.* Special printing of *Plants and gardens.* 8 (3). New York: Brooklyn Botanic Gardens.

30

Under Lights

by Margery Edgren

Rock gardeners, perhaps more than any other group of plant enthusiasts, continually attempt to grow plants from environments entirely different from conditions in their own gardens. We do much to alter garden soil and moisture to match natural conditions for alpines, but daylength and temperature can play important roles as well. Chances are the Rocky Mountain alpine you take home would benefit from a cool respite from an East Coast heat wave, or the three or four rare seeds you waited years to obtain would have a better chance to grow in a clean, stable environment. Plants shipped from distant sources are often difficult to establish, especially those airlifted from midsummer to midwinter in 24 hours. Prolonging their natural season through control of daylength and temperature and subsequently providing a gradual transition to their new climate may be important keys to their survival.

I have grown rock plants near Philadelphia, New York, and San Francisco, with a brief pause in Michigan in between. At present, in the Mediterranean climate near San Francisco, I find more members of the animal kingdom ready to satisfy their gourmet appetites with my rock plants than ever before. Fungus diseases abound and insect pests such as scale have no severe winter to reduce their numbers. While we can grow many species here that are not hardy in temperate climates, many of the true alpine species miss the low temperatures necessary to satisfy dormancy requirements or produce good flowering. Late summer months are so dry and sometimes so hot that maintaining adequate moisture in the soil is extremely difficult; humidity levels fall dangerously low for many plants. In addition, the growing season is much too long for mountain flowers. In spring, temperatures warm enough for active growth combine with days too short for species that are adapted to renew growth in midsummer. Summers drag on endlessly compared to the few short weeks some plants get in the mountains. Here, more than ever, I rely on creating artificial conditions that allow me to enjoy some of my favorite alpines. Fortunately, many beautiful rock plants are small enough to make this possible. The following suggestions are designed to improve your chance of success with the rare, the difficult, the imported and the uprooted.

Often the first challenge in growing a new species is the attempt to unlock that tiny embryo from the seed in which it was efficiently packaged for distribution by the parent plant. If a species is rare, choice, and desirable, its seed is usually in short supply. Sometimes less than five seeds may be

Margery Edgren earned two degrees in biology from Northwestern University, but her interest in alpines was not sparked until she visited the Chelsea Flower Show where the exhibits included a magnificent rock garden. She first grew rock plants under lights to produce exhibits for the early spring Philadelphia Flower Show. Her experimentation with control of daylength and temperature to induce flowering proved so fascinating and successful that she expanded her experimentation to other phases of plant development. She now lives in Woodside, California.

provided, making the options for experimentation pretty limited.

By placing the seeds on moist paper toweling in a plastic sandwich bag, it is easy to observe whether they germinate, rot, or appear unchanged. I usually chill half the seeds in a household refrigerator, while the rest are kept warm at room temperature. If no germination results after 3 months, the temperatures are reversed, that is, the warm bag moved to the cold, and the refrigerated one warmed. Some seeds germinate when warm and moist, some when cold and moist; some need a warm-cold sequence or 2 cycles of warm followed by cold; others require fluctuating temperatures. Stratification requirements vary from 1 month or less to more than 6 months. For any given species, old seed may require longer chilling than fresh seed. Cold requirements of individual seeds within a species may vary greatly, so some seeds germinate rapidly, while others need many months. For these recalcitrant species and for those from which seed is rarely available and always in short supply, the seeds are allowed to germinate in the plastic bag and then planted carefully with forceps. This is very time consuming and often not necessary. In most cases, once germination requirements have been determined under close observation, seeds can be given any necessary treatment and planted in the usual way before germination occurs.

A soilless mixture provides a clean medium for planting. I rely heavily on sand, especially for species at risk in wet soil, since the moisture content can be rapidly and closely controlled. On the other hand, it must be constantly monitored, or plants will dry out completely. Sand is also a convenient medium for roots and bulbs you wish to harvest when dormant, because it is easy to clean off the living plant tissues. Varying amounts of peat and perlite are useful additions to maintain moisture and aerate the soil. However, if you plan to harvest any small white bulbs, avoid adding perlite to the soil mix, because finding a white bulb in perlite is like finding a needle in a haystack.

All the plants while small seedlings or part of the indoor collection get surface watering with a hydroponic fertilizer. There are several of these available with all known trace elements provided, as well as the usual N-P-K (nitrogen-phosphorus-potassium) components. They are available in a buffered solution in concentrations safe for bare roots, so they can be used on seedlings and rooted cuttings. Completely chelated formulas may be better for plants with special pH requirements. Tap water is usually satisfactory for mixing the solution.

I grow seedlings under fluorescent light in an enclosed space that is unheated. Special plant-growth lights can be used, or a 1:1 mixture of warm and cool colors. A warm white and daylight combination gives a good spectrum for vegetative growth and flowering, and it produces natural color in foliage and flowers. Gro-Lux tubes grow healthy plants, but can cause abnormally intense colors in foliage and flowers. Cool white tubes, readily available and inexpensive, are quite satisfactory as a light source for seedling growth.

Lewisia pygmaea
Photo by Margery Edgren

Lewisia brachycalyx. Photo by Margery Edgren

I use 3 daylengths to create artificial seasons for my plants: a continuous light at warm temperatures (CONT); a 16 hour long day with a refrigerated cold night (LDR); and an 8 hour short day with a cold night (SDR). The cold night is provided by actually placing the potted seedlings, enclosed in a plastic bag, in a household refrigerator. Each species is tested under each of the three conditions. Some plants grow on all three; some plants die on all three. Most do better on one regimen than the others. Most LDR plants do well on CONT in winter when temperatures are around 55°F. Seedlings can be kept under lights until mature enough to plant in the garden, as with cold frame or greenhouse cultivation. Some plants, like small shooting stars, should remain inside for several seasons. Others can be part of a permanent indoor collection like those in alpine houses.

On the other hand, once requirements for germination and seedling growth have been determined, further planting can then be carried out under natural conditions at appropriate times of the year to provide the best chance of survival for the seedlings. Thus, for a plant like *Dodecatheon pulchellum (D. pauciflorum)*, which requires several months of stratification for seed germination and long days with cool nights for optimal seedling growth, refrigerate the seeds in late winter and plant to a cold frame or cool greenhouse in spring.

For mature plants, control over daylength and temperature may be desirable to induce flowering for display or hybridization. Perhaps you have wished you could bring a rare May-flowering specimen into bloom for a February study weekend or cross two species that bloom in different months. One can often produce bloom for a specific date by providing artificial seasons, but the requirements for each species must be determined individually. Some plants mature and bloom on CONT within a few months (the European *Papaver radicatum*). Others flower after several months on SDR (*Lewisia rediviva*) or several weeks on LDR (*Dodecatheon pulchellum*). Some require several weeks on SDR to set buds, and then open flowers after several weeks on LDR or CONT (*Viola pedata*). A few examples follow, showing the use of these methods to grow certain species from germinated seed to flowering plant. In most cases, although hand pollination of the flowers is necessary, the plants produce viable seed, making it possible to maintain or establish these forms in cultivation.

Like most members of its genus, *Dodecatheon pulchellum* has seeds that require stratification for germination, and almost all seeds sprout readily after 3–6 months of refrigeration. Seedlings grow best on LDR, seldom producing much vegetative plant beyond the seed leaves during the first season, while a fat root develops under the soil. Roots may be harvested as soon as the leaves go dormant. After washing, they are placed on moist paper toweling in a plastic bag for immediate refrigeration to stimulate a new season of growth. About 3 months is adequate, after which the roots are planted again to LDR for another season. New shoot growth is usually evident before the roots are removed from the cold. After several seasons a vigorous vegetative rosette is formed, and flowering results during the LDR growth period without a shift in daylength.

Most *Dodecatheon* species can be forced to go dormant under CONT at warm temperatures. With timely attention to the length of the seasons, allowing 3–4 months for growth and 2–3 months for refrigeration, one can hurry the seedlings through 2 seasons in one year. On the other hand, if you wish to shift the flowering season to coincide with an exhibit, the roots can be left warm and slightly moist for 1–2 months after going dormant to delay the next growing season. Roots (or growing plants) can also be held cold in the refrigerator to delay the start or progress of the next season, but they tend to develop and flower faster than usual after prolonged periods of refrigeration.

Although their cultivation is more difficult, and rewards more ephemeral than members of the *L. cotyledon* group, I still prize the *Lewisia* species *pygmaea, rediviva,* and *brachycalyx.* Growing in containers is recommended for all three of them. *Lewisia pygmaea* seed requires only a brief period of stratification. About 6–8 weeks in the cold will suffice for 90 percent of the seed. Daylength of choice is CONT, and plants can be grown rapidly to flowering without any changes in daylength or temperature. Some specimens reach full bloom in 9 months.

Lewisia rediviva seed also germinates well after about 4–8 weeks of refrigeration. Seedlings grow best on SDR for 4–5 months and produce a fat tap root. When vegetative growth slows or stops, one should move the plant to CONT and keep it fairly dry until it goes completely dormant. Then chill the bare root on moist paper toweling in a plastic bag. New shoot growth will appear after 1–2 months in the cold, indicating it is time to plant the root to SDR again. Seedlings may bloom in their third season toward the end of their growth period on SDR and set seed well on CONT after flowering.

Lewisia brachycalyx is cultivated in the same manner. Seeds chilled for 2 months germinate very well. Plants grow vigorously and roots are larger at comparable stages than *L. rediviva.* Some of the plants begin to flower in their fourth year, and viable seeds are set as they go dormant on CONT. Generally speaking, with all lewisias it is essential to keep dormant roots dry during warm weather to avoid rot. Moisture is all right during vigorous growth or for dormant roots at low temperatures, as during refrigeration or winter months. Good drainage is important always, and soil should never stay soggy. My lewisias thrive in pure sand with hydroponic fertilizer and top watering. However, they are repotted for each new growing season.

Lewisia rediviva. Photo by Margery Edgren

Viola pedata, without doubt the queen of the violets, is a good example of a species providing very little seed for distribution. If one is lucky enough to obtain a packet, there may be only four or five seeds inside. This species, unlike many of its genus, does not produce cleistogamous flowers in late summer. That is unfortunate, as these apetalous flowers can be a bountiful source of seeds, especially if long warm days are prolonged with artificial light. My plants have consistently failed to set seed after blooming, until last year when one was hand pollinated. The shining white pollen concealed within the flower was easily exposed by pulling off one of the petals. During development of the seed pods, the plant was protected inside on CONT. For germination, the seeds of this plant should be moistened and held at warm temperatures for 1–2 months before being placed in the cold. As long as 5 months of refrigeration may be necessary. Young seedlings grow well on LDR. Plants can be brought into flower by 3–6 months of growth on SDR, followed by 5–8 weeks on LDR. *Viola pedatifida* is much easier to grow than *V. pedata,* but is less beautiful. *Viola adunca* seed also responds well to a warm-cold temperature sequence for germination. Vegetative growth is rapid on LDR or CONT. This species does form cleistogamous flowers. If left on CONT, it will continue forming pods of viable seeds for many months, thus producing an ample supply with very little effort.

Androsace chamaejasme and *Papaver radicatum* have flowered from seed under fluorescent light. Seeds of both species start to germinate in less than 2 weeks without stratification, and young plants have flowered when less than 6 months old. However, I have not kept either one long as a specimen plant. Seeds of *Aquilegia jonesii* are quite variable in their requirements for chilling. About 5 months of cold is often sufficient. Seedling growth is best on LDR and young plants have flowered under lights about 6 months after planting. I have raised this plant from seed to flower several times, but have never maintained mature specimens for many seasons.

Some species resist all my efforts to grow them. *Eritrichium nanum* seed has germinated after a month of refrigeration, but seedlings have not survived. Virtually all *Calochortus nuttallii* seeds germinate vigorously after 2–4 months of cold, but have not produced good bulbs. One always hopes next year will bring success with a new species. Whatever your location, it is possible you may be able to apply some of this information to certain problems or activities in your own area to achieve greater success with your favorite plants.

References

Bickford, Elwood D., and Stuart Dunn. 1972. *Lighting for plant growth.* Kent, Ohio: Kent State Univ. Press.

Elliott, Roy C. 1966. *The genus Lewisia.* London: Alpine Garden Society.

Emery, Dara E. 1964. *Seed propagation of native California plants.* Santa Barbara Botanic Garden Leaflet. 1:81–96.

Emery, Dara E., ed. n. d. *Seed germination of rock garden plants.* Santa Barbara: American Rock Garden Society.

Hills, Lawrence D. 1976. *The propagation of alpines.* Sakonnet Point, R.I.: Theophrastus.

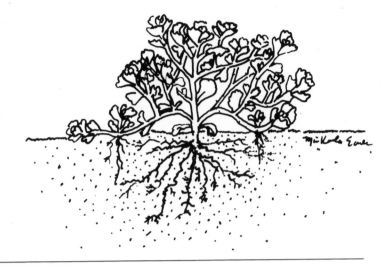

31

In Dry Sand

by Norman C. Deno

Plants moved from the Rocky Mountains to central Pennsylvania experience major environmental changes. The intense sunlight of elevations of 6,000–11,000 ft. is replaced by the lower light intensity (a factor of about 3 on the light meter) here at 1,000–2,000 ft., including a much lower intensity of ultraviolet light. Annual rainfall increases from 10–20 in. to 40–50 in. Wind is reduced from the relentless 30 miles per hour on the Wyoming plains to gentle 5–10 mph zephyrs. Daytime humidity in summer increases to 80 percent at times, partly because of more rain but equally because of reduced diurnal temperature changes. Finally, the chill of the night air is replaced by balmier blankets.

Since all these changes increase the activity and variety of molds, fungi, and bacteria, plants are subjected to much higher levels of stress from these organisms. The result: Plants of the Rockies soon rot in eastern gardens. Clearly, the challenge is to create conditions designed to thwart or inhibit these new stresses.

Our garden is at 1,000 ft. in the geographical center of Pennsylvania. My desk is surrounded by windows that look out through the treetops to the 2,000 ft. ridges of the Bald Eagle, Nittany, and Tussey Mountains. To the north the Alleghenies barely peep over the Bald Eagles. These modest mountains cause diurnal temperature ranges of 30°. Day temperatures never exceed 92°F, and night temperatures always fall below 70°F. The uplift associated with eastern, southern, and western winds gives us our fair share of cloudy days. Nevertheless, rot is still the big problem with Western plants.

There are tour-de-force methods of inhibiting rot: refrigerated soils and air-conditioned alpine houses as practiced at Kew Gardens or spraying with fungicides every two weeks. The latter is used successfully by many orchid growers, including Paul Keisling of Massachusetts who uses it for growing hardy orchids. Marge Edgren, of Woodside, California, puts the pots in the refrigerator every night. All these methods require effort and expense and are not suited to our goal of growing breeding populations.

Dry sand beds were conceived on the following principles. If ordinary soil is overlaid with 10 in. of sand, rotting organisms are inhibited by the relatively sterile, low-nutrient nature of the sand and by the fast-drying character of its surface. Additional advantages are the absence of frost-heaving and the easy friability that makes planting and weeding a pleasure.

The sunniest and breeziest site was chosen to test these principles, and 15 tons of sand were

Norman C. Deno is a retired Pennsylvania State University chemistry professor. He started his first rock garden in Wilmette, Illinois, at the age of 10. He and his wife, Virginia, garden on several acres in State College, Pennsylvania. The garden includes extensive woodlands, steep screes and a unique "sand garden" where xerophytic plants from the western United States and central Asia are grown to perfection. He has lectured throughout the country on rock and alpine gardening and chemistry.

ordered from the local lumber yard. This great sand pile was spread to a depth of 10 in., and planting began. Our first experiment used masonry sand, the kind used in making mortar. We have had 15 years experience with this bed. Last year a second 15 tons of sand were added. This time a coarser sand was used, the kind used in making concrete. So far there has been little difference in the performance of plants in the two types of sand, although we expect the coarser sand may be more suitable for plants, like Oncocyclus iris, which crave summer dryness.

Rock gardeners will notice that the word drainage is conspicuously absent in the above description. Since good drainage is highly recommended and dry sand beds drain well, an explanation is in order. Plants do not directly "care" whether water runs rapidly past the roots (good drainage) or slowly (poor drainage). What is critical is good soil aeration, which works in two ways. First, plant roots are rapidly metabolizing and require a ready supply of oxygen for good results. If there is poor aeration, the roots suffocate and die. The sensitivity of plants to this factor varies greatly, but no plant will root under completely anaerobic conditions. The second effect of good soil aeration is to destroy organic matter rapidly by oxidation. The molds and rots are starved out, as is commonly seen on sandy beaches. We think this second factor is particularly important with Western plants. Incidentally, it is possible to have good oxygen levels with zero drainage as in hydroponics and in a type of wet sand bed with which we are now experimenting. These wet sand beds have proved ideal for certain primulas such as the rare *Primula pamirica* and certain gentians such as *Gentiana linearis*, but that is a topic for another time.

Returning to dry sand beds, the eriogonums have been very successful there. A plant of *Eriogonum compositum* has formed a 10 ft. mat in 10 years. Photos have been taken of people standing on it, sitting on it, and lying on it. The mat, a uniform 4 in. high, roots as it spreads. This form produces its massive flower clusters largely on the periphery of the mat, but other clones have formed looser mats that flower throughout. Unfortunately, the flower color is usually an undistinguished creamy white, though some forms age to a coppery rose. The flower heads last for weeks in good condition.

The two good eriogonums are *Eriogonum caespitosum* (from seed collected by Paul Palomino in Nevada) and a form of *E. flavum* with flat, buttercup yellow flower heads that are 3 in. across on 3 in. stems. The later was collected and sent by Claude Barr. Despite ministrations of the camel's-hair brush, neither has set viable seed, a particular disappointment with *E. caespitosum* because it has not propagated vegetatively. The original seven have dwindled to two over the years.

All of the eriogonums have foliage that functions over the winter, though it can hardly be called evergreen since it produces various shades of coppery red and green with varying amounts of silver fur. Already there is a rich variety of foliage with plenty of room for selection and breeding.

The flower color will be a problem. The *Eriogonum flavum* group produces fine yellows, but the remaining species gravitate toward creamy white with little variation except for some coppery rose tones. Another problem is nomenclature. Harold Rickett's *Wildflowers of the United States* shows four photos of *Eriogonum umbellatum*, three of *E. ovalifolium*, three of *E. flavum*, and two of several other species, all depicting different plants. Another problem in this vast genus is that many of the species are no more than weeds with tiny flowers scattered along the stems or in flimsy open umbels.

The penstemons have also been successful in dry sand. The majority of these are short-lived so breeding populations are necessary. As with the eriogonums, their nomenclature is a jungle. The larger penstemons such as *Penstemon grandiflorus* (*P. bradburii*) and *P. palmeri* have done well, but their tall stature, short blooming period, and nearly monocarpic nature have led us to discard them in favor of the more dwarf species. *Penstemon glaber* and its allies do well and can be spectacular if they are a foot tall and have clear light blue to dark blue flowers. Some forms grow taller, however, and some forms have indeterminate pinkish blue flowers. The complexes of *P. angustifolius* and *P. nitidus* are usually under a foot tall and have glaucous foliage. Like the *P. glaber* group, the flowers can be beautiful blues, but are not always.

Penstemon caespitosus and *P. virens* love the dry sand. The blue flowers of *P. caespitosus* are a good size and held on short 3 in. crowded racemes. The flowers of *P. virens* are small, but they are a good blue. They are held on 6–12 in. spikes over small neat rosettes. *Penstemon virens* is common in woodlands immediately west of Denver. A third dwarf blue penstemon is one sent out by Claude Barr labeled *P. caespitosus*. It is extremely dwarf, being under an inch high with oval, evergreen leaves. In general appearance it resembles a member of the Ericaceae such as chiogenes or a dwarf cranberry. The flowers are a good blue but so scattered on the tight mat they have little effect. Another group of good performers are the hybrids with flowers in shades of pink. They appear to have *P. barbatus* "blood" in them and are 12–18 in. tall.

A most pleasant surprise has been the success of *Penstemon davidsonii* and its allies such as *P. rupicola* and *P. fruticosus*. They are evergreen mats, and many forms have been selected for deep

Penstemon ambiguus. Photo by Bob Heapes   *Oenothera caespitosa.* Photo by Roberts

purple, rose red, and white flower colors. Even in dry sand beds, some clones are troubled with leaf blights, a problem that can be reduced by shearing spent flower stems and old stems. One peculiar problem has been the non-flowering of some *P. fruticosus* seedlings. They make nice evergreen shrublets and grow for years, but never bloom.

There have been failures among the penstemons. The salmon pink *Penstemon laricifolius* is one of the most beautiful plants in all the world growing on the western escarpment of the Bighorns in Wyoming. It grows in the dry sand beds and forms little shrublets smothered with flowers almost as well as in Wyoming, but it has not been possible to keep it going. The same can be said for the beautiful *Penstemon eriantherus, P. albidus* and the less attractive *P. l.* ssp. *exilifolius* (a scrawny white *P. laricifolius*). Finally, the gorgeous *P. ambiguus* has thwarted us because viable seed has never been obtained.

The Eastern *Phlox bifida, P. nivalis, P. subulata, P. stolonifera,* and the vast *Phlox pulchra* complex do superbly in dry sand, and *P. bifida* will not grow well elsewhere. *Phlox pilosa* is also a success despite its transient nature and the necessity of breeding populations. As a result, the Western phlox are against stiff competition to merit space, particularly since so many resemble the Eastern phlox. *Phlox alyssifolia* and *P. andicola* are permanent but do not bloom with the freedom of the Eastern phlox. *Phlox longifolia* finally died out after a number of years. *Phlox muscoides* is good. *Phlox hoodii* has some merit because it develops a mosslike tuft, more so than in the wild, but the flowers are mediocre and the plant is transient. Unfortunately the *P. condensata* group, which flowers gloriously in the Rockies, has failed here.

The one group of phlox that merits full attention is the Mexican and Southwestern phlox centering on *P. mesoleuca* (sometimes considered *P. lutea, P. purpurea*), *P. nana*, and their relatives. Paul Maslin and Panayoti Kelaidis of Colorado have selected forms that are becoming famous for their exciting colors of yellow, orange, rose-reds, and vibrant purples as well as their habit of flowering all summer. Our experience is limited. Anita Kistler has grown several near Philadelphia in dry stone chips. A pink form of *P. mesoleuca* (collected in New Mexico by Richard Clinebell) has grown here in dry sand for fifteen years. It flowers every year, but it keeps dying back and threatens to depart. Western growers like Kelaidis and Mineo are successful with these. It would seem that dry sand is the way to try them in the East. A collection was planted this year. They are growing well and blooming. The questions: Will they last and will they be hardy?

The oenotheras make an outstanding display in dry sand. A hybrid swarm derived from *Oenothera brachycarpa,* and *O. fremontii* has 4 in. yellow flowers facing upwards from small 6 in. mounds of linear foliage. This moundlike habit makes them preferable to the rambling and more common *O. missouriensis.* The flowers open in the evening, and they remain open the next day or even two days in cool weather. This is more likely in the flush of September–October bloom than in June. Also with 4 in. flowers facing up from small mounds is the glistening white *O. caespitosa,* the gumbo lily. It, too, holds its flowers open through the next day in cool weather.

A stunning beauty is *Oenothera lavandulifolia* with square, dark yellow flowers. One plant grew and flowered for several years but finally died, and a source of seed has not been found. A number of other oenotheras have done well, the most attractive being the rambling, smaller, white-flowered species like *O. albicaulis* and *O. nuttallii*. They are short-lived and need to be renewed from seed regularly.

The remaining plants will be discussed in the order they appear in Rickett's Volume 6. Calochortus likes the dry sand. *Calochortus nuttallii* and *C. nitidus* perform well, but that scourge of the East, the chipmunk, prevents an honest test of these beauties. *Erythronium mesochoreum* spreads slowly by seed, but the off-white flowers and unmottled foliage are not exciting. *Leucocrinum montanum*, the sand lily, got raves from Farrer. It slowly increases vegetatively, and old clumps will have 10 to 15 white, crocuslike flowers open at once. All efforts to set seed have failed. *Agave utahensis* and *A. toumeyana* have survived three winters, but growth is slow.

Claude Barr sent a fine strain of *Nemastylis geminiflora* which carries four flowers or more per stalk and which he called *N. acuta*. It propagates only by seed, and the seedlings take about five years to flower. The heavenly blue 2 in. flowers, narrow pleated foliage, and 1 ft. stature make an exciting plant, but the flowers open at 11 AM and close with finality at 4 PM.

Sisyrinchium campestre is a glistening white, blue-eyed grass only 6 in. high. Counterbalancing its attractiveness are the fleeting nature of the flowers and the alarming rate of spread by self-seeding. The fault of fleeting flowers also hangs heavily over the tradescantias. *Tradescantia longipes*, rose-pink, and *T. bracteata*, blue-purple, hold their flowers only 3–6 in. above the ground. Their dwarf stature and upfacing flowers make attractive plants during the week they are in bloom. Claude Barr found a pure white *T. bracteata*. It spreads rapidly by stolons with a character not seen in the blue *T. bracteata* nor in *T. longipes*. Another fleeting bloomer is *Mirabilis multiflora*, the perennial four o'clock. It is too big and lush to be a rock plant.

Unlike the above group of fleeting bloomers, the dwarf Western delphiniums have long-lasting flowers and are all beautiful. The most successful has been *Delphinium bicolor*, which has formed a self-seeding colony. Most individuals do not live more than several years, but their persistence seems to be increasing. It is possible there has been some crossing with the indestructible Eastern *D. tricorne*, which grows here by the thousands and is much like *D. bicolor* in form and stature.

Some plants, like the famous aquilegias of the Rockies, do not like dry sand. *Aquilegia saximontana* persisted in sand if watered regularly and self-sowed a bit. It always appeared starved so some were shifted to north-facing rocky limestone slopes. Here they do much better with 5 to 10 flowers open all at once. *Aquilegia jonesii* failed in dry sand; perhaps it, too, should be tried on the limestone slopes. *Mertensia lanceolata*, Barr's dryland mertensia, dies out in dry sand, but forms a breeding colony in moist shade. The same is true of *Viola rugulosa* and *V. pedatifida*.

Anemone caroliniana has been a tragedy. This is a rare plant. Edgar Wherry, eminent botanist and "dean" of the ARGS, told me that in all his travels he saw it only once in the sand hills in Oklahoma. Barr would never tell me where he found his plants, but he said they were rare. It is a beautiful anemone closely resembling *A. blanda*. Both have big, flat flowers that come in pink, white, and blue. Barr sent many tubers. They would bloom beautifully, self-sow a bit, threaten to spread by branching rhizomes, and then suddenly die. *Anemone caroliniana* differs from *A. blanda* in that the pedicel is more rigid and upright, and ground-hugging winter foliage is produced. The loss of the last plant of *A. caroliniana* made for a very sad day.

Pulsatilla (Anemone) patens is short-lived, but so are the European *P. vulgaris* and *P. halleri*. (*Pulsatilla albana* is long-lived.) Perhaps *P. patens* has contributed genes to the hybrid swarms that bloom here by the hundreds every year. *Anemone multifida* in a deep rose-red form persists here by reseeding, but it is of modest attractions.

Dryas octopetala forms great mats in dry sand, but they are probably garden-selected forms of European origin. The mentzelias and argemones grew well, but were tall and prickly. Their big flowers nearly saved them.

Cacti are not everyone's alpine plants, but dry sand is the answer if you are interested. Most desirable are the large pink and rose flowers of hybrids of *Echinocereus pectinatus* and its relatives. The flowers last only two days. The first day the anthers ripen; the second day the stigma ripens. Several generations have been grown, and resistance to rot is improving. *Echinocereus viridiflorus* is a willing, abundant bloomer, but the greenish-yellow flowers are not impressive. The red flowers of *E. triglochidiatus* are smaller, but they last four days and Panayoti Kelaidis says they will cross with the *E. pectinatus* group. *Pediocactus simpsonii* has nice pink flowers and is permanent. The gorgeous *Coryphantha vivipara* blooms well but winter kills. The opuntias are ungainly despite the big flowers, so all have been discarded but three. *Opuntia* 'Desert Splendor' was selected and named by Claude

Arenaria saxosa. Photo by Norm Deno

Barr. It has very big pink flowers. *Opuntia imbricata,* from Barr, is a 3 ft. branching cholla cactus that is hardy and has fine red flowers. Unfortunately, it is a shy bloomer. *Opuntia clavata,* with papery bracts instead of spines, is of some interest, but it is slow-growing and shy-blooming. I can remember standing beside Claude Barr and sharing his joy when it bloomed for him for the first time after twenty years.

Among the Cruciferae there are fine drabas, erysimums, lesquerellas, and physarias. Those tried usually bloomed, but there were too few to establish breeding populations, and all were short-lived. The dwarf *Lepidum nanum* received much praise some years ago. Several were grown from seed collected by Paul Palomino in a remote valley in Nevada. They persisted for 5 years and had dwarf, congested foliage; but the small, pale, lemon yellow flowers were disappointing.

Among the Caryophyllaceae, *Silene acaulis* does well, but again they are garden-selected forms of European origin. One is from Mongolia. *Arenaria saxosa* (*A. lanuginosa*) grows vigorously, similar to the European *A. montana,* but it is darker green with more evergreen foliage. *Arenaria saxosa* is recommended as a beautiful plant. *Arenaria hookeri* persisted for 10 years, but the flowers are not the equal of *A. saxosa.* A very dwarf mosslike arenaria, probably *A. (Minuartia) obtusiloba* has grown well for ten years and produces scattered white flowers.

Paronychia sessiliflora is an unusual member of the pink family. It forms a mat only a half-inch high. The needlelike foliage is the color of juniper foliage so its appearance is that of a minute juniper. Yellow insignificant flowers lie flat on the mat.

Sedum lanceolatum (formerly *S. stenopetalum*) is a good yellow sedum. *Saxifraga oppositifolia,* again of European origin, will not grow in dry sand. It struggles on north limestone slopes or in well-watered sand beds, but despite some bloom, does not prosper.

The most noteworthy failures have been the genera *Astragalus* and *Oxytropis. Oxytropis halleri* flowered and even self-sowed a bit, but it was a shadow of its resplendence on the Bighorns. A particularly sad loss was *Astragalus barrii,* named after my old friend Claude Barr. A group of three grew and flowered for several years. Despite hand pollination, seed would not set and the group died out. Not all legumes fail. *Thermopsis rhombifolia* spreads like wildfire. It is a favorite because of its large trusses of yellow sweet pea flowers, intense honey fragrance, low 1 ft. height, and good foliage all summer. It should be grown in a bed by itself since it makes great patches.

Townsendia parryi
Photo by Norm Deno

Dodecatheons bloom by the acre on top of the Bighorns and all over the West. Even in Barr's baked gumbo a species prospered, and he selected two fine forms, 'White Comet' and 'Prairie Ruby.' After many trials of these in various sites, all that can be said is that their behavior is erratic. They bloom and seed, but the attrition rate exceeds the propagation rate, partly because they develop so slowly from seed, having only cotyledons and no true leaves their first year. They are probably not suited to dry sand beds.

The Rockies are rich in composites, but their success in dry sand beds has been limited. An aster labeled *A. kumleinii (A. oblongifolius)* by Barr is the best dwarf fall aster. It spreads rapidly by seed and stolons. The flower color is usually a good pink or lavender blue. It stays under a foot tall. Flowers open all at once to make a show, but the show lasts only a week. *Townsendia formosa*, a lavender daisy of 10 in. stature, persists by self-seeding. *Microseris cuspidata*, a dandelion with flat, undulate foliage, and *Hymenoxys acaulis* are long-lived. The dwarf, high alpine forms of *Hymenoxys acaulis* die out. A few seedlings of *H. grandiflora* are near blooming in the dry sand. Their flowering would be a joy since this plant is such a prominent feature of the high alpine meadows in the Rockies.

Townsendia exscapa, white-tinged-pink; *T. grandiflora*, white; *T. parryi*, lavender; and *T. montana*, vibrant magenta, are all beautiful with big daisies over huddled tufts. Several generations of each of these were grown, but all died out when attention was not given to collecting seed and starting the seed in pots. The same was true of *Erigeron eatonii* and *E. scribneri*. *Erigeron caespitosus* and *E. compositus* are still here after a dozen years, but attention must be given to renewal seeding. *Melampodium leucanthemum* is a fine bush of white daisies, but the initial supply was insufficient to start a colony. *Machaeranthera (Aster) tanacetifolia* is a beautiful blue dwarf aster over pinnate foliage, but it is an annual, and one must decide whether to have a field of it or none. *Lygodesmia grandiflora*, a low pink chicory with terete foliage, would be worth growing, but seed has not been available, and I did not have the fortitude to try collecting their deep taproots. As a group, Compositae have been disappointing.

Several groups of plants merit a brief comment. The true high alpines such as *Claytonia megarhiza, Polemonium viscosum, Primula angustifolia,* and *Eritrichium nanum* have failed with so many gardeners that only a plant or two were tried with the usual result. However, the high alpine *Douglasia montana* should be tried. It grows on Waterworks Hill in Missoula, Montana, on the highest and driest sand at the top. Its relatives, *D. laevigata* and *D. vitaliana*, are great successes in dry sand.

PLATE 27

Phlox hoodii and cushion
of *Eriogonum caespitosum*
Photo by Sharon Sutton

Eriogonum clavellatum
Photo by Elizabeth Neese

Bryce Canyon, Utah
Photo by Pat Pachuta

Eriogonum caespitosum
Photo by Sharon Sutton

PLATE 30

Cryptantha jamesii
Photo by Jim Borland

Opuntia 'Claude Arno'
Photo by Anthony Taylor

Opuntia phaeacantha
Photo: DBG Collection

Opuntia imbricata
Photo by Allan Taylor

Some plants such as *Primula parryi* are plants of moist places and were not attempted. The gentians such as *Gentiana (Pneumonanthe) affinis, G. puberulenta,* and *Gentianopsis thermalis* need more study. The parasitic castillejas have on rare occasion grown up and bloomed from seed in the dry sand, but they are uncertain.

Conclusion

From the above experiences, it is evident that many of the plants of the Rockies are not long-lived and must be cultivated as breeding colonies. Most gardens cannot afford the space that this requires nor do most gardeners like the constant realignment and wildness of such colonies. But if you yearn for the wide open spaces and the plants that grow there, do try a dry sand bed. Be sure to make one large enough to accomodate the wandering free spirits that will grow there. Even vegetative propagators like *Phlox mesoleuca* wander widely, sending up tufts of foliage spaced several feet apart.

It may help enthusiastic plantspeople to mention that plants from other dry areas of the world often do their best in dry sand beds. Acantholimons, Oncocyclus and Juno iris, and *Douglasia vitaliana* all do well. Some of the annuals from the Western deserts have prospered. Among these are nemophilas, linanthus, and phacelias.

But most of all, dry sand beds are a joy to work with because they are easy to weed and easy to plant. In a sand garden you'll be a kid again, playing in the sandpile.

References

Dannen, Kent, and Donna Dannen. 1981. *Rocky Mountain wildflowers.* Estes Park, Colo.: Tundra Publications.

Dodge, Natt N. 1967. *Roadside wildflowers of Southwestern uplands.* Phoenix: Arizona-Messenger Printing Co.

Gabrielson, Ira N. 1932. *Western American alpines.* New York: Macmillan Co. (Reprinted in 1972 by Theophrastus, Sakonnet Point, R.I.).

32

On Hummocks

by Lee M. Raden

About nine years ago I purchased a gently sloping property in Charlestown Township about 35 miles northwest of Philadelphia, elevation 110 ft. above sea level. Located in Chester County in southeastern Pennsylvania, the climate falls somewhere within USDA zones 6b and 7a. Our climate is tempered by the Atlantic Ocean 75 miles to the east and the Chesapeake Bay 30 miles to the south. Average rainfall is 40-plus in. Our rainfall is relatively heavy in early spring and fall months, with periods sometimes approaching drought in July and August. We do not enjoy periods of long snow cover in the crucial January and February months. Some years we have plenty of snow; other years we have freezing rains; and still other years, near drought conditions.

To make my horticultural fantasy work, a series of six hummocks, facing as many directions as possible, was constructed, all placed relatively close together so that they would create microclimates among themselves. Each of the six hummocks has 20,000 pounds of 2 in. crushed granite as a base. Over this was spread topsoil, coarse river sand and subsoil mixed at approximately a 1:1:1 ratio. (The hummocks devoured sand in 20 ton increments; the largest used 60 tons.) I was fortunate that a good gardening friend, Claire Muller, was available for a full week, the time necessary to construct the hummocks. She sat on the front-end loader with the operator and developed the hummocks. This mixture of topsoil, sand and subsoil gave us an almost neutral pH. The largest hummock faces north and south with the northern exposure on a very gradual grade and the southern exposure very steep, carved in the semicircular shape of a miniature alpine cirque like those formed by glacial action. This hummock is approximately 6 ft. high, 110 ft. long and 110 ft. wide. The west hummock is 10 ft. high and approximately 80 ft. wide. A third hummock, which is devoted exclusively to succulents, runs north and south and is 3 ft. high and 40 ft. long. All six hummocks were then mulched with 120,000 pounds of washed river gravel.

Inside of two months I realized I had overindulged my horticultural stomach, and the other three hummocks were planted to *Juniperus horizontalis* cv. 'Wiltonii', *Juniperus conferta,* and *Cedrus deodora* cv. 'Pendula'. The cedrus died within three years. The rigors of our climate plus the general southeastern exposure of that hummock did them in. In the spring of 1982 we planted *Juniperus procumbens* 'Nana' (*J. chinensis* var. *p.* 'Nana').

Living in the country, we can never irrigate since our water source is a well. All our planting has

Lee Morris Raden is currently serving as vice president of the American Rock Garden Society, has served in the same capacity with the Pennsylvania Horticultural Society, and is active in a host of horticultural organizations. He is best known as a connoisseur of choice alpines, which he grows superbly not only in his innovative alpine house, but in bulb frames and on the famous naturalistic hummocks of Alpineflora, which capture the texture and feel of tundra in the suburbs of Philadelphia. His ambitious displays at the Philadelphia Flower Show have inspired many rock gardeners.

North slope of central hummock, author's garden. Photo by Lee Raden

to be done knowing that only rainfall and snow will be the water source for the plants growing on the hummocks. After many years of experience with an irrigated garden, it was apparent that we would have to drastically change the types of plants grown on the hummocks in Charlestown.

Consequently, every effort was made to create superb drainage in a soil mixture that would also be moisture-retentive. Since we were dealing with a climate where long summer periods of 90 percent humidity and 95°F temperatures could mean disaster for many alpines, the hummocks were placed to catch any breeze that might be moving through our valley. The Chester Valley runs west and east, and the prevailing winds are from the west. The venturi effect is considerably in evidence even in the hottest and most humid periods; the wind is compressed as it comes up our shallow valley, and because it is compressed, its velocity increases. As an example, the central hummock is 6 ft. high. The southeast slope on its weather side faces north and west, and there is a 20 percent increase in wind speed over the top of the hummock (see Figure 32.1). The spill is 20–25 ft. downward on the lee side. This is especially important during January, February and March when we have high winds that give us a lot of desiccation of south-facing plants. The plants in the cirque, because of wind spill, get very little desiccation, thereby insuring their weather hardiness.

We grow as many plants as possible from all over the world. Needless to say, we have killed them by the thousands as well. The problems, of course, are: (1) altitude—we are 110 ft. above sea level; (2) lack of a consistent and dependable snow cover in the winter months; and (3) that terrible combination of temperature and humidity when they both hover around 95. Yet as we all know, rock gardeners are an optimistic group. We forget our failures quickly and dwell on our successes.

Growing plants native to the Rocky Mountains is a challenge we try to meet in many ways. The perfect drainage of the hummocks contributes to our limited successes, and we have some leeway in where the plants are placed. Plants that need extremely dry conditions can be planted as high as 119 ft. above sea level, whereas some high desert and high meadow plants can be planted at the base of the hummocks at a mighty 110 ft. above sea level. While there may be some levity in my descriptions, there is no question that the higher I go on the hummocks the better for the dryland plants.

The list of Rocky Mountain alpines we are growing has habitats from Canada to Mexico. They are all planted with either a western exposure (our very hottest and driest hummock) or on the gentle north slope of the cirque. Do not be lulled into believing that the north side does not get full sun. It does, but I would guess that the temperatures are somewhat cooler in the summer, and at this latitude in the winter the snow definitely remains 1–4 days longer than on the west hummock and the south-facing cirque. Also, generally speaking, silver or gray plants are planted on the west hummock.

As a matter of principle, I take as many cuttings as possible of any new plant material. I do this so I can plant these propagations in a number of locations to see if they will successfully handle our

Central hummock looking
east to west, author's garden.
Photo by Lee Raden

climate or my microclimates. *Planting a single plant in the single area that you think is best is fraught with peril.* As a glaring example, penstemons like root company; if I plant a solo penstemon off by itself I generally lose it. Consequently, most of the penstemons are grown together, jammed as close as possible. I haven't really discovered the secret of growing the peas. Western astragalus and oxytropis are plants near and dear to my heart. Yet, while I have listed them, it is only with a certain amount of limited success that I have grown them.

The Western phlox have been a tragedy. *Phlox nana* lingered on for three or four years. *Phlox* cv. 'Tangelo,' *P. purpurea* cvs. 'Arroyo,' and 'Mary Maslin' (some or all sometimes considered *P. mesoleuca*) have all been badly winter-killed after only one growing season. Deer and rabbits also created havoc in the first few years of this garden. Bulbous material and the penstemons were eaten to the ground by the rabbits. The deer don't eat, but their hooves are like razors, and in walking from one hummock to another they make literally hundreds of cuttings of dianthus and phlox. This has been overcome by laying chicken wire flat over large expanses of the garden from November through March. Believe it or not, after it has weathered for a season or two, chicken wire is rather unobtrusive, and deer will not walk on it, and the rabbits are discouraged. Another deer deterrent is the playing of rock-and-roll music from dusk to dawn. It's directed at the garden during the months of December through March—one advantage of living in the country with no neighbors.

Lastly, weeding is not done seriously until mid-June. Each successive year we enjoy a tremendous crop of self-sown seedlings of many of the rarest plants. A great deal of this is attributed to the pebble mulch and the lack of disturbance of the growing areas by cultivation. There have been some serious weed problems in the past. Generally these are taken care of mid-June, mid-July, and mid-August with a hand-held sprayer of herbicide. Forms which become inert on contact with the soil are a boon to all serious gardeners.

South slope of central hummock, author's garden. Photo by Lee Raden

References

Bates, Carlos G. 1944. *The windbreak as a farm asset.* Farmers Bulletin 1405. Washington, D.C.: United States Dept. of Agriculture.

Carborn, J. M. 1957. *Shelterbelts and microclimate.* Forestry Commission Bulletin no. 29. Edinburgh: Forestry Commission.

Halstead, M. H. 1952. *The relationship between wind structure and turbulence near the ground.* Geophysical Research Papers no. 19:97–129. Cambridge, Mass.: United States Air Force, Cambridge Research Center.

Ortho Books ed. staff. 1974. *Weather wise gardening.* San Francisco: Ortho Book Division.

Raden, Lee Morris. 1983. "The hummocks of Alpineflora." *Green Scene.* 11:7–9.

Robinette, Gary O. 1972. *Plants, people, and environmental quality; a study of plants and their environmental functions.* Washington: United States Dept. of the Interior, National Park Service.

U. S. Forest Service. 1911. *Windbreaks: their influence and value.* Bulletin 86. Washington: U.S. Government Printing Office.

Table 32.1. Rocky Mountain Alpines in the Hummocks at Alpineflora

Agave utahensis var. *kaibabensis*	*Oxalis grayii (O. decaphylla)*
Antennaria arida (A. microphylla)	*O. metcalfei (O. alpina)*
Artemisia frigida	*Penstemon alpinus*
A. spinescens (Picrothamnus desertorum)	*P. ambiguus*
Astragalus purshii	*P. crandallii*
Castilleja integra	*P. linarioides* ssp. *coloradoensis*
Chrysothamnus sp. (Colorado)	*P. linarioides* ssp. *linarioides*
Draba asprella	*P. teucrioides*
Echevaria (Graptopetalum) rusbyi	*P. wilcoxii*
Ephedra sp. (Colorado)	*Phlox muscoides*
Erigeron compositus	*P. pulvinata* 'Black-eyed form' *(P. caespitosa* ssp. *p.)*
Eriogonum strictum ssp. *proliferum*	*P. woodhousei (P. speciosa* ssp. *woodhousei)*
Haplopappus (Tonestus) lyallii	*Potentilla thurberi*
Hedyotis (Houstonia) pygmaea	*Sedum cockerellii (S. wootonii)*
Lesquerella arizonica	*S. stelliforme*
L. intermedia	*Senecio longilobus (S. douglasii* v. *l.)*
L. purpurea	*Sisyrinchium longipes*
Lewisia brachycalyx	*Townsendia exscapa*
Opuntia clavata	*Tradescantia pinetorum*
Oxytropis sericea	*Tritelia (Brodiaea) lemmonae*

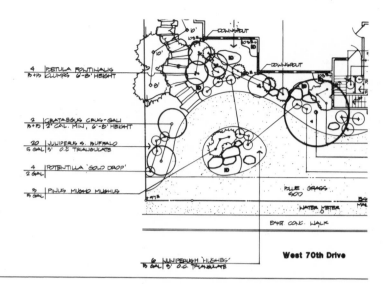

33

In the Overall Design of Private Gardens

by Herbert R. Schaal

Many Rocky Mountain gardens possess a quality that is recognized as unique to the region. This special quality is the result of using design responsive to specific environmental and cultural characteristics of the region and of incorporating native plants and building materials.

The most influential environmental factor is the area's climate. Although the growing season is short, the Rocky Mountain region is blessed with abundant sunshine and low humidity, yielding many comfortable days and nights, even in winter. However, being a midcontinental climate, the region is dry, with evaporation exceeding precipitation; it is given to extremes of temperature, and is often subject to severe weather with high winds, hail, torrential rain, and heavy spring snow. The region's lack of moisture, together with certain geological conditions, has resulted in generally alkaline and sometimes saline soils at the populated lower elevations. The establishment and flourishing of woody plants here is largely dependent upon imported water.

The cultural factors which most influence design are a general desire to be out-of-doors as much as possible and an appreciation of the natural mountain landscape. Although most of the region's population is only near and not actually in the mountains, the inhabitants yearn for qualities of the mountain landscape. Irrigation technology allows the designer to combine the feeling and materials of the foothills and montane zones with qualities of the landscape found along streams in the plains zone to produce a highly livable, low maintenance garden. A discussion of the main elements that contribute to this special garden image and the factors upon which they are based follows.

Outdoor Living

Because of the region's generally agreeable climate and the outdoor values of the inhabitants, outdoor spaces for eating, cooking, sunning, lounging, visiting, play, bathing, and horticulture are typical garden requirements. These functions are usually sited adjacent to the residence for

---

Landscape architect **Herbert R. Schaal** is officer-in-charge of EDAW's Rocky Mountain regional office in Fort Collins, Colorado. Since establishing this office in 1974, he has been involved with numerous area projects, including the award-winning Rock Alpine Garden at Denver Botanic Gardens. During the course of this project, he personally selected and directed the placement of more than 600 tons of rock. Nine major projects under his direction, including the Rock Alpine Garden, have won awards from the American Society of Landscape Architects.

Rock Alpine Garden,
Denver Botanic Gardens.
Photo by Herb Schaal

convenience and can extend the form, style, and materials of the house into the garden. The outward edges of these elements facilitate transition to the more naturalistic environment. Where possible, the edges accentuate natural features, such as rock outcrops or trees, by terminating into or partially surrounding them. A portion of the edge is given to partial enclosure to help define the space, provide privacy, and direct the outward view. Along this edge and in key locations, the most detailed and interesting planting arrangements are positioned.

For comfort, the primary outdoor living area is partly shaded in the summer and mostly in sun during the other seasons. A covered extension of the house allows the continuation of outdoor living during the frequent, but brief, summer afternoon showers.

Expansive Views

The region is characterized by openness, unlike the densely wooded eastern United States. It is common to enjoy a vista of 50 to 100 miles (80–160 km); mountains typically provide a skyline, and dramatic skies usually occupy a large portion of the scene.

In order to capitalize on this truly regional quality, it is common to orient and frame the best views, while keeping an openness in the middle ground of the garden. Generous "windows," or breaks, in perimeter plantings focus views to high peaks or other interesting skyline features. Adjacent development is screened out by landform, fences, or plantings. These screens are placed close to the viewer and frequently are more effective in preserving the open feeling than those placed at the perimeter of the garden.

Landscape Zoning

Landscape zoning is a response to many considerations, but primarily to the rising cost and scarcity of water for irrigation in the region. During drought years, it is becoming more common for municipalities to ration water for landscape irrigation. Landscape zoning is a conservation technique to reduce supplemental water requirements by concentrating plants requiring the most water in small selected areas, usually in the most used portions of the garden.

Bluegrass lawns are kept to a minimum, and ground covers, shrub beds, or native grasses are used in place of lawn to cover ground surface.

On large estates, the zoning may resemble the Rocky Mountain life zones, with perimeter areas corresponding to plains, intermediate areas to foothills, and higher use areas around the residence to the montane zone. Gardening enthusiasts extend this concept to include the Sonoran or the alpine zones as special features. The juxtaposition of these zones actually captures the natural feeling of the region, where radical differences in plant communities commonly occur in close proximity due to soil conditions, aspect, and drainage.

Each of the zones is irrigated by a separate system according to the differing precipitation needs. The plains zone may be unirrigated, except for tree and shrub establishment, which is accomplished by drip irrigation.

Severe Weather

Short, stout, and small-flowered varieties of common bulbs, annuals, and perennials are often selected for their ability to withstand wet spring snows and occasional severe summer weather associated with thunderstorms.

Taller and heavy-headed herbaceous plants are planted on the lee side of fences and are staked to prevent them from being blown over.

Alpines, ideally suited to the severe conditions of the Rockies, are an alternative to the more traditional herbaceous garden plants and are gaining in popularity with greater commercial availability.

One measure for dealing with sudden severe weather and the relatively short growing season is the use of containers, which can be moved to protection until the threat of damage is over. Garden structures and arbors are sometimes used to protect selected plants from hail.

In order to counteract the visual impact of plant attrition due to severe weather, mixed naturalistic plantings are preferred over formal monocultures.

Native Plants

Native plants are perfectly adapted to the region and, after establishment, thrive with just a little extra water and a minimal amount of care. When these plants are used throughout the garden, a plant community is created which is unique to the region, characterized by coarse open trees and shrubs, low ground covers, wildflowers, and short grasses. The foliage of many of these plants has a xeric look and tends toward gray and blue-green coloration.

Although most gardens are located below 6,000 ft. in the plains life zone, plants from several of the region's life zones are used in order to get the desired variety, seasonal interest, and levels of comfort. See Table 33.1 for commonly used native plants for typical garden uses.

Native Building Materials

Rock is abundant throughout the region and has many applications in the garden. Quarried sandstone, of both buff and red coloration, is used for paving, stepping stones, walls, steps, and capping. The same material, weathered and collected from the surface, supports several colorful lichens and may be pocked with "bird baths" and interesting crevices. Large boulders (sometimes over 10 tons) of this sandstone, placed judiciously, are important features in many gardens. Limestone is usually found in the foothills interbedded with sandstone. The blocky nature of limestone pieces makes the material easy to stack and compose into large masses. This quality and the many cracks and solution cavities in the rock make it a choice material for rock gardens. Granite and schist are used less often, but are more naturally associated with the alpine plants of the region.

Round river rock and river cobbles are used for dry streams and as a coarse mulch, whereas smaller gravels and crushed rock are used as a fine mulch. Mulching with rock is a common practice because of occasional high winds which can blow organic mulches away. Rock mulches are used primarily as a temporary measure to aid in maintenance, water conservation, and erosion control, and to provide a clean, managed look until plants become established and cover the entire ground surface.

Summary

Although the Rocky Mountain garden may take many forms and follow a variety of styles, use of the area's native materials and response to the area's special environmental and cultural factors result in an image undeniably unique to the region.

The Lang residence, Arvada, Colorado

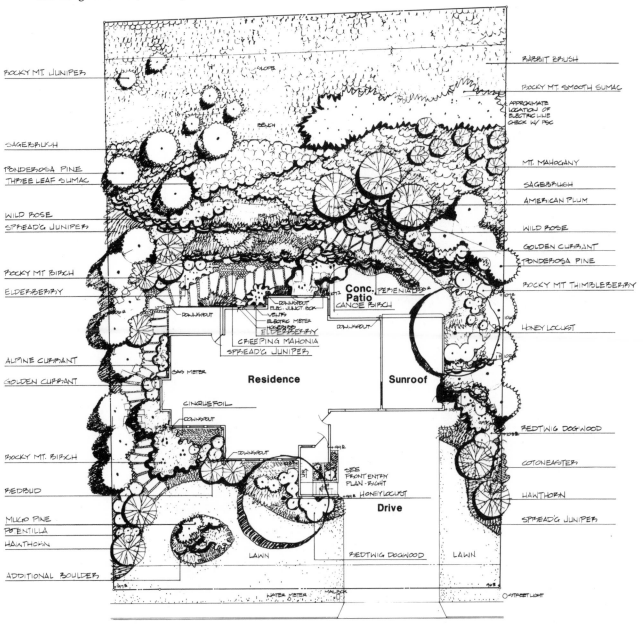

West 70th Drive

References

EDAW, Inc. Eckbo, Dean, Austin, and Williams. 1973. "A landscape design guide for the citizens of Pueblo, Colorado." *Pueblo Design Quarterly* 1 (March):1–37. Pueblo, Colo.: City and County of Pueblo.

Huddleston, S., and M. Hussey. 1975. *Grow Native.* Ft. Collins, Colo.: Apple Tree Image Publishers, Inc.

Kelly, George W. 1981. *Flowers for the Rocky Mountains.* Cortez, Colo.: Rocky Mountain Horticultural Publishing Co., Inc.

———. 1958. *Rocky Mountain Horticulture.* Boulder: Pruett Publishing Co.

———. 1979. *Shrubs for the Rocky Mountains.* Cortez, Colo.: Mountain Horticultural Publishing Co., Inc.

Lang garden
Photo by Herb Schaal

Rock Alpine Garden, DBG
Photo by Herb Schaal

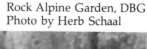

Table 33.1. Rocky Mountain Native Plants for Typical Garden Uses

COMMON NAME**	BOTANICAL NAME	COMMON NAME**	BOTANICAL NAME
Shade Trees		***Accent Shrubs***	
Common Western Cottonwood	*Populus sargentii*	Soapweed	*Yucca glauca*
Narrowleaf Cottonwood	*P. angustifolia*	Thimbleberry	*Rubus deliciosus*
Willow	*Salix* sp.	Serviceberry	*Amelanchier* sp.
Green Ash	*Fraxinus pensylvanica*	Waxflower	*Jamesia americana*
Boxelder	*Acer negundo*	Rocky Mountain Maple	*Acer glabrum*
Hackberry	*Celtis occidentalis*	Sandcherry	*Prunus besseyi*
Evergreen Tree Screens, Windbreaks, and Solid Masses		***Herbaceous Flower Borders and Beds***	
		Gayfeather	*Liatris punctata*
Ponderosa Pine	*Pinus ponderosa*	Yarrow	*Achillea millefolium*
Colorado Blue & Green Spruce	*Picea pungens*	Aster	*Aster* sp.
Pinyon Pine	*Pinus edulis*	Penstemon	*Penstemon* sp.
Bristlecone Pine	*P. aristata*	Sulphur Flower	*Eriogonum umbellatum*
Limber Pine	*P. flexilis*	Gaillardia	*Gaillardia aristata*
Colorado Juniper	*Juniperus scopulorum*	Goldenrod	*Solidago* sp.
White Fir	*Abies concolor*	Brown-Eyed Susan	*Rudberckia hirta*
		Colorado Columbine	*Aquilegia caerulea*
Small Accent Trees		***Low Spreading Plants for Ground Cover***	
Quaking Aspen	*Populus tremuloides*	Mountain Common Juniper	*Juniperus communis*
Scrub Oak	*Quercus gambelii*		
Rocky Mountain Birch	*Betula occidentalis*	Kinnikinnick	*Arctostaphylos uva-ursi*
Hawthorns	*Crataegus* sp.	Oregon Holly Grape	*Berberis (Mahonia) repens*
Wild Plum	*Prunus americana*		
Mountain Alder	*Alnus tenuifolia*	Pussytoes	*Antennaria* sp.
Big Tooth Maple	*Acer grandidentatum*	Wild Strawberry	*Fragaria americana*
Tall Shrubs for Foundation or Background Plantings		***Climbing Plants for Fences and Walls***	
Red Twig Dogwood	*Cornus stolonifera (C. sericea)*	Western Virgin's Bower	*Clematis ligusticifolia*
		Western Clematis	*C. columbiana*
Buffaloberry	*Shepherdia argentea*	Riverbank Grape	*Vitis vulpina*
Western Chokecherry	*Prunus melanocarpa*	Virginia Creeper	*Parthenocissus vitacea (P. inserta)*
Ninebark	*Physocarpus intermedius*		
Rocky Mountain Sumac	*Rhus glabra* var. *cismontana*		
Mountain Mahogany	*Cercocarpus* sp.	***Turf***	
Buffalo Currant	*Ribes aureum*	Buffalo Grass	*Buchloë dactyloides*
Low Shrubs for Foundation Plantings, Beds, and Borders		***Ground covers and low perennials for rock gardens***	
Sage	*Artemisia* sp.	Alpine Columbine	*Aquilegia saximontana*
Potentilla	*Potentilla fruticosa (Pentaphylloides floribunda)*	Wild Yarrow	*Achillea lanulosa*
		Kinnikinick	*Arctostaphylos uva-ursi*
		Shooting Star	*Dodecatheon pulchellum*
Three Leaf Sumac	*Rhus trilobata*	Sulphur Flower	*Eriogonum umbellatum*
Native Rose	*Rosa* sp.	Gentian	*Gentiana parryi*
Rabbitbrush	*Chrysothamnus nauseosus*	Broomweed	*Guttierezia sarothrae*
		Perky Sue	*Hymenoxys acaulis*
Squaw Currant	*Ribes cereum*	Mat Penstemon	*Penstemon caespitosus*
		Townsendia	*Townsendia exscapa*
		Zauschneria	*Zauschneria californica*

** All names used here are consistent with nomenclature in *Meet The Natives,* by M. Walter Pesman (1975).

Section III

Around the World:
Adapting to Different Climates

Photo by Deane Hall

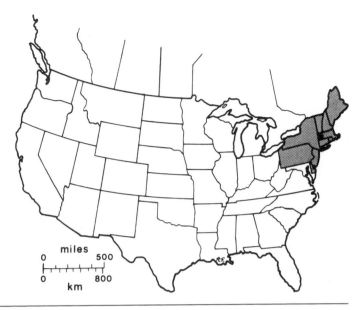

34

In the Northeast

by Geoffrey Charlesworth

Take a mountain, and crush into rocks of various size. Mix with ice and roll southward from Canada until smoothish. Add an equal amount of acid sand; stir until randomly distributed, and pile into heaps. Cover with enough white pine, maple and trash trees to form a rooty mat. Settle with a boatload of Englishmen, and get the worst of the visible mess piled into stone walls. Open up good farmland in Ohio, and sell out to weekend yuppies from New York. This is the New England we have to garden with: wornout farmland, cleared second-growth woodland, rounded boulders too big for one man, too small for two or not worth the trouble of moving at all. And everywhere you dig, large lumpy rocks. Lucky people get a bit of exposed ledge.

What was poor farmland turns out to be quite good rock gardening country. There are as many methods of using this terrain as there are gardeners, so I shall establish my own point of view. First, you can introduce other kinds of rocks if you wish, but they would look as foreign here as they do at Kew or Wisley. Moreover, the expense would be possible only for an institution or an institutionlike person. This applies to tufa even more than just rock. Second, you can work with the rocks you dig up or find on the stone walls. This means lumps of smoothish granite, not slices of stratified sandstone or delicious parallelepipeds of Farrer limestone. So for a combination of reasons I have turned away from conventional rock gardening and in doing so have perhaps invented a few aesthetic justifications for doing the inescapable. The Japanese-inspired miniature landscapes that may look fine, say, in a Czech backyard, are all wrong in a very large field in western Massachusetts. And here I must finally admit that no rock garden with a rockscape as its framework has ever looked quite natural to me, and this includes even Edinburgh and all the "greats." The conventions they observe, though they were developed for historic and aesthetic reasons, are simply not needed if all you want to do is to grow alpines. This, of course, is merely an excuse for my own obsession. Raised beds may not be the best garden design or even the best way to grow alpines, but they offer an acceptable compromise for both. Raised beds, of course, are not new. There are beautiful examples in the Savill Gardens and at Kew, and they are often incorporated into a larger garden design and nearly everybody has at least part of their garden raised. Even the "almond pudding" is a raised bed of sorts.

Some of the advantages of raised beds are: increased visibility of plants, improved drainage, unimpeded light, separation of small plants from ground level clutter to act as a picture frame, exclu-

Geoffrey Charlesworth is a retired mathematics professor who first gardened in the backyard of a New York City brownstone. His gardening interests expanded when he moved to Hempstead, Long Island, near Hofstra University where he served as associate dean. His suburban garden was filled with azaleas, dogwoods and perennials. He later expanded to a 90-acre summer home in the Berkshire Hills of Massachusetts where he now lives year-round. He is an active member of a host of specialist societies.

sion of weeds that walk in from grass verges, possibility of vertical niches with all aspects of the compass. Finally, they offer the possibility of growing plants that have proved difficult to grow otherwise, including plants from the Rocky Mountains.

The plants I grow come from all parts of the world, and I have never enjoyed the luxury of segregating them geographically. Rocky Mountain plants stand check by jowl with Europeans, Asians and a few New Zealanders.

I have tried many methods of construction. The first raised beds I coveted were those Frank Cabot of Cold Spring, New York, had built by a swarm of professional masons using dressed stone. Four or five courses high, they stood like Mexican temples next to the parking lot. These monuments aroused a great deal of envy, and I could see Frank was on to a good thing. With limited resources, however, I knew I would have to modify his design. Here I must confess that my philosophy of gardening is totally present-directed with no thought that posterity will wish to preserve my contraptions. In fact, I fully expect to outlive the raised beds I have made. Since every bed seems destined to be replanted or redesigned every four to seven years, it is a matter of indifference that one of my walls may collapse or dissolve in ruins.

The general principles are as follows: the ground is cleared of sod and a course of stone, wood or concrete is laid out in a rectangle or some other shape, and slightly sunk into the ground for stability. You may then fill the outline with material of your choice, lay another course and fill again, continuing until high enough. The fill can be rocks and small stones at the bottom to give drainage and extra height. For the middle layers I usually mix good compost with peat moss, sand and fertilizer. The top layer is coarse, sharp sand. The depth of these layers varies, but I have had best results with Western plants when the top layer is at least 3 in. and as much as 6 in. deep. The theory is that the roots go down through the sand into the richer compost mixture. For a taprooted plant this is a fine arrangement; some fibrous rooted plants that don't make it all the way down sometimes suffer in drought, and without care, you will lose them. Since the plants are growing very lean, it is sometimes hard to tell the difference between 'tight' and 'dying.' Irrigation is minimal since the sand tends to retain some moisture. Average rainfall is over 40 in. with quite a bit coming as summer thunderstorms. I may have to water these beds two times a year. This is usually when I feel desperate, not when the plants are telling me anything special. Other variations on the theme: some raised beds have been made starting with a "compost heap" of upturned sod with no ground level rock. This is the easiest to make, but building up the pile can take a year or so. In one bed I have incorporated tufa donated by a kind friend; this is the nearest I have gotten to making a miniature landscape. It "fits in" because it looks like one of the exposed boulders the lawn is full of. In another shortlived experiment I made the walls of bales of hay. This had rotted down to mush by the next spring, and I replaced the hay with logs.

For the winter, which begins in November and normally continues until April, I have usually attempted some form of protection. At first, I used evergreen boughs on every bed. They keep the deer off quite well. Deer will eat anything uncovered. Last year I used the previous year's boughs with no needles left on them. These also keep off the deer, hold the snow, and keep off most of the winter sun in a snowless period. Many alpines do not need protection from severe weather, but some definitely rely on it for survival. In 1984–85 I used a canopy open at the sides to keep off winter wetness. That very snowless winter no snow settled on the bed as I had planned, and the resulting wind tunnel had an effect like the top of Pikes Peak. My theory was that most alpines do not live in crevices but in places where snow regularly gets blown off. At the time of writing this seems to have partially worked; the *Eritrichium howardii* survived but *E. nanum* var. *jankae* succumbed. However, *Eritrichium argenteum (E. nanum)* was kept under a light aluminum frame laid directly on the bed; this came through the winter looking greener than the survivor under the canopy.

Generalizations about the Northeast are dangerous, and each of our gardens is unique. The rainfall is certainly adequate with over 40 in. in most places; this has obvious advantages, but it is a hazard when it comes to growing xerophytes, and it makes good drainage imperative. The natural soil drains very quickly in my garden, and I believe soggy soil is the exception in most gardens of the Northeast. Another advantage we have is a strongly seasonal climate, with enough cold to ensure winter dormancy and a spring late enough so that the growing season is not unduly prolonged. The negative aspects of this are the unreliability of the winter. Sometimes there are dangerous thaws, and the snow cover varies a lot from year to year. My garden is 1,400 ft. high, so it tends to escape some of the summer mugginess, and the snow is usually deeper and stays longer.

A disadvantage of a good winter for plants is the effect it has on humans. Too short a growing season and too long a winter could make one consider alternative pursuits. Perhaps the most discouraging aspect of gardening in New England is wildlife depredation. This is inevitable, continuous and without solution; the toll of plants and records (labels) is severe. Perhaps every

PLATE 31

Opuntia polyacantha
Photo by Pat Pachuta

Opuntia basilaris
Photo by Sharon Sutton

Echinocereus reichenbachii var. *perbellus*
Photo by Deane Hall

Opuntia erinacea
Photo by Sharon Sutton

PLATE 32

Taylor desert garden
Photo by Pat Pachuta

Taylor desert garden
Photo by Joel Spingarn

Coelogyne ramossisima in Arizona desert
Photo by Deane Hall

Mystery Valley, Arizona
Photo by Deane Hall

Arenaria obtusiloba
Photo by Karen Trout

region has a similar problem, Mercifully, we do not have the slugs of Seattle to contend with. The region is also blessed with trees. I believe Rocky Mountain plants should not be grown near trees—not in their shade nor below their drip and their droppings. Convention has it that gardeners require privacy and summer shade; worse, that their rock gardens should be cluttered with dwarf conifers and rhododendrons. Mountain plants ought to get plenty of light, and this problem may also be without solution other than to limit one's plants to those that tolerate semiwoodland conditions. This obviously eliminates *Eritrichium howardii.*

As for specific results, there have been successes with plants from all parts of the region, from Arizona and New Mexico up to southern Alberta—also many failures. I shall end with a list of plants I have tried at various times with mixed success; they are roughly grouped according to difficulty.

First, a group of plants that could be grown in the Northeast with normal care:

Arenaria fendleri and *A. kingii* are a foot tall and grassy and introduce a clumpy look into the rock garden. *Arenaria (Minuartia) obtusiloba* and *A. hookeri* form mats.

The anemones and pulsatillas seem to require no special care. *Anemone cylindrica, A. drummondii* and *A. multifida;* also *Pulsatilla (Anemone) patens* and *P. (Anemone) occidentalis.*

Artemisia frigida is a flat mat.

Callirhoe involucrata is an easy garden plant.

Draba oligosperma, D. crassifolia, D. fladnizensis, D. lonchocarpa, D. densifolia are all very good but not great.

Gaillardia aristata is a beauty and easy, though I lost it after three years.

Geum (Erythrocoma) triflorum and *G. rivale.* Interesting.

Hymenoxys (Actinea) acaulis and *H. (Tetraneuris) argentea.* The latter may be annual, the former is a beautiful horse.

Ipomopsis (Gilia) aggregata is worth growing even though biennial; it self-sows in gravel and returns. This is 3 ft. tall so needs the right place. There are other gilias, but I don't know their provenance.

Iris missouriensis. I grow this rather inappropriately under a maple, but it has lasted for years and flowers faithfully.

Phacelia sericea is easy enough from seed though I have not kept any one plant for long. Some of the forms are exquisite, others just run-of-the-mill. The best form I ever had was a tight, white-green mat with a 3 in., powder blue spike.

Silene acaulis doesn't flower every year for everybody.

Saxifraga oppositifolia is OK if you have a place where kabschias will grow.

Townsendia eximia, T. parryi, T. exscapa are easy from seed. *Townsendia parryi* is not permanent and so far there is no self-sowing.

Next, some plants worth growing which probably need raised bed treatment at least; some may be better off in a container that can be put in a cold frame for the winter.

I am growing *Androsace chamaejasme* in a pot which is pushed under the eaves in winter.

Aquilegia saximontana. Although variable in form, some plants are reliable.

Calyptridium (Spraguea) umbellatum now self-sows in a raised bed. This was hard to get going.

Claytonia megarhiza. You have to get hold of it first. Grows in a pot.

Chrysopsis villosa needs a raised bed.

Eriogonums. If you can get the seed to germinate and the seedlings transplanted, some are straightforward. *Eriogonum flavum, E. ovalifolium, E. umbellatum* are good.

Lewisia brachycalyx and *L. pygmaea* are easy enough. I had the disconcerting experience of a whole batch of *Lewisia brachycalyx* flowering spectacularly one year and looking miserable the next. Sonia Lowzow of Arizona claims they need a very sandy habitat.

Lesquerellas. I think these need sun and very well-drained soil.

Linanthastrum nuttallii is very capricious. This died out in several locations and produced a gigantic bush in another. No explanation.

Lithospermum multiflorum has a protected spot.

Opuntia fragilis, O. phaeacantha, O. polyacantha, O. rhodantha (O. erinacea var. utahensis), O. humifusa need a raised bed if only to control weeds. They will grow at ground level but quickly become infested with rumex and other creeping weeds. It is not easy to weed out the dandelions. You may have to start again with new pads.

Oenothera caespitosa. I don't know whether this is permanent or not. It is a ravishing beauty whenever you can get the seed.

The penstemons are glorious and vary in difficulty. From the Rockies, using this term loosely, I have grown the following: *Penstemon alpinus, P. angustifolius* (pale bluish leaves and gray-blue flowers), *P. eriantherus* (glorious), *P. aridus, P. albertinus, P. ambiguus, P. fruticosus, P. haydenii* (a weird tangle of ropy stems), *P. humilis, P. procerus, P. confertus, P. caryi, P. cobaea, P. caespitosus, P. eatonii, P. lyallii, P. secundiflorus, P. unilateralis (P. virgatus* ssp. *asa-grayi), P. virens, P. moffattii, P. ellipticus*. The only evergreen shrubby listed above is *P. fruticosus*. Most of the shrubbies winter-burn and take until flowering time in late May to green up in the Northeast. The variety of growth habit makes this a fascinating genus. It is a pity most rock gardeners only grow the *Dasanthera* section and the Eastern weeds.

Zigadenus elegans has flowered here.

Yucca baccata and *Y. glauca* from seed have survived two winters.

Finally, a group of plants to try and try again. Some year success will come.

Aquilegia jonesii has only bloomed once for me. After it bloomed it died. May need coddling indoors to get it to behave, something I am unwilling to do.

Balsamorhiza hookeri germinates without difficulty. Seedlings do not grow very big the first year, survive one winter and fade out during the summer or the following winter. *Mentzelia decapetala* follows a similar routine.

Wyethias likewise.

Douglasia montana. I am sure this is possible; the other douglasias do quite well. I just haven't kept it long.

Hymenoxys grandiflora
Photo by Loraine Yeatts

Iris missouriensis
Photo by Vernon Tomppert

Echinocereus triglochidiatus and *Pediocactus simpsonii.* These are ball cacti and not as easy as some of the opuntias. Opuntias recover from a hard winter without cover, but these two may end up as mush. Well worth trying, though perhaps with a winter cover. They take years from seed.

Eritrichiums. Limited success outside with *E. argenteum* and *E. howardii.* I had one flower that lasted three days. Some people in the East have grown these in pots to the flowering stage but never kept them long.

Hymenoxys grandiflora. When it flowers it is great. It usually dies before flowering and always dies after flowering. When it sets seed it isn't viable.

Kelseya uniflora has been grown in the East (but not by me) once from a cutting and once from seed. To my knowledge it didn't flower and died young.

All lupines worth growing are difficult. I have had many flower but the tendency is for them to die the following spring. Curiously enough, there is often life in the plant at the end of the second winter. *Lupinus argenteus* is a good one.

Mertensia alpina I have had only a short time. *Mertensia franciscana* and *M. paniculata* seem easier. The blue-leaved mertensias attract an insect or a virus that deposits brown blotches on the leaves.

Oxytropis and *Astragalus. Oxytropis campestris, O. deflexa, Astragalus caespitosus (A. spatulatus),* and *Astragalus alpinus.* The easier astragali can be rampant, and I haven't pigeonholed these Rocky Mountain plants yet.

I am growing *Phlox condensata* (*P. caespitosa* ssp. *condensata*), *P. hoodii* and *P. longifolia.* These are very hard to get hold of; very few people have the patience to collect the seed. *Phlox woodhousei* (*P. speciosa* ssp. *w.*) seems easier. *Phlox nana* and the southern forms have not survived for me. Others have kept them going with cuttings.

Polemonium viscosum is easy from seed but doesn't often want to bloom.

Polemonium delicatum is very easy.

I have had *Primula angustifolia* to the seedling stage and *P. parryi* to the flowering stage but not yet for keeps.

Besseya alpina and *Telesonix (Boykinia) jamesii.* Nobody I know has flowered these yet; both are worth growing for the foliage, and of course, the romance.

References
Bailey, Liberty Hyde. 1976. *Hortus third.* Revised and expanded by the staff of the Liberty Hyde Bailey Hortorium. New York: Kashong Publishers.

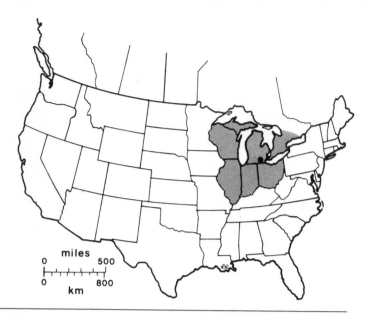

miles
0   500
0   800
km

35

In the Midwest

by Betty Blake

The Midwest seems an unlikely place to grow plants used to the cool air, sharp drainage and high altitudes of the Rocky Mountains, but as many enthusiastic growers know, some of them do very well here.

The low hills and hummocks of the southernmost part of Michigan were formed by debris left by melting glaciers 10,000 years ago. The sand, gravel and clay they carried, along with assorted round rocks, were left in no discernable order. For gardeners of today, this means very good drainage indeed in some places, only tolerable in others. There is little in the way of topsoil, usually only a few inches.

The growing season is 150–160 days long. Annual rainfall, I'm told, averages about 34 in., although it seems to me this has been running behind average ever since I started gardening. Temperatures get as high as 100°F and as low as −20°F; in short, we are in zone 5. Humidity can be high in summer, but not so high that an alpine house is considered a necessity. Snow cover is erratic. Some years there is only a little; other years will see us blanketed from Christmas until mid-March. March is the month when many plants on the borderline of hardiness cross the line and give up the fight. It may be the uncertainty that does them in, the alternate freezing and thawing of standing in melted snow water that cannot drain away because the soil beneath is still frozen solidly.

Altitude is around 900 ft., making it impossible for the high mountain plants to get their full quota of ultraviolet light. This is something we can do nothing about, of course. The tendency is to think that increasing the amount of light will compensate for the lack of intensity, but this does not often work because of the summer heat. Plants are likely to be heated well beyond their capacity to cope. This is where the contour of the land becomes important. Soil on a north-facing slope stays cooler than soil on the level, and the slope also helps to provide good drainage and improved air circulation. In Michigan summers, air often needs a bit of a push. High shade during the hottest part of the day is standard procedure, and it works as well here as anywhere. Some of the successes and a few of the failures—how soon we forget these—among the Rocky Mountain plants I have tried are these:

Germination was good the only time I was able to get seed of *Androsace chamaejasme.* I planted out and saw flowers on ten of them, all the size of marbles. The fragrance was wonderful, and I thought the hardest part was over, but before the summer was gone, all had disappeared. They were

Betty Blake was born and educated in Kansas where she earned a BA degree in botany. She began gardening in Michigan where she joined AGS in 1960, ARGS a year later, and "has not had a plant-free moment since." Her large Michigan garden includes natural woodland, numerous screes, rock walls and extensive rockwork. North American plants form an important nucleus in the garden, which contains plants from all over the world. She now serves on the ARGS board.

on the north slope, but without enough shade—a hard way to learn.

Androsace septentrionalis looks like a dear in the mountains, but after the first day or two of bloom, like a weed in Michigan. It is a self-sowing annual.

Aquilegia caerulea is a stunner. It is really too large for the rock garden, but the gorgeous blue and white flowers carried so gracefully are hard to resist. Nothing could be easier.

Aquilegia formosa is also easily grown and too large, but the perky shape of the flowers and their bright red and yellow colors ensure it a place somewhere in the garden.

If you must have problems, *Aquilegia jonesii* is just the plant for you. In the wild, where it grows to 8 in. across, covered with bloom, it looks easy. In the Midwest we have found it possible to grow, and some have even seen a few flowers. It stays a 2 or 3 in. huddle of blue-green leaves, which are beautiful in themselves, but it seldom looks really happy. The best bloom on the happiest plants I have seen were growing in a trough with other lime-lovers. The rich purple flowers are worth a bit of a bother to see.

Aquilegia saximontana is another tiny one from the high mountains, easier to grow and to flower than *A. jonesii*. Bright green leaves set off blue-and-white flowers on a 4 in. plant. It has not been long-lived, staying only two years.

My experience with *Aquilegia scopulorum* has been somewhat happier, though I am still learning how much shade it will take and still flower. The foliage makes a gray-green mound 5 in. in diameter. Flowers are borne just above and are fully 3 in. long. A soft blue and white, it is a sight to behold. In full sun, there are many more flowers than in shade, but the plants tend to die shortly after bloom.

Calochortus maweanus (*C. tolmiei*) was with me long enough to bloom, and *C. nuttallii* lived another year, but these are not for us.

Caltha leptosepala, the beautiful marsh marigold of the Rockies, has not done well at all. It bloomed one year, its first, and that was the end of that. I am trying it from seed now, and hope for better results. It needs a wet place.

Campanula lasiocarpa is 4 in. high when in bloom, and is said to wander about among rocks. Mine bloomed very well, with good blue bells held nearly upright on 4 in. stems, but did not live long enough to wander. I have grown it several times from seed, so it is possible, if not for very long.

Clematis pseudoalpina from the Beartooths grows to only 4–5 in. there, but in Michigan the height has been more like 2 in., perhaps less. My plant is very small, but has persisted for several years. I hope to see it flower someday.

Corydalis aurea is an annual with grayish finely cut foliage and clear yellow flowers. It seeds itself about and is attractive in the spring, not so attractive later.

Dodecatheon pulchellum is just one of the many shooting stars. They are all easy to grow, to flower and to keep. A more elegant, less fussy group of plants would be hard to find. They will even grow in a wall, but do like moisture in the growing season.

Douglasia montana, from the Beartooths, needs careful attention in our hot summers. High shade is essential, and it is helpful to have a rock to the southwest of it to help keep the roots cool. It blooms well—bright pink flowers right on top of the clump of short pointed leaves. But I have not seen a large plant growing well in Michigan. Mine tend to stay about the size of a quarter.

Draba densifolia is one of the better drabas. It comes easily from seed and produces light yellow flowers on 2 in. stems above a compact bun of gray-green leaves. Mine does well on tufa with a little filtered shade in the afternoon. I have not had difficulty with any of the drabas; the difficulty is in identifying them.

It is easy to grow *Dryas octopetala* and *D. drummondii* from seed, and easy to keep them. I have a dwarf form of *D. octopetala* which is a little less easy, but it has been with me for six or seven years, so is not really difficult. It appears to require a bit more moisture and shade than the others. Transplanting must be done when the roots are growing, which is in early spring or late August. The little oaklike evergreen leaves are attractive most of the year.

Erigeron aureus has yellow daisylike flowers borne singly on 3–4 in. stems. Leaves are gray-green, narrow, forming a loose rosette. It likes the sun and does well here, blooming in the spring, but has not been long-lived.

Erigeron linearis is another yellow one, with truly linear leaves, gray-green, 2 in. long. The flowers are on 5 in. stems, and the whole effect is one of some elegance. It grows in full sun and is perennial with us.

Nice to have, but not extraordinary, are *Erigeron pinnatisectus* and *E. compositus*. These little white, sometimes lavender, daisies are up to 5 in. high, both with finely cut grayish foliage. There was a time when it seemed my whole garden would be taken over by these, but they have lost that first fine frenzy and are well behaved now, growing in sun or part shade.

Erigeron ursinus is a lavender daisy with narrow green leaves. It is quite hardy and has persisted

Erigeron aureus
Photo by Betty Blake

for many years on a north slope between limestone rocks. Nice, but not flashy.

Eriogonum umbellatum is a tiny plant with whitened leaves and beige turning orange-red flower heads on lax 2 in. stems. It was collected from Idaho and lived here two years, blooming once. It probably got too hot, but another has now been installed on a north-facing limestone hill, and I am hoping for the best.

There are other species of *Eriogonum* growing here but without proper names. Some make lovely, large weed-free mats with 10 in. flower stems. Not special, but useful.

Fritillaria pudica, in Montana, has rich yellow bells on 8 in. stems. In Michigan I feel lucky to have kept the plant for three years and to have seen bloom twice in that time. Stems were only 2 in., but that doesn't matter. There are tiny offset plants coming up around the original, evidence that something is going right. There is afternoon shade and full morning sun on a flat area of the usual sand, gravel and clay that underlies everything.

Heuchera hallii has leaves 0.75 in. across with pointed scallops all around. The flowers look like little lilies of the valley, strung along the upper third of an 8 in. stem. A woodland plant, it is easy to grow in a variety of soils and positions.

Lesquerella alpina was here only long enough to show its yellow flowers and to set a seed or two in the inflated seed pod.

Lloydia serotina, a tiny white lily, will have nothing to do with us at all.

The evergreen lewisias with substantial leaves are the ones that survive here: *Lewisia columbiana*, *L. cotyledon* and *L. tweedyi*. The first two have pink, somewhat striped flowers, several on a long stem. *Lewisia tweedyi* produces large pale apricot flowers in profusion, each on a single stem. These have been growing in east-facing situations, and do much better when some compost is worked in nearby.

Lewisia brachycalyx, *L. nevadensis*, *L. oppositifolia*, *L. pygmaea* and *L. rediviva* are sometimes very good indeed, but they are not usually long-lived. They need summer dryness, not always easy to provide. Flowers tend to be thinner in texture than those of the evergreen sorts.

Linanthastrum nuttallii, from Idaho, makes a good show of white phloxlike flowers on 8 in. stems in early summer. It did not reappear the following year, and in general behaved like an annual. Possibly misidentified.

Mertensia lanceolata, a 10 in. high charmer with blue-blue hanging bells, has not been easy to keep. The likely problems: too much heat and too little moisture. This is a real beauty.

An unidentified mimulus from the Sawtooths in Idaho keeps its flat-on-the-ground habit here in the Midwest and produces half-inch yellow flowers over a long period in full sun and moist soil.

Mimulus primuloides has larger yellow flowers on thin 3 in. stems with smooth narrow leaves. This is quite welcome to spread, but does so only slowly, in the same moist soil and sun as the unknown mimulus above.

Penstemon ambiguus
Photo by Betty Blake

Oenothera caespitosa is almost too big and beautiful with its 3–4 in. white flowers on an 8 in. plant. The leaves are long and slender, and the whole thing makes a big splash indeed. Easy to grow but not reliably perennial, it does best in full sun and a fast-draining soil.

Oenothera greggii has large, lemon yellow flowers just above a somewhat untidy collection of leaves and decumbent stems to 4 in. high. It is seldom without a flower during the summer, but is slow to show up in spring.

Penstemons are everywhere in the Rockies, and a surprising number of them do quite well here in the Midwest.

Penstemon ambiguus has phloxlike, glittery-white flowers with a pink reverse on an 18 in. plant. Leaves are gray-green and needlelike. Flowers are produced in profusion over a long period in June and July. This is one of the best for a hot sunny spot—a real beauty.

Penstemon aridus has blue flowers on an 8 in. stem over narrowly spatulate leaves. It is a permanent resident of the garden, but does not increase in size noticeably.

Penstemon caespitosus never gets above 2 in. and has tiny, glossy leaves among which appear 0.5 in. blue-lavender flowers. Here in Michigan, we do not lose it, but even the Denver Botanic Gardens form ('Claude Barr') has been damaged by our winter weather.

Penstemon crandallii, P. linarioides and *P. laricifolius* have needlelike leaves, the first two with decumbent stems and light blue flowers down among the leaves. Not particularly showy, but long in bloom and dependable, despite their delicate appearance. *Penstemon laricifolius* is a wonderful sight in the Bighorns where pink flowers on 8–10 in. stems grow in such large masses that their color can be appreciated. In the garden it is seldom possible to grow them in quantity, and after two years, the plants decline and in another year or two are gone.

Penstemon cyaneus and *P. cyananthus* have some of the best blue flowers to be found, the former on 8 in. stems, the latter on stems a good 12 in. tall. They do not live long here, but usually set enough seed to keep things going.

Penstemon procerus in several varieties as well as *P. virens* produce somewhat similar stems of small blue flowers that are effective in some quantity. Perennials, all.

Petrophytum caespitosum makes a slowly spreading mat of small grayish leaves. The mat is 2 in. high and 10 in. across after five years. Spikes of pale cream flowers appear in July. There have been no problems, only delight, with this evergreen plant for sun and scree.

Phlox diffusa grew slowly from seed to bloom in three years but never had the look of a plant satisfied with life and faded away not long after. Flowers were white, faintly flushed with pink.

Phlox muscoides has mosslike foliage and small white flowers. I am encouraged that it has lived in a north-facing scree for an entire year. This is the first of the mountain phloxes that looks as though it might settle down here.

Phlox purpurea 'Arroyo' spent the winter under a pot filled with oak leaves and is alive, but only

Chaenactis alpina. Photo by Betty Blake

just. *Phlox* 'Tangelo,' with the same treatment, did not survive. (These are sometimes called *P. mesoleuca*.)

Potentilla nivea, from Colorado, stays flat on the ground, its silky, small leaves the main attraction, as I have seen no flowers. It increases very slowly indeed and is thoroughly perennial.

Salix reticulata grows at great heights in the Rockies, and also grows here in the Midwest, given a moist soil and a little protection from sun at its hottest. It will probably never be serious competition to other plants, however.

Silene acaulis does not grow well nor for very long for me, and has bloomed only twice. I have given up on it.

Synthyris missurica has been with me for many years without increasing in size, but it seldom fails to bloom in early spring, producing 8 in. racemes of dark purple over leathery 2 in. round, scalloped leaves.

Townsendias have been great successes here. *Townsendia exscapa* (*T. wilcoxiana*) makes a dense mound of narrow dark green leaves 3 in. high and only a little wider. The large white, or in some years lavender, daisies have stems only long enough to clear the leaves. Soundly perennial, they have started to sow themselves around a bit. *Townsendia rothrockii* was somewhat similar, but did not live another year after blooming. Seed collected in the Bighorns produced very large pink-lavender daisies on 6 in. stems that fell over with the weight of the flower. This was monocarpic, but resowing kept it going for a long time. Seed collected on Galena Summit in Idaho has produced plants with gray-green leaves and large, blue-lavender daisies on 4 in. stems. Flowering continues off and on most of the summer, and the plants are perennial.

Valeriana arizonica is a tiny, spreading-but-not-weedy ground cover with many small, pale pink flowers on 4 in. stems in early spring.

Viola pedatifida is another ground cover, but not always a welcome one. It is attractive, with large violets just above bird's-footlike leaves. It grows in full sun and could easily carpet the entire garden.

Zinnia grandiflora is not much like the multicolored hybrids. It is a perennial, with linear leaves and makes a 10 in. sphere of small yellow flowers from late June until frost. It is blooming here on a limestone scree.

Among the ferns, *Aspidotis densa*, *Cryptogramma crispa* and *Pellaea glabella* grow especially well here. None exceeds 5 in. in height.

Three wishes: I wish it were possible to grow *Chaenactis alpina*, *Eritrichium nanum*, and *Primula angustifolia* right here in my garden.

References

Bailey, Liberty Hyde. 1976. *Hortus third.* Revised and expanded by the staff of the Liberty Hyde Bailey Hortorium. New York: Macmillan Publishing Co.

Harkness, Bernard. 1980. *Seedlist handbook.* 3rd ed. Bellona, N.Y.: Kashong Publishers.

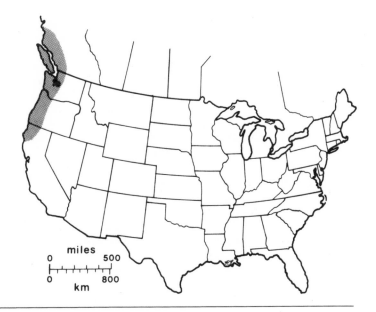

36

In the Northwest

by Betty J. Lowry

The Northwest includes not only maritime climates from Oregon to British Columbia, but also continental east of the Cascades. Since growing conditions and gardeners' experiences over this area vary so much, I cannot speak for the entire Northwest. But I would like to tell you about our garden and climate, and share my experiences with some Rocky Mountain plants and a bit of my philosophy about growing them.

When I think of plants of the Rockies, two types come to mind. The first is the high alpine-dweller, covered with snow for much of the year. Upon emerging, it experiences a short growing season with intense light, cold nights, and cool soil. The second is a plant of the high plains or intermountain valleys at somewhat lower elevations. This plant encounters the continental extremes of a cold, dry winter and a long, hot, dry season with semidormancy in summer. As will be seen, conditions here are very different. Fortunately, many plants are adaptable. Our job is to find the most suitable ones and to make them as happy as we can.

Western Washington is known for its moderate temperatures and high precipitation. In our garden at a 550 ft. elevation, temperatures below 15°F or above 85°F are not common, but they have reached extremes of 0°F and 101°F. Annual precipitation averages 53 in. How and when this moisture falls is where the problem lies.

Most of the precipitation occurs during the winter months, averaging about 35 in. from November through March. Incoming storms carry warm Pacific air, and so most of the precipitation falls as rain. The overall mild conditions encourage many plants to keep their foliage into the winter. The coldest periods are dry and clear and usually without snow cover, and what snow does fall is usually of short duration. Instead of even, dry winter conditions, plants are subjected to long wet periods as well as alternate freezing and thawing. Such stresses, if not actually fatal, damage plants and are especially hard on the hairy-leaved ones. In late winter, some injury results from the frosting of new growth. The worst winter for alpines started with an early period of record cold (0°F) and was followed by torrential warm rains. The best was very dry and more uniformly cold, and gave the

---

Betty J. Lowry and her husband, Ned, have made their home east of Renton, Washington, about 20 miles from Seattle, since 1964. Her gardening interests were first directed toward border plants and gladiolus, but 12 years ago she was bitten by the alpine gardening bug. Since then she has converted most of the lawn and available garden space into rock gardens. The Lowrys have hiked the Washington mountains for 25 years and now extend their travels, plant hunting and seed collecting to other Western states in their search for rare and unusual plant material.

bonus of a protective snow cover during the coldest periods. So the welfare of sensitive alpines in our winter depends on the whims of a particular season. The extreme winter wetness is our greatest problem here. Many plants do not fare well under such open conditions.

Rain can come any time of the year, but occurs frequently in spring, a little bit at a time, so we typically have many cloudy, drizzly days relieved by occasional much-appreciated clear periods. The shock of sudden hot sunny weather following weeks of dull weather is sometimes a problem. Summer is the driest season, with low humidity during clear weather. Storm systems from the Pacific moderate summer temperatures so that we seldom experience the deadly combination of extreme heat and humidity. But no year is average; we may have a wet summer or dry spells in any season.

While winters may be the greatest threat to survival of alpines here, it is the number of dull days during the growing season that makes it difficult to keep them in character. Light intensity reduced by atmospheric filtration at low elevations and the large number of cloudy days produce inadequate insolation, resulting in lush, elongated growth. For plants from dry sunny areas, moist conditions and limited sunlight are more foreign yet, and as a group these are the most difficult of all.

Other common garden problems become magnified here, the corollaries of a mild, high-rainfall area. Slug depredation is the most serious of these, and complete control by baiting never seems possible. Warm moist conditions favor plant diseases, and fungal infections probably account for the collapse of some species. High rainfall and acid soil favor a variety of troublesome cryptogams, of which liverwort and polytrichum mosses are the worst. Fertility, especially in scree soils, decreases rapidly, presumably the result of leaching of nutrients by so much rain.

One way to protect plants from the vagaries of weather is to grow them as pot plants in frame or alpine house. I do this when all else fails, and I also carry winter stock of susceptible species in the frame for insurance. Most of these plants are given no overhead protection during the growing season. Troughs are easily moved or covered in winter, and suit certain plants better than frames or open ground, so these containers are becoming a valuable adjunct to the garden. Plants in the open may also be protected by a pane of glass, or by some cover during cold spells, but I personally use little such *in situ* protection.

My objective is to grow plants in the open garden if at all possible. In the beginning, I needed to decide how best to convert our flat yard of poorly drained, acid clay-loam into a suitable home for alpines. In this climate, we obviously needed to provide excellent drainage and as much sun as

Part of the Lowry garden. Photo by Betty Lowry

possible to keep the plants compact. From the start, *sun* and *drainage* were the watchwords; today, I would add *food* to the list. Our slow-draining soil was clearly unsuitable for alpines, so I chose to excavate this soil to a depth of 1–2 feet, totally replacing it with various mixtures of sand, gravel, and humus or black topsoil. Onto this, the rockwork was laid and more scree piled up, resulting in a system of mounded gardens.

This process of construction, carried out over several years, eventually produced an undulating appearance that relieved the flatness of the site and, more importantly, provided considerable depth of scree. The design offers a variety of exposures, various soil mixtures and some crevices to work with. A small rocky area with underground watering capabilities, euphemistically called the moraine, and a slightly limed tufa garden were also constructed. All these are top-dressed with gravel, which protects the crowns of plants from excess moisture, keeps soil from splashing, and helps control most moss and liverworts which in time grows even on the sunny screes. Other areas of richer, peaty soils complete the spectrum of sites available for experimentation: sunny or shady, moist or dry, rich or lean, heavy or light. From these I try to choose a situation suitable for each Rocky Mountain plant alongside its international cousins. There is never time to experiment as much as I would like. Certain plants have been hard to establish in the garden, but once done, grow nicely for years, so if at first you don't succeed, try again. The season of transplantation and the subsequent weather, until the plant is thoroughly established, are important factors here.

Each of the screes gave excellent results at first, but after a few years, plants failed to grow and flower well. Feeding helps. The oldest of the screes is troubled with ants, whose activity has killed several plants. During dry spells in summer it is necessary to water the screes, but no more so than richer soils elsewhere in the garden. In the future I hope to set aside an area for plants disliking summer moisture that is never artificially watered.

The heavy representation of species from the northern Rockies in this garden is not surprising, since quite a few have been brought home as cuttings or seed. The mountains of Idaho, Montana and Wyoming are more familiar to us than the more distant southern Rockies, but more importantly, the range of many of the northern plants extends to the nearby Cascade and Olympic Mountains. Perhaps such wide distribution also infers a degree of adaptability which makes these more growable in the garden.

Let's start with some plants of the northern Rockies that are amenable to culture in the Northwest. In this category the ericaceous plants are of primary importance, from the forms of *Arctostaphylos uva-ursi*, so valuable a ground cover in a variety of soils, to the choice little shrublets for cool peaty areas. One of my favorites is *Kalmia microphylla*. A superb little glossy-foliaged shrub with typical puckered pink flowers, it is happy in full sun in a damp peaty spot near a pool. The reddish *Phyllodoce empetriformis* and creamy *P. glanduliflora* grow and flower well here, too, but I find *Cassiope mertensiana* and *Gaultheria humifusa* more difficult. Sharing cooler soils are such species as *Erythronium grandiflorum* in the red-anthered form, the little white orchid *Spiranthes romanzoffiana*, the incomparable *Cornus canadensis*, and *Mitella stauropetala*, an elegant species with long one-sided racemes of palest pink snowflakes.

One of the easiest high alpines for scree soils is *Silene acaulis*. Of circumpolar distribution, it is characteristic of the arctic-alpine flora of the Rockies. It is spotted about the garden, a bit from

Silene acaulis
Photo by Betty Lowry

Wyoming here, or Utah there—always a fine green mossy cushion sparingly bespangled with rose pink flowers. A form called *S. acaulis* 'Pedunculata' is the only one that covers itself in bloom every spring as it would in the mountains. The specimen that interests visitors most is an 18-year-old plant from seed (Park Seed Co.!) started long before I was hooked on alpine gardening. Finally given a sunny location on slightly mounded rich scree, this plant is now a rough oval of green mossiness of about 40 in. diameter. This form has quite small flowers, never making a sheet of pink, but offering a sprinkling of bloom from time to time throughout the season, usually after a cool, cloudy spell. This big old plant has been showing signs of decline, and some repair now needs to be made annually. I will be sorry to see it go.

Dryas octopetala and its relatives are very valuable alpines for this area. The larger forms of this species, including its subspecies *D. o.* ssp. *hookeriana,* cover ground alarmingly fast, so I prefer *D. octopetala* 'Minor,' a rock plant of the first order. Smaller yet, and choice enough for a container, is *D. integrifolia,* which is characterized by its entire, revolute leaves and dense habit. Mine has nicely rounded creamy white flowers on 1–2 in. stems. Quite distinct from these is *D. drummondii,* whose deeper green, glossy mats are adorned with half-opened, beguilingly declined flowers of primrose yellow backed by the black, hairy calyx. This plant holds its foliage better through the winter than *D. octopetala,* which is semideciduous.

Other amenable plants of the Rockies which provide excellent mats and cushions of evergreen foliage and flower in most seasons are the white-flowered species *Arenaria (Minuartia) obtusiloba, Petrophytum caespitosum, Saxifraga bronchialis,* and *Thlaspi fendleri* var. *idahoense.* The last is soundly perennial, and has tiny, dark green foliage. Lovely little *Douglasia montana* is more sensitive. Disliking our winter wet, it favors us with its pink flowers only after a dry winter.

It's hard to beat the genus *Draba* for marvelous cushions and buns. Six Rocky Mountain species are represented in our garden. The first two are variable, pectinate-haired species and are sometimes hard to distinguish. *Draba incerta* is an easily grown, tufted gray plant with light yellow flowers, nice but not exciting. *Draba oligosperma* is smaller of leaf, at its best making compact gray cushions and large, deep yellow flowers on short stems. An especially good caespitose form from high elevations of the White Cloud Peaks in Idaho has not settled down in the open garden, but other forms seem easy enough. *Draba ventosa* sports short-stemmed, yellow flowers over a handsome, gray cushion of thick, rounded leaves. *Draba paysonii* var. *treleasii* is similar, but smaller in its parts, forming dense gray buns. This one tends towards rather small, bright yellow flowers that do not open widely. Both of these do best with winter protection. *Draba densifolia* is another yellow-flowered one with a tight, finely textured bun, this time greenish and impervious to all weather. Quite different from all these is *D. oreibata,* an interesting newcomer which shares limestone cliffs with *Kelseya uniflora* in Idaho. In a frame, its small green tufts produce an abundance of relatively large white flowers on 2 in. stems.

Some of the smaller *Aquilegia* species are outstanding among herbaceous Rocky Mountain alpines. Little *Aquilegia saximontana* (the true species) is one of the best, and I also like the small form of *A. shockleyi,* a very dainty red and yellow species. Even *A. jonesii* is not difficult to grow, but flowering it is another matter! I have grown it on scree without protection, in troughs and pots with and without protection, and even in heavily limed pots sunk in scree. Over the years, only three flowers have been produced, and each time the plant has died afterwards. However, its lovely characteristically twisted, bluish foliage is a joy in itself.

Collomia debilis is a fascinating member of the Polemonium family—smelling skunky like one too—which in all its forms dwells strictly on talus slopes. The compact Western *C. d.* var. *larsenii* is probably best known, but it is the large-flowered, deep rose variety from the mountains of western Wyoming that has made itself most at home on our moraine. This variety has been listed as *C. d.* var. *ipomoea* (Hitchcock et al. 1971), but is now included in *C. d.* var. *debilis* (Cronquist et al. 1984). Part of its considerable value lies in its late flowering in July to August. As grown here, the loose, glandular hairy plants may be as much as 4 in. tall. Brought home from the mountains as cuttings, it now seeds itself sparingly. Each plant is fairly short-lived. A good lavender-blue form recently brought back from low elevations of Idaho has kept its foliage though the winter and flowers in May. Whether it will seed itself remains to be seen, but all are relatively easy from cuttings. The dark blue anthers of all forms add considerably to the attraction of the flowers.

If I were granted the ability to grow just three genera of the Rocky Mountain plants, I would choose *Penstemon, Phlox,* and *Eriogonum,* and how well-stocked the garden would be! Each of these is rich in choice species suitable for the rock garden, and to me they most represent the essence of western American mountain plants. Alas, many of these cannot be called easy in cultivation.

One of my first loves was the genus *Penstemon.* The Northwestern members of the Dasanthera (shrubby) group have been a cornerstone of our garden, but of these, only *Penstemon fruticosus* reaches the Rockies. This is an easy and floriferous plant in its various forms, and it benefits from hard

Collomia debilis var. *ipomea.* Photo by Betty Lowry

shearing to help keep it compact. Regretfully, attempts to introduce *P. montanus,* with its large mats of purple, and the smaller, gray-haired gem *P. montanus* var. *idahoensis,* have failed.

In my opinion, the major contribution of Rocky Mountain penstemons comes not from the shrubby group, but from several other sections, each represented by small exciting species, often vivid blue. To me, the most desirable of all are the Ericopsis penstemons, which have mats of small, sometimes needlelike foliage and rather characteristic, wide-mouthed, short-tubed flowers. One of the great joys in the early years was *Penstemon crandallii* ssp. *glabrescens,* which flourished briefly on a south-facing scree. Its mat of narrow green foliage adorned with sky blue flowers was lovely. *Penstemon laricifolius,* with more upright stems of pale lavender flowers, was happy in a container without winter protection for several years. More recently, Ericopsis penstemons have refused to accept our screes so troughs are the safest place for them. Three distinct types currently grown in this way are *P. caespitosus* 'Claude Barr,' with flat mats of deep green, oval foliage, *P. caespitosus* ssp. *suffrutescens* (now *P. tusharensis*), with looser mats of oval, gray foliage, and *P. linarioides* ssp. *coloradoensis,* with glaucous, needlelike foliage. All these are blue-flowered.

Many other desirable small penstemons have come and gone in our garden. Several outstanding kinds accepted a newly constructed sunny section which consisted of several inches of sand and gravel mixture over a well-drained soil. One of the most outstanding was *Penstemon caryi,* with dark green basal foliage and 8 in. stems of large, bright blue flowers. *Penstemon angustifolius,* blue-flowered over narrow glaucous foliage, was also very fine for a time. There was enough success with *P. nitidus*—that unforgettable little species with piercing azure flowers over gray-blue leaves—to ensure that the struggle goes on. In the same bed, even *P. ambiguus* grew and flowered. It is a unique linear-leaved species with pale lavender pink flowers, each with face so round and flat that it looks more like a phlox than a penstemon except for the oblique tube. It was possible to grow these dryland species here once, so their cultivation in the Northwest is well worth attempting.

The smaller phlox of the Rockies offer so much promise in the wild; minutely foliaged mats and buns are covered with fragrant, near-stemless flowers large for the size of the plant. They also offer a big challenge, at least to me. Most of these plants have not taken kindly to sunny screes in the open garden, but troughs or containers please some of the more fussy ones, or at least make their survival possible. As much as any genus, phlox grow out of character here, whether in garden or trough.

Of these species, *Phlox diffusa* is the easiest to establish in the garden. It makes good green mats with white-to-blue flowers, but seldom flowers profusely for me. *Phlox hoodii,* a tiny-foliaged drylander, was difficult to establish on scree, but now one plant of the blue form has firm footing, and flowers regularly. For a time, a lovely dwarf Arizonan with marvelous deep pink flowers edged white, tentatively identified as *P. amabilis,* grew and flowered in the open garden, but sadly has now departed.

Cultivation in troughs gives the best results for some phlox. Two mat-forming species, white *Phlox pulvinata* and an unidentified deep purple one from Idaho, possibly *P. kelseyi,* can be quite floriferous. More than other species, the dense little buns of *P. muscoides* and *P. condensata* lose their uniquely congested form in cultivation. These two also are sparsely flowered.

Eriogonum offers a number of choice mat- and cushion-forming species, many of them with excellent silver foliage. The new flowers are attractive, but sometimes secondary to the wonderful foliage. However, one of the most striking plants I have ever seen was *Eriogonum ovalifolium* var. *nivale* with its old flowers aged bright red over the white cushion. Acquiring these plants has been rather slow because cuttings seem more difficult to root than most other natives, and seed is not easily obtained.

Two distinct varieties of *Eriogonum umbellatum* have established in the garden and flower each year. *Eriogonum umbellatum* var. *umbellatum* forms rather loose mats of green foliage bearing numerous heads of bright yellow flowers. The leaves take on burgundy tints in winter. *Eriogonum umbellatum* var. *subalpinum (E. subalpinum)* is much more compact, with smaller leaves appearing lighter green from the denser tomentum beneath. Its red flower buds open into heads of cream. *Eriogonum ovalifolium* var. *nivale* is one of the whitest-foliaged plants in our garden, and makes an especially pretty picture as the red buds emerge. Unfortunately, in the garden its cream flowers never age to red, just a rusty color. Difficult to establish at first, this species now seems secure, although its foliage looks rather bedraggled in winter. *Eriogonum caespitosum* is another very desirable, small, silver-foliaged species, but it abhors the open screes so far. In the meantime it is a handsome trough dweller to accompany the fussy phlox and penstemon. Several other gray-leaved eriogonums from dry areas of the Pacific states look promising on the scree, which bodes well for the introduction of more Rocky Mountain species in the future.

Eriogonum ovalifolium var. *nivale.* Photo by Betty Lowry

Like any alpine buff given the chance, I have tried my hand at growing some of the traditionally touchy, elite plants needing winter protection. *Eritrichium nanum* and *E. howardii* are so sensitive to winter moisture that a simple roof over their heads is not enough in a wet winter; the moisture content of the air is enough to kill them. After growing a Wyoming form of *E. nanum* alongside two seed-grown European forms, I cautiously suggest that the European forms are more difficult. *Kelseya uniflora*, that superb pink-flowered polster, is another fine plant that requires close attention to detail; I've lost mine. The exciting, diminutive peas of *Trifolium, Astragalus* and *Oxytropis* form another elite class deserving royal treatment. The exquisite forms—furry white cushions, hard gray pads, pancake-thin green films—all studded with jewellike flowers, are truly compelling. All have so far resisted my attempts to grow them outside. There are many other fine species which prefer and deserve winter protection, of which *Polemonium viscosum*, most of the townsendias, and *Primula rusbyi* and *P. angustifolia* are only a few.

I have reserved one container protected from winter wet for plants of the Great Basin. *Oenothera lavandulifolia* is of small stature, with exceptionally beautiful, bright yellow blossoms, crinkled and rather square in shape. *Lesquerella tumulosa*, such a tight gray bun in Utah, grows loosely, but is generous with its yellow flowers. Two varieties of *Silene petersonii* also seem happy in this container, both small plants with large deep pink flowers and narrow, glandular leaves. Both from Utah, the smaller greenish *S. p.* var. *minor* comes from red limestone areas at sunbaked lower elevations, while the grayer variety *S. p.* var. *petersonii* inhabits white limestone slopes at alpine heights. Neither has probably ever seen a slug in nature, but here they are sought by these pests like the choicest campanula.

It would be a pity to do without the huge pink or white cactuslike blooms of *Lewisia rediviva.* All it asks is total dryness in summer. It is spectacular each year when given a container of its own which is dried off completely from the time seeds mature until about November, when it is exposed to all weather until the growth cycle is again complete.

My original approach—trying to grow most plants on scree—seems to have its limitations. Many fascinating plants dwell in very heavy soils, so shouldn't such soils be tried if drainage can be provided? The dry wall or sloping site with a surfacing of gravel or grit to ensure dryness at the crown are two possibilities. Encouraging results with several silver-foliaged Western plants in a dry wall and with *Penstemon caespitosus* and *Hymenoxys acaulis* var. *glabra* in heavy, unimproved soils at the top of the wall suggest that this approach is worth pursuing.

I have much to learn about new plants and new techniques, by more experimentation of my own and by sharing other gardeners' experiences. One has only to look at the magnificent container plants grown by Steve Doonan and Phil Pearson at Grand Ridge Nursery in Issaquah, Washington, to understand that excellent specimens of some tricky plants can be grown without protection, so winter wetness alone cannot be blamed for some failures. These innovative growers freely share their knowledge and ideas about soil components, drainage, watering, feeding, and control of disease and pests. Anyone who experiments and pays strictest attention to detail will surely succeed with many of these plants. No plant is unsatisfactory, only the conditions for growing it. For those incomparable cushions for which this climate is irreconcilable, we must be content with our best efforts to grow them in pots with protection, and must visit them in their native homes to see them at their best.

37

In Great Britain

by Eric Hilton

The range of American plants I grow is determined by the contents of nurserymen's catalogs and, more importantly, by the availability of seed in society exchanges. Nurserymen tend to look to European and Asiatic species for their main stock, and I know of none in Britain specializing in New World plants. Though typical genera like *Phlox, Penstemon* and *Lewisia* are widely grown, they are more frequently represented by cultivars than species.

The seed exchange lists do something to correct this deficiency, but they leave large areas relatively untouched and many genera seriously undersubscribed. The reason is not far to seek: it is our pleasure to see plants while they are in flower. A much more dedicated effort is needed to seek them out when they are in seed, and then comes the problem of identity. Both botanical skill and local knowledge are needed, and this lack of knowledge—ARGS membership is much too thin in some crucially important states—is a serious handicap to a wider appreciation of the Western flora.

I must also refer to the geography of my garden. We are on a limestone ridge overlooking the valley of the River Severn at a point where the river is broadening into its estuary. Though only 400 ft. above the river level, we seem to catch every wind that blows, making it a cool garden in a part of the country generally regarded as one of the milder areas. The high pH, around 8.2, and the fact that so many Rocky Mountain plants are from acid soils creates problems that can be met only by providing special conditions for those intolerant of lime. Lime-free soils and grits can be obtained at a price from other areas and used in troughs, planters and raised beds. In the latter I use sheets of polythene to separate the native soil below from the imported mixtures above. This sheeting can be used to advantage since, laid on a slope, it provides a relatively dry soil at the top of the slope and, by arranging a lip at the bottom, a moist, even wet area for such plants as *Mimulus tilingii* and *Caltha leptosepala* at the bottom. Larger lime-free beds are more difficult to provide, and they depend heavily on the use of large quantities of peat into which pockets of nutritious composts are placed for the accommodation of the plants. Here there are no polythene barriers. My assumption is that once a plant is established, its roots can penetrate the 9–10 in. acid layer into the limy soil below without serious ill-effect. But this is not an ideal arrangement, and deep-rooted subjects sometimes show signs of chlorosis.

Our 30–35 in. of rain are spread unpredictably throughout the year. Summers are particularly untrustworthy. One year I may lose many plants that will not tolerate drought, and the next, many of

---

A retired schoolmaster, **Eric Hilton** has become a full-time gardener on his large garden overlooking the Severn River near Bristol, England. He attended the First Interim International (Seattle-Vancouver) Conference and was so captivated by what he saw that he has since paid five long visits to the American Mountain West, visiting dozens of Western mountain ranges. He has described his travels in a series of articles for the bulletin of the Alpine Garden Society of England, and is a well-known lecturer on American plants in that country.

Phlox hoodii. Photo by Loraine Yeatts

those which prefer to be dry. Temperatures, too, fluctuate widely, and a mild winter with little snow may be followed by one in which plants are at the mercy of long spells of low temperatures and bitter winds, often without the protection of snow.

My glass houses are now devoted entirely to propagation. Mature plants must go outdoors. While I endeavor to shield vulnerable plants that cannot easily be replaced, the majority must cope as best they can. Growing much from seed and cuttings, I usually have enough stock for experiments, so in potting up young plants I like to try different soil mixtures. I am particularly interested in testing adaptability to limy conditions. The results are sometimes curious. Species phlox clearly resent lime, but cultivars are usually quite indifferent, yet of 24 cuttings of *Phlox* 'Kelly's Eye'—12 of which were put into an acid mix and the other 12 into a calcareous one—all the former grew strongly while all the latter died. But the parent plant grows on a limy bed.

Of the species, I have *Phlox missoulensis* (*P. kelseyi* var. *m.*), grown from seed given me by Klaus Lackschewitz who lives in Missoula, Montana; *P. bifida,* which grows well in both its blue and white forms; and *P. diffusa* and *P. hoodii,* which are only shadows of the magnificent plants I have seen in the wild. *Phlox kelseyi* flourishes, but I sometimes suspect that it is not the true species. I have *P. nana* from Paul Maslin's seed, and it has almost taken over the trough in which it grows, but for the last two years my own seed has been infertile. This seems to have resulted from unusually dry growing conditions. I have *P. ensifolia* and *P. lutea* too, but by comparison their growth is weak. I am more hopeful about *P.* 'Mary Maslin.'

The related polemoniums present strong contrasts. While the pretty *Polemonium pulcherrimum* is over-enthusiastic and provides more adventitious seedlings than I like, *Polemonium viscosum* has so far refused to flower, and *P. brandegei* never provides the display that Conference visitors will see on the Trail Ridge Road. *Polemonium delicatum* seems impermanent, though I feel sure that it should not be so, and *P. carneum* has also not been long-lived.

Of the many *Ipomopsis* species, I have had only *I. aggregata* (formerly *Gilia*). This can be more effective in the garden than in the wild; a concentrated stand gives a much finer display than one that is more dispersed. I do not find it a true perennial, however, and this year my efforts to maintain continuity have been defeated by the loss of young plants over-wintering in frames. But old seed has germinated.

It is scarcely possible to grow more than a selection of the many penstemons that are available, and one tends to favor the more compact species. Nevertheless, I find these more difficult to grow, and while I have no trouble with such vigorous types as *Penstemon serrulatus, P. procerus, P. rydbergii, P. richardsonii, P. secundiflorus, P. venustus, P. wilcoxii, P. alpinus* and *P. jamesii,* I have not succeeded with *P. caespitosus, P. newberryi* and *P. crandallii. Penstemon hallii* seed seems reluctant even to germinate. *Penstemon rupicola* has now established itself, but has only recently begun to flower satisfactorily.

Lewisia rediviva. Photo by Betty Lowry

Penstemon rupicola and *P. pinifolius* seem to resent lime but usually penstemons accept it; *P. heterophyllus* appears to enjoy it.

In the same family, I have never kept *Synthyris pinnatifida* for very long, but *S. missurica* and *S. reniformis* are stayers. The pedicularis species seem to be impossible, but I sometimes get good germinations of castillejas and try to associate them with what might be suitable host plants, but I have not yet flowered one. *Mimulus tilingii* grows with abandon in a really wet spot.

The lupines are notorious for their aversion to lime. The tall species remind one too much of the dowdy pre-Russell lupines, and for me they are not worth garden space. But the small ones are challenging treasures, and I grow what I can get under such names as *Lupinus lepidus*, *L. lobbii* (*L. lepidus* var. *lobbii*), *L. breweri* and *L. aridus* (*L. lepidus* var. *aridus*). I am never quite sure which is which, but all respond to trough rather than pot treatment. Even so, they seem to be almost monocarpic and need to be constantly regenerated from seed. Indeed, they will often self-sow given a gritty mix.

I have to take particular care with plants that in nature are accustomed to dry summer conditions. The lewisias that aestivate—*Lewisia brachycalyx*, *L. rediviva*, *L. nevadensis*, *L. pygmaea* and *L. sierrae*—I cannot grow in the open garden but must restrict them to troughs over which plastic sheeting can be placed during their vulnerable months. *Lewisia tweedyi* must be treated similarly or the caudex quickly rots. The various forms of *L. columbiana* are much tougher (even more so than the *L. cotyledon* forms), and I do not find protection at all necessary. No protection is needed for *Claytonia megarhiza* nor *C. nivalis* (*C. m.* var. *n.*), though drainage must be kept very sharp. With *C. lanceolata* I have had no success, but this year I have flowered *Hesperochiron pumilus* and *H. californicus* for the first time. *Calyptridium (Spraguea) umbellatum* always delights me, but it does not persist, and I am at present without it.

One could devote a great deal of space to the composites; there are some very worthy plants among them. *Erigeron aureus* I rate as one of the best plants in my garden, often in flower as early as April and as late as December. Another yellow species, *E. linearis*, is not so weatherproof though almost equally attractive, and I must take care to have plants in reserve. Of the blue erigerons, *E. pinnatisectus* is an excellent grower, and of the whites, *E. flettii*, *E. simplex*, *E. leiomerus* and *E. compositus* are also attractive, though the rayless form of the latter, *E. compositus* var. *discoideus*, has little merit. I am now trying out some taller species including *E. coulteri* and *E. speciosus*. I am doing better with the townsendias than I used to, but still find them short-lived. The asters seem less distinguished, and though *A. alpigenus* is a first rate plant, I'm afraid I threw out *A. porteri*, which was once recommended to me. *Eriophyllum lanatum* always earns its keep—a tough plant if ever there were one—but I have to put it where its virile seedlings can do no harm. *Haplopappus (Tonestus) lyallii* and *Heterotheca villosa* are two more valuable space fillers, but *Hymenoxys acaulis* and *H. grandiflora* flower and then die—a pity, for they give an excellent display. *Ratibida columnifera* and *Helenium (Dugaldia) hoopesii* need to be

Saxifraga serpyllifolia ssp. *chrysantha*. Photo by Loraine Yeatts

accommodated in the herbaceous border. I once had *Arnica nevadensis*, *A. chamissonis* and *A. cordifolia* there too, but their rapacious root systems soon made them unwelcome, and I grubbed them out though they did not yield without a struggle. *Solidago spathulata* is worthwhile, however, especially in its variety *nana*.

The Liliaceae contain some of the most desirable of plants and also some of the more difficult, and of the fritillaries I have been modestly successful only with *Fritillaria pudica*. I am inclined to think that in the past I have been too cautious with the calochortus species, growing them under cover and with dry periods probably too rigidly observed, but I now have *Calochortus weedii* and *C. leichtlinii* growing well in a raised bed, and I wish I could resurrect some others I have lost.

Trilliums do well in the peat gardens. The commonest Rocky Mountain species, *Trillium ovatum*, has now made a good patch in a drier position than I would have chosen with hindsight. There is no problem with *Smilacina racemosa* or *S. stellata*. The latter was introduced adventitiously and is now spreading quickly under dwarf shrubs in a peat garden to make quite good ground cover, though it lacks the scent and grace of *S. racemosa*. *Disporum hookeri* is slowly taking hold but does not grow as freely as its relative *Uvularia grandiflora*, which is completely happy both in sun and in shade. My only complaint with it: its seed pods are invariably empty. *Zigadenus paniculatus* flowers freely, and *Tofieldia glutinosa* is now reaching that stage. *Erythronium americanum* once multiplied generously but never flowered, and now it seems to have died out, but I have a very good patch of *E. grandiflorum*. Many of the *Brodiaea-Triteleia* genus complex are almost too easy and threaten to become a nuisance. But there are some charmers, especially the *Brodiaea coronaria* var. *macropoda* collected by Wayne Roderick of El Cerrito, California. I am wary of alliums, and since *Allium cernuum* began to proliferate, it has had to be banished; but *A. geyeri* has been well behaved, and I am pleased with a pretty newcomer, *A. siskiyouense*. The loss of a strong plant of *Xerophyllum tenax*, probably a consequence of the dry summer of 1984, was a disappointment.

For many years I have had the two forms of *Telesonix (Boykinia) jamesii*—that from Pikes Peak and the limestone version that festoons the limestone crevices of Medicine Wheel in the Bighorns. Both flower well, but not all Saxifragaceae have flourished. I cannot grow *Saxifraga chrysantha* and *S. flagellaris*, though *S. bronchialis* and *S. integrifolia* do well. The heucheras grown in the United Kingdom are usually the colorful hybrids developed by the nurserymen Blooms of Bressingham Nursery, Norfolk, England, but the species have a quiet charm, and *Heuchera hallii*, *H. grossularifolia*, *H. bracteata* and *H. cylindrica* all have their places in the garden. Their cousin *Lithophragma parviflorum* can be rather invasive and another relative, *Tellima grandiflora*, is a positive menace unless it can be restricted to an area where it can colonize at will.

The Primulaceae are best represented in my garden by the dodecatheons, and I have all the Rocky Mountain species with the exception of *D. redolens* (*D. jeffreyi* var. *r.*). The primulas, androsaces

Papaver kluanense
Photo by Loraine Yeatts

and douglasias are a different story. Of the androsaces I have none. The douglasias come and go, though a good stock of young plants gives hope for the future of *Douglasia montana*. *Primula angustifolia* is making progress too, and I am hoping it will be less reluctant to flower than *P. parryi* which does not get the plentiful moisture at the roots which it so obviously enjoys in nature. *Primula ellisiae* and *P. rusbyi* are easier, and I usually manage to collect a pinch of seed.

I wish I had a wider range of the American violas. *Viola pedatifida* flowers well, and now that I grow it in a very sandy soil, *V. pedata* has established itself. But I have lost *V. canadensis,* have *V. adunca* only in white, and *V. nuttallii,* though it is growing well, has not yet bloomed. Over the rest I will draw a veil.

The Ranunculaceae are so well represented in the Rockies that there is much to choose from, but of the genus *Ranunculus* proper, I have only a tiny creeping species that may be *R. natans.* Seed of the aquilegias is much more easily available, and I have *Aquilegia brevistyla, A. caerulea* and its variant *A. c.* var. *daileyae, A. elegantula, A. formosa, A. triternata, A. saximontana, A. scopulorum, A. scopulorum* var. *perplexans,* and *A. shockleyi.* I am making yet another effort with *A. jonesii.*

I am very fond of the dwarf delphiniums. The one that grows best came to me under the name *Delphinium orfordii,* apparently a small form of *D. nuttallianum.* After years of patient waiting my plants of *Clematis hirsutissima* are now flowering, but *Pulsatilla (Anemone) occidentalis* and *Anemone drummondii* never seem to get beyond the seedling stage. I have occasional success with *Pulsatilla (Anemone) patens,* but *Anemone parviflora, A. zephyra, A. multifida* and *A. cylindrica* are my standbys. What I felt to be a minor triumph this year was the flowering of *Caltha leptosepala.* I had waited a long time!

The western United States has some very good drabas, and I am glad to have a number of them, though I am not always sure that they are what they purport to be. The general likenesses are such that in cultivation there is much mistaken identity. However, I believe that my *Draba densifolia, D. ventosa, D. crassifolia* and *D. oligosperma* are true to name. I used to have *D. paysonii* but found it difficult to keep. Another crucifer, *Erysimum asperum,* is over-exuberant, but it is a gay thing, and I am content to allow a few to flower each year. *Erysimum nivale* also appears to be monocarpic, but there are no bonus plants here, and it would quickly disappear if I did not collect seed. Our climate does not suit the lesquerellas and physarias, and though I had *Smelowskia calycina* for some years, it has now departed.

Mertensia viridis
Photo by Loraine Yeatts

I take pains to keep the delicate *Papaver kluanense*, though it is desperately vulnerable and short-lived. The wild *Potentilla fruticosa (Pentaphylloides floribunda)* is so much excelled by cultivars that I have ceased to grow the species, but other worthy potentillas have escaped the attention of hybridizers. I once obtained *Potentilla gracilis* when I applied for seed of *Pulsatilla occidentalis,* but I have never regretted the mistake. It is not a spectacular plant, but it has a long flowering season, and seedlings accommodate themselves in odd corners spurned by other tenants. *Geum (Erythrocoma) triflorum* is always around, and *Luetkia pectinata* also does well. *Kelseya uniflora* I cannot grow unprotected, though I have tried it in the tufa which it should enjoy. I like the American form of *Dryas octopetala,* a neater plant than the commonly grown European form, but I cannot get it beyond the seedling stage.

I try to keep *Linnaea borealis* but cannot easily reproduce the rich woodland mold through which it loves to spread. I have given up attempting *Chimaphila umbellata* and the pyrolas, but *Berberis (Mahonia) repens* is now well established in the partial shade of peat-loving shrubs. *Maianthemum dilitatum (M. kamtschaticum)* has a reputation for aggressiveness, but one cannot deny its attractiveness. I have it in a well-drained sunny position on limy soil, and these are probably not optimum conditions, so in fifteen years I have not had to curb its activities.

Phacelia sericea is something of a problem plant in the garden, but I have a good crop of seedlings, and having seen much of it in the wild, I shall attempt to emulate as closely as possible the conditions under which it grows and hope for success. The rather pretty annual *P. franklinii* maintains itself acceptably, but my *P. magellanica (P. heterophylla)* is a dowdy type scarcely worth growing.

I rarely collect plants in the wild nowadays, but in 1976 I brought back a small *Kalmia polifolia* var. *microphylla* along with the wad of soil in which it was growing. It prospered, but it soon had growing with it a seedling *Cassiope mertensiana* and a tiny picea, both of which grew so rapidly that disentanglement became necessary. Alas, only the spruce survived the disturbance, and my only ericaceous species now are the widely distributed *Arctostaphylos uva-ursi, Phyllodoce empetriformis* and, from the Cascades, *Kalmiopsis leachiana,* though this does not thrive.

Many useful plants are too tall for the rock garden, of course, and the herbaceous border is the home of *Iliamna rivularis, Ratibida columnifera, Helenium (Dugaldia) hoopesii, Sidalcea candida* and the taller mertensias. I am very fond of *Mertensia ciliata,* but this has not yet reached the stage of seeding about as does the Eastern *M. virginica.* I am not very successful with the smaller species, for *M. viridis* flowers only sparingly, and the fine *M. alpina* will not even germinate for me. I have grown mentzelias and argemones to the point at which they resent our unwelcome rain, and I have never flowered them. It is either the rain or the cold which causes me to lose sphaeralceas, though one which is new to me promises to be more permanent. *Tradescantia bracteata* is impervious to the weather, but it is so untidy that it is in danger of exclusion. I would like more of the eriogonums for I have only *Eriogonum umbellatum* and one which was supplied (almost certainly erroneously) as *E. jamesii,* but seed is not easy to get. The arenarias, too, can be very desirable, and there are many of them; but there is a certain similarity, and I have restricted myself to four of the most useful species: *Arenaria capillaris, A. congesta, A. (Minuartia) obtusiloba* and the rather taller *A. kingii.*

I look forward to future trips to the American Mountain West, to many successful seed exchanges and to an increased stock of Rocky Mountain plants in the future.

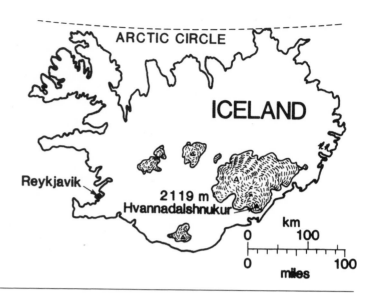

38

In Iceland

by Olafur B. Gudmundsson

Gardening is a fascinating hobby—especially the kind of gardening we could call botanical gardening, that is, collecting and growing wild species from all over the world. Of course, every kind of gardening has its own charm—growing fruits and vegetables, trees and shrubs, annuals and exotic flowers. But I think alpine gardening comes nearest to that previously mentioned category. The alpine gardener is always looking far and high, seeking new acquaintances. This kind of gardening also demands substantial knowledge of such things as botany, geography and geology, so that its practitioners can understand and meet the needs and requirements of plants from different climates, latitudes and elevations. A collector of alpine plants, the botanical gardener is dealing with more plants than those usually listed as garden plants or plants of horticultural value. He may even be interested in plants normally labeled of no horticultural value, or even weeds!

The term alpine is difficult to define. We may say that it is a plant growing in, or on, mountains. That depends on many things, mostly climate, latitude and locality. In northern countries the high alpines of more southern latitudes may be dethroned. For example, the mountain avens, *Dryas octopetala,* or the moss champion, *Silene acaulis,* that you may have to climb a thousand feet for in Colorado, we can pick at our doorstep in Iceland. Even a typical high alpine like the glacier crowfoot, *Ranunculus glacialis,* goes right down to sea level in the northernmost parts of Iceland and in Greenland.

One of the many exciting things in gardening is finding and trying out new plants—new to the area and the climate. The incredible adaptability of many plants to climates and soils quite different from their own is most surprising. I often think of *Anemone blanda:* Who would seriously think of going to Greece for plants to grow in Iceland? Nonetheless, the Balkan anemone has become a beloved garden plant in Iceland, a true and dependable perennial.

Hunting for new plants and trying them out in a horticulturally underdeveloped country like Iceland is an exciting and rewarding hobby. As a member of long standing in the American Rock Garden Society, I could not escape the temptation of Western plants, especially alpines—and here the Rocky Mountains come into the picture. The only way to get hold of these remote plants was to grow them from seed. Through the seed exchanges of the ARGS, the Alpine Garden Club of British

Olafur B. Gudmundsson is a 67-year-old pharmacist, born and brought up in northern Iceland, now living in Reykjavik. He and his wife Elin Mariusdottir have four children and nine grandchildren. He is secretary of the Icelandic Horticultural Society and editor of its annual journal. Of himself he says, "From childhood, as far back as I can remember, I have been interested in flowers. On the farm, where I grew up, I hardly could be used for anything, I always got lost in nature. Finding a new plant, I was almost sure of losing one of the cows! Later on, getting hold of a garden of my own, I became a passionate gardener and plant collector, always trying something new from almost every corner of the world."

Columbia, and a few others, I have been able to get acquainted with some of the gems among American alpines. Of course, there have been a lot of failures, but there have also been successes when least expected—and this pays the bill. This collection and the trials of Rocky Mountain plants in Iceland were made in a very haphazard way, purely for the enjoyment of a hobby. Therefore, the results are equally incomplete, but they may be of interest to some.

Iceland, the Problems and Advantages

Iceland, situated in the North Atlantic between Norway and Greenland just south of the Arctic Circle, is, after Great Britain, the largest island in Europe. Geologically, it is a very young country, thrust up from the mid-Atlantic ridge some 15 million years ago by a series of violent volcanic eruptions.

Until recently Iceland has been remote and little known except possibly for its Viking sagas, its hot springs, and its cold name. Now, in the age of flight, it has become a stepping stone between two continents.

Although its northernmost point just reaches the Arctic Circle, the climate is not as cold as the name of the country implies. It is an oceanic, cold-tempered, island climate. A branch of the Gulf Stream embraces its shores, and that warm embrace makes all the difference. Summers are cool, and the average temperature in July is 51°F. On the other hand, winters are mild with an average temperature in January of 30°F (in the South). That is, I think, almost the same as in New York. Rainfall is heavy in the South, an average of 51.5 in. annually, especially in autumn and winter. Climatic conditions are quite variable, and the weather changes quickly and often. Snow rarely lies long in the lowlands, but on the highland plateau the climate is similar to that in arctic countries.

Growing southern heat-loving plants can be difficult, especially trees and shrubs, due to the lack of warmth during the short summer. But when it comes to growing high alpines, the climate is in many ways favorable, although the long, wet winters often make overwintering these plants difficult. Warm spells during the winter months—long periods of thaw in which growth starts, followed by hard frost—are often catastrophic to young growth.

Many plants are common both to Iceland and to the Rocky Mountains, the so-called circumpolar plants. To name a few, I mention: moss campion, *Silene acaulis;* mountain sorrel, *Oxyria digyna;* black crowberry, *Empetrum nigrum;* purple saxifrage, *Saxifraga oppositifolia;* arctic poppy, *Papaver radicatum; Sibbaldia procumbens;* and of course the koenigia, *Koenigia islandica.* These plants are all very common in Iceland, right down to our doorstep.

Soil and Growing Methods

Our garden is situated on the outskirts of Reykjavik, about 150 ft. above sea level, facing northwest. The soil is mostly rather heavy clay that needs liberal incorporation of peat and sand or grit for growing high alpines. Also, the rock garden beds must be elevated, at least a foot, to ensure adequate drainage. The topsoil in the rock garden beds usually consists of equal parts of clay soil, peat, and fine grit (or coarse grade volcanic pumice). This makes a light, open, friable soil that seems to suit most alpines. In addition, the surface of the beds is covered with 0.5–1.0 in. of grit. This helps to protect the basal leaves and rosettes from too close, often destructive, contact with the wet soil.

Most of our Rocky Mountain plants are grown from seed. Sowing begins in March or April when the weak winter sun begins to warm up the unheated greenhouse on bright days. The species are sown separately in small pots and placed in a box with a plastic dome. The sowing medium is always the same: equal parts sterilized Finnish peat (not fertilized) and fine grade Hekla pumice sand (about ½ pea-size), thoroughly mixed and moderately moistened. At first there are great fluctuations in temperature in the greenhouse, from hard frost in cold spells and up to 70–80°F on bright, sunny days, but soon the temperature becomes more even as spring approaches. Now a slight bottom heat is given, and things begin to happen.

As soon as the seedlings appear, the pots are transferred to a frost-free house ("the Kindergarten"), given a weak fertilizer solution, and eventually receive some artificial light in dark periods. Germination can be very erratic, so seedpots showing no sign of life in the first summer are set aside and kept moist; this operation is repeated the second year, or even the third. This demands a lot of patience, but often it pays off. Who does not know the old story about the lost sheep!

After the usual process of transplanting into flats, the seedlings are either planted individually into small pots, or—if they are big, strong and sturdy—into a coldframe where they spend their first arctic winter under glass. To me it seems a sound practice to let the young plants spend one winter in the shelter of a frame, acclimatizing and forgetting their homelands and origins.

Two kinds of coldframes are in use—one with a regular soil-mix, mentioned before, where plants are planted directly, and another with a pumice-gravel mix, where pots are plunged up to their rim. Both are covered with glass windows during winter. These two kinds of frames, along with the cold greenhouse and the cool greenhouse (insulated and kept just above the freezing point by a small automatic electric fan-heater), supply a kind of life insurance for the new and unfamiliar plants. Some are not even admitted to the open garden for the first two or three years, while they are tried and tested for hardiness in the houses and frames. But sooner or later the big jump has to be taken, and here looms the big question: Is the plant hardy enough to take the Icelandic winters unprotected? Will we have a new, reliable plant for our garden and our climate?

Of course the answer is often negative, but that doesn't mean that we have to abandon the plant altogether—far from it. It can be given some kind of cover during the winter months, or it can be transferred to the frames or the greenhouses and returned to the garden each spring. Choice potted plants can even be transferred from the plunge-frame to a cozy corner in the rock garden, where the rim of the pot is easily covered with the top layer of grit. This isn't cheating—just a sound practice in a harsh world. And the ends justify the means.

By these methods, we have come to know and cherish a great number of foreign species, among them some of the gems of the Rocky Mountain plants. The following is a brief account of the results of our "fiddling" with some of these plants.

Plants, Descriptions and Results

The Jacob's ladder, *Polemonium delicatum*, was, I think, the first of the Rocky Mountain plants tried here in our garden. This beautiful, delicate plant has now made itself at home here and has proved a hardy, reliable garden plant. Later came the skypilot, *P. viscosum*, that now seems equally at home.

Kings crown, *Rhodiola (Sedum) integrifolia*, a close relative to our own native roseroot, *R. (Sedum) rosea*, has also been with us here for many years and proved extremely hardy, as has the blue-eyed-grass, *Sisyrinchium angustifolium*, that seeds itself all around.

The high alpine *Saxifraga adscendens*, with its snow white flowers on slender stems, seems to be monocarpic but keeps going by self-sowing. We would also like to try the snowball saxifrage, *S. rhomboidea*, but we have not yet had the opportunity.

Old-man's whiskers, *Geum (Erythrocoma) triflorum* is quite hardy here, but after roaming the Rocky Mountain alpine tundra, we also would like to try *G. (Acomastylis) rossii*, the alpine avens, to see how it fares in Iceland.

The shooting stars, *Dodecatheon pauciflorum* (*D. pulchellum* ssp. *pauciflorum*) and *D. alpinum*, have both been favorites for many years. They seem to like the climate and perform beautifully.

Some of the fleabanes, erigerons like *Erigeron compositus, E. pinnatisectus* and *E. simplex*, seem quite happy here, too.

A low-growing "*Solidago* sp. from the Rocky Mountains" (so the seed-packet was labeled) has proved very hardy, free-flowering and a splendid rock garden plant. I think it may be *Solidago multiradiata* ssp. *scopulorum*, but I am not sure.

A single plant of *Anemone multifida* var. *globosa*, given to us some years ago, is really enjoying itself in our garden. It is a strong, stout plant with red-tinged flowers, and globose, wooly seed heads.

Some years ago a single, unexpected seedling popped up from one of our seedboxes where some seed from the ARGS had been sown. For a while we could not identify this plant by any means, and even after it had flowered, we could only state that it was a relative of the saxifrages. It was not until we had a visit from a friend from the Rockies that this mystery was solved.

"This is *Boykinia (Telesonix) jamesii* from Pikes Peak in Colorado," he said. And so it was! We had not even dreamt of getting hold of such a rarity. Sometimes we are lucky. This plant is doing quite well in our garden, and also potted in the greenhouse. It seems to like being divided often, and it demands perfect drainage. We like this plant except for touching it, because it is sticky all over with glandular hairs. So, no touching, just looking!

A newcomer to our garden is *Trollius laxus*, a gracious plant, with big, boldly open, golden yellow, long-lasting flowers that come quite early in the spring. I predict that this plant will, in a short time, become very popular in Icelandic gardens. Now we must try to get hold of the Rocky Mountain type, *T. laxus* var. *albiflorus*, to see how well it will take our conditions.

Polemonium viscosum var. *grayanum*. Photos by Loraine Yeatts

Rhodiola rhodanthum

Lewisia pygmaea

Let's now turn to our favorite Rocky Mountain plants, the lewisias. My first meeting with the genus *Lewisia* was some 15 years ago on a clear morning during a stroll through the Botanical Garden in Reykjavik. There my attention was drawn to a glistening white flower on a tiny plant with narrow succulent leaves. This turned out to be *Lewisia nevadensis*, and although this one is not among the showiest of the lewisias, it was love at first sight!

I started by reading all I could find about this genus, and the quest for seed began. In the years following it arrived from far and wide, from friends in Scandinavia, Britain and the United States, from clubs, botanic gardens and various firms such as Jack Drake in Scotland and Far North Gardens in the United States. Out came the seed pans and compost every spring, and this exciting experiment began. How would those "aristocrats of the Rocky Mountains" behave on an island in the shade of the Arctic Circle?

Lewisia nevadensis was an easy prey, setting a lot of seed and prospering everywhere. More difficult was *L. brachycalyx*. I don't even know for sure if we have ever come upon the true *L. brachycalyx*. After trying seed from many sources, we often have ended up with something like *L. nevadensis* on our hands. But we have not given up. Perhaps, someday we will obtain this species.

Lewisia pygmaea is a very variable species. The seedlings are variable both in color and stature, from "dirty" pale pink to rose pink, and some are obviously hybrids. Some years ago the late Don Havens of Milwaukee sent us some roots labeled *L. pygmaea*, collected in the Colorado mountains. Those plants came out with beautiful dark purple flowers. They come true from seed and seem quite hardy.

Lewisia pygmaea ssp. *longipetala* has proved a reliable plant that flowers well, at least in the greenhouse. We have not tried it in the open garden yet.

Lewisia sierrae, a tiny little thing with purple-striped light pink flowers and threadlike leaves seems to thrive in small pots in the greenhouse.

Lewisia columbiana is perhaps the hardiest of the whole lot. That goes for both varieties, *L. c.* var. *rupicola* and *L. c.* var. *wallowensis*. In our rock garden *L. c.* var. *rupicola* has been prospering for the last 10 years and has now sown itself to make a big colony. The larger *L. c.* cv. 'Rosea' seems to do best in pots in the cold house, but can also easily take the winter outside.

Lewisia leana and *L. cantelowii* we have only tried once, and we were not able to keep them alive for more than a year. Better luck next time! From the seed of *L. oppositifolia* we have gotten quite variable plants. It seems difficult to obtain seed of the true species.

Lewisia cotyledon is a chapter in itself. The infinite variety in size, shape and color makes every sowing an exciting event, for one never knows what forms and hybrids may show up. Although typical examples of the species itself and its two named varieties—*L. c.* var. *heckneri* and *L. c.* var. *howellii*—can often be picked out of the flock of seedlings all kinds of intermediates appear. We have long ago quite given up separating them. We just take them as they come and enjoy their company.

Germination of the *L. cotyledon* seed is, in my experience, rather uneven. Sown in early spring, perhaps half the seeds germinate in a few weeks, but the rest not before the next winter or spring. Therefore, we carefully prick out the seedlings for transplanting, trying not to disturb the surface of the seedbox holding the remaining seed. This, of course, demands very thin sowing.

We grow most of these plants in pots in our cold greenhouse where they literally cover themselves with flowers, sometimes two or three times during the spring and summer. They also do reasonably well outside in the open garden, provided they are given perfect drainage. Here on the southwest corner of Iceland, we cannot count on much snowcover during winter and, in my experience, the best cover we can give them is a piece of wood, tilted over the rosettes. But not too close; they need adequate aeration. This seems to me just as good, or even better, than the sometimes recommended pane of glass. Of course, there are winter losses among those "outgoers," but in the houses we also have problems overwintering the potgrown plants. The rosettes frequently rot away from the caudex during the long, damp winter.

The potting soil, used for the whole line of our lewisias, is made up of even parts clay soil, and fertilizer-balanced Finnish peat and grit, sometimes with the addition of some horse or sheep manure. On top of the soil we usually put a 0.5–1 in. layer of fine grit or pumice. Repotting of established plants is usually done every second year. Watering is done from below, using a weak fertilizer while the plants are in growth.

Most of those cotyledon hybrids are very reluctant setting seed (at least in the greenhouse), but hand-pollination seems to give some results. The flowers are very long-lasting, and a vase of cut lewisia flowers is unrivaled.

Lewisia tweedyi is the dream of every rock gardener, or so I am told. Well, it is not my *first* choice. Actually this plant puzzled us a little. We had thought it impossible except under glass, potted in the greenhouse. At first the plants did very well, but in the next 2–3 years they dwindled away one after another. Then we lost our patience and transferred the remaining potted plants to the rock garden—giving them the chance to fall with dignity in the Icelandic winter. But to our surprise almost every one stood the winter—and still do. Of two evils, they chose the arctic winter over the pots! Usually their leaves are badly battered during winter, even more or less rotted and eaten by slugs, but the plants recover amazingly every spring and flower reasonably well, although maybe not quite as well as in their early days in their hated pots.

Finally, I will mention the "grand old lady" of the lewisias, the bitterroot, *Lewisia rediviva.* This plant has not proved as difficult to grow as we had thought. It seems to like a cool root run, so clay pots are a must because plastic pots, allowing no evaporation, get too hot. Also, great care must be taken in watering. In the open garden it has not been too happy (too much drink, I think!), so a pot in the greenhouse is where it belongs. There it has flowered very well. Sowing usually results in many inferior plants so one has to select the sheep from the goats, retaining only the very best—the *crème de la crème.* Good plants can display fine big flowers more than 4 in. in diameter. After flowering we usually transfer the pots to the highest shelf in the greenhouse to sunbake for the rest of the summer.

Well, now. This has been a long list and much talking. But all those Rocky Mountain plants I have mentioned here—and many, many more—have given us untold moments of joy and pleasure. Let me, therefore, finish this with a quotation from one of Nobel Prize-winner Halldor Laxnes's poems:

> But what is a house, and wealth, and power,
> if in your pot does not grow a flower?

References

Elliott, Roy C. 1966. *The genus Lewisia.* London: Alpine Garden Society.

Marinos, Nic, and Helen Marinos. 1981. *Plants of the alpine tundra.* Estes Park, Colo.: Rocky Mountain Nature Association.

Porsild, A. E., and Dagny Tande Lid. 1974. *Rocky Mountain wildflowers.* Ottawa, Canada: National Museum of Natural Science.

Willard, Betty E. and Chester O. Harris. 1976. *Alpine wildflowers of the Rocky Mountains.* Estes Park, Colo.: Rocky Mountain Nature Association.

294

39

In Czechoslovakia

by Otakar Vydra

Czechoslovakia is a small country in the heart of Europe where rock gardening is very popular. Some Czechoslovakian rock gardeners are members of AGS, ARGS, SRGC and other rock garden organizations of international consequence.

The climate of Czechoslovakia is generally mild with irregular rainfall and temperatures. Summers are sometimes dry and hot, sometimes cold and humid. Winters are often very mild with much rainfall and little snow, but sometimes very hard and long with severe frosts and temperatures falling to −30°C for several days. From the rock gardener's point of view this wide variety of climate, temperatures, and humidity is a source of much consternation.

Most Czechoslovakian rock gardens are at the lower elevations near their owners' homes, weekend houses or cottages. I am one of the few lucky rock gardeners who has a garden in the mountains. The altitude of my garden is about 800 meters. The first snow comes generally at the end of October or the beginning of November and lasts until late March or April. A good winter may have snow cover of 1–1.5 meters—very good for the plants and also for cross country or downhill skiing. A bad winter has rain, and sometimes the snow cover is only a few centimeters deep. In January 1985, after a mild December and a snow cover of only 5 cm, we had a period of severe, long-lasting frosts with temperatures descending to −30°C. The summer of 1983 had only a few cloudy days, and the climate in my garden seemed more Californian than Czechoslovakian. Under these variable climatic conditions we are obliged to grow our plants, keep them alive and try to help them adapt to the changes.

I grow all my plants outdoors without any protection. It is very difficult to keep a wide variety of plants from different climates and all parts of the world alive and healthy in a small rock garden (almost 50 m²) on a hillside facing south, fully exposed to the sun, rain, snow and wind. Yet, under these conditions many plants that are considered difficult grow and flower. I attribute these good results to a rock gardening method that seems to be more effective, offer more possibilities and give better results than the classical one.

The method is crevice rock gardening, and it consists mainly of placing the stones very close together. Between the stones there is only a small space to be filled with the proper soil mixture for the plant that is to grow there. Rockwork thus constructed also gives a more natural impression of an

Born in 1930, **Otakar Vydra** is a technician living in Prague. He has been interested in rock gardening since 1971 and has travelled in Sweden, the European Alps, Greece, Spain, the United States and the Pamir and Tian Shan Mountains of central Asia studying and collecting plants for his extensive garden near Prague. He successfully introduced *Potentilla lignosa* and *P. biflora* from the Soviet Union, and is an innovator in rock garden construction, helping to develop the naturalistic technique of crevice gardening. Among other special interests: baroque music.

actual outcrop so that the highest aesthetic values of rock gardening can be reached.

The plants live practically on the rocks, which dry rapidly after each rainfall. Crevices allow a deep, cool root run, maintain even moisture and keep the plants compact. This method prevents the fast growth of weeds, because crevices are occupied by good plants, and the only place weeds can grow is on the surface of the stones. Finally, in any good crevice rock garden there are vertical, horizontal and inclined crevices facing all cardinal points and creating a variety of exposures.

Along with the American plants, under the open sky with the same climatic conditions and without any cover or protection, I grow other plants from all parts of the world. I mention this only to show the wide variety of plants and the wide possibilities of crevice rock gardening.

Crevice rock gardening is not a new method. It was described before the second World War by English gardeners and rock garden builders Symons-Jeune and Gertrude Jekyll, but there are only a few such gardens in my country. However, many Czechoslovakian gardens built in a variety of styles have introduced a wide range of American plants. The following notes relate some experiences growers in our country have had in introducing American plants to the European climate.

Author's garden
Photo by Otakar Vydra

Aquilegia. The most exciting of all, *Aquilegia jonesii,* is a very difficult plant which, in our conditions, will never reach its natural size or be free-flowering as it is at home. It is grown with difficulty by a few growers both in pots and in the garden. It flowers with few flowers and sometimes gives fertile seed. It is hardy in winter but doesn't adapt to the very humid summer. My plant was raised from seed from Mr. Hans Asmus of Milwaukee, Wisconsin. Regular seed propagation will be necessary to maintain it because plants here die after 5–7 years. *Aquilegia scopulorum* var. *perplexans* seems to be easier and is also very beautiful. *Aquilegia saximontana* grows very well and a hybrid, *A. saximontana* × *A. jonesii,* is by some growers considered a weed.

Arenaria. Nice, small plants adapt well to our conditions and seem to be long-lived. *Arenaria congesta, A. kingii, A. hookeri* and others, because of their compact growth, are used by many growers for troughs. The best of all seems to be *A. (Minuartia) obtusiloba,* which is very beautiful and shows signs of good adaptation to our area. In a friend's garden it has lived 7 years, and has reached a size of about 18–20 in.

Aster. Good results are reported for *Aster alpigenus,* but the plant is considered large for small gardens.

Astragalus. Very good, exciting plants but very difficult in cultivation. Some adult specimens in a friend's garden could be considered adapted to our conditions: *Astragalus utahensis,* which received a prize in the 1985 Rock Garden Club Exhibition in Prague; *A. crassicarpus* which is now 6 years old and about 5 in. across; *A. purshii; A. barrii;* and *A. ceramicus. Astragalus purshii* is now 5 years old. Other friends consider American species of *Astragalus* very difficult to grow. Seeds germinate regularly—*A. spatulatus, A. podocarpa* and others—but seedlings soon perish.

Boykinia (*Telesonix*). Good results are reported by many growers in the adaptation of *Telesonix jamesii,* which grows without difficulty in open gardens.

Calochortus. Results are often disappointing. Seed germinates regularly, but the plants disappear rapidly after a hard or humid winter. They survive if kept in the alpine house.

Caltha. *Caltha biflora* and *C. leptosepala* are good, long-lived plants if kept moist and grown in a sheltered position. Not suitable for small rock gardens because of their size.

Claytonia. *Claytonia megarhiza* is rarely seen in cultivation and then mostly in pots or in alpine houses. When hiking with Marvin Black, of Seattle, Washington, in 1983 on the summits of the Wenatchee Mountains, he allowed me to take two cuttings of *C. megarhiza* var. *nivalis.* They survived a long transport to Prague, and these two plants flowered for the first time in the spring of 1985. Another plant of *C. megarhiza* was raised from seed, and grows and flowers in a vertical crevice in my garden.

Claytonia megarhiza var. *nivalis*
Photo by Otakar Vydra

Clintonia. Good results are reported in growing and adapting *Clintonia uniflora*.

Collomia. Collomia debilis var. *larsenii* is a very attractive plant but very difficult. Seeds germinate regularly, but seedlings disappear a year later. A friend grows *C. debilis* v. *ipomoea*, a very attractive plant that does well in full sun and seeds itself freely. This 6-year-old plant seems to be established to perfection in his garden.

Diapensia. Many consider the circumpolar *D. lapponica* a plant that refuses all efforts of cultivation. I have two 12-year-old plants growing in a very deep horizontal crevice. They are now about 2 in. across. They have flowered four times in the past 12 years. I didn't find any seeds.

Dicentra. Dicentra oregana grows without any problems and can be considered a good plant for adaptation to bigger gardens. *Dicentra uniflora*, which I consider a very desirable plant, did not survive.

Dodecatheon. Very popular in many gardens, dodecatheon is easily grown in our climate. *Dodecatheon dentatum*, which received a prize in the 1983 Exhibition of the Prague Rock Garden Club, is a highly regarded plant.

Douglasia. These desirable cushion plants adapt well to European conditions. They live in several gardens in different positions, are free-flowering and give fertile seeds. In my garden, *D. laevigata* var. *ciliolata* is now 8 years old and about 6 in. across. *Douglasia nivalis* disappeared after 6 year's cultivation when about 8 in. across.

Draba. These good cushion plants adapt well to the European climate. *Draba paysonii*, which I consider the best of all, reached a size of about 8 in. in 5 years. *Draba oligosperma* and *D. incerta* are well suited to small rock gardens or troughs.

Dryas. Dryas drummondii gives good results in outdoor European culture. The recent introduction of *D. octopetala* var. *alaskensis* is a welcome addition to our gardens.

Epilobium. Many seeds of *E. obcordatum* and *E. rigidum* received in various exchanges are not true to their names. The true forms are good plants adaptable to European conditions.

Eriogonum. Some eriogonums are extremely attractive plants and the smaller forms quite suitable for rockeries and troughs. If well-established, they are long-lived. Their culture under our conditions is difficult but possible. An *Eriogonum jamesii* in a friend's garden is more than 20 years old. *Eriogonum ovalifolium* and *E. kennedyi* have been grown by another friend in tufa rock for more than 14 years. My plant of *E. siskiyouense*, received from Lawrence Crocker of Jacksonville, Oregon, is now about 12 years old. Even the plants from semidesert areas can be grown outdoors in our climate. With Margaret Williams I collected in July, 1983, near Sparks, Nevada, seeds of *E. ovalifolium* ssp. *williamsii*, which grows there in sand and in semidesert conditions. Several seedlings perished, but two plants are now growing outdoors in the humid and rainy 1985 summer in a very narrow, inclined, south-facing crevice. Another young plant of *E. ovalifolium* I collected myself in 1983 near Yosemite survived the long transport to Prague. It is now the living souvenir of my trip to the United States. There are many other species in cultivation such as *E. douglasii, E. caespitosum, E. heracleoides, E. thymoides, E. umbellatum.*

Eritrichium. I consider the eritrichiums the most attractive alpine plants for small rock gardens, but even European forms are very difficult for us to cultivate. The American *E. howardii* and *E. argenteum* (*E. nanum*) grow in a friend's garden in a vertical position in tufa stone. Since few seeds of these desirable plants have been available very long, there is very little experience with them. My plant of *E. nanum* has grown outdoors for several years in an inclined crevice and flowers profusely. *Eritrichium howardii* perished when 3 years old.

Erysimum. It seems to us that *E. amoenum*, introduced from Denver Botanic Gardens in 1983 by Z. Zvolanek, will be a good, pretty, free-flowering plant. The color of the flowers varies from cream white to dark pink.

Erythronium. Many species of *Erythronium* are very popular in our gardens. There are no problems of adaptation if they are given humid, sheltered positions. The fact that the seeds require 3–4 years to germinate in some cases is very disappointing.

Gentiana. The American gentians are not very popular in our gardens because the European forms are considered prettier. Nevertheless, *Gentiana* (*Pneumonanthe*) *calycosa, G. parryi, G. newberryi* and others that adapt well to our conditions are in cultivation. The best of all, *G. algida* is rarely seen here.

Haplopappus. There are only few reports concerning *H. acaulis*. In outdoor culture it survived only a few years.

Hesperochiron. Hesperochiron californicus and *H. pumilus* are grown only by a few people in pots and alpine houses.

Hymenoxys. Hymenoxys grandiflora is rarely seen in cultivation. A new introduction, *H. acaulis* var. *caespitosa*, seems promising. Small silver leaves and reduced form make this plant very suitable for small rockeries.

Kalmia. My plant, introduced from Lawrence Crocker under the name *K. polifolia* ssp. *microphylla* 'Nana' (*K. microphylla* 'Nana', *K. nana*) is actually about 12 years old, grows well and flowers freely.

Kelseya uniflora. It is too early to consider this very desirable, exciting, small cushion plant adaptable to our conditions, since there is little experience with it as yet. Some growers have their first few-years-old plants in pots. My two small plants grow outdoors in a vertical crevice.

Lepidium. *Lepidium nanum* is a small, mysterious plant, not very showy, grown only by a few people. For me it was not long-lived, perishing after three years of culture.

Leptodactylon. First efforts at introduction of *L. pungens* were made in 1983. It seems to be very difficult to cultivate under our conditions.

Lewisia. Lewisias are very popular, common plants in our gardens with no troubles of adaptation. *Lewisia brachycalyx, L. cantelowii, L. columbiana, L. cotyledon, L. leana, L. nevadensis, L. pygmaea, L. rediviva, L. sierrae, L. tweedyi* and many hybrids of these are grown.

Luetkia. *Luetkia pectinata* is a good plant that grows well under our conditions and can be used as a ground cover.

Lupinus. *Lupinus lyallii, L. breweri* and *L. lepidus* are occasionally grown in a few gardens. Best results are from pot culture, but they are generally not long-lived here.

Mertensia. *Mertensia alpina* is very attractive and interesting even for smaller gardens. Introduced some years ago, it is considered a promising plant with good possibilities for adaptation to our climate.

Oenothera. Some, like *O. missouriensis, O. fremontii, O. pallida,* and *O. caespitosa,* grow well in our conditions though they are not suitable for a small crevice rock garden because of their size. *O. lavandulifolia* from Colorado is very desirable, but no seeds have germinated yet.

Oxytropis. *Oxytropis* is rarely seen in our gardens, but a friend grows *O. lambertii, O. sericea, O. multiceps* with good success.

Penstemon. Popular plants grown in many Czech gardens, penstemons from the section Dasanthera are quite adaptable to our conditions. Those from section Ericopsis are more difficult to cultivate. There are some surprises. *Penstemon gairdneri,* which lives in semidesert conditions, didn't survive the hot, dry summer days in a friend's garden. *Penstemon eriantherus* var. *eriantherus* is considered the best of all. It has grown in a friend's garden for 5 years and received a prize at the Prague Rock Garden Club Exhibition.

Petrophytum. Petrophytum can adapt well to our conditions. *Petrophytum caespitosum,* grown rather frequently in our country, seems not to be true to name. *Petrophytum cinerascens* is not very common in Czech gardens, and *P. hendersonii* is rarely seen. My free-flowering *P. hendersonii* is about 9 years old, and when in flower, is the conversation piece of the American section of my garden. My *P. cinerascens,* introduced in 1983 from Oregon growers Baldassare Mineo and Jerry Cobb-Colley, grows and flowers to perfection.

Petrophytum hendersonii
and *Lewisia cotyledon.*
Photo by Otakar Vydra

Phlox caespitosa
Photo by Otakar Vydra

Phlox. Various species of *Phlox* are grown. Most, due to their size, are not suitable for small gardens. The cultivars of *P. douglasii* are showy and nice, have special colors and are grown without problems. Other phloxes such as *P. caespitosa, P. diffusa, P. borealis, P. hoodii, P. bifida, P. adsurgens,* and *P. missoulensis* can be sometimes seen. Some very small semi-desert phloxes would be extremely desirable introductions. We have good first reports from the introductions of *P. bryoides, P. condensata* and *P. pulvinata. Phlox bryoides* was introduced in cuttings from a friend in East Germany, who grows a 15-year-old plant about 15 in. across. *Phlox condensata* and *P. pulvinata* were introduced from Denver Botanic Gardens by Zdenek Zvolanek in cuttings and seeds. I myself dream about one phlox I have seen with Margaret Williams on the summit of Red Rock near Sparks, Nevada—a tight small cushion 2–5 in. across completely covered with snow white flowers. Does anyone grow it or have seed?

Physaria. *Physaria didymocarpa* and *P. condensata* are good plants for small gardens, but unfortunately not long-lived. My *P. condensata,* which flowered in a dark yellow color, did not survive the hard winter of 1985.

Polemonium. *Polemonium delicatum* grows in some gardens. *Polemonium viscosum* is more difficult and not long-lived. *Polemonium brandegei* was introduced 5 years ago thanks to Denver Botanic Gardens and grows in a friend's garden to perfection.

Primula. The American primroses are interesting, desirable plants. *Primula angustifolia* gives early signs of accepting our conditions; it flowered for a friend for the first time in 1985. *Primula rusbyi* grows and flowers for another friend in East Germany. *Primula parryi* is rarely seen in our gardens. Very desirable is *P. cusickiana,* which perished after 3 years of cultivation in a friend's garden. There are very few seeds of this species available.

Saxifraga. There are numerous saxifrages all over the world, but not many in America. In 1983 in Issaquah, Washington, at Grand Ridge Nursery, owned by Phil Pearson and Steve Doonan, I saw a small wonder: a tight, hard, compact cushion of *S. oppositifolia* from the Wallowa Mountains. This plant looked like *Raoulia eximia.* I got a few cuttings which did not survive and a few seeds. Now I am very happy to have one 2-year-old rosette of this plant, which gives signs of very slow growth in a vertical crevice facing west.

Sisyrinchium. Several species of *Sisyrinchium* are grown in our gardens and are well-adapted. Some friends report failures with *S. douglasii,* which gets frozen sometimes during hard winters. *S. idahoense* v. *macounii* (*S. macounii*) is considered very nice but seems not to be hardy in winter. The best of all is *S. macrocarpon* which flowers with very big yellow blossoms. It has grown in a friend's garden more than 10 years and reached a size of about 5 in. across.

Spraguea (*Calyptridium*). *Spraguea umbellata* is rarely seen in cultivation. My plant, which is 4 years old, grows outdoors in a narrow, horizontal crevice and seeds itself.

Talinum. *Talinum okanoganense* is a miniature plant suitable for small rockeries or troughs. A nice cultivar introduced under the name *T. okanoganense* × *T. spinescens* 'Zoe' is the same size but has very big violet flowers. There are others growing here such as *T. rugospermum* and *T. spinescens,* which could all be considered well-adapted to our conditions.

Townsendia. *Townsendia exscapa* is a popular, often cultivated plant. *Townsendia grandiflora, T. incana, T. rothrockii* and *T. hookeri* are seen rarely. Townsendias are not long-lived plants, and propagation by seeds is necessary. Sometimes they seed themselves freely.

Townsendia exscapa
Photo by Otakar Vydra

Trifolium. *Trifolium nanum* and *T. macrocephalum* are very rarely seen in our gardens. They are very slow-growing plants. I have never seen any plant in flower.

Trillium. Trilliums are very well-adapted and make no trouble in cultivation. The most popular in our country are *T. ovatum* v. *hibbersonii, T. chloropetalum, T. nivale* and *T. rivale.*

Viola. Many American violas grow well in a friend's garden. He mentions the following: *Viola beckwithii, V. douglasii, V. halli, V. adunca, V. nuttallii, V. pedata, V. pedata* var. *bicolor, V. pedatifida, V. flettii, V. trinervata.* He has good results growing them outdoors.

Not all of the plants mentioned above grow in my garden. Information on the performance of American plants in Czechoslovakian gardens was supplied by enthusiastic growers and gardeners, including Mrs. O. Duchacova; Mr. J. Grulich; F. Holenka, Ing.; J. Holzbecher; J. Jurasek; Dr. J. Kazbal, Ing; J. Klima, C. O. Vlasak; R. Zeman; and Z. Zvolanek. From East Germany, R. Schlamm and G. Duhrkopp told me about American plants in their gardens.

Many years ago some of the American plants, such as the lewisias, were considered very difficult and practically impossible to grow in our area. Now they have found new homes in our gardens, and they have chosen to live, grow and be happy with us.

Naturally, we want to make progress in our efforts to introduce more American natives, whether from the high country or semidesert areas, and we hope that one day even *Kelseya uniflora, Phlox pulvinata* and other American beauties will be content in our gardens and give us lasting pleasure in growing them.

References

Clark, Lewis J. 1976. *Wild flowers of the Pacific Northwest, from Alaska to northern California.* Sidney, British Columbia: Gray's Publishing.

Wherry, Edgar T. 1955. *The genus Phlox.* Philadelphia: Morris Arboretum.

Tokyo
Kyoto
Osaka
Awaji Island

40

In Japan

by Atsushi Kuyama

Japan, like the United States, is rich in a variety of wild flowers. Like the United States also, it has a variety of climates. It is a narrow country but a long one. It extends from 45 to 26° north latitude, from the subarctic zone to the subtropical zone. The Japanese first began to cultivate wild plants found near their homes—plants such as orchids, epimedium, tricyrtis, and iris. Then they started to climb to the high mountains to find alpines such as *Dicentra peregrina* and *Cypripedium macranthum.* They also started to collect those genera which have many variations like *Calanthe* and *Cymbidium.* Today, thanks to the introduction of foreign plants, people in Japan love to see and grow not only Japanese natives but also alpines from abroad.

Because of a concern for nature conservation, people grow many plants from seeds. However, though I have learned of many fine plants from the Rocky Mountains, only a few have been introduced from that area because, compared to plants from the eastern United States, they are not easy for us to grow. The American botanist, Asa Gray, mentions the similarity between plants of the eastern United States and Japanese plants.

I would like to explain the method of cultivating alpines in Japan. I have just planned and installed a large rock garden on Awaji Island. In the spring of 1985, Awaji Farm Park, located about 2.5 hours from Kobe or Osaka by boat and car, was opened to the public. Two thousand species were planted in the 5,000 m² rock garden. A cooling system was installed in the 6 × 14 m alpine house to keep the air below 25°C and the soil below 15°C so that cool-loving plants such as meconopsis and primula can be grown. In this locality it is hot and dry in summer; the temperature reaches over 36°C. In winter, it is mild with temperatures down to −4°C. Annual rainfall is approximately 155 cm. We have monsoons in June, about 25 cm, and we have about 17 cm of rain from December to February.

Native plants in this area include *Cymbidium goeringii, Liparis nervosa, Calanthe discolor, C. sieboldii,* and *Arisaema tosaense.* We might say that we have no cultivation problems in the wintertime, but in summer it is necessary to find the best way of growing plants away from the heat. In our area we cannot use fine soil for pot culture or for rock gardening. We have tried using many kinds of coarse sand, and we have discovered that a mixture of 5–10 mm coarse pumice sand and granite is our most suitable material for pot culture. For rock gardening we use coarse sand 30–50 cm deep piled over pebbles. Essential needs for rock gardening are good drainage, proper moisture and fresh

Atsushi Kuyama, floriculturist of Hyogo Prefectural Farm Park and designer of Awaji Farm Park rock garden, has conducted plant explorations in 35 countries and has described his travels in many gardening publications. He now serves as assistant secretary of the Japan Alpine Rock Garden Society and is Honorary Associate Editor of the Himalayan Plant Journal. He belongs to plant societies throughout the world and is a member of Old Kewites.

air circulation. In this way I can insure that the roots of plants go downward, and the plants themselves will be able to endure the heat and dryness of the top soil. I can also save water for irrigation.

Before I planned this huge rock garden at Awaji Farm Park, I tried to grow plants from abroad in my small private rock garden. I realize that many alpines and mountain plants can be grown even in our hot area.

I keep the plants in geographical groupings such as the United States, the Soviet Union, China, Japan, Europe, and Africa as well as five other areas. The U.S. section is located in the central part of the garden. It is covered with *Picea pungens,* lewisia and 300 other species. In the alpine house, penstemons, dodecatheons, and *Cypripedium reginae* are displayed for the enjoyment of visitors.

Now I will explain how Rocky Mountain plants are grown in Japan, mainly in the rock garden of Awaji Farm Park. Dwarf conifers should not be omitted from the list of rock garden plants. There are *Picea glauca* 'Albertina Conica' and *P. pungens,* called Colorado spruce. The 30 Colorado spruce trees in our rock garden are very attractive, and they are something new for the visitors, because dwarf conifers which have whitish blue leaves are not familiar to most Japanese. I planted 300 *Chamaecyparis pisifera* 'Aurea Nana' beside *Picea pungens* for the combination of the two color tones. Dwarf conifers grow well even in a hot area.

In the Portulacaceae I chose *Lewisia cotyledon, L. brachycalyx, L. rediviva, L. nevadensis, Montia parvifolia,* and *Claytonia megarhiza.* All of these are easy plants to grow in the garden. Because the color of *Lewisia cotyledon* is conspicuous among the wildflowers, some nurseries propagate this species as a pot flower using meristem culture to keep a uniform color and flower size. *Montia parvifolia* is quite lovely and lively, like a weed.

Anemone narcissiflora is the same species as in Japan. It hates to be kept in a dry place and is not an easy plant to establish.

Most of the *Aquilegia* species are easy to grow. We have *A. flavescens, A. formosa, A. shockleyi* and *A. saximontana* in the rock garden, but because of hybridization between the species, I am not sure the species are correctly identified.

Plants of the Berberidaceae are numerous in China and Japan. *Jeffersonia diphylla* and *Vancouveria hexandra* were chosen for the rock garden. I do not know why *Jeffersonia diphylla* does not bloom frequently compared to the Korean or Chinese *J. dubia* which has a noble pale purple flower. I realize that both species in the genus *Jeffersonia* have unique qualities other than the color of flowers.

In the poppy family, *Dicentra cucullaria* and *D. formosa* are easier to grow than *D. peregrina.* I have heard that the American species are found in the woodlands, but *D. peregrina* in Japan and the Soviet Union must be grown in full sunshine on an alpine scree.

Arabis blepharophylla grows well.

Empetrum nigrum is native to Japan as well as to the Rockies, but it hates hot conditions, and we cannot keep it long.

In Violaceae, I grow *Viola pedata* and *V. palustris. Viola pedata* is highly regarded in Japan because of the beauty of its flowers and leaves. Reginald Farrer, the "father of rock gardening" was unhappy when he missed *V. eizanense* (*V. disseeta* v. c) in Japan. If I had missed *V. pedata* in the United States, I would have had the same feeling.

Part of rock garden at
Awaji Farm Park.
Photo courtesy Atsushi Kuyama

American plant area,
rock garden at
Awaji Farm Park.
Photo courtesy Atsushi Kuyama

Cassiope mertensiana and *C. tetragona* are easier to grow in pot culture and in rock gardens than *C. lycopodioides*, which is native to Japan.

Primulaceae are one of the fascinating families to lovers of alpines. Dodecatheon is loved as the emblem of the American Rock Garden Society. *Dodecatheon jeffreyi* is nice to grow and *D. meadia*, which grows in the central part of the United States, is common and easy to cultivate.

We grow *Polemonium pulcherrimum, P. acutiflorum,* and *P. haydenii. Polemonium boreale* blooms for a long time with many flowers. It is highly recommended.

I had a chance to grow *Eritrichium howardii* of the Boraginaceae. It is an extraordinarily difficult plant, like *E. nanum* and *E. nipponicum*. We have not yet found a method for their cultivation.

Mimulus, which keeps its flowers for a long time, gives us a cheerful feeling grown with lysichitons, lobelias, primulas and calthas in a wet place.

Though the genus *Penstemon* is rich in the western part of the United States, we have only *P. frutescens* (now *Pennellianus*) in Japan. Most of the members of this genus are quite popular among alpine enthusiasts. *Penstemon serrulatus* is not a difficult species in our area, but it is hard to keep *P. davidsonii* and *P. newberryi* in a good condition in our rock garden.

Japan and China are rich in species of the genus *Asarum*. There is no difference in the cultivation between asarums native to Japan and those from the United States. *Asarum caudatum* and *A. hartwegii* have been grown in the woodland garden for a long time. Though their flowers are not especially beautiful, their leaves and the smell of the roots are lovely.

Heuchera sanguinea has remarkable flowers on its racemes. It is sold by some nurseries as an ornamental pot flower. Other *Heuchera* species such as *H. cylindrica* and *H. ovalifolia* are easy to grow.

Saxifraga oppositifolia has flowers of unusual color for this genus. I have tried to grow this species; unfortunately, it did not survive for very long.

Thermopsis montana is quite a vigorous plant in our area, and we have a similar one named *T. lupinoides* in the northern part of Japan.

Parnassia palustris, Cornus canadensis, and *Linnaea borealis* occur not only in the United States but also in Japan. However, they are not easy plants to grow.

Lobelia cardinalis is a handsome plant. As we only have the pale blue flowered *L. sessilifolia* in Japan, *L. cardinalis* attracts people's attention with its red flowers.

Campanula rotundifolia is a common plant not only in the United States but also in Europe. Though the bell-shaped flowers are common, but they always attract us.

Erigeron compositus is about 20 cm high and it grows well. We have *E. alpicola* and *E. thunbergii* in the mountains. They are not difficult to grow in our area.

Lysichiton americanum is grown here beside the waterfall. In the United States and Japan the white flowers of *L. camtschatcense* can be found in the bog in cool areas. I think *L. americanum* has a stronger odor than *L. camtschatcense*.

Liliaceae are also one of the interesting families. Members of the genera *Smilacina, Maianthemum, Clintonia, Erythronium, Fritillaria, Trillium* and *Allium* are also native to Japan.

The Japanese native, *Clintonia udensis* is not an easy plant to grow in our area, but it is a good woodlander in cool areas in Japan. *Clintonia uniflora* of the Rocky Mountain area is also difficult to grow except in the cooled alpine house.

Erythroniums have various colors. *Erythronium grandiflorum* has a yellow flower, so most of the Japanese visitors cannot believe that it is the same genus as the pink flowered *E. dens-canis* var. *japonicum*.

Fritillaria lanceolata and *F. camschatcensis* are easy plants to grow. *Fritillaria camschatcensis* has two types in Japan. *Fritillaria camschatcensis*, which is native to alpine zones, is fertile, but the one in the lowland in the northern part is infertile.

We have only three species of *Trillium* in Japan, and their natural hybrids are very rare even in Hokkaido. *Trillium ovatum* and *T. chloropetalum* from the western United States are not difficult to grow.

The nodding onion, *Allium cernuum*, is suitable for rock gardens. We grow a large number of *Allium* species and each has a different character when the flower is blooming and when it dries.

Many *Dichelostemma pulchellum*, *Triteleia laxa* (both formerly species of *Brodiaea*) and *Camassia quamash* were planted in our rock garden. I have read that at the time of the Lewis and Clark 1805 expedition, there were blue meadows of *C. quamash*. I expect such a meadow in our rock garden.

To me calochortus is one of the gems, and I keep *Calochortus uniflorus* in the scree, but it does not look well.

The genus *Iris* is an easy group to grow; we grow *Iris hartwegii* and *I. chrysophylla*. *Iris chrysophylla* has yellow dwarf flowers; we have no native yellow iris in Japan. We often grow *I. gracilipes* and sometimes *I. rossii*, a dwarf type of iris.

Finally, it is not possible to forget the orchids. We have *Calypso bulbosa* and *Goodyera repens* in Japan. *Calypso bulbosa* is a woodland orchid in cool areas, so it is one of the difficult orchids to grow. *Cypripedium calceolus* is an easier plant to cultivate than the Japanese *C. macranthum*.

We have not introduced many plants from the Rocky Mountains. We need more exchange of proper information. We hope our Japanese Alpine Rock Garden Society and the botanical garden of Awaji Farm Park will be able to play an important role in the future among all people who are interested in plants.

References

Niehaus, Theodore F., and Charles L. Pipper. 1976. *A field guide to Pacific states wild flowers.* Boston: Houghton Mifflin.

Spellenberg, Richard. 1979. *The Audubon Society field guide to North American wildflowers, Western Region.* New York: Alfred A. Knopf.

Cassiope tetragona
Photo by Atsushi Kuyama

Afterword

by Audrey Williams

With the opening, in late June 1986, of the Second Interim International Rock Garden Plant Conference in Boulder Colorado, we celebrate the 50th anniversary of the First International Rock Garden Conference held in London, England, in 1936. Enthusiastic gardeners from around the world will gather for the second time in North America to discuss the subject which for many is the dominant interest in their lives.

Rock gardening is more than a hobby, for it encompasses everything from the art of garden design—the placement of rocks, screes and pools, the arrangement of plants with regard to color, texture and pattern of foliage and flowers—to the scientific study of plants in the wild and in cultivation. It involves the search for new species as well as the practice of propagation and the technique and artistry required to produce prize-winning plants for the show bench. The rock gardener who is also painter or photographer captures for all time those fleeting moments of perfect bloom.

Although the late E. B. Anderson, well-known English alpine gardener, said in the report of the Second International Conference in 1951 that modern rock gardening began in Britain in 1870, the year of publication of William Robinson's early book, *Alpine Flowers for English Gardens,* shows us that mountain plants were being grown in specially constructed rock gardens at a much earlier date.

In his book, "written to dispel a very general but erroneous idea that the exquisite flowers of alpine regions cannot be grown in gardens", Robinson enunciated the fundamental principles of rock garden construction that remain sound to the present day. In his book *The Wild Garden,* he advocated the use of hardy exotic plants in the natural landscape "in conditions where they will thrive without further care."

The magazines that Robinson started, *The Garden* and *Gardening Illustrated* (eventually incorporated in *Gardeners' Chronicle*) gave him the opportunity to advance his ideals of naturalistic gardening and to attack his pet hatred, the then current fashion of 'carpet bedding'—the use of tender perennials in a riot of color, imitating Persian or Turkish carpets. Robinson visited America in 1870 and with Dr. Albert Kellogg and Nicholas Bolander saw mountain plants in California. Henry Correvon, a Swiss alpine gardener, conservationist and writer, recorded that European mountain plants such as *Rhododendron ferrugineum* were being grown in Boston as early as 1872.

Audrey Williams, born in Yorkshire, England, began collecting plants by pressing wildflowers in an old wallpaper sample book as a child. She came to Canada in 1954 and now lives in a house she built with her husband, Geoffrey, on the lower slopes of Mount Seymour overlooking Burrard Inlet in North Vancouver. The Williams love to hike mountains—a pursuit that has led them to many of the world's high places. Accounts of their travels have appeared in the bulletin of the Alpine Garden Club of British Columbia, which Geoffrey edited with Audrey's assistance for nine years. The Williams' garden is considered a garden for connoisseurs, featuring woodland as well as alpine plants.

Correvon wrote of gardens and of the plants of his beloved Alps in numerous books that were translated into several languages. In *Alpine Flora,* translated into English and enlarged to suit that market, he wrote of gardens like that of the botanist, Edmond Boissier, built in 1857 to accommodate his collection of alpine plants. He also wrote of gardens he himself had helped to establish, such as La Rambertia at over 2,000 meters elevation at Rochers de Naye near Montreux, where a Congress of Alpine Gardeners, presided over by Prince Roland Bonaparte, was held in 1904.

The early days of rock gardening coincided with the great age of plant collecting: the period when the large English nursery firms sent their collectors to the far corners of the earth to look for new plants beautiful and hardy enough to grace the gardens of their wealthy clients. It was a period of comparative peace in the world and a gentleman of means could arrange his own collecting trip, either going to the area himself or sending his collectors. Interested officials in the diplomatic service and missionaries in far away places might fill their idle hours by collecting plants and seed.

Businesses were established which specialized in alpine plants from around the world. Their lists are as mouth-watering today as when they were written, in spite of the absence of Asian plants, for the collections of George Forrest were not in cultivation until 1908. In 1864, Backhouse of York was offering *Campanula cenisia* and *C. zoysii,* as well as two species of *Cassiope.* In 1879 one could order *Aciphylla lyallii* from New Zealand, *Asphodelus acaulis* from North Africa, *Conandron ramondioides* from Japan and *Mertensia alpina* from the American Rockies.

In Britain, alpine gardening attracted well-to-do and leisured gardeners, including members of the aristocracy and clergy. Among a distinguished group of horticultural friends whose names are remembered through plants still popular today were E. A. Bowles, Ellen Wilmott, Canon Ellacombe and the young Reginald Farrer.

Farrer was not only a gardener who could grow difficult plants successfully and an entertaining writer who could present the essential of a plant succinctly, but a plant explorer who travelled widely in search of new species. He was not a professional botanist but a discriminating gardener who disdained plants he deemed unworthy or too difficult to transplant. He is perhaps best described as a plantsman—a subtle blend of botanist, horticulturalist, explorer, plant collector, writer and painter. His enduring contribution to rock gardening is the two-volume reference book, *The English Rock Garden,* completed in 1911 which, despite the numerous new plant introductions since, is still the bible for many alpine growers today.

The English Rock Garden was not published until after the end of the first world war when growing alpine plants rapidly gained popularity in Europe and America. Farrer's ideas on moraine and bog gardens were being put into practice, as were those of Murray Hornibrook, who had described his peat-rock garden in 1914, and Clarence Elliott, who pioneered the use of troughs, tufa rock and pavements for growing alpine plants.

Elliott was among the enthusiasts who founded the Alpine Garden Society in 1929. In 1933 the Scottish Rock Garden Club was formed, to be followed a year later by the American Rock Garden Society. Founded even earlier, the flourishing Vancouver Island Rock and Alpine Garden Society celebrates its 60th anniversary in 1986. These societies placed great emphasis on shows which attracted new members. The alpine house and adjacent cold-frames were much used to cultivate newly introduced rarities for the show bench.

In 1936 the Alpine Garden Society and its big brother, the Royal Horticultural Society, jointly sponsored the First International Rock Garden Plant Conference in London. It was 15 years before a second conference was held, sponsored by the English and Scottish societies, partly in London, partly in Edinburgh. This conference was attended by a large number of overseas visitors and an impressive array of international speakers like E. B. Anderson, Aymon Correvon, Wilhelm Schacht, Harold Epstein, and Kathleen Marriage, who spoke on "Flowers of the Rocky Mountains."

A pattern of conferences at ten year intervals was established, with lectures, shows and garden visits. In 1971, the large number of overseas visitors from the newer societies in New Zealand and Canada, as well as from old established groups, generated enthusiasm for another conference in less than ten years. This resulted in the First Interim Conference held in Seattle and Vancouver in 1976.

This meeting was the first such conference to be held outside Europe. The theme of the conference was 'Alpines of the Americas.' An ambitious program of lectures and displays on plants of both North and South America was supplemented by a day-long field trip to Mount Rainier National Park. Pre- and post-conference tours enabled many rock gardeners, especially the large contingent from Europe, to see North American plants in the wild for the first time. North Americans became aware that their native plants were highly prized elsewhere and could compete with the traditional European alpines for beauty and hardiness.

Since then all of the societies have grown. The American Rock Garden Society has new chapters like the flourishing Arizona group, while the Rocky Mountain Chapter which has grown from a handful of members in 1976 to approaching 200, has accepted responsibility for the Second Interim International Rock Garden Plant Conference. Paralleling the growth of the chapter has been that of the Rock Alpine Garden at Denver Botanic Gardens, an inspiration to all who would make a rock garden in a most difficult climate.

This Second Interim Conference has as its theme 'The Rocky Mountains—Backbone of a Continent.' Because of its location at Boulder, Colorado, the conference is able to use the living world of mountain plants in the Southern Rockies, as well as slide programs, to focus attention on the wild species, and to use Denver Botanic Gardens to show the plants in cultivation.

Traditionally, International Rock Garden Plant Conferences have been followed by the publication of a Conference Report based on papers submitted by the speakers. *Rocky Mountain Alpines* is a departure from that custom, having been written before the conference by many plantspeople, including the speakers. It provides an overall view of the Rocky Mountains and its plants and will be welcomed by far more than the limited number of enthusiasts who are able to be at the conference.

What can the gardener learn from the thousands of words written by the naturalist, botanists, horticulturalists and gardeners who have contributed to *Rocky Mountain Alpines*?

Most important are the plants in their infinite variety; some well-known in the wild and in cultivation, others newly introduced, rare or endemic, as they are seen through the eyes of naturalists and gardeners. We learn of their preferred habitat, be it on limestone or acidic rocks, in crevices or scree slopes, in woodland or meadow, bog or arid plain.

The naturalist, for instance, may be fascinated by the similarity in leaf, flower and reproductive bulbils of *Romanzoffia sitchensis* and *Suksdorfia ranunculifolia*, members of different families occupying the same habitat. The gardener sees horticultural potential in unusual forms of well-known species like *Dryas drummondii* and *Cornus canadensis* and comments on the garden performance of the plant he sees in the wild. Both gardener and naturalist add to our knowledge of, and interest in, Rocky Mountain plants and may perhaps enhance the plants' chances of survival in the wild as well as facilitating their introduction to gardens.

The patterns of distribution of alpine plants in the Rockies become apparent as we follow the writers from northernmost British Columbia to southern Arizona. Circumpolar arctic alpine plants such as *Saxifraga oppositifolia* and *Silene acaulis* occur again and again at high elevations as we go southward. In the northern Rockies many of the plants are well known, widely distributed and often cultivated. Farther south the numbers of species increase markedly with newly-discovered endemics in the Yellowstone region such as *Antennaria aromatica* and new stations for such very rare plants as *Aquilegia jonesii* and *Kelseya uniflora*. There is even a new genus, named *Shoshonea* by Erwin Evert, which promises to be a fine rock garden plant.

A rock gardener could list enough challenging new plants from those described in the Yellowstone region to last a lifetime, without even looking at Elizabeth Neese's discoveries in the Great Basin. The wealth of plants she describes includes several very dwarf penstemons, which with cryptantha, eriogonum, astragalus and oxytropis, promise to be some of the most sought after rock garden genera of the future.

Many rock gardeners who live in temperate climates have regarded the plants of the southern Rockies as resentful of winter wet and marginally hardy at best. Accounts of the wild plants of the White Mountains of Arizona, the Sandia Mountains of New Mexico, and the Canyonlands of southeast Utah reveal some plants already well established in cultivation, examples being *Gentiana affinis, Philadelphus microphyllus* and *Mahonia (Berberis) fremontii*. Gardeners should be encouraged to try such interesting plants as *Hedyotis (Houstonia) pygmaea, Mertensia franciscana, Mimulus eastwoodiae* and *Chilopsis linearis* in the hope that they may be just as adaptable.

Rocky Mountain Alpines provides the interested lover of mountain plants with an exciting guide to the best flower areas whether he drives a car, explores the meadows on foot or scrambles up the highest ridges. The book should also serve as a warning that the plants of the Rocky Mountains are not indestructible.

Remarks such as, "This is a sadly overused area" and "just outside the upper terminal (Whistlers' Peak) much of the original vegetation has vanished", occur frequently enough to give us pause for reflection on the subject of conservation.

Early in rock gardening history, Henry Correvon and other members of the Swiss Alpine Club became concerned about the destruction of alpine plants when "peasants of Savoy and Valais might be seen bringing baskets full of uncommon species for sale in the Geneva market and it was only too certain that several classical habitats of rarities were becoming exhausted."

Deploring the practice of collecting plants in the wild, Henry Correvon said, "We see them flowering; promptly admire and as promptly tear them up. When their charms disappear, we cannot tell one from another and no longer care about possessing them".

As a result of this concern, the Association for the Protection of Plants was formed in 1883. In an effort to lessen the destruction, "by encouraging professional gardeners to raise these species from seed and sell them at low prices to amateurs", a garden of acclimatization was established at Planpalais. The nursery distributed plants and seeds throughout the world for eighteen years until it was moved to Chêne Bourg to become the commercial nursery Floraire, operated by Correvon.

In spite of Correvon's extensive writing and the efforts of the Association, the idea that a plant species could be collected out of existence was not recognized by most rock gardeners.

In 1907 Reginald Farrer wrote in his book, *Among the Hills,* of his collecting expeditions in the French Alps, with little regard for conservation. He could not have foreseen the development of tourism for the masses that now endangers alpine plants when he wrote, "the haunts of *Saxifraga florulenta* are very high, very remote, very expensive, very tedious and difficult to come at" and "Therefore in such grim high places I do not fear for that grim and thorny treasure any danger from the trowel of the itinerant spinster or casual tourist."

Of *Campanula bellardii* he said, "in half ten minutes you might have packed a washing basket full, and not the slightest difference made to the luxuriant lavishness of the slope."

Farrer does seek to justify himself in the afterword to the book: "For strange, stray women have gone about accusing me of devastating regions and valleys of the Alps," and goes on to reason that, "the misconception of alarmists appears to be entirely based on the rooted inability of the public to realize the vastness of the mountains and the innumerable laughter there of even the rarer species. . . . No, what you take or I take or five hundred others of us might take in reason and decency from the flanks of the enormous Alps would never be able to make a petal's difference to their glory".

In the early days of the rock garden societies, and until as recently as twenty years ago, it was considered perfectly acceptable to dig wild plants for one's garden. Publications such as *Plant Hunting in Europe* by Hugh Roger-Smith described the places to see rare plants. While advocating restraint and suggesting that certain plants are best grown from seed, Roger-Smith gave detailed advice on digging, wrapping and re-establishing collected plants. Twenty years after his book was published we looked in vain for *Cypripedium calceolus* "in real abundance so that specimens could be collected without any qualms of conscience," which he had seen in the woods around Campitello in northern Italy. A. E. Porsild writes in *Rocky Mountain Wildflowers* that this orchid, once common near Banff in the Canadian Rockies, has been "exterminated by excessive picking."

Although in recent years the subject of collecting whole plants has been played down, either totally avoided or glossed over, in the publications of the rock garden societies, there is no doubt that collecting by individual members continues. Those with an eye to winning prizes at the shows seek, find and collect rare plants in the wilds of less developed countries which have an abundance of endemics not yet in cultivation, and a dearth of laws to protect them.

In 1975, and again ten years later, the Alpine Garden Society published an article by Anthony Huxley, "The Ethics of Plant Collecting," in which he presented the arguments for and against plant collecting, and outlined the steps being taken to preserve endangered species. He suggested that gardeners can help in plant conservation by, "exercising personal restraint; spreading the gospel among acquaintances and even, by the strong-minded, among strangers." He later added the suggestion that plants should be bought only from firms known to propagate their stock.

Mr. Huxley presents a depressing picture of the future for wild plants. Of the approximately 250,000 species of higher plants in the world, 10 percent are endangered, and it is probable that one species becomes extinct each day. If destruction of habitat continues, the rate may reach one per hour by 1990.

Immediately preceding the article in 1985 was the long overdue statement, "the Society does not lend its name to the collecting of living plants in the wild except by means of seed." The Scottish Rock Garden Club also made clear its position with regard to collecting. The Alpine Garden Club of B.C. has among the objects written into their constitution, "To promote an interest in the native plants of British Columbia and their conservation." Is it not time that the American Rock Garden Society passed a strong statement on conservation into its bylaws?

Nevertheless, the collecting of rock plants by a relatively few individual gardeners plays a very small part in the escalating rate of extinction of species. The enormous increase in world population in this century—resulting in expansion of agriculture to lands previously considered unsuitable, clear-cutting of forests and growth of cities—plays an increasingly greater role.

In the Rocky Mountains, population pressure at this time seems insignificant compared to many other parts of the world, but new developments involving large tracts of land, flooding associated with hydro-electric projects, widespread irrigation for agriculture, open cast mining such as that in the Crowsnest Pass in the Canadian Rockies, and oil exploration are cause for concern. However, oil exploration in the Great Basin has revealed new species. It would be ironic if they were to become extinct just as they are being described.

Naturalists and gardeners can rescue a limited number of species by bringing them into cultivation when destruction seems imminent, but the preservation of large numbers of plants and animals within their original habitat is required to assure their continued existence beyond being specimens in some living museum.

Thanks to the foresight of earlier generations of nature-lovers, national parks such as Rocky Mountain, Yellowstone, Glacier and the Canadian parks have preserved areas of exceptional natural phenomena and outstanding beauty. But other areas of unique plants such as the Beartooth and the Bighorns remain largely unprotected. Recently there has been considerable pressure to increase tourist accommodation within some Canadian National Parks that are already suffering from overuse.

The Nature Conservancy in the United States and Canada has jurisdiction over certain areas of such rare plants as the carnivors of the Green Swamp in North Carolina. In British Columbia, largely because of the work of Dr. Vladimir Krajina, there are ecological reserves typical of the various biogeoclimatic zones of the province established on public lands. Nature reserves on private lands have been preserved by the fundraising efforts of local groups, an example being the Antelope Valley California Poppy Reserve near Bakersfield. In Canada, the Honeymoon Bay Wildflower Reserve was donated by the forest company that owned the land.

Unfortunately, any protected area on government land may be subject to political pressure. In these times of recession and its accompanying restraint, governments may be tempted, with some justification, to propose development that could provide jobs.

In North America, all-terrain vehicles, mountain bikes and snowmobiles penetrate ever more deeply into the wilderness which was once regarded as a safe place for wild plants and animals. Worldwide, the ever-extending networks of ski-lifts may not in themselves damage the habitat of alpine plants when they are in use, but their construction and maintenance does. The building of steel towers and the shaping of runs, as well as the removal of trees all create barren scars on the mountainsides that take years to recover.

It may be that such developments are inevitable, but would it not be possible to preserve an equal area of wilderness for every new resort area?

There is still time to dedicate natural areas rich in plant life in the Rocky Mountains, often on National Forest land, as nature reserves or ecological areas. Plant societies such as the American Rock Garden Society, the American Penstemon Society, and the Carnivorous Plant Society should consider raising funds toward the acquisition and preservation of areas rich in plants of particular interest to them.

On a smaller scale, the digging of plants for direct sale to the public continues despite the existence of international laws that restrict their export to other countries. Collecting is most prevalent in less developed countries where, for example, rare bulbs may be the only source of real income for the poor. Even in the United States there is considerable collecting of difficult to re-establish woodland plants like *Epigaea repens,* as well as cactus and orchid species. The University of North Carolina Botanical Garden encourages nurserymen to propagate desirable native species and its list of wildflower growers excludes those who sell collected plants. In theory it should be possible, by using all available methods of propagation, to make most collecting in the wild unnecessary.

Both rare and common species are at risk from those who should be their protectors. We have met college botany students, each making a collection of 50 herbarium specimens to complete a first year course. Even botanic gardens have been criticized for setting a bad example by digging whole plants for their collections instead of taking seed or cuttings.

It is important that the hundreds of rock garden plants already in cultivation should continue to be propagated and distributed, for many of these species are rare and endangered in the wild. Gardeners have always known that the best way to keep a treasured plant is to give it to as many good growers as possible. The local botanic garden is not the only safe place for rare plants.

Rock gardeners can cooperate with naturalist groups and botanic gardens to increase public awareness of the native plant heritage, especially those who use the outdoors for recreation. This may be achieved through public lectures, articles and letters to newspapers and magazines, and displays of wildflowers in gardens, as well as at flower shows. In British Columbia, a joint effort of garden and naturalist societies resulted in a wildflower poster depicting some endangered species with the slogan, "Look, Enjoy, Let them be".

Rock garden societies, like mountaineering clubs and naturalist groups, need special committees to seek ways to actively support conservation. How many gardeners have offered to help in the restoration of damaged areas in national and other parks that the public has loved too well? Is it possible that rare plants propagated in gardens could be used to increase populations in the wild? Plant societies must be seen as supporting conservation seriously if they are to avoid criticism of the kind seen in a 1982 issue of *Garden,* a publication of the New York Botanical Garden. In a guest column titled "Plant Societies Please Join Us," Faith Thompson Campbell says, ". . . certain plant organizations are conspicuous by their absence from the ranks of the conservation organizations." The author draws attention to societies devoted to particular types of plants such as cacti, orchids and carnivorous plants, some of whose members "are recognized experts, knowledgeable about habitat, range and status of particular species." These members, she says, are primarily interested in growing plants in their collections and "tend to perceive conservation programs as adversaries." While conceding that individual members may be conservationists, and while not criticizing the American Rock Garden Society, the American Primrose Society, or the American Penstemon Society directly, Ms. Campbell does list all three among the societies which have not yet committed themselves, as organizations, to the cause of conservation.

One method of conservation is the introduction and maintenance of collections of wild plants in cultivation. The valuable information on propagation from seed contained in *Rocky Mountain Alpines* encourages the introduction of new plants without further depleting wild populations. Pre-sowing treatments and the care of young seedlings are described for over 400 species of Rocky Mountain plants from trees to alpines.

Gardeners can learn much from the chapters on landscaping in the book. Although the authors describe the situation as it applies to Denver, the ease of maintenance (especially minimal watering and the sense of regional identity achieved by using native plant material) makes sense to all but the most dedicated plant collector who will attempt to grow everything from alpines to South African bulbs wherever he lives.

The experiences of gardeners growing even a limited number of Rocky Mountain alpines in other parts of the world (including other parts of the United States), in situations as varied as troughs, dry sand beds and even indoors, using time-controlled artificial lighting, challenge us to try these plants in locations other than the traditional scree or alpine house.

Judging from the experiences of the writers, Rocky Mountain alpines in cultivation appear to fall into three categories. About 50 percent of the plants grown are from a wide area of North America, not solely from the Rockies, or else are circumpolar arctic alpines. Among those (Rocky Mountains) endemic plants grown many are legendary species such as *Aquilegia jonesii* and *Kelseya uniflora.* Not surprisingly the highest percentage of "Rocky Mountains only" plants are grown in the Rock Alpine Garden at Denver Botanic Gardens where the curator lists dozens of choice species.

Rocky Mountain plants are rarely available commercially. Even Siskiyou Rare Plant Nursery offers only twenty species in a list of 1000. Claude Barr's "jewels of the plains" are being grown in a memorial garden in South Dakota, but where can one buy his *Dodecatheon* 'White Comet' and 'Prairie Ruby' or *Astragalus barrii?* As a result of this book, many more Rocky Mountain alpines will be brought into cultivation but when, and even whether, they will be available commercially is much less certain. Few new specialist nurseries are being opened to replace those lost when their owners are forced to retire.

Rocky Mountain Alpines gathers together a wealth of information about the plants of a vast mountain range, focusing on those most attractive to gardener and naturalist alike. Although it describes the habit and habitat of many wild plants and directs us to methods by which they may be grown in gardens, this book is only a starting point for plant explorers, propagators and cultivators.

Ten years from now the knowledge of Rocky Mountain plants resulting from research inspired by this book could well fill another volume. It might even speed the publication of an up-to-date flora of the Rocky Mountains.

Other great mountain ranges of the world, such as the Andes and the Alps, merit the attention of writers as able as those who have contributed to Rocky Mountain Alpines. The floral wonders of individual areas of the Alps have been described well and often but no overall view has appeared as yet.

The history of Rocky Mountain alpines in cultivation is short; the number of species available commercially is a small fraction of the multitude in the wild as yet untried. Rock gardeners attending this conference have the opportunity to see the Rocky Mountain alpines that are presently in cultivation and to admire the way they are being used at Denver Botanic Gardens.

As a result of this conference and this book which is a part of it, the flowers of the Rocky Mountains will be better known. The great genera of the central and southern Rockies: *Penstemon, Astragalus, Eriogonum* and *Cryptantha* may soon take their place, with *Kelseya* and *Telesonix,* among the classic alpines of Europe as supreme rock garden plants.

References

Anderson, E. B. 1951. *Retrospect.* In *Report of the second international rock garden plant conference.* London: Alpine Garden Society.

Bacon, Lionel. 1979. *Mountain flower holidays in Europe.* London: Alpine Garden Society.

Campbell, E. T. 1982. "Plant societies please join us." *Garden* 6 (5):2–3, 31–2.

Correvon, A. 1971. *Rock gardening in Switzerland.* In *Report of the fourth international rock garden plant conference.* ed. Roy C. Elliott. London: Alpine Garden Society.

Correvon, Henry, and Phillipe Robert. 1911. *The alpine flora.* Geneva: Atar.

Farrer, Reginald. 1907. *My Rock Garden.* London: Edward Arnold.

———. 1907. *Among the Hills.* London: Swarthmore Press.

———. 1919. *The English Rock Garden.* London: E. C. Jack.

Healey, B. 1975. *The Plant Hunters.* New York: Scribners.

Huxley, Anthony J. 1965. "The ethics of plant collecting." *Alpine Garden Society Bull.* 43 (2):109–118.

———. 1975. "The ethics of plant collecting." *Alpine Garden Society Bull.* 53 (2):114–123.

———. 1978. *Illustrated History of Gardening.* New York: Paddington Press.

Hyams, Edward S. 1971. *A history of gardens and gardening.* New York: Praeger Publishers.

Shelgren, Margaret. 1983. A poppy paradise. *Garden* 7 (3):15–16, 32.

Watts, May Thielgaard. 1957. *Reading the Landscape of America.* New York: MacMillan Publ. Co., Inc.

Bibliography

compiled by Solange G. Gignac, Librarian, Helen C. Fowler Library, Denver Botanic Gardens

BOOKS

1. Floras and wildflower books

Andersen, Berniece A. 1970. *Mountain plants of northeastern Utah.* Logan: Utah State University.

Arnow, Lois Aileen Goodell. 1980. *Flora of the central Wasatch Front, Utah: a manual of the ferns, fern allies, conifers, and flowering plants growing without cultivation in Salt Lake and Davis Counties.* Salt Lake City: University of Utah Printing Service.

*Craighead, John J., Frank C. Craighead, and Ray J. Davis. 1963. *Field guide to the Rocky Mountain wildflowers.* Cambridge, Mass.: Riverside Press.

*Cronquist, A., A. H. Holmgren, N. H. Holmgren, and J. L. Reveal. 1972. *Intermountain flora: vascular plants of the Intermountain West, USA.* Vol. 1. New York and London: Hafner Publishing Co.

*_____ , A. H. Holmgren, N. H. Holmgren, J. L. Reveal, and P. K. Holmgren. 1977. *Intermountain flora: vascular plants of the Intermountain Region, USA.* Vol. 6. New York: Columbia University Press.

*_____ , A. H. Holmgren, N. H. Holmgren, J. L. Reveal, and P. K. Holmgren. 1984. *Intermountain flora: vascular plants of the Intermountain Region, USA.* Vol. 4. Bronx: New York Botanical Garden.

Dorn, Robert D. 1977. *Manual of the vascular plants of Wyoming.* New York: Garland Publishing.

Eastwood, Alice. 1893. *A popular flora of Denver, Colorado.* San Francisco: Zoe Publishing Co.

*Harrington, Harold David. 1954. *Manual of the plants of Colorado, for the identification of the ferns and flowering plants of the State.* Denver: Sage Books.

*Hitchcock, C. L., A. Cronquist, M. Ownbey, and J. W. Thompson. 1955. *Vascular plants of the Pacific Northwest.* 5 vols. Seattle: Univ. of Washington Press.

_____ , and A. Cronquist. 1973. *Flora of the Pacific Northwest.* Seattle: University of Washington Press. (Condensation of *Vascular plants of the Northwest.*)

Komarkova, Vera. 1979. *Alpine vegetation of the Indian Peaks area: Front Range, Colorado Rocky Mountains.* Vaduz, Lichtenstein: J. Cramer.

Kearney, Thomas Henry, and Robert H. Peebles. 1951. *Arizona flora.* Berkeley: University of California Press.

McDougall, Walter Byron. 1956. *Plants of Yellowstone National Park.* Yellowstone Park, Wyo.: Yellowstone Library and Museum Association.

---

*Starred references were most referred to by the authors of this book, and should serve as excellent guides to the Rocky Mountain flora.

Marinos, Nic, and Helen Marinos. 1981. *Plants of the alpine tundra.* Estes Park, Colo.: Rocky Mountain Nature Association.

*Nelson, Ruth Elizabeth Ashton. 1979. *Plants of Rocky Mountain National Park.* 3rd ed. Estes Park, Colo.: Skyland Publishers.

———. 1976. *Plants of Zion National Park wildflowers, trees, shrubs, and ferns.* Springdale, Utah: Zion Natural History Association.

Pesman, M. Walter. 1975. *Meet the natives.* 7th ed. Denver: Denver Botanic Gardens.

*Rickett, Harold W. 1973. *Wild flowers of the United States.* Vol. 5, 6. New York: McGraw-Hill Book Co.

Tidestrom, Ivar. 1925. *Flora of Utah and Nevada.* Washington D.C.: U. S. Government Printing Office.

*Weber, William Alfred. 1976. *Rocky Mountain flora: a field guide for the identification of the ferns, conifers, and flowering plants of the southern Rocky Mountains from Pikes Peak to Rocky Mountain National Park and from the plains to the Continental Divide.* 5th ed. Boulder: Colorado Associated University Press.

Welsh, Stanley Larson. 1971. *Flowers of the Canyon country.* Provo, Utah: Brigham Young University Press.

Willard, Beatrice E. 1979. *Plant sociology of alpine tundra, Trail Ridge, Rocky Mountain National Park, Colorado.* Golden: Colorado School of Mines.

Young, Robert Glen. 1977. *Colorado West: land of geology and wildflowers.* Grand Junction, Colo.: Wheelright Press.

2. Tundra Ecology

Bliss, L. C., O. W. Heal, and J. J. Moore, 1981. *Tundra ecosystems: a comparative analysis.* Cambridge, Eng. and New York: Cambridge University Press.

*Zwinger, Ann, and Beatrice Willard. 1972. *Land above the trees: a guide to American alpine tundra.* New York: Harper and Row.

3. Alpine and Rock Garden Plants

*American Rock Garden Society, Northwestern chapter, and the Alpine Garden Club of British Columbia. 1980. *Alpines of the Americas: the report of the first interim International rock garden plant conference.* Seattle: American Rock Garden Society, Northwest Chapter.

*Barr, Claude A. 1983. *Jewels of the plains.* Minneapolis: University of Minnesota Press.

Brooklyn Botanic Gardens. 1952. *Handbook of rock gardens.* Special printing of *Plants and Gardens,* Vol. 13. New York: Brooklyn Botanic Gardens.

Gabrielson, Ira Noel. 1932. *Western American alpines.* New York: The Macmillan Co.

McCully, Alice Woodruff (Anderson). 1931. *American alpines in the garden.* New York: The Macmillan Co.

Preece, William Hugh Arthur. 1937. *North American rock plants.* New York: Macmillan.

4. Rock Gardens

Foster, H. Lincoln. 1982. *Rock gardening: a guide to growing alpines and other wildflowers in the American garden.* Portland, Ore.: Timber Press.

Klaber, Doretta. 1959. *Rock garden plants: new ways to use them around your home.* New York: Holt.

Kolaga, Walter A. 1966. *All about rock gardens and plants.* New York: Doubleday.

Schacht, Wilhelm. 1981. *Rock gardens.* New York: Universe Books.

Schenk, George Walden. 1964. *How to plan, establish, and maintain rock gardens.* Menlo Park, Calif.: Lane Book Co.

Tanner, Ogden. 1979. *Rock and water gardens.* Alexandria, Va.: Time-Life Books.

Titchmarsh, Alan. 1983. *The rock gardener's handbook.* Portland, Ore.: Timber Press.

5. Botanical Nomenclature

Bailey, Liberty Hyde. 1976. *Hortus third.* Revised and expanded by the staff of the Liberty Hyde Bailey Hortorium. New York and London: MacMillan Publ. Co., Inc., and Collier MacMillan Publishers.

Kartez, J. T., and R. Kartez. 1980. *Synonymized checklist of the vascular flora of the United States, Canada, and Greenland.* Vol. 2. Chapel Hill, N.C.: University of North Carolina Press.

Periodicals

1. Bulletin of the Alpine Garden Society of Great Britain

Ferns, Francis. 1984. "Denver Botanic Gardens—rock alpine garden." 52:180–1186.
Foster, H. Lincoln. 1959. "The challenge of comparison." 27:187–190.
_____ . 1966. "Waterworks Hills." 34:222–227.
_____ . 1970. "The genus Phlox." 38:66–90.
_____ . 1972. "Off-season cuttings." 40:95–97.
Hilton, Eric. 1985. "Western American mountain flowers." 53:170–180.
Ingwersen, Will. 1938. "Plant hunting in the Rockies." 6:131–147.
_____ . 1938. "Plant hunting in the Rockies." 6:203–218.
_____ . 1955. "Plants of the Rocky Mountains." 23:393–398.
Marriage, Kathleen. 1937. "Back again in the Colorado Rockies." 5:118–123.
_____ . 1938. "Plant collecting in the Colorado Rockies." 6:112–120.
_____ . 1945. *Boykinia jamesii.* 13:8–9.
Nelson, Aven. 1940. *Mertensia viridis.* 8:257–258.
Regan, Mrs. William J. (Clare). 1943. "Phlox of the northern Rocky Mountains." 11:136–140.
_____ . 1948. 6:11
_____ . 1948. 6:40
_____ . 1952. "Something a little different in 1951." 10:8–11.
Ripley, Dwight. 1942. "Rarities of western North America." 10:73–80.
_____ . 1944. "More western Americans." 12:65–74.
_____ . 1947. "Searching high and low." 15:18–32.
_____ . 1948. "The Paunsagunt Plateau and other wonders of the West." 16:15–28.
_____ . 1948. "Three days in Leadville." 17:26–30.
_____ . 1951. "Colorado, 1950." 19:38–48.
_____ . 1972. "Notes from Long Island." 40:182–187.
_____ . 1973. "Notes from Long Island." 41:125–131.
Rose, Frank. 1948. "Montana cacti." 6:62–3.
_____ . 1950. "Afield with a plant collector." 8:87–89.
_____ . 1962. "Storm Lake." 20:39.
_____ . 1964. "Montana's dodecatheons." 22:86–7.
Seligman, Richard. 1941. "A week-end in the Rocky Mountains." 9:8–22.
Worth, Carleton R. 1950. "The North American aquilegias." 18:241–254.

2. Bulletin of the American Rock Garden Society.

Barr, Claude A. 1946. "The life span of penstemons." 4:59–60.
_____ . 1946. *"Viola montanensis,* a gem." 4:107–108.
_____ . 1946. *"Violas nuttallii* and *vallicola."* 4:108–109.
_____ . 1947. "Dwarf western asters." 5:65–68.
Callas, Panayoti Peter (Kelaidis). 1978. "Two dryland ferns." 36:65–69.
_____ . 1980. *"Heuchera hallii:* in the wild and in the garden." 38:36–39.
Long, Lucian M. 1981. "Pikes Peak—and how the tundra got there." 39:136–139.
Maslin, T. Paul. 1979. "The rediscovery of *Phlox lutea* and *Phlox purpurea."* 37:62–69.
_____ . 1983. "Some fall blooming bulbs." 41:32–35.
Pierce, Andrew. 1981. "Plants for Denver's new rock garden." 39:21–23.
_____ . 1982. "Rocky Mountain high." 40:18–22.
Ripley, Dwight. 1952. "Garden notes, 1952." 10:68–70.
_____ . 1953. "A miniature bog garden." 11:87–89.
_____ . 1955. *"Ranunculus hystriculus."* 13:69.
Schaal, H. R. 1981. "In the making: Denver Botanic Gardens' alpine and rock garden." 39:18–20.
Taylor, Allan, and Panayoti Callas (Kelaidis). 1979. "Cacti: America's foremost rock plants, part I." 37:157–164.
_____ . 1980. "Cacti: America's foremost rock plants, part II." 38:1–101.
_____ . 1980. "Cacti: America's foremost rock plants, part III." 38:59–66.
Worth, C. R. 1967. "Plant collecting expeditions." 25:3–7.

3. The Green Thumb.

Kelly, George. 1952. "Better gardens with less water." 9 (8):23.

———. 1949. "A mountain trip in October." 6 (10):7–9.

Marriage, Kathleen. 1946. "Rock gardens." 3 (2):11.

———. 1952. "Letters from Kathleen Marriage to Ruth Nelson: spring, 1951, excerpts." 9 (4):28.

———. 1952. "The loveliest gardens anywhere, and jolly people." 9 (5):11.

More, Robert E. 1959. "Mrs. G. R. (Kathleen O'Neil) Marriage." 15 (3):109.

Pesman, M. Walter. 1948. "Landscape that mountain home." 5 (9):18–21.

———. 1950. "Why gardens differ." 7 (12):21.

———. 1960. "What do you learn when you look at gardens?" 17 (6):201–202.

———. 1966. "Above timberline . . . where flowers commune with the clouds." 23 (4):121–23.

———. 1968. "Early botanists in the Rockies." 25 (2):64–66.

Woodward, Wes, ed. 1972. "A tribute to S. R. DeBoer." 29 (5):143–225.

———. 1974. "George Kelly: the man who taught us how to garden." 31: (2):42–7.

———. 1975. "M. Walter Pesman: He made the plants our friends." 32 (3):74–83.

Index

compiled by Stan Metsker and Gwen Kelaidis

Index consists primarily of scientific names, place names, proper names and references to illustrations. Italics indicate scientific names, boldface type denotes photographs or drawings, and asterisks mark entries that refer to maps, tables, or charts.